CITY AND C
NORM

CW01566971

This pioneering study of urban society in twelfth-century mainland Norman Italy examines the self-governing role of urban communities and explores their social ordering, identities and communal activities. Drawing on charters, chronicles, annals and other sources, Paul Oldfield uncovers notable continuities in a range of cities across southern Italy throughout a period of regime change and disruption. Unlike traditional interpretations which suggest that the Normans, and the creation of a monarchy in 1130, stifled urban development, this book argues that South Italian urban communities were still able to enjoy a level of autonomy under the Norman monarchy. By emphasising the fluidity of the social structures and groups found in these cities, alongside the influential role of both the Church and civic consciousness, the author sheds new light on the multi-layered complexity of the urban communities of Norman Italy and provides a more balanced comparison with the cities of northern Italy.

PAUL OLDFIELD is a Lecturer in Medieval History at the Department of History and Economic History, Manchester Metropolitan University.

Cambridge Studies in Medieval Life and Thought
Fourth Series

General Editor:

ROSAMOND McKITTERICK
Professor of Medieval History, University of Cambridge, and Fellow of Sidney Sussex College

Advisory Editors:

CHRISTINE CARPENTER
Professor of Medieval English History, University of Cambridge

JONATHAN SHEPARD

The series Cambridge Studies in Medieval Life and Thought was inaugurated by G.G. Coulton in 1921; Professor Rosamond McKitterick now acts as General Editor of the Fourth Series, with Professor Christine Carpenter and Dr Jonathan Shepard as Advisory Editors. The series brings together outstanding work by medieval scholars over a wide range of human endeavour extending from political economy to the history of ideas.

A list of titles in the series can be found at:
www.cambridge.org/medievallifeandthought

A charter from Bari of 1202, with the 'wolf' signature of the protonotary Lupo. Perg. 1169, Biblioteca Statale di Montevergine.

CITY AND COMMUNITY IN NORMAN ITALY

PAUL OLDFIELD

CAMBRIDGE
UNIVERSITY PRESS

CAMBRIDGE UNIVERSITY PRESS
Cambridge, New York, Melbourne, Madrid, Cape Town,
Singapore, São Paulo, Delhi, Tokyo, Mexico City

Cambridge University Press
The Edinburgh Building, Cambridge CB2 8RU, UK

Published in the United States of America by Cambridge University Press, New York

www.cambridge.org
Information on this title: www.cambridge.org/9781107403079

© Paul Oldfield 2009

First published 2009
First paperback edition 2011

A catalogue record for this publication is available from the British Library

Library of Congress Cataloguing in Publication data
Oldfield, Paul, Ph.D.
City and community in Norman Italy / Paul Oldfield.
p.   cm. – (Cambridge studies in medieval life and thought : fourth series)
Includes bibliographical references and index.
ISBN 978-0-521-89804-1 (hbk.)
1. Italy, Southern–History–535–1268.   2. Normans–Italy, Southern–History.
3. Italy, Southern–Social life and customs.   4. Italy–Social life and customs–To 1500.
5. City and town life–Italy, Southern–History–To 1500.   6. Community
life–Italy, Southern–History–To 1500.   7. Cities and towns–Italy, Southern–
History–To 1500.   8. Italy, Southern–History, Local.   9. Italy, Southern–Politics and
government.   10. Italy–Politics and government–476–1268.   I. Title.   II. Series.
DG867.2.O55 2009
945′.703–dc22   2008053263

ISBN 978-0-521-89804-1 Hardback
ISBN 978-1-107-40307-9 Paperback

To KB, my wife and best friend, and to
Finlay Samuel, *il mio piccolo tesoro*

CONTENTS

ACKNOWLEDGEMENTS

I would like to express my thanks for the help of so many different people, without which this work would not have been possible. The funding of the AHRC and the support of the history departments at the University of Leeds and Manchester Metropolitan University have all been crucial. The team at Cambridge University Press has been equally invaluable – Michael Watson and Helen Waterhouse have skillfully guided me through, while Jonathan Shepard's expertise has been vital. I am grateful too for the general support, advice, articles and responses to silly questions generously offered by Edoardo D'Angelo, Wendy Childs, Donald Matthew, Alex Metcalfe, Rosemary Morris, Günter Prinzing, Patricia Skinner, Elisabeth Van Houts, Vera von Falkenhausen and Chris Wickham. Thanks are due also to Jean-Marie Martin for his continual eagerness to provide guidance, send papers and to discuss the subject. Ian Moxon deserves particularly warm thanks for innumerable afternoons spent poring over troublesome Latin, for reading drafts and for just chatting! Last, but not least, I am hugely indebted to the support, understanding and endless efforts of Graham Loud, who supervised the thesis out of which this book is formed. His knowledge of and energy for the subject have been infectious, and his generosity in offering me useful material and personal translations of key sources/documents will never be forgotten. It was as an undergraduate taking Graham's special subject on the Normans in southern Italy, and spending more and more time in the wonderful Brotherton Library at the University of Leeds, that I realised (to the fascination/perplexity of family and friends!) the extent of my desire to pursue my interest in medieval southern Italy further.

My family and friends have been so important throughout. They have all offered, in their own unique ways (!), enormous encouragement, time, laughter, drinks and other welcome distractions. Finally, and above all, I would like to thank my wife. I have been so lucky to

Acknowledgements

write this book with her arms around me every step of the way. Having spent years searching for the right words to say the right things in my work, now I cannot find even one suitable to describe how much her love, belief and support has meant to me. I will be for ever touched by her and grateful for everything.

ABBREVIATIONS

Alex. Tel.	*Alexandri Telesini Abbatis Ystoria Rogerii Regis Sicilie Calabrie atque Apulie*, ed. L. De Nava, *FSI* CXII (Rome, 1991).
Amatus	*The History of the Normans by Amatus of Montecassino*, trans. P. Dunbar and G. A. Loud (Woodbridge, 2004).
BISME	*Bulletino dell'istituto storico italiano per il medio evo.*
Cattedrale di Benevento	*Le più antiche carte del capitolo della cattedrale di Benevento (668–1200)*, ed. A. Ciarelli, V. de Donato and V. Matera (Rome, 2002).
CDBI	*Le pergamene del duomo di Bari (952–1264)*, ed. G. B. Nitto de Rossi and F. Nitti di Vito, *Codice diplomatico barese* I (Bari, 1867).
CDBIV	*Le pergamene di S. Nicola di Bari. Periodo greco (939–1071)*, ed. F. Nitti di Vito, *Codice diplomatico barese* IV (Bari, 1900).
CDBV	*Le pergamene di S. Nicola di Bari. Periodo normanno (1075–1194)*, ed. F. Nitti di Vito, *Codice diplomatico barese* V (Bari, 1902).
CDBVI	*Le pergamene di S. Nicola di Bari. Periodo svevo (1195–1266)*, ed. F. Nitti di Vito, *Codice diplomatico barese* VI (Bari, 1906).
CDNA	*Codice diplomatico normanno di Aversa*, ed. A. Gallo (Naples, 1926).
CDS	*Codice diplomatico salernitano del secolo XIII*, vol. I *(1201–1281)*, ed. C. Carucci (Subiaco, 1931).

Abbreviations

CDSA	*Codice diplomatico svevo di Aversa* [parte prima], ed. C. Salvati (Naples, 1980).
Conversano	*Le pergamene di Conversano, I (901–1265)*, ed. G. Coniglio, *Codice diplomatico pugliese* XX (Bari, 1975).
Falcandus	*The History of the Tyrants of Sicily by 'Hugo Falcandus', 1154–1169*, trans. G. A. Loud and T. Wiedemann (Manchester, 1998).
Falco	*Falcone di Benevento, Chronicon Beneventanum*, ed. E. D'Angelo (Florence, 1998).
FSI	*Fonti per la storia d'Italia.*
JMH	*Journal of Medieval History.*
Malaterra	*De Rebus Gestis Rogerii Calabriae et Siciliae Comitis, Auctore Gaufredo Malaterra*, ed. E. Pontieri, *RIS* V (Bologna, 1927–8).
MGH SS	*Monumenta Germaniae Historica Scriptores.*
Montevergine	*Codice diplomatico verginiano*, 13 vols., ed. P. M. Tropeano (Montevergine, 1977–2000).
Peter of Eboli	*Liber ad honorem Augusti di Pietro da Eboli*, ed. G. B. Siragusa, *FSI* XXXIX (Rome, 1906).
PBSR	*Papers of the British School at Rome.*
PL	*Patrologia Latina*, 221 vols., ed. J. P. Migne (Paris, 1844–64).
QF	*Quellen und Forschungen aus Italienischen Archiven und Bibliotheken.*
Rich. S. Germano	*Rycardi de Sancto Germano Notarii Chronica*, ed. C. A. Garufi, *RIS* VIII part ii (Bologna, 1937).
RIS	*Rerum Italicarum Scriptores.*
Romuald	*Romualdi Salernitani Chronicon*, ed. C. A. Garufi, *RIS* VII part i (Città di Castello, 1935).
San Modesto	*Le più antiche carte dell'abbazia di San Modesto in Benevento (secoli VIII–XIII)*, ed. F. Bartolini (Rome, 1950).
Taranto	*Le pergamene dell'archivio arcivescovile di Taranto, i (ii) (1083–1258)*, ed. F. Magistrale (Lecce, 1989).

Trani	*Le carte che si conservano nello archivio dello capitolo metropolitano della città di Trani (dal IX secolo fino all'anno 1266)*, ed. A. Prologo (Barletta, 1877).
Troia	*Les Chartes de Troia. Edition et étude critique des plus anciens documents conservés à l'archivio capitolare, I (1024–1266)*, ed. J-M. Martin, *Codice diplomatico pugliese* XXI (Bari, 1976).
Will. Apulia	*Guillaume de Pouille, La Geste de Robert Guiscard*, ed. and trans. M. Mathieu (Palermo, 1961).

MAP OF SOUTHERN ITALY

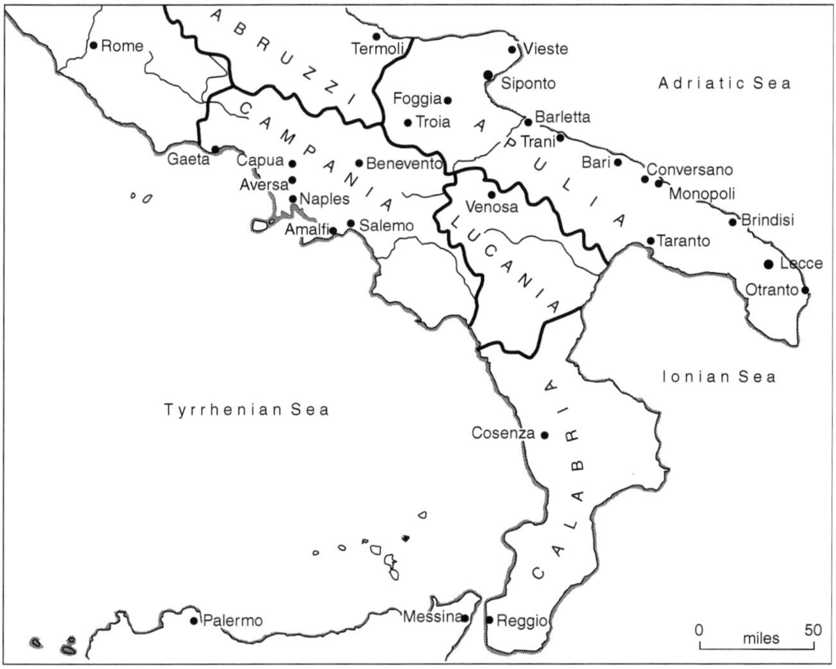
ABRUZZI
CAMPANIA
APULIA
LUCANIA
CALABRIA
Rome
Termoli
Vieste
Siponto
Adriatic Sea
Foggia
Troia
Barletta
Trani
Gaeta
Capua
Benevento
Bari
Conversano
Monopoli
Aversa
Naples
Venosa
Brindisi
Amalfi
Salerno
Taranto
Lecce
Otranto
Ionian Sea
Tyrrhenian Sea
Cosenza
Palermo
Messina
Reggio
0 miles 50

INTRODUCTION

At first glance the fractious political history of medieval southern Italy, stretching from the Abruzzi to Sicily, makes a study of the region's urban societies a problematic endeavour. From the mid-eleventh to the early thirteenth century the political map of mainland southern Italy was in an almost unabated flux. A snapshot of the region in 1050 would see the zones of Apulia and Calabria under the distant rule of the Byzantine emperor, Lombard principalities centred on Benevento, Capua and Salerno and some small, but independent, duchies on the Tyrrhenian coast at Amalfi, Gaeta and Naples. In the backdrop were bands of Norman adventurers, who had been slowly infiltrating the region for the previous half-century. Initially appearing around 1000 as a mixture of pilgrims and mercenaries, these Normans soon settled and placed increasing pressure on the existing governing authorities. By 1100 the Normans had transformed the South Italian political landscape immeasurably. Byzantine rule was no more, and the Lombard principalities were without their Lombard princes. Apulia, Calabria (along with the island of Sicily, which was previously under Muslim rule), the duchy of Amalfi and the principality of Salerno were controlled by Norman dukes of the Hauteville dynasty. Capua was still governed by a prince, but one from the Norman Quarrel kin-group, while Benevento had placed itself under papal rule. Naples retained a precarious independence under its ancient ducal rulers. In 1139, after twelve years of conflict, all of these lands, except for Benevento, were united, with Sicily, into one central kingdom. The architect of this new realm was Roger II of Sicily, a 'scion' of the Hauteville lineage.[1] Roger's direct descendants ruled the kingdom until 1189, when conflict over the succession erupted. The contest for the throne was finally settled in 1194 with the successful invasion of the German emperor, Henry VI, who took the crown. But

---

[1] *Alex. Tel.*, Bk I.I, p. 6.

I

the death of Henry in 1197 and that of his Sicilian wife, Constance, in 1198 left a three-year-old son, Frederick II, and a huge political vacuum. The resultant anarchy in the region was not fully quelled until after Frederick's return to southern Italy in 1220.

Despite the manifest instability, southern Italy's urban centres stand out as a notable constant. While political boundaries moved and regimes fell the city and its community remained. Civic life did not merely subsist though, and particularly in the twelfth century it evolved and thrived. This dichotomy of political volatility and urban evolution was found throughout Europe. However, in its European, and even Italian, context southern Italy (often termed the *Mezzogiorno*) has received limited attention, both in broad terms and especially in relation to the study of its urban society. Even Nicholas's immense work, *The Growth of the Medieval City*, barely refers to the southern part of the Italian peninsula.[2] There is, of course, a relative plethora of studies on Italian urban life – though in most cases Rome is as far south as the coverage is taken.[3] The concentration on the centre and north of the peninsula is understandable not only because of the vast source material available. It was in this part of Italy where the majority of the significant developments in medieval urban life evolved into their most dynamic formats – communal government and consular administration by the twelfth century, the rise of the *popolo* in the thirteenth and striking inter-city rivalry. Moreover, wider historical developments, notably the Renaissance, owe much to the evolution of the independent city-states of central and northern Italy.[4]

By contrast the emergence of the Normans and the establishment of a strongly centralised kingdom in southern Italy (the type of which was absent further north) are considered to have oppressed the vitality of urban society and to justify passing over an examination of the region. The formation of the kingdom in 1139 is presented as a significant but disruptive watershed. Analyses of the development of urban society before that date are tinged with a sense of a fast-approaching and fateful decline, an 'if only' scenario. After 1139 this 'decline' was supposedly in progress – the cities were economically, politically and even culturally

---

[2] D. Nicholas, *The Growth of the Medieval City: From Late Antiquity to the Early Fourteenth Century* (New York, 1997).

[3] See for a typical example D. Waley, *The Italian City-Republics* (London, 1969); P. Jones, *The Italian City-State: From Commune to Signoria* (Oxford, 1997), where some South Italian evidence is intermittently incorporated.

[4] C. Wickham, 'City society in twelfth-century Italy and the example of Salerno', in *Salerno nel XII secolo. Istituzioni, società, cultura. Atti del convegno internazionale* [June 1999], ed. P. Delogu and P. Peduto (Salerno, 2004), p. 12; J. H. Mundy, 'In praise of Italy: the Italian republics', *Speculum* 64 (1989), p. 816.

smothered by the kingdom – and the community lost its voice. As Hyde set the parameters for his work on civil life in medieval Italy we are informed that 'the growth of the *vita civile* is the centre of interest throughout and for this reason the South largely drops out of the picture after the Norman conquest.'[5] This is a common supposition. It is equally common to find descriptions of southern cities in the twelfth century saturated with pejorative adjectives such as 'doomed', 'repressed' and 'stunted'. Kreutz maintains that the Normans did not 'live progressively and creatively with cities' and 'deliberately extinguished' their 'spirit'.[6] Even Evelyn Jamison asserted that 'genuine city life was killed' by the Norman monarchy.[7]

It would seem that this over-simple representation of urban society in southern Italy is linked to the way the region has been understood in broader terms. Some scholars have seen medieval southern Italy as a channel through which Byzantine and Islamic culture was transmitted to Western Europe. Others have focused admiringly on the constitution of the Norman kingdom as a precursor to the modern state.[8] For the most part, however, attention on southern Italy has focused on the region as a 'problem area' which confusingly embodied luxury and poverty in equal measure. It appears that this interpretation of the medieval South had its origins in the early Renaissance period, and was accentuated by the works produced in northern Italy during the era of Italy's unification (the *Risorgimento*), achieved in 1870. The scholars writing them worked in an age in which the North's drive towards an Italian state was considered to have been obstructed by the 'reactionary' Bourbon kingdom in southern Italy and the perceived apathy of its inhabitants.[9] The invectives aimed at the 'absolutist' Bourbon kingdom presented 'the people and society of southern Italy as "corrotto" (corrupted) and "abbrutito" (become brutish) by centuries of bad government'.[10] A host of cultural stereotypes developed in the North (and elsewhere in Europe)

---

[5] J. K. Hyde, *Society and Politics in Medieval Italy – The Evolution of Civil Life, 1000–1350* (London, 1973), p. 9.

[6] B. Kreutz, *Before the Normans – Southern Italy in the Ninth and Tenth Centuries* (Philadelphia, 1991), p. 157.

[7] E. Jamison, 'The Norman administration of Apulia and Capua more especially under Roger II and William I, 1127–1166', *PBSR* 6 (1913) [reprinted as a separate volume, Aalen, 1987], p. 235; B. Croce, *History of the Kingdom of Naples*, trans. H. Stuart Hughes (Chicago, 1970), believed that the Norman monarchy repressed 'with the severest vigour all signs of communal formation', p. 11.

[8] A. Marongiu, 'A model state in the Middle Ages: the Norman and Swabian kingdom of Sicily', *Comparative Studies in Society and History* 6 (1963–4), pp. 307–20.

[9] H. Hearder, *Italy in the Age of the Risorgimento 1790–1870* (Harlow, 1983), pp. 125–53, 218–51.

[10] N. Moe, ' "This is Africa": ruling and representing southern Italy, 1860–61', in *Making and Remaking Italy – The Cultivation of National Identity around the Risorgimento*, ed. A. R. Ascoli and K. von Henneberg (Oxford, 2001), p. 126.

which emphasised the South's backwardness and saw Europe as ending at Naples. A moral map of Italy gradually emerged depicting the North as progressive and virtuous and the South gripped by vice. After the South's integration into the Italian state, some northern politicians saw themselves as 'doctors' healing the 'wound' of an uncivilised South incapable of self-government.[11] It was possible to link the Bourbon kingdom's roots with the twelfth-century monarchy and to trace the origins of southern Italy's so-called modern socio-economic problems back to the Norman period. As foreign misgovernment and a lack of civic spirit were put forward among the many reasons for the South's 'problems' the finger was often pointed at the Normans. More so because the exact opposite seemed to be occurring from the late eleventh century in the Centre and North, where an independent and energetic civic consciousness was visibly contributing to free enterprise and progress in areas which were subsequently seen as more developed in the modern era. Historians writing in the socio-political milieu of the nineteenth century could easily interpret evidence from the medieval period within the framework of a persistent North–South imbalance.

This understanding was underlined further by the intellectual tradition known as *Meridionalismo*, which addressed the so-called 'southern question' through comparisons with the North. The resultant analyses of the South 'essentially consisted of noting the absence of features found in the North [and] portraying the *Mezzogiorno* through a northern prism'.[12] As an approach it carries obvious negative consequences for an understanding of urban societies in the medieval South, as it encourages an interpretation through the framework of their more glamorous Northern counterparts. While *Meridionalismo* has recently begun to be questioned, its influence on the medieval period remains strong. In short, this period of history in the South has largely been seen as an abortive phase in the general framework of Italian history and has often been isolated from it. Even the hugely influential Neapolitan Benedetto Croce considered the history of the Norman monarchy as not identifiable with the history of southern Italy and lamented 'I can find no admirable traits among the peoples of southern Italy during the great period of Norman-Swabian domination, no stimulus to local pride, no comfort in examples of patriotic virtue.'[13] Later, Giovanni Tabacco

---

[11] Moe, '"This is Africa"', pp. 120–9, 133–7, 140.

[12] J. Morris, 'Challenging *Meridionalismo*: constructing a new history for Southern Italy', in *The New History of the Italian South – The Mezzogiorno Revisited*, ed. R. Lumley and J. Morris (Exeter, 1997), p. 10.

[13] Croce, *History of the Kingdom of Naples*, p. 23. For a stimulating discussion of these interpretative problems and a cogent argument for the Norman period to be placed within the South's history

depicted the medieval South in part as 'more a passive object than an actor in history', a region that was often marginal to European events, 'following its own different rhythm, sometimes even in an opposing direction'.[14]

The stigma attached to the Normans, their 'omnipotent' kingdom and its successor's later dilatory contribution to Italian nationhood has influenced the study of medieval urban life in the South, even of the period before the Normans appeared. Perhaps, partly as a result, scholars of urban society have more regularly been attracted to the Centre and North, increasing the *corpus* of works and maintaining the sense of disparity with the South. This has been exacerbated by the fact that of the smaller body of works dedicated specifically to Norman southern Italy few have adequately examined urban life. Within the South Italian historiographical tradition a great deal of research has been carried out upon various aspects of Norman southern Italy.[15] The region's political organisation, religious establishments, settlement patterns, arts, social composition and legal and administrative structures have all received superb treatment. Yet few detailed works, modern or otherwise, exist on South Italian urban government and society. Carabellese's 1905 edition of *L'Apulia ed il suo commune nell'Alto Medio Evo* provides an invaluable background to urban government, but it must be used with caution. It focuses solely on Apulia, is over a hundred years old and was written in the generation following Italian unification.[16] In the 1920s Calasso produced an important study on South Italian urban legislation, the aim of which was to explore the nature of civic liberties but not to investigate urban society as such.[17] Later, M. Caravale added a useful chapter in his *Il regno normanno di Sicilia*, but its emphasis is largely on administrative structures.[18] More recently J-M. Martin published *La Pouille du VI au XII siècle*, a remarkable work that approached the study of medieval Apulia using an exacting methodology.[19] The work, however, is limited again to the region of Apulia and is not primarily an

---

see G. Galasso, 'Considerazioni intorno alla storia del Mezzogiorno d'Italia', in his *Mezzogiorno medievale e moderno* (Turin, 1965), pp. 13–59.

[14] G. Tabacco, *The Struggle for Power in Medieval Italy – Structures of Political Rule* (Cambridge, 1989), pp. 6–7.

[15] J-M. Martin, 'Historiographie récente de l'Italie Méridionale pendant le haut moyen age', *Cahiers de Civilisation medievale X–XII siècles*, 41 (1998), pp. 331–51.

[16] F. Carabellese, *L'Apulia ed il suo comune nell'Alto Medio Evo* (Bari, 1905); there is also a less well-known follow-up volume published posthumously from the author's notes, F. Carabellese, *Il comune pugliese durante la monarchia normanno-sveva* (Bari, 1924).

[17] F. Calasso, *La legislazione statutaria dell' Italia meridionale: le basi storiche; le libertà cittadine dalla fondazione del regno all'epoca degli statuti* (Rome, 1929).

[18] M. Caravale, *Il regno normanno di Sicilia* (Rome, 1966), pp. 325–82.

[19] J-M. Martin, *La Pouille du VI au XII siècle* (Rome, 1993).

urban history. There are some more general works covering this period of South Italian history which do touch upon urban government and society. Most notable is Chalandon's *Histoire de la domination normande en Italie et en Sicilie*, published in 1907. Within its two huge volumes a good quantity of the material for a comprehensive study of urban life is included. Unfortunately it is mostly dispersed throughout the work in various chapters without a compact analysis on urban society. The more modern work, *The Norman Kingdom of Sicily*, by Matthew, also covers various important themes for an urban history, but, like Chalandon's, its focus lies elsewhere.[20] On the other hand one could compile a reasonable catalogue of modern works, mostly journal articles, which have explored individual cities or wider aspects of urban society.[21] These individual works have been particularly important in highlighting the wide regional differences throughout southern Italy and cautioning against making generalisations.

In short, there has not been a broad study of urban government and society in southern Italy during the Norman period; and certainly not one that has drawn together the wealth of source material with the latest research, which tends to emphasise the need for certain revisions in our understanding. It is my aim to take a tentative step towards filling what is a significant void, to build on the wave of new works on individual cities and to challenge some of the assumptions that surround the subject by exploring these emerging ideas in greater detail. Did the Normans stifle urban autonomy and civic life in the South, and if so to what extent? Was the region developed economically and commercially? How complex was the social ordering of urban communities, and is there evidence for a sense of civic identity? What continuities or inter-ruptions can be found in the cities? To answer these questions, an extensive range of charter material will be analysed, in order to reveal the minutiae of quotidian life in the city, without which we cannot begin to understand the bigger pictures in urban society. Hopefully such an investigation will bridge the gap that exists between the general histories of medieval southern Italy, which allude briefly to urban society, and those works which have looked exclusively at particular cities. While the need to apply 'historical specificity' to the South is clear, there should, and will, be room for constructive comparisons with the North.

The huge and relatively accessible quantity of material available to carry out an extensive analysis of medieval South Italian urban life means

---

[20] F. Chalandon, *Histoire de la domination normande en Italie et en Sicilie*, 2 vols. (Paris, 1907); D. Matthew, *The Norman Kingdom of Sicily* (Cambridge, 1992).

[21] For which see the Bibliography.

that the present study has had to impose certain limitations on itself, for obvious reasons of space. Most importantly the work concentrates primarily on the twelfth century, for the reasons already touched on. The decades immediately before and after the twelfth century have also been covered in order to provide a stronger framework. A steadily increasing body of charter material from the twelfth century facilitated this analysis, along with some fascinating narrative sources. The study's geographic scope focuses primarily on the most urbanised areas of southern Italy, Campania and Apulia, although Lucania will not be ignored. To avoid the work becoming gargantuan and overstretched, the areas of Calabria and Sicily had to be discounted. Not only is the source material for Calabria, an area with few urban centres, rather sparse, but both it and Sicily, with their stronger Greek and Muslim influences, would require an extensive survey in themselves. It is to be hoped that future research can explore both of these regions in the same way. Therefore, the present work essentially concerns itself with the traditional 'Latin' areas of the mainland. Within this area, as wide a comparative survey as possible has been undertaken of urban society. However, adopting such an approach is not intended to overlook the diversity of each individual city, shaped by its own unique history, culture and topography, or to minimise the regional heterogeneity of southern Italy.

It is worth briefly being precise about certain terminology. The use of the term 'Norman' is not intended to deny the existence of other 'French' groups subsumed within that label. Equally, for simplicity, the terms 'Norman' monarchy and 'Norman' Italy have been retained, although how 'Norman' South Italian society or the monarchy actually was is open to question. It should be acknowledged that this study on 'Norman' Italy also touches on the years 1194–1220, during which the term 'Norman' technically should be replaced by 'Staufen'. When used, the word 'communal' is employed as an adjective meaning 'that which relates to or benefits the community'. It is not to be associated with the commune as an institution, unless this is specifically indicated. Where the term 'urban/local government' has been frequently employed it is to denote the system of administration for the city which had both formal (a hierarchy of local public officials often linked to higher provincial ones) and informal (the role of private individuals/the citizenry) components. The powers of urban government varied, at times in connection with the city's position in any higher governmental framework. The urban government had a range of basic responsibilities: collection of various taxes and dues which were incumbent on the urban population and their transfer to a higher authority (if there was one), supervision of low criminal and civil justice, the regulation of trade and local customs, the organisation of civil order and defence. According to circumstances these powers could be notably extended to include, for example, high criminal justice, military and political policy and the control of public revenues.

Finally, in a medieval South Italian context what do we mean by a 'city'? A city could be defined by a combination of some, but not all, of the following: its size, its heritage, its function and its possession of a bishopric. It would seem too that a city is characterised by a reasonably dense population distribution and that a sizeable share of the inhabitants was devoted to non-agricultural occupations. But this is rarely straightforward, and there are variations and ambiguities inherent in the vocabulary employed for the region's urban settlements.[22] Fortunately this mostly applies only to the lesser urban centres, some of which could actually be smaller than a *castellum* and were usually of more recent foundation (often from the tenth and eleventh centuries). Indeed some of these 'cities' were not endowed with a bishopric, which was often regarded as a key indicator of urban status.[23] The only reliable option is to follow Fasoli's simple criterion – 'to accept as cities those to which contemporaries awarded the title of *civitas*'.[24] In this case we can only adopt the usages found in the sources at our disposal. However, this does not always clarify the marginal point at which the city and the country, in a physical, legal, economic or psychological sense, locate their boundaries. A population of 2,000 is generally considered the minimum size at which a settlement could have an urban and not a rural status.[25] Yet one suspects that those smaller urban centres in southern Italy, which medieval sources considered as 'cities', may not even have surpassed that

---

[22] J-M. Martin, 'Les communautés d'habitants de la Pouille et leurs rapports avec Roger II', in *Società, potere e popolo nell'età di Ruggero II. Atti della terza giornate normanno-svevo. Bari 23–25 maggio 1977* (Bari, 1980), 73–98; V. von Falkenhausen, *La dominazione bizantina nell'Italia meridionale dal IX all'XI secolo* (Bari, 1978), pp. 145–8.

[23] Foggia and Eboli were both settlements which were rapidly developing in the twelfth century and which at times were designated as a *civitas* without obtaining episcopal rank.

[24] G. Fasoli, 'Città e ceti urbani nell'età dei due Guglielmi', in *Potere, società e popolo nell'età dei due Guglielmi. Atti delle quarte giornate normanno-sveve. Bari, 1979* (Bari, 1981), pp. 148–9. The title *urbs* was also occasionally adopted, for example at Aversa, *CDNA*, p. 24 no. 16. According to J. F. Niermeyer, *Mediae Latinitatis Lexicon Minus* (Leiden, 1976), it was 'used as a variant of *civitas* chiefly with reference to major cities', p. 1051.

[25] K. A. Lynch, *Individuals, Families, and Communities in Europe, 1200–1800. The Urban Foundations of Western Society* (Cambridge, 2003), pp. 25–7, in which a distinction is made also between town and city. Such a division does not seem entirely relevant in a South Italian context and is not made in the present study. The nearest intermediate term in the peninsula could be the rather infrequently used *oppidum*. In the preface to his comprehensive study Nicholas noted that 'English is the only west European language that distinguishes "town" from "city" functionally', Nicholas, *Growth of the Medieval City*, p. xiv.

figure. The 'city' certainly extended beyond its walls, to include any suburbs and the immediate surrounding lands, but how far exactly remains unclear. Galasso has highlighted the fact that city and country were symbiotic, not separate, spheres and that the former could have strong rural characteristics.[26] The medieval use of the word *civitas* and *civis* (citizen) was certainly much more imprecise than the Roman conception. In consequence, the status of the wider territory assigned to a city was especially vague, as it was riddled with overlapping jurisdictions and inexact limits.[27]

With all this in mind, a sample of urban centres, which qualify through having the title of *civitas* along with most of the other urban characteristics just discussed, has been selected and examined in depth as case studies (Aversa, Bari, Benevento, Capua, Conversano, Salerno, Trani and Troia). Significant evidence has also been drawn from other cities (most notably Amalfi, Gaeta, Melfi, Monopoli, Naples and Taranto). The main case studies were selected as they offer a representative survey of urban life in twelfth-century southern Italy and also possess the vital intensity of documentation. The case studies provide an even geographic distribution (four each from Apulia and Campania) and in terms of size comprise relatively small (Conversano, Troia), medium (Aversa, Capua, Trani) and large (Bari, Benevento, Salerno) agglomerations. The diversity of the cities' political and cultural histories was equally significant in their selection. Bari, Trani, Troia and Conversano had all been under Byzantine rule in the eleventh century. Indeed Bari had been the Byzantines' capital city in southern Italy, although all four cities had mostly Lombard populations. In Campania, Aversa was from its foundation in 1030 a military base for Norman mercenaries, ruled by a Norman count, and later incorporated into the principality of Capua. It had a strong Normanno-French population and was heavily influenced by their customs and practices. Capua, Benevento and Salerno had for centuries been the capitals of Lombard principalities until their Lombard princes were replaced in 1058, 1077 and 1076/7 respectively. The inclusion of Benevento in this study is important. All the cities chosen as case studies succumbed to the invading Norman bands in the course of the eleventh century, while Benevento avoided this fate by placing itself under papal rule (where it remained until 1860). For this reason Benevento, an effective papal enclave in Norman southern Italy, has often been dealt with separately from the rest of the region,

---

[26] Galasso, 'Le città campane nell'Alto Medioevo', in *Mezzogiorno medievale e moderno*, pp. 83–4.
[27] Often called its *contado*, while Latin sources use phrases such as *in territorio, pertinentia, finibus, confinibus civitatis*.

9

and especially so after 1139. However, having a papal rather than a Norman lord does not alter the fact that the city was South Italian.[28] A comparative study can only benefit from incorporating Benevento, where illuminating developments took place in the twelfth century. Fortunately some of these were recorded in great detail in the remarkable work of Falco of Benevento, one of the earliest genuine civic chronicles of the medieval period.

Much of the primary material for the main case studies has been assembled from cartulary collections, which have provided thousands of private and public documents. For Apulia most of these charters have been edited in the *Codice diplomatico barese* series (of which later volumes are known under the title of *Codice diplomatico pugliese*). Collectively these volumes have yielded a wealth of documentation on Bari, Conversano, Monopoli, Trani and Troia. Numerous other collections provide additional charter evidence for the cities of Apulia: for example volume IV of *Le colonie cassinesi in Capitanata* provides around 40 documents on Troia, and Prologo's edition of the metropolitan archive at Trani contains some 100 charters for that city.

There is a similar abundance of material for the cities of Campania. For Aversa the main charter collections are contained in the *Codice diplomatico normanno di Aversa* and the *Codice diplomatico svevo di Aversa*. These two sources also provide a handful of charters on Capua although the core material for this city is in *Le pergamene di Capua* (volumes I and II), *Le pergamene normanne della Mater Ecclesia capuana*, *Le pergamene sveve della Mater Ecclesia capuana* (2 volumes) and the *Regesto di S. Angelo in Formis*. For Benevento and Salerno, as well as a host of printed collections, there is still a sizeable quantity of unpublished documents. At Benevento these are mostly deposited in the Fondo S. Sofia at the Museo del Sannio and in the Pergamene Aldobrandini, formerly at the Biblioteca Apostolica Vaticano.[29] The main printed collections for the city are found in *Le più antiche carte del capitolo della cattedrale di Benevento*, *Le più antiche carte dell'abbazia di San Modesto in Benevento*, the *Chronicon Sanctae Sophiae* and the *Codice diplomatico verginiano* (13 volumes up to the year 1210, which also provide documents on Aversa, Capua, Salerno and

---

[28] A point argued by G. A. Loud, 'Politics, piety and ecclesiastical patronage in twelfth-century Benevento', in *Cavalieri alla conquista del Sud. Studi sull'Italia normanna in memoria di Léon-Robert Ménager*, ed. E. Cuozzo and J-M. Martin (Bari, 1998), pp. 283–312 [reprinted in G. A. Loud, *Montecassino and Benevento in the Middle Ages* (Aldershot, 2000)].

[29] G. A. Loud, 'The medieval records of the monastery of St Sophia, Benevento', *Archives 19* (1991), pp. 363–73 [reprinted in Loud, *Montecassino and Benevento*]. Translations of unpublished documents from Benevento were obtained courtesy of the generosity of G. A. Loud.

Troia).[30] In addition, the *Obituarium Sancti Spiritus* provides further detail on Beneventan society in the twelfth and thirteenth centuries. For Salerno, many relevant documents are housed in an immense collection in the archives at the monastery of Cava. The majority of these remain unpublished, although the charters up to 1080 have been printed in the *Codex Diplomaticus Cavensis* series.[31] Other Cava documents have found their way into print in collections such as *Le pergamene di S. Nicola di Gallucanta (secc. IX–XII)*, *Documenti per la storia di Eboli. I (799–1264)* and in the volumes on the monastery of S. Giorgio of Salerno by Cassese and Galante. There are other additional and significant published collections of Salernitan charters, namely the *Pergamene salernitane (1008–1784)* and the *Codice diplomatico salernitano del secolo XIII*. Moreover, compilations of charters relating to the nearby city of Amalfi, such as *Il codice Perris. Cartulario amalfitano. Sec. X–XV* and the *Codice diplomatico amalfitano*, supply useful material pertaining to Salerno. Garufi's edition of the necrology of S. Matteo of Salerno, which contains details on the leading members of the civic community, is a valuable resource to be used in conjunction with the charter material.

General compilations of charters that are not specific to a particular city or region have also formed an integral part of the source material and offer some key documents. The first, and as yet only, volume of the *Recueil des actes des ducs normands d'Italie* provides ducal diplomas for the earlier period of 1047–87. The *Codex Diplomaticus Regni Siciliae* contains a variety of royal charters from the twelfth century, while the *Acta Imperii Inedita Saeculi XIII et XIV* and the multi-volume *Historia Diplomatica Friderici Secundi* supply some useful documents from the Staufen period. Papal collections have proved useful, most notably volumes VIII and IX of the *Italia Pontifica* series and Vendola's edition of papal acts concerning Apulia from the pontificate of Innocent III to that of Nicholas IV. Volumes VI to IX of Ughelli's eighteenth-century *Italia Sacra*, a regional historical survey of Italy's bishoprics, include copies of documents not found in print elsewhere.

Chronicles, annals and other sources have been employed alongside this extensive charter documentation. The works by Amatus of

---

[30] There is also a seven-volume register of the documents of Montevergine, of which the second volume is relevant to our period, *Abbazzia di Montevergine. Regesto delle pergamene*, vol. II, 1200–49, ed. G. Mongelli (Rome, 1957).

[31] To do justice to this wealth of material on Salerno, most of which remains unpublished, would require a thesis in itself. The present study has utilised all the published material available on the city as well as a good quantity of unedited documents from the Cava archive, kindly provided by G. A. Loud. These are extensive enough to permit detailed conclusions on the city, even if they cannot be inclusive of the full body of documentation.

Montecassino, Geoffrey Malaterra and William of Apulia, as well as the Montecassino Chronicle and that which is widely attributed to Archbishop Romuald II of Salerno, contribute vital material on South Italian urban life during the chaotic period of Norman infiltration in the eleventh century. The key twelfth-century chronicles composed by Alexander of Telese and Falco of Benevento enhance our understanding of the critical early decades of that century and of the civil war that broke after 1127, a time that saw substantial evolution in civic government. Falco's work offers a comprehensive look at the functioning of urban life at Benevento that is without parallel elsewhere. Unfortunately, Alexander's work ends in 1135, while Falco's halts abruptly in 1140.[32] Thereafter, aside from the continued work of Romuald of Salerno, which in places is pan-European in scope, the coverage for the mainland becomes thinner. The survival of a legal code attributed to Roger II, often incorrectly called the Assizes of Ariano, throws some light on life in the kingdom. The *History of the Tyrants of Sicily*, attributed to the so-called Hugo Falcandus, offers a wonderfully intricate insight into the political machinations at the royal court in Palermo over the years 1154 to 1166. The author's attention does turn at times to the mainland and its cities, but Sicily always remains the focus. Useful, but relatively brief, information can be drawn from outside Italy in the works of the Greek John Kinnamos and the German Otto of Freising, who both recorded the mainland rebellion in the kingdom in 1156 which enveloped the urban centres. Despite the continuation of Romuald's chronicle until 1178 it is frustrating how little of this type of material exists for the reign of King William II, particularly for the 1180s. The Catalogue of Barons does offer some assistance for tracing administrative procedures and leading figures at least for the early part of William II's rule. The Catalogue is a royal register assembled in the 1150s, and possibly revised in the late 1160s, which listed the military service due to the crown on the mainland. In addition, the Constitutions of Melfi, promulgated by Frederick II in 1231, provides some insight into legal and social practices that were current at the time of William II (and his predecessors). After 1189 we can use the chronicle of Richard of S. Germano, which continues beyond the chronological limits of this study, and also the Deeds of Pope Innocent III (*c.* 1198–*c.* 1208). More specifically the period of conflict for the throne (1189–94),

---

[32] It seems that Falco's chronicle did continue until at least 1144, and a rudimentary version of the last section has survived in the *Chronicon Ignoti Monachi Cisterciensis Sanctae Mariae de Ferraria*, ed. A. Gaudenzi (Naples, 1888); also see G. A. Loud, 'The genesis and context of the Chronicle of Falco of Benevento', in *Anglo-Norman Studies 15. Proceedings of the Battle Conference 1992*, ed. M. Chibnall (Woodbridge, 1993), p. 179.

in which the mainland cities were heavily involved, formed the subject of a long and engaging poem by Peter of Eboli. Separating fact from fantasy in Peter's *Liber ad honorem Augusti* is not easy, but some remarkable scenes of urban life are provided not only by the author's verse but also by superb, appended illuminations. As the outcome of the succession dispute linked the fortunes of the kingdom of Sicily more closely to those of the empire, from the 1190s certain works of German writers, such as the Chronicle of Otto of St Blasien and the Marburg Annals, also took an interest in South Italian affairs. Finally, throughout the whole period of this study an array of brief annal sources can be utilised. Among the many are the annals of *Lupus Protospatharius* and the *Annales Barenses*, which are useful for Bari and Apulia in the eleventh century, the *Anonymous Barensis Chronicon*, which offers otherwise unattested information on urban disorder within Bari in the 1110s, and the *Annales Beneventani*, which are valuable for the city of Benevento in the decades either side of 1100. One can also add the *Annalista Saxo*, for the conflict in the 1130s, and the *Annales Casinenses*, a work continued into the early-thirteenth century.

In using this range of source material, alongside the body of modern research, it has been possible to construct a deeper, more nuanced understanding of urban society and community in twelfth-century mainland southern Italy.[33] Such an understanding, in turn, suggests the need to revise 'traditional' interpretations of the Norman kingdom.

---

[33] See the Bibliography for the complete references for all the aforesaid primary works and a full list of all the others used, excluded here for reasons of space.

Part I

URBAN GOVERNMENT AND COMMUNAL INDEPENDENCE

Chapter 1

BEFORE 1085: THE ARRIVAL
OF THE NORMANS

Norman adventurers had been appearing on the South Italian mainland since the first decades of the eleventh century, possibly even as early as *c.* 1000.[1] Some perhaps entered the peninsula originally as pilgrims, others as opportunistic warriors. The newcomers, exuding military prowess, were swiftly recruited as mercenaries by native rulers as part of their endless internecine conflicts.[2] The South at this point was a patchwork of competing petty rulers. In Campania, Lombard principalities were centred on Benevento, Capua and Salerno. On the Tyrrhenian coast, Amalfi, Gaeta and Naples were all effectively independent states that only nominally acknowledged Byzantine overlordship.[3] In these cities, government was more personalised and somewhat unadorned, being largely based around the ruling princely or ducal families. A small group of leading functionaries (counts, *gastaldi, comites palacii*) and other advisers, largely drawn from the most influential inhabitants, orbited around the ruling dynasty and oversaw public authority. A typical example can be seen in a donation by Prince Gisulf II of Salerno to the monastery of Cava in 1072, which was completed in the sacred palace of the city before a single judge, and 'with several *fideles* around him as was usual'.[4]

---

[1] *Amatus*, Bk I.17, p. 49; E. Joranson, 'The inception of the career of the Normans in Italy – legend and history', *Speculum* 23 (1948), pp. 353–96; J. France, 'The occasion of the coming of the Normans to Italy', *JMH* 17 (1991), pp. 185–205.

[2] Excellent coverage of the early impact of the Norman 'infiltration' into southern Italy is provided by: G. A. Loud, *The Age of Robert Guiscard. Southern Italy and the Norman Conquest* (Harlow, 2000); V. von Falkenhausen, 'I ceti dirigenti prenormanni al tempo della costituzione degli stati normanni nell'Italia meridionale e in Sicilia', in *Forme di potere e struttura sociale in Italia nel Medioevo*, ed. G. Rossetti (Bologna, 1977), pp. 321–71.

[3] For the relationship between these Campanian polities and Byzantium before 1000 see J-M. Martin, 'L'Occident Chrétien dans le *Livre des Cérémonies*, II, 48', *Travaux et mémoires* 13 (2000), pp. 617–46.

[4] C. A. Garufi, 'Sullo strumento notarile nel Salernitano nello scorcio del secolo XI', *Archivio storico italiano* 46 (1910), appendix, pp. 324–6 no. 3.

In lower-status cases, judges, notaries and *idonei homines* conducted affairs. It seems that the Lombard prince of Salerno was able to maintain public power far more successfully than his counterparts in Capua and Benevento, where the local communities may have participated more in government.

Apulia and Calabria were still Byzantine-controlled lands split into 'themes', each with an important centre at Bari and Reggio.[5] However, these territories were on the margins of the empire, and Constantinople allowed local customs, officials, and structures of power to remain in place. Byzantine policy was marked by flexibility, countenancing the continuance of varied legal, linguistic and religious practices among the native Lombard and Greek communities. Yet at the same time, the locals could, and did, avail themselves of an effective overarching imperial legal system.[6] Apart from the leading provincial officials, the *catepan* and the *strategotus*, lower officials, such as *turmarchi* and the Lombard *gastaldi*, were drawn from the indigenous population. Thus, below a thin but largely efficient Byzantine superstructure, internal government was essentially left to the local communities.[7] While Calabria and parts of southern Apulia and Lucania had large Greek populations, the other regions under Byzantine rule, central and northern Apulia, had a Lombard majority and were not 'Hellenised' as such. This was especially evident in the network of defensive hill-forts founded by the Byzantines in the Capitanata region of northern Apulia around the year 1000, where the new settlers were predominantly Lombard.[8] However, in the major Apulian coastal cities, Byzantine culture, official titles (which could be passed down through families) and symbols were influential and acted as channels through which the local population could express allegiance and position.[9]

If Byzantine southern Italy appears to have been regularly hit by troubles and revolts, it seems that this was largely linked to temporary dissatisfaction over excessive fiscal exactions and the need for greater security, rather than a direct desire to secede from Byzantine government. Troubles often had at their root internal power struggles among

---

[5] There may have also been a theme of Lucania; see generally von Falkenhausen, *La dominazione bizantina*.

[6] R. Morris, 'Dispute settlement in the Byzantine provinces in the tenth century', in *The Settlement of Disputes in Early Medieval Europe*, ed. W. Davies and P. Fouracre (Cambridge, 1986), pp. 146–7.

[7] C. Holmes, *Basil II and the Governance of Empire (976–1025)* (Oxford, 2005), pp. 429–47.

[8] J-M. Martin and G. Noyé, *La Capitanata nella storia del Mezzogiorno medioevale* (Bari, 1991).

[9] For more see below pp. 26–7, 34–5, 169; good background on the cities of Byzantine Italy is provided by V. von Falkenhausen, 'Die Städte im byzantinischen Italien', *Mélanges de l'école française de Rome* 101 (1989), pp. 401–64.

South Italians and are not evidence of attitudes towards Constantinople.[10] That said, the nobleman Melo of Bari may have been aiming at some form of independence when leading the Apulian revolts which began in 1009. Different Norman bands played increasingly key roles in these Apulian insurrections and also fought (at times against other Normans) in the fluctuating border skirmishes between the Campanian rulers. By 1030 one band of Normans had settled in a small *casale* called Aversa (between Capua and Naples) and eventually developed it into an important urban settlement in what became known as the county of Aversa. Others established themselves in 1041 at Melfi in Lucania. By the 1050s the political landscape of the South Italian mainland was in a palpable ferment. While the power and independent action of some of the Norman bands was continually increasing, that of the local authorities (including distant Byzantium) was weakening. This was confirmed at the Battle of Civitate in 1053, when a coalition of Norman bands defeated a combined force of South Italian and papal troops which had aimed to rid the peninsula of their presence. A prompt reversal in papal policy led to the formal investiture in 1059 of two of the leading Normans: Richard Quarrel, count of Aversa, was recognised as prince of Capua, and Robert Guiscard, of the Hauteville family, received the new designation of duke of Apulia, Calabria and in the future Sicily. The support of the papacy, which claimed ancient jurisdiction over southern Italy, provided legitimacy and was significant, as neither Richard nor Robert had full control of the territories that were bestowed upon them.[11] Richard had successfully besieged Capua in 1058, ousted the princely family and received recognition from the inhabitants as the new *princeps Capuanorum*. However, he did not have at that point full power over Capua; its populace was able to keep control of the city defences. It would take another siege of the city in 1062 before Richard was able to receive the city fully into his hands.[12] The next year Richard extended his authority over the small independent state of Gaeta, where a Norman duke was installed, but it would take further campaigning to subdue the entire principality. Indeed this process was still continuing under Richard's son and successor, Jordan I (1078–90).

Likewise Robert Guiscard might have controlled most of Calabria in 1059, but its principal city, Reggio, held out until 1060. Sicily was still under Muslim rule and the protracted conquest of that island (1061–91),

---

[10] J-C. Cheynet, *Pouvoir et contestations à Byzance (963–1210)* (Paris, 1990), pp. 385–7; V. von Falkenhausen, 'A provincial aristocracy: the Byzantine provinces in southern Italy (9th–11th century)', *The Byzantine Aristocracy IX to XIII centuries*, ed. M. Angold, BAR international series 221 (Oxford, 1984), pp. 211–35.
[11] Loud, *Age of Robert Guiscard*, pp. 130–45. [12] *Amatus*, Bk IV.28–9, pp. 120–2.

under his younger brother Roger I, was yet to commence. In Apulia, Bari and most of the region's southern territories remained under Byzantine control, albeit one that was largely collapsing as a result of problems at the centre of the empire. Guiscard did capture the northern Apulian city of Troia (*c.* 1060), which became a quasi-ducal capital, but his general progress in the region was sporadic in the 1060s. While Guiscard was distracted by Sicily and family squabbles, other Norman counts were able to make independent inroads into Apulia during this period. For example Geoffrey, Guiscard's nephew, created a large power base in Central Apulia and by the early 1070s had established himself at Conversano, from where he subsequently took his comital title. Therefore, when Guiscard later attempted to consolidate his position in Apulia he met resistance and revolts (1067–8, 1072–3, 1079–80, 1082–3) led by these Norman nobles, who largely considered themselves the duke's equals.[13] The insurrections also received external support from Byzantium and the Norman princes of Capua. However, on each occasion the uprisings were suppressed, and confiscations of rebel territories enabled Guiscard to extend his authority (for example, Trani in 1073 and Taranto in 1080 were acquired from the rebel Count Peter II of Andria).[14] An important turning-point for Guiscard's rule was the capture of Bari after a lengthy siege (1068–71); with its fall the last vestige of Byzantine rule in southern Italy was eradicated. Furthermore, in 1073 the city of Amalfi voluntarily accepted Guiscard's authority on condition that he would offer security against the threats of the nearby Lombard Prince Gisulf II of Salerno.[15] Indeed soon afterwards, following another protracted blockade (1076–7), Guiscard extended his power in Campania with the important seizure of Salerno. Gisulf II fled into exile at the papal court. By Guiscard's death in 1085 he ruled a composite territory incorporating Apulia, Calabria, most of Sicily, parts of Campania and the Abruzzi. He had achieved it partly through conquest, partly through confiscation and partly through the submission of other Normans who had previously taken over lands independently.

However, two cities retained a semblance of independence from the Norman advances. Naples, ruled by an ancient ducal family, resisted a blockade in 1077 by Prince Richard of Capua. The siege was lifted after Richard's death in April 1078, though it appears that Prince Jordan I received tribute from the city, and established some sort of protectorate

---

[13] Loud, *Age of Robert Guiscard*, pp. 234–46.
[14] *Will. Apulia*, Bk III lines 372–89, p. 184, lines 670–2, p. 200.   [15] *Malaterra*, Bk III.3.

over it.[16] The other city was Benevento, which had briefly been under papal rule around 1050, though this arrangement collapsed soon afterwards. However, in 1073 the city's prince, Landulf VI, placed Benevento once again under papal authority, most likely to find security from Norman attack.[17] When Landulf died without heir in 1077, the city passed to direct papal rule. It held out against Guiscard's siege (1077–8) and was to retain its autonomy from the Normans.

The political disruption of this period of Norman 'conquest' severely tested southern Italy's urban communities. Byzantine influence in its South Italian territories was waning, and the power of the Lombard princes was receding to the immediate orbit of their principal cities. But the subsequent Norman take-over was rarely smooth or immediate. Power voids lasted for sizeable periods, during which urban government was essentially in the hands of the local population. In many cases prior to a final submission there were preliminary hazy phases in which cities accepted some sort of Norman domination, often indirectly via tribute payment. This was often the case in Apulia. Troia paid tribute to Guiscard in the 1050s, as perhaps also did Bari, Trani and Otranto, which suggests that the urban community organised its own finances.[18] At Capua, between 1058 (if not earlier) and 1062, citizens retained control of civic defence and clearly much else besides. Also at Benevento, which resisted the Normans, events by the mid-eleventh century imply an active role for the urban community. The inhabitants of Benevento had refused to recognise Emperor Henry III during his expedition of 1046–7 in southern Italy, resisted his siege and received papal excommunication for their pains.[19] Pope Leo IX renewed the sentence when he arrived at the city in 1050, and it was only lifted the following year. By this point the Beneventans, no doubt fatigued by the papal sanctions and continued Norman pressure, had exiled their prince and appealed for the pope to rule Benevento. This the pope did, but in the name of Emperor Henry III. Yet after Leo's defeat at Civitate and his death in 1054, the citizens by 1056 had recalled Prince Pandulf III. It was clear that papal/imperial protection was not safeguarding the city from the Normans.[20]

---

[16] *Malaterra*, Bk IV.26; Loud, *Age of Robert Guiscard*, p. 141; for evidence of the effects of the Norman attacks on Naples, *Codex Diplomaticus Cavensis*, ed. S. Leone and G. Vitolo (Cava, 1990), vol. x. no. 103.

[17] *The Register of Pope Gregory VII – 1073–1085*, trans. H. E. J. Cowdrey (Oxford, 2002), pp. 20–1, 1.18a; one Beneventan charter of 1076 is actually dated by the ruling years of both Pope Gregory VII and Prince Landulf, *Montevergine*, i. 291–2 no. 74.

[18] *Will. Apulia*, Bk II lines 294–6, p. 148.

[19] *Chronicon Monasterii Casinensis*, ed. H. Hoffman, *MGH SS* XXXIV (Hanover, 1980), II.78, p. 323.

[20] O. Bertolini, 'Gli 'Annales Beneventani'', *BISME* 42 (1923), pp. 137–40; Loud, *Age of Robert Guiscard*, pp. 110, 115, 121; G. Intorcia, *Civitas beneventana. Genesi ed evoluzione delle istituzioni*

Although local communities were eager to self-govern, our sources do not show any official, or institutionalised, form of popular participation in the region's cities at this stage.

In a period of regular conflict and siege the communities, particularly in Byzantine Apulia, were left with even more scope than before to organise their own defence and government. At Guiscard's siege of Troia (*c.* 1060) the inhabitants 'took counter measures, though they did not refuse the customary tribute [to Guiscard] and had even promised to add to it gold and horses from Greece'.[21] The citizens held out until famine induced surrender. Recognised authority within cities fluctuated in this early phase. A charter from Troia of 1065 carried the name of the Byzantine emperor, only to be followed by one from 1068 again recognising Duke Robert.[22] At Bari it seems that in 1064 the citizens and Guiscard had exchanged some sort of mutual oath.[23] Nevertheless the city remained under Byzantine control and, when besieged by Guiscard in 1068, vigorously resisted for three years. Narrative accounts stress both the influential role of leading citizens and the unsuccessful attempts at Constantinople to succour the city. Factions in Bari were, according to Amatus, formed around pro-Byzantine and pro-Norman movements, but one suspects that local familial rivalries were at the root of the split.[24] Indeed we are told that Argirizzus, apparently the leader of the group that favoured accommodation with Guiscard, had 'more relatives and friends than Bisantius', his chief rival, whose murder he arranged.[25] On the other hand Malaterra's shorter account of the siege includes the assertion that Argirizzus actually 'governed the city of Bari for the emperor' and suggests that he acted loyally towards his Byzantine lord.[26] William of Apulia's more detailed version states that Guiscard targeted with promises 'those who form the most noble and powerful section of the city', believing that their seduction would lead ineluctably to that of the 'lesser' people.[27]

---

cittadine nei sec. XIII–XVI (Benevento, 1981), pp. 8–12; a papal charter of 1052 records the 'wrongful behaviour and arrogance' of the Beneventans in rebelling against the pope and the emperor, *Chronicon Sanctae Sophiae*, 2 vols., ed. J-M. Martin, *Fonti per la storia dell'Italia medievale* (Rome, 2000), ii. 620–3 no. v.2 (*hereafter Chron. S. Sophiae*).

[21] *Amatus*, Bk V.6, p. 135; but Romuald suggests that the inhabitants of Troia actually invited Guiscard to be their lord, *Romuald*, p. 184.

[22] *Troia*, no. 12; *Le colonie cassinesi in Capitanata. IV. Troia*, ed. T. Leccisotti, *Miscellanea Cassinese*, XXIX (Montecassino, 1957), no. 10.

[23] *Anonymi Barensis Chronicon (855–1149)*, ed. C. Pellegrino, *RIS* V (Milan, 1724), p. 152.

[24] *Amatus*, Bk V.27, pp. 143–6.

[25] *Amatus*, Bk V.27, p 144; see also *Lupus Protospatharius, Annales*, ed. G. H. Pertz, *MGH SS* V (Hanover, 1845), p. 272 and *Anonymi Barensis Chronicon*, p. 153.

[26] *Malaterra*, Bk II.40, 43.

[27] *Will. Apulia*, Bk II lines 533–6 p. 160, and for the full account, Bk II lines 479–572 pp. 158–62, Bk III lines 112–66 pp. 170–2.

If we follow Amatus, Argirizzus did indeed eventually hand over the city to the Normans, despite the protestations of many of the citizens, who had clearly not been swayed by the 'provisions' and 'gifts' which he had offered to the 'lesser people' and the 'poor'. William of Apulia called Argirizzus 'the first citizen of Bari' (*urbis primus*) and explained that one of the reasons for his success was that 'the *maiores* [were] able to lead the spirit of the *minores* to whatever end they wished'.[28] At Amalfi, in 1073, it was 'the leading men with the agreement of the citizens' who handed the city over to Guiscard.[29] Later, during Richard's blockade of Naples, the Neapolitans offered 'fierce resistance' and 'prepared the city with provisions and kept a sharp watch from the towers'.[30] We can only guess at the losses inflicted upon the urban communities. In addition, in most cases, surrender was induced by famine, with the Normans finding it difficult to take cities by other means. The result was extreme hardship for the besieged, which was described by Amatus for Salerno (1076–7) in graphic detail.[31] Similarly Trani submitted to Guiscard in 1073, as it was 'left in the grip of famine and other afflictions' by his siege.[32]

While there was evident bloodshed and prolonged periods of disruption we should not underestimate the underlying fibres of continuity that remain a significant feature of South Italian urban life during this period. Above all it is clear that the Normans, for all the damage they wrought and the difficulties in distinguishing them from natives in the source material, were a minority group. Their number may only have been around 2,000 to 2,500. Moreover, there was not on the mainland any notable exodus of the local population to other lands. More importantly, the Norman newcomers predominantly settled in rural areas, and it was among the native rural landowning elite that the main appropriations took place. There was only a slow and gradual importation of new tenurial structures.[33] The charter documentation shows little evidence of Normanno-French inhabitants settled within cities, and as a result the urban population, and its elites, were not displaced.[34] The

---

[28] *Will. Apulia*, Bk III lines 144–8 p. 172.   [29] *Malaterra*, Bk III.3.

[30] *Amatus*, Bk VIII.25, p. 200.   [31] *Amatus*, Bk VIII.16, 18, 19, 20, 24, pp. 194–200.

[32] *Amatus*, Bk VII.2, pp. 115–16; *Wil. Apulia*, Bk III lines 372–89 p. 185.

[33] See below p. 170.

[34] Von Falkenhausen, 'I ceti dirigenti prenormanni', pp. 327–30; L-R. Ménager, 'Pesanteur et étiologie de la colonisation normande de l'Italie' and 'Inventaire des familles normandes et franques émigrés en Italie méridionale et en Sicile (XIe–XIIe siècles)', both in *Roberto il Guiscardo e il suo tempo (Relazioni e communicazioni nelle prime giornate normanno-sveve, Bari 1973* (Bari, 1975), pp. 189–215, 259–390 [reprinted with additions in his *Hommes et institutions de l'Italie normande* (London, 1981)]. Examples like Herbius de Lohec of Brittany at Troia in 1087 (*Colonie cassinesi*, no. 14) and Robert Curteray 'ex genere normannorum' at Conversano in 1093 (*Conversano*, no. 54) are infrequent.

Normans did not notably alter the urban landscape, and we do not find Norman quarters within cities. This was particularly the case in the larger cities possessed of a strong civic tradition and more complex urban topography.[35] But castles were erected, usually on the city's periphery, and this was a novel imposition on the urban landscape. It theoretically ensured the ruler's control of the community and acted as a visible reminder of it as well as a potential target for disaffection. However, it is clear that the existence of a castle and garrison was not sufficient to prevent communities from rebelling and conducting their own military activities. The exception to all this was Aversa, a small *casale* with no previously established civic ordering or high population density, which was developed by the Normans into one of their key centres.[36] Charters from the city in the eleventh century contain a large proportion of identifiable Normanno-French individuals, and speak of 'frankish law', while those of the twelfth century regularly applied French-influenced vocabulary to social groupings.[37] Elsewhere, a small Norman elite was grafted onto existing urban structures. Unfortunately a detailed understanding of urban government at this period is barely possible. Limited charter material, and the undoubtedly confused process of regime change, leaves a hazy picture. At Capua, aside from the introduction of a *vicecomes*, the pre-existing Lombard administration remained, along with Lombard officials and law; Lombards were also found in the Norman prince of Capua's entourage. At Benevento, another former capital of a Lombard principality in southern Italy, the city's Lombard heritage remained strong under papal rule; judges still carried the Lombard title of *gastald* and the city's administrative centre continued to be the sacred palace.[38] The pope did not have the inclination, the capability or the time to restructure the functioning of urban government. The only significant alteration was the appointment of a supreme official to represent papal interests in the city. But the first two incumbents of that post were both drawn from the local elite and had close links to the previous Lombard regime. Of the two men, Stephen Sculdascio (*sculdahis* is a Lombard administrative title) was a former agent of the last Lombard prince, Landulf VI, and Dacomarius may well

---

[35] P. Delogu, 'I Normanni in città: schemi politici ed urbanistici', *Società, potere e popolo nell'eta di Ruggero II. Atti delle terze giornate normmano-sveve, Bari, 1977* (Bari, 1980), pp. 176, 187, 192–3.

[36] Melfi, although not to the same extent as Aversa, was also subject to relatively strong Norman influence. Founded by the Byzantines in 1018, it later became a key centre for the Normans.

[37] For example *CDNA*, pp. 309–11 no. 37, pp. 341–2 no. 19, pp. 386–7 no. 43, pp. 389–90 no. 45, pp. 399–401 no. 53.

[38] *Montevergine*, i. 292 no. 74 refers to the use of Lombard law (1076), 324 no. 81 ter., refers to city customs and a *gastald* (1085).

have been a *fidelis* of the prince.[39] Although the pope visited the city as often as possible, he had to rely largely on these two figures to maintain his interests. Both men initially seemed to share power. In a document of 1082, referring to both of them, Stephen alone seems to carry the title of rector; however, he stated that the 'highest authority' had placed them both in charge of 'managing the city' and its people.[40] What is clear is that a wider circle of citizens participated in urban affairs. In 1075, among those present at a case held by Milo, archbishop of Benevento, were Prince Landulf, Stephen Sculdascio and 'several of the Beneventan nobility (*nobilitas*) who had the authority of a witness'.[41] In the document of 1082 we see Dacomarius and Stephen before 'a great crowd of noble Beneventans', and other *boni homines*, 'investigat[ing] the minds of all the citizens standing by', over a donation to the Beneventan monastery of S. Sofia.[42]

At Salerno, Guiscard did not assume the princely title, perhaps because the papacy had not initially supported the city's conquest. However, he ruled in the same way as his Lombard predecessor; the *sacrum palatium* remained the centre of administration, and similar ecclesiastical establishments continued to be patronised.[43] Sensitivity towards matters of local importance was evident. The rebuilding of the cathedral and the invention in 1080 of the city's patron, St Matthew, were astute moves, assisted by the support of the hugely influential archbishop, Alfanus I. This association was important for Norman rule. For some time the city's archbishop had actively exalted Salerno's cultural splendour and opulence, primarily through his poetical works and the cult of St Matthew. The effect was to play down the regime change and make it easier for the citizens to accept.[44] The old Lombard comital elites remained in powerful positions, and judges who served under Gisulf II continued to do so under Guiscard. Sico *comes et iudex* was attested from 1065 (and perhaps as early as 1050) to 1091.[45] The *vesterarius* Gratian, son

---

[39] *Chron. S. Sophiae*, ii. 683–90 no. vi.4, 744–50 vi.24–5; Stephen owned property in and around Benevento, *Montevergine*, i. 312–4 no. 78; for more on the Sculdascio family see below p. 220.

[40] *Chron. S. Sophiae*, ii. 744–7 no. vi.24.   [41] *Chron. S. Sophiae*, ii. 683–90 no. vi.4.

[42] *Chron. S. Sophiae*, ii. 744–7 no. vi.24.

[43] For a donation by Guiscard to the monastery of Cava see *Recueil des actes des ducs normands d'Italie* [1046–1127]: *I., Les Premiers ducs (1046–1087)*, ed. L.-R. Ménager (Bari, 1980), pp. 105–8 no. 33; for grants to the archbishopric see pp. 108–10 no. 34, pp. 110–13 no. 35.

[44] P. Delogu, *Mito di una città meridionale (Salerno, secoli VIII–XI)* (Naples, 1977), pp. 181–90; *I carmi di Alfano I Arcivescovo di Salerno*, ed. A. Lentini and F. Avagliano, *Miscellanea Cassinese* XXXVIII (Montecassino, 1974); Pope Gregory VII congratulated Alfanus on the discovery of St Matthew, *Register of Pope Gregory VII*, pp. 373–4 no. 8; See also below p. 239 for Alfanus' poems.

[45] On Sico's activities see *Documenti per la storia di Eboli. I. (799–1264)*, ed. C. Carlone (Salerno, 1998), p. 15 no. 30; *Nuove pergamene del monastero femminile di S. Giorgio di Salerno. I. [993–1256]*, ed. M. Galante (Salerno, 1984), pp. 18–19 no. 7; *Le pergamene di S. Nicola di Gallucanta (secc. IX–XII)*,

of Roderisius, undoubtedly Lombard and described as *fidelis*, received property from Guiscard in 1079.[46] On a broader social scale, it has been estimated that the necrology of the *Liber Confratrum* of the city's cathedral, dated to the eleventh and twelfth centuries, contains only 93 Norman names among its list of 1,059.[47]

In Apulia at the highest level there was a restructuring of the administrative ordering. In Benevento, Capua, and to some extent also Salerno, the new ruler simply replaced the old dynasty. In Byzantine Apulia there had been no such thing, and the region was incorporated into a new superstructure comprising Sicily, Calabria and (after 1077) the principality of Salerno. The latter city seemed to take precedence over Bari, the former Byzantine provincial capital. But within the cities of Apulia we can trace continuities with what is found elsewhere. As in Capua and Salerno with the Lombard administration, the Normans retained the more advanced Byzantine governmental machinery. The Byzantine offices of *catepan*, *strategotus* and *turmarch* all still appeared in cities, but with geographically and administratively reduced competences. Whereas the Byzantine *catepan* and *strategotus* had originally been provincial governors with military and civil duties, under the Normans their orbit was essentially restricted to a particular city as supervisors of the ducal demesne and local administration.[48] Guiscard had a disparate agglomeration of lands to rule and wide-ranging concerns, notably his invasion plans for Byzantium and his relationship with the papacy. Delegation of power was necessary, and this was yet another reason for retaining local leading figures and offices. Narrative sources suggest that Argirizzus, who held a leading position at Bari in the pre-Norman period, may have retained his status after 1071 and perhaps also for a while after his role in the city's rebellion in 1079–80.[49] However, there is no documentary proof for this, and a charter of 1075 shows two key officials acting on behalf of Guiscard in the city: Maurelianus with the Byzantine title of *patricius et catepanus*, who was probably native, and Lizius the viscount, who was perhaps a Norman.[50] In many cities, especially Bari, leading citizens continued to sport Byzantine official

---

ed. P. Cherubini (Salerno, 1990), pp. 189–90 no. 72, pp. 260–2 and note 1 no. 102, pp. 280–3 no. 111; *Codex Diplomaticus Cavensis*, ed. S. Leone and G. Vitolo (Cava, 1984), vol. ix no. 71; Other officials who served under Lombard and Norman rule are discussed in Garufi, 'Sullo strumento notarile nel Salernitano', pp. 53–80, 291–343.

[46] *Recueil des actes des ducs*, pp. 97–8 no. 28 and below p. xxx.

[47] *Necrologio del Liber Confratrum di S. Matteo di Salerno*, ed. C. A. Garufi, *FSI* LVI (Rome, 1922); von Falkenhausen, 'I ceti dirigenti prenormanni', p. 362.

[48] Von Falkenhausen, 'I ceti dirigenti prenormanni', pp. 339–43.

[49] *Will. Apulia*, Bk III lines 655–8 p. 200.

[50] *CDBV*, no. 1; Loud, *Age of Robert Guiscard*, p. 136.

titles – showing that they maintained their position and that they were not isolated as a result of their former attachment to the empire. In the city in 1078 Sifandus *protospatharius et kritis Italias*, who had carried the same title in the Byzantine period, bought a *tarpito* before *Cricorius imperialis protospatharius et manglabiti atque critis Italias* and John *imperialis protospatharius.*[51] Moreover, already in 1071 Guiscard had granted the Baresi 'liberty and tranquility', restoring their property and exempting them from tribute.[52] At Troia, where Guiscard regularly resided, we can trace the long careers of judges; John de Sabbo (1039–65), John of Luponi (1064–83), who only belatedly added the 'ducal' epithet to his title in 1078, and John, son of Franco, who began his career as a notary in 1059 and was still active as a judge in 1085.[53]

Uprisings against ducal rule at Trani, Bari and Taranto (1079–80) and Troia (1082) may be evidence of an incipient communal participation in civic affairs and certainly shows that southern Italy was far from a settled land. We can only speculate on the motives behinds these revolts: dissatisfaction with the new regime; sympathy for Byzantine rule; the influence of rebellious Norman counts; a hope that by playing off Norman rivals they could retain the freedom that they had enjoyed in the preceding power vacuum. It is certainly the case that Norman rule was initially more intense for the South Italian population than that which they had experienced in the decades before their take-over. Exactions were made and military service required from the citizens. The anonymous Bari Chronicle records in the early 1080s Guiscard's levy on the inhabitants of Bari of 'many thousands of *solidi* (coins)', which caused them 'great tribulation'. Combined with the duke's taking of prisoners/hostages (*captiones*), this may suggest that there had recently been another uprising in the city.[54] After the fall of Bari in 1071, some of its inhabitants were ordered to join Guiscard's fleet and were probably among the 'Apulians' who took part in the siege of Palermo. In 1080, after Guiscard had put down an uprising in Bari, he besieged Trani with a contingent of Baresi.[55] Yet Norman rule was not able fundamentally

---

[51] *CDBIV*, no. 45; *CDBV*, no. 3; for a discussion of the Byzantine legacy in Norman southern Italy see J-M. Martin, 'L'Empreinte de Byzance dans l'Italie normande. Occupation du sol et institutions', *Annales. Histoire, Sciences Sociales* 4 (July–August 2005), pp. 733–65.

[52] *Will. Apulia*, Bk III lines 149–66 p. 172.

[53] *Will. Apulia*. Bk III lines 487–501 p. 190; John de Sabbo: *Troia* nos. 5, 12; *Colonie cassinesi*, nos. 2, 6, 8; John of Luponi: *Troia* nos. 17, 18; *Colonie cassinesi*, nos. 9–13; *Chron. S. Sophiae*, ii. 705–7 no. x.vi.10; John, son of Franco: *Troia* nos. 11, 18, 19; *Colonie cassinesi*, nos. 5, 9–11; *Chron. S. Sophiae*, ii. 705–7 no. x.vi.10; *Recueil des actes des ducs*, pp. 76–9 no. 18.

[54] *Anonymi Barensis Chronicon*, a.1083 p. 154; the entry for 1084 mentions more *solidi* being exacted in Bari.

[55] *Will. Apulia*. Bk III lines 163–6, 187–8 pp. 172–4, Bk III lines 668–9 p. 200; *Malaterra*, Bk II.45.

to transform urban life, and surely did not aim to do so. While the Normans brought regime change they broadly left underlying continuity. The dynamics of the conquest actually acted as *stimuli* for urban communities to grow more accustomed to self-government as their previous rulers weakened, and their new ones soon showed themselves unable to be overly intrusive. This was to be an important formative experience for later developments, as we shall shortly see.

Chapter 2

THE FRAGMENTATION OF POWER
(1085–1127)

As we have seen, urban communities showed signs of a greater engagement in self-government during the power vacuum produced in the Norman take-over. Moreover, once the take-over was complete, the Norman rulers, largely on account of their numerical weakness, maintained the existing administrative hierarchies and local customs within the cities. This had also been the case in Benevento, where its papal overlord had changed little. The deaths of Robert Guiscard, duke of Apulia, in 1085 and Jordan, prince of Capua, in 1090, in depriving the South Italian mainland of its two most authoritative figures, only further accentuated this general process. The ensuing period witnessed the evolution of a variety of urban governments in the region which displayed clearer tendencies towards wider self-government, while everywhere traditional local mechanisms of civic rule were increasingly relied upon.

The chronicler Geoffrey Malaterra outlined the 'disorder' that followed Guiscard's death. It was only in 1089 that his two warring sons, Roger Borsa, the new duke, and Bohemond, agreed on their respective inheritances, Roger having to concede direct rule to Bohemond in Bari and the Terra di Otranto. But this period of conflict between the brothers had allowed many to strive for 'their own gain . . . and profit', and it must have proved difficult for either brother to regain the usurpations at which Malaterra hints.[1] Recent scholarship has somewhat rehabilitated Roger's reputation.[2] But the duke's position was clearly weaker than his father's, some of his subordinate counts acted as if independent and his activities were largely confined to the principality of Salerno. Bohemond, although a more dynamic figure, was often absent from southern Italy (having participated in the First Crusade)

---

[1] *Malaterra*, Bk III.41–2, p. 82.   [2] See especially Loud, *Age of Robert Guiscard*, pp. 246–60.

from 1096 until his death in 1111.[3] The frequent papal visits to southern Italy during this period were indicative of the weakening political environment and aimed at bolstering the local rulers, who were needed as papal counter-balances to the empire.[4] Urban II was present in 1098, as mediator, when the prince of Capua was attempting to regain his principal city and was also a regular visitor to Salerno (in 1091, 1092, 1093 and 1098).[5] Nor were his successors, Paschal II and Gelasius II, strangers to the region and its cities. Numerous papal councils were held throughout southern Italy (at Melfi in 1089, Troia in 1093, 1115 and 1120 and Bari in 1089 and 1098) and the Truce of God was preached in the region.

Roger Borsa and his son and successor William (1111–27) focused their activities primarily in and around Salerno. Ducal courts were regularly held in the city and the dukes enjoyed a substantial urban patrimony. In 1100 Roger donated a tenth of the dues collected from trade within certain of the city's squares (*plateatici platearum Salerni*) to the important nearby monastery of Cava. In 1105 he confirmed a donation of lands and houses in Salerno and in 1110 provided Cava with further exemptions and rights in the city.[6] Duke William confirmed his father's donation of the *plateaticum* to Cava and also added the right to exact gate dues (*portaticum*), sustaining the Lombard princely tradition of patronage of Cava.[7] The close and important alliance with the city's archbishopric also continued. Duke Roger donated lands, Salerno's Jewish community, a tenth of the city's port revenues and, significantly, ratified all the privileges of previous Lombard princes.[8]

It soon became evident that the new political order initiated in 1077 was not to be lamented but rather embraced. The city appeared to be developing into a ducal capital, but the duke's government in Salerno was neither overly intrusive nor innovative. The beneficent rule inaugurated

---

[3] See R. B. Yewdale, *Bohemond I, Prince of Antioch* (Princeton, 1917).

[4] Loud, *Age of Robert Guiscard*, pp. 223–33.

[5] H. Houben, 'Urbano II e i normanni', in *Mezzogiorno normanno-svevo: monasteri e castelli, ebrei e musulmani* (Naples, 1996), 115–43.

[6] Cava dei Tirreni, *Archivio della badia di S. Trinita: Arm[arii] Mag[ni]* D.33 (perhaps forged in its present form, the document is edited in P. Guillaume, *Essai historique sur l'abbaye de Cava* (Cava dei Tirreni, 1877), pp. xvii–xviii, appendix E.VI), E.1, E.14. The Cava archive is divided into two sections, the *Armarii Magni* (hereafter *Arm. Mag.*) and the *Arcae* (hereafter *Arca*), which are arranged in chronological order. Each *armarium* contains *c.* 40–50 documents, while each *arca* holds 120 documents.

[7] Cava, *Arm. Mag.*, F.2, F.30.

[8] *Antiquitates Italicae Medii Aevi*, ed. L. A. Muratori, 6 vols. (1738–42), i. 899–900; *L'archivio diocesano di Salerno. Cenni sull'archivio del capitolo metropolitana*, ed. A. Balducci (Salerno, 1959–60), pp. 22–3 nos. 33, 35, 38. For more on the relationship between the dukes, the archbishop of Salerno and the monastery of Cava see V. Ramseyer, *The Transformation of a Religious Landscape. Medieval Southern Italy 850–1150* (Ithaca, 2006).

by Guiscard continued. Malaterra censured Roger Borsa for 'believing that the Lombards were just as loyal to him as were the Normans' and for his equitable treatment of both groups, behaviour which the chronicler ascribed to Roger having a Lombard mother.[9] This pro-Lombard orientation correlates with the naming patterns that Drell discovered in local charters. It was still socially and politically acceptable well into the twelfth century for many families to trace their descent back to the Lombard princely family or its comital offshoots.[10] Civic life and government remained remarkably similar to that of the Lombard era. New offices (chamberlain, *strategotus*, *vicecomes*) had been installed in the region by the Norman rulers, but they were filled by Lombards, such as Peter the chamberlain and Romuald the viscount.[11] Peter was succeeded in his office by Alferius Guarna, a member of an influential Salernitan kingroup, whose father was a civic judge, his brother an archdeacon and another relation a *strategotus*.[12] This local family proved to be a bastion of the city's administration and would provide important officials in local and royal government later on in the twelfth century.[13] Under Duke William's reign various offspring of the previous generation of Lombard officials maintained their standing. The judge John had a sizeable landed patrimony and was the son of Disedeus *comes palatii*.[14] A document from 1117 shows that the son of Granatus, who had been a *vestararius* of Robert Guiscard and was surely Lombard, was still a sizeable landowner near Salerno.[15] Perhaps also important for the Salernitans was the Norman dukes' development of their city into the capital of a region larger than any ruled over by a previous Lombard prince.[16] Ducal rule was weak in Apulia, and in the wider region, but its faint existence, with Salerno at its centre, gave the city a certain prestige. It is perhaps in this light that we should interpret Duke Roger's and Duke William's

[9] *Malaterra*, Bk IV.24, p. 102.
[10] J. Drell, 'Cultural syncretism and ethnic identity. The Norman conquest of southern Italy and Sicily', *JMH* 25 (1999), pp. 193–6.
[11] Loud, *Age of Robert Guiscard*, pp. 140, 282–3; Cava, *Arca* xvii.13.
[12] Loud, *Age of Robert Guiscard*, p. 283; Alferius: Cava, *Arca* xviii.24, xx.19, xx.iii.63, xxix.99.
[13] For the Guarna genealogy see Loud, *Age of Robert Guiscard*, p. 305. See also below p. 193.
[14] *Documenti per la storia di Eboli*, pp. 47–8 no. 100.
[15] *Documenti per la storia di Eboli*, p. 42 no. 87; Granatus was attested as ducal *vesterarius*, alongside Guiscard's wife Sichelgaita and the archbishop of Salerno, at an important case held at Salerno in 1083, *Recueil des actes des ducs*, pp. 136–41 no. 43; it is possible that Granatus was the *vesterarius* Gratian, son of Roderisius, attested in 1079 (see above pp. 25–6) and also related to a former chaplain of the Lombard princes who was later apparently the victim of Gisulf's tortures, *Amatus* Bk VIII.21 p. 197 and n. 30.
[16] D. Matthew, 'Semper fideles. The citizens of Salerno in the Norman kingdom', in *Salerno nel XII secolo*, p. 29.

adoption of the new title of duke *and* prince.[17] When William died he was placed, like his father, in the city's cathedral and 'never had any duke or indeed emperor been buried with such lamentation'.[18] If we delve below Falco of Benevento's hyperbole it would seem that the citizens of Salerno had genuine reason to mourn the passing of a man considered to be a native and munificent ruler.

However, a city like Troia, previously a favoured residence of Guiscard's, may have represented a more typical model of urban government in the ducal lands after 1085. The city remained nominally part of the demesne, and outward signs of the duke's control of Troia were still present – such as the castle built in the 1060s and private charters dated by the years of ducal rule. However, during Roger's reign there is little clear evidence of ducal activity in the city, few of his officials appeared there and Troia must have profited from the political fragmentation, if only in an indirect manner.[19] Local officials intermittently dropped their ducal title, using instead effusive epithets like *prudentissimus* and *doctissimus*.[20] Such men were undoubtedly enjoying a more prominent role in the government of their native city. This stemmed not only from the duke's absence, but also from the extremely close and influential relationship that these officials had with the urban populace.[21] Duke Roger, reluctant to lose the city's support, must have tacitly sanctioned the increasing role of native elements in the city's internal affairs. This was probably shrewd, given the memory of Roger's ruthless suppression, on his father's behalf, of a rebellion in the city in 1082.[22] Kingroups like the Alberice and Caccise maintained their wealth and status into the twelfth century.[23] It would be plausible to suggest that civic officials were largely elected as a result of local influences, followed by later ratification by the duke. While there is no evidence that the city's inhabitants officially acquired any political or public powers, their growing control of internal affairs must have increased their role in this sphere.

Roger retained some influence at Troia through cultivating links with the city's bishops. Bishop Walter signed a ducal privilege in 1087, and his successor Gerard met the duke for 'secret' discussions in Calabria in 1095.[24] In 1092 Roger conceded two rural settlements to the bishop of Troia, in 1095 he added some pasturage revenues and in 1105 offered

---

[17] For an example of this title, Cava, *Arca* xix.101.   [18] *Falco*, pp. 84–6.
[19] J-M. Martin, 'Troia et son territoire au XI siècle', *Vetera Christianorum* 27 (1990), pp. 175–201.
[20] *Troia*, nos. 23, 24, 37.
[21] Calasso, *La legislazione statutaria*, pp. 76–7.   [22] *Will. Apulia*, Bk IV lines 506–20 pp. 230–2.
[23] Alberice: *Troia*, nos. 11, 19, 24, 26, 38, 42, 51, 59; *Colonie cassinesi*, no. 25; Caccise: *Troia*, nos. 25, 29, 40, 42, 46, 49, 51, 59, 78; *Colonie cassinesi*, no. 30.
[24] *CDBI*, no. 32; *Troia* no. 31.

a massive territory in the east of the city's *contado*.[25] In fact it is only through this connection with the Church that we see Duke Roger in direct contact with Troia. Around 1090 Bishop Gerard was chosen by Roger with the consent of a papal legate and the clergy and people of Troia, while in 1093 he attended the papal council held in the city.[26] It seems that the bishops of Troia, of whom, significantly, at least four in this period were non-native, acted as unofficial mediators between the duke and the local government hierarchy.[27]

It may be possible to apply this model of civic government to other cities. Although we cannot be sure, given the meagre source material, Melfi and Venosa, which like Troia had both been key ducal centres under Guiscard, no longer seemed to form part of the limited itineraries of his ducal successors. Yet at the same time some evidence suggests that the duke continued to patronise these cities' bishoprics.[28] This fits with Romuald of Salerno's depiction of Roger as ruling 'more by the generosity of his gifts than by the harshness of his power'.[29] More interestingly Malaterra's observation that in 1098 'they [the Apulians] were insubordinate towards the duke, as if at that time they had no ruler at all, [and] several places rose up against him', may be the Sicilian-based chronicler's misunderstanding of the nature of Roger Borsa's relations with the region's cities.[30] Similar, if potentially more volatile, developments were taking place at Bari after 1085, a city with a tradition of unrest which had never fully acquiesced to Guiscard's regime. The famous translation of the relics of St Nicholas from Myra to the city in 1087 highlighted the (often violent) civic pride that was burgeoning in the Apulian port as well as the urban population's cognisance of political affairs.[31] The translation was an entirely civic enterprise, independent of ducal initiative. In the subsequent armed conflict over where to house the relics, the sources reveal factions within the city and a group of 'most noble and sagacious leaders', who were clearly the principal figures in local government.[32] Perhaps aware of these trends, in the few

---

[25] *Troia*, nos. 27, 28, 31, 36. [26] *Troia*, no. 27; *Romuald*, p. 200.

[27] N. Kamp, 'The bishops of southern Italy in the Norman and Staufen periods', in *The Society of Norman Italy*, ed. G. A. Loud and A. J. Metcalfe (Leiden, 2002), p. 193.

[28] In 1093 Roger Borsa gave the bishop of Melfi jurisdiction over the city's Jewish population, *Italia Sacra*, ed. F. Ughelli (2nd edn by N. Colletti, 10 vols., Venice, 1717–21), i. 923; Houben, 'Melfi e Venosa: due città sotto il dominio Normanno-Svevo', in *Mezzogiorno normanno-svevo*, pp. 319–36.

[29] *Romuald*, p. 197. [30] *Malaterra*, Bk IV.26, pp. 104–5.

[31] F. Nitti di Vito, *La ripresa gregoriana di Bari (1087–1105); e i suoi riflessi nel mondo contemperaneo politico e religioso* (Trani, 1942).

[32] From the account of Nicephorus, cleric of Bari, Vat.MS. Lat. 5074, fos. 5v–10v in C. W. Jones, *Saint Nicholas of Myra, Bari and Manhattan. Biography of a Legend* (Chicago, 1978), pp. 189–91.

years prior to 1089 in which Duke Roger was Bari's nominal lord, it appears that he consented to a similar style of local government to that at Troia. Two identical themes surface: the devolution of urban rule into the hands of prominent locals who recognised the token authority of the duke, while at the same time cushioning this loss of ducal influence by tightening links with the city's religious institutions. Between 1086 and 1089 the duke granted to the archbishop of Bari jurisdiction over the city's Jewish population, and a range of lands.[33] As at Troia, Roger assisted, alongside the people and clergy of Bari, in electing Elias as the city's archbishop in 1089.[34] At the same time, the city's government included, among others, a judge Nicholas, a member of the influential Melipezzi family. A man with Nicholas's local connections, carrying the title of *ducalis iudex*, the only instance of such a designation at Bari, supports the idea of a 'bargain' between ruler and ruled over the city's government.[35]

There is little evidence of this arrangement altering much when Bari passed into Bohemond's hands shortly after September 1089. However, later evidence attesting to a castle in the city shows that Bohemond reneged on a previous agreement made between his brother and the citizens of Bari not to build one there. It seems that this castle replaced the Byzantine *catepan* court as Bari's administrative headquarters.[36] Additionally, by 1094, the office of *catepan* had been adapted into Bohemond's highest representative in the city. These *catepans* seem to be non-native: one appeared to be from Flanders, another from Gallipoli, while two had the Norman name William and one was called Godfrey.[37] But the power of this official, whose responsibilities covered Giovinazzo too, should not be overstated. It was confined to the administration of Bohemond's goods in the city, confirmed by the appearance of *catepans* only in private charters, without any wider jurisdiction over the city's judges or its judicial system. Moreover, before authenticating any private act the *catepan* had to show 'to many men of the city' the *sigillum* in which Bohemond conferred his power to the official; a clear statement of the active role played by elements of the urban populace.[38] The maintenance of the office of *catepan* in Bari, more than any other city in southern Italy, carried connotations of continuity with its Byzantine past and was surely meant to pacify. This was significant, as there was still an entire class of people carrying official Byzantine ranks and titles,

[33] *CDBI*, nos. 30–2.   [34] *CDBI*, no. 34.
[35] *CDBV*, no. 13; von Falkenhausen, 'I ceti dirigenti prenormanni', pp. 343–4. A private tower belonging to Nicholas was mentioned in 1117, *Anonymi Barensis Chronicon*, p. 154.
[36] See *Malaterra*, Bk IV.10, p. 91 and references to a Fulco *curialis notarius castelli barini* in *CDBV*, nos. 51, 52, 54.
[37] *CDBV*, nos. 18–20, 22, 43, 47, 51, 52, 54.   [38] *CDBV*, nos. 52, 54.

such as *imperialis kritis, protospatharius, protovestarius* and *turmarch*.[39] Whether these designations still denoted functions (like the city's judges, who employed the title *critis*) or were now purely honorific, their continued appearance is important. They show that large sections of Bari's Byzantine ruling class survived with their status intact, and that it was still acceptable to emphasise links to a Greek past. This 'group' was among the city's wealthiest and was undoubtedly active in its government.

Other signs of continuity are not lacking. In 1094, Bohemond's *catepan* sold some vines near Bari which belonged to the former 'pro mortizzo', a Lombard legal term for properties that escheated to the lord's demesne.[40] In 1108, a man released from the semi-free status of *affidatus* by the *catepan* Godfrey was henceforth to be considered among the *autopii*, possibly Greek for free citizen.[41] Indeed the same act states further that the man, Aldebertus, 'should have the power to judge [his] matters and to act freely according to the customs of the Baresi'. Here then is confirmation that under Bohemond, Lombard, Byzantine and civic customs endured. A fragmented document from 1105 also shows that the citizens had received some, still effective, *capitularia* from either Guiscard or one of his sons.[42] The civic elite responsible for local government also endured and despite (or because of) their freedom of action remained loyal. This should not be underestimated; city judges were important civic figures who also often acted outside the city walls.[43] Their status was occasionally echoed, as at Troia, in their grandiloquent titles, like that of Grifo who called himself judge of Bari and Apulia.[44] The judge Nicholas Melipezzi was prominent, and it is significant that he recognised, for example, that a sentence pronounced in 1100 (when Bohemond was in the Holy Land) was made in the court, and through the authority, of 'glorius noster dominus Boamundus'.[45] The aforesaid judge Grifo was described as *fidelissimus* when receiving a donation from Bohemond's *catepan* Godfrey in 1107, who a year later gave to the notary Fulco a house 'on account of the love and loyalty' which he had shown to Bohemond, as well as 'the many good services' rendered.[46] In 1109 a certain Gemma received a donation from the aforesaid Godfrey on account of the fidelity that her husband, presumably an influential person, had shown to Bari's lord.[47] Bohemond had the co-operation of the city's leading individuals.

[39] For example *CDBV*, nos. 13, 16, 46.   [40] *CDBV*, no. 19
[41] *CDBV*, no. 51; Martin, *Pouille*, p. 313.   [42] *CDBV*, no. 43.
[43] For example see *CDBV*, no. 40.   [44] *CDBV*, no. 42.
[45] *CDBV*, no. 32.   [46] *CDBV*, no. 47, 52.
[47] *CDBV*, no. 54. It could be that Gemma's husband, in the document called Sclavus son of Melus, was Stephen Sclavus son of Melus, a wealthy money lender, who had various links with the city's urban elite; for more on Stephen see below pp. 71, 256.

Bohemond's approach to governing Bari, like that of his brother Roger elsewhere, was pragmatic and sensitive. The city neither rebelled nor descended into factional strife and was willing to recognise his 'gentle' domination (although private charters at Bari were not dated by the ruling years of any lord between 1085 and 1111). This understanding worked especially well alongside the role that the famous Archbishop Elias played in the city until his death in 1105. Elias had an excellent relationship with the *populus* of Bari, its ruling urban aristocracy and also Bohemond, from whom his archbishopric and the basilica of S. Nicola (where Elias remained the abbot) received donations. It is doubtful whether Elias was able to operate any jurisdiction over the city government outside that which pertained to the property and men of the Church, mostly because Bari's strong tradition of civic administration did not require him to do so. However, his unifying role as the moral leader of the city bestowed upon him greater power than any political office could have done.[48]

There are then some examples, which may be extended to other less well-documented cases, of how South Italian cities were able to reach a *modus vivendi* with their lord. 1111 saw the deaths of both Roger Borsa and Bohemond and the succession of their sons as minors. Roger's son William, a minor until 1114, was not able to increase ducal power outside the principality of Salerno and in fact barely maintained it.[49] In many places urban government continued virtually unchanged. For example, at Troia William understandably followed his father's policy. The city's bishop continued to receive large donations of territory from the duke.[50] Although William attended the two papal councils held in the city in 1115 and 1120, he generally does not appear to have actively intervened in the city's internal organisation.[51] As we shall see, the development of Troia as an ostensibly self-governing city under the guidance of an increasingly wealthy and influential bishop was to have important consequences when Duke William died in 1127.

Conversano provides another example, at the comital level, of a similarly gradual and stable evolution of urban government. The city's ruler, Count Geoffrey of Conversano, collaborated and allied with prominent local figures, a policy which he had adopted from the outset of his control of the city (*c.* 1072). It was to continue more visibly after the death of Robert Guiscard, his theoretical superior. Geoffrey was

---

[48] According to one source, in 1095, the Barese people swore a general oath to Elias, *Anonymi Barensis Chronicon*, p. 154; Nitti di Vito, *La ripresa gregoriana*, especially pp. 521–6, 576–8.

[49] Chalandon, *Histoire de la domination normande*, i. 313–26; see an episode in *Falco*, pp. 66–8.

[50] *Colonie Cassinesi*, nos. 24, 26.   [51] *Troia*, no. 102.

supposedly placed under the lordship of Bohemond in 1086 by Roger Borsa, but in reality the count had been acting independently in his lands for most of the previous decade, and his freedom of action only further increased.[52] The count's territory also included, amongst others, Monopoli, Noicattaro, Brindisi and Nardo.[53] Private charters at Conversano did not recognise any higher ruler after 1085, and Geoffrey seemed to control public power throughout his lands by administering justice, collecting taxes and maintaining public order. This was achieved by using the previous administrative structure run by local officials such as David *imperialis spatharius kandidatus et critis* (1072–89), Maio *turmarch* (1079–89) and Leo *vicecomes et turmarch* (1081–98?), whose double title signals an interesting integration of Norman and Byzantine offices.[54] By the time Geoffrey had died around the year 1100 the count disposed of a more advanced administration; documents speak of his own court, procurator and notaries in the city, while examples of men ambiguously carrying two offices were becoming rarer. But government was still largely executed according to Lombard law and local custom. In 1089 Count Geoffrey claimed some goods in Conversano according to the Lombard practice of *mortizzo* and in doing so actually quoted the eighteenth chapter of the law code of 'dominus Liudprand excellentissimus rex'.[55] It is unclear where the urban administration at Conversano ranked in relation to those of the other cities within the county. Before 1100 there had been occasional signs that high justice was dealt with at Monopoli, and indeed in 1087 and 1095 a judge from that city was present at Conversano when Geoffrey made significant donations to the monastery of S. Benedetto.[56] But a picture of the county's administrative jurisdictions is severely confused by the division of its lands after 1100. Geoffrey's successor and eldest son Robert retained Conversano, but Brindisi seems to have been held by his mother, Nardo by his brother Alexander and Montemilone and Ruvo by another sibling called Tancred. Thus the southern portion of the county was detached from the centre and the count's powers reduced.[57] Alexander succeeded Robert at some point between 1113 and 1119, though perhaps 1114–16 may be more accurate. Within these dates there appeared in the city a judge Maio with the specific geographic qualifier of Conversano and in 1115 a certain Arechis designated as judge of Conversano *and* Nardo; both perhaps hinting at an administrative restructuring required by the

---

[52] *Malaterra*, Bk IV.4, p. 87.   [53] Loud, *Age of Robert Guiscard*, p. 247.
[54] David: *Conversano*, nos. 41, 43, 45, 48–50; Maio: *Conversano*, nos. 43, 45–47, 49, 51; Leo: *Conversano*, nos. 45, 49, 50, 53, 58.
[55] *Conversano*, no. 49.   [56] *Conversano*, pp. xxxviii–xliv and nos. 48, 57.
[57] Martin, *Pouille*, pp. 737–8.

reintegration of some of Alexander's lands into the comital demesne.[58]
Also in 1114 a notary with the title of *magnus* was found at Conversano
for the first time, and these officials begin to participate more in private
acts.[59] But in truth the civic administration and its officials remained
largely unaffected by the change of counts. Private transactions still
required the counsel of *boni homines*, and some of the city's leading men
in this later period, like Grisantus son of the judge Petracca and Nardus
son of Leo the viscount, were the progeny of the previous generation's
civic elite.[60]

Just as was the case at Troia, Bari and perhaps Melfi and Venosa,
Conversano's lord forged a close relationship with local religious institutions. The wealthy urban monastery of S. Benedetto received a series
of donations from the count including the village of Castellana (in 1087),
tax exemptions when trading in the city market and the right to receive
affidati.[61] This connection allowed the Norman count to bind himself to
Conversano's civic traditions, as did his promotion of the city's defunct
ancient bishopric which was re-established by 1081. Enhancing the
status of the city was clearly a policy intended to legitimate the count's
rule, and it successfully reinforced his control of Conversano.[62]

On the other hand, at Bari the functioning of civic government under
Bohemond's lordship did change after his death in 1111 and the ensuing
regency of his wife, Constance, on behalf of their minor son, Bohemond II. Significant transitions in the structure of urban government
and society took place in Bari in a unique manner to which we will
return later. But the breakdown in the *modus vivendi* at Bari in 1111 had
not been the first in Apulia. Trani, a city that had been incorporated
with difficulty into the duchy of Apulia at a late stage and had always
retained strong cultural ties to Byzantium, did not even make the pre-
tence of recognising ducal power after 1085. Whereas private charters at
Trani in the 1070s and 1080s had been dated by the ruling years of
Robert Guiscard, thereafter, until the 1130s, they were dated by the rule
of the Byzantine emperor.[63] Dukes Roger and William had no visible
representation in this emerging port city. As the Byzantine emperor
could not have held any authority across the Adriatic at this period,
it seems that the city had made the quiet transition to a *de facto* independence. Corporate municipal institutions and purely local administrative structures must have governed Trani to have enabled the city to
function independently for the half-century before the 1130s, although

---

[58] *Conversano*, nos. 66, 69.   [59] *Conversano*, no. 67.   [60] *Conversano*, nos. 67, 68, 74, 75.
[61] *Conversano*, nos. 45, 48, 59.   [62] Delogu, 'I normanni in città', pp. 182–7.
[63] *Trani*, nos. 19, 21, 23, 24, 26, 27, 29, 30.

charters from the city do not refer specifically to them. A letter from Urban II in the late 1090s was simply addressed to the city's religious officials as well as to its *nobiles* and *plebs*.[64] The coastal city of Monopoli seems to have been in a comparable position; however, its limited documentation prevents definitive conclusions. The city had been incorporated in an uncertain way into the county of Conversano and probably functioned as its judicial centre.[65] But by 1100 Monopoli appears as a city without an effective superior authority. Private charters recognised the Byzantine emperor, while some documents give the impression of a structured urban society accustomed to acting collectively under the direction of an urban elite. In 1098 a donation was made to the monastery of S. Lorenzo of Aversa 'by all the noble men and the whole population' of Monopoli.[66] An ambiguously worded document of 1099 also refers to a noble or elite class.[67] Again the city's leading men are attested over long periods. The judge Leo seems to have been in office from 1074 to 1099, and the son of a *turmarch*, active in Monopoli in 1054, was found in the city as a monastic advocate in 1099.[68] Communal activities appear most pronounced in Apulia's coastal cities, and it is perhaps the events of this period that are responsible for the later literary *topos* of the disloyalty of Apulia.[69] These cities were certainly aided by the fragility of central authority. But also, at this time of great commercial and demographic growth, their links to the Mediterranean and trends emanating from northern Italy cannot be discounted.[70]

Instances of this more obvious form of a break between a city's lord and his subjects can also be seen, although they were more fleeting, in Campania. At Amalfi, a small duchy on the Tyrrhenian coast which had voluntarily submitted to Robert Guiscard in 1073, there was a revolt against Roger Borsa's rule in the 1090s.[71] Roger besieged the city in 1096, but it seems not to have been brought back under ducal authority until *c.* 1100. Although it was restored, ducal rule was only irregularly recognised in the city's charters thereafter, while the duke seems to have entrusted the local administration to men from leading Amalfitan

---

[64] *Trani*, no. 25.   [65] See above p. 37.
[66] *CDNA*, pp. 16–8 no. 11, although there are doubts over part of the document's authenticity.
[67] *Conversano*, no. 60.   [68] *Conversano*, nos. 40, 42, 60
[69] For an early example see *Malaterra*, Bk IV.26; in the mid- to late twelfth century the so-called Hugo Falcandus inveighed against the 'people of Apulia [who] are utterly disloyal, and vainly hope to win their independence', *Falcandus*, p. 66 (Latin translation: *La Historia o Liber de Regno Sicilie e la Epistola ad Petrum Panormitane Ecclesie Thesaurium di Ugo Falcando*, ed. G. B. Siragusa, *FSI* XXII (Rome, 1897)). In the 1190s an anonymous author, perhaps Falcandus, penned a letter to the treasurer of the Church of Palermo, in which the Apulians were said to 'constantly plot revolution because of the pleasure they take in novelty', an additional text in *Falcandus*, p. 254.
[70] Calasso, *La legislazione statutaria*, pp. 31–5.   [71] *Malaterra*, Bk IV.24, p. 102.

families.[72] More prominent cases can be identified at Capua and Benevento. The power of the Capuan prince had been slowly declining, especially in the northern part of the principality, during the last years of Jordan I. Meanwhile, the administration continued to be shaped by its Lombard inheritance. A chamberlain was attested in 1085, but he was probably a revised version of the old Lombard *thesaurarius*.[73] Moreover, the prince's treasury (*camera*) eventually reverted to its former Lombard title of *sacrum palatium*. Indeed the Norman princes often dwelled in the *sacrum palatium*, the old Lombard princely residence found at the centre of Capua, rather than the *castrum lapidum* built by Richard I around 1065.[74] The rule of the Norman princes continued to stress continuity with the past, while not being overly burdensome. Nevertheless this did not prevent an uprising. The rule of the minor Richard II, who succeeded his father in 1090, was inevitably fragile, and in the following year the Capuans rebelled.[75] Richard took refuge in his second city of Aversa, surrounded by a court of Normanno-French supporters, but, apart from a brief period in 1093, he was unable to regain the city until 1098.[76] The rebellion was clearly a significant one; in a diploma of 1096 Richard lamented the 'multitude of enemies' he had to combat, 'who after the death of [his] father attempted to impede and have [his] *honorem* [inheritance?]'.[77] This presupposes that the people of Capua were well organised, able to govern themselves for nearly a decade, perhaps through communal institutions.[78] One such institution was surely a civic militia, as Prince Richard needed the aid of Duke Roger Borsa and Count Roger I of Sicily to besiege the city. Another corporate body is intimated in the way the Capuans defended themselves at the judicial hearing with Prince Richard, organised by Pope Urban II in 1098, to ascertain which party was in the wrong (it is interesting to note that the

---

[72] P. Skinner, *Family Power in Southern Italy: The Duchy of Gaeta and Its Neighbours 850–1139* (Cambridge, 1995), pp. 202–5; for a discussion of civic consciousness in Campania see A. Leone, 'Particolarismo e storia cittadina nella Campania medievale', *Quaderni Medievali* 9 (1980), pp. 236–56.

[73] G. A. Loud, *Church and Society in the Norman Principality of Capua, 1058–1197* (Oxford, 1985), pp. 86–118. For mention of a chamberlain, G. A. Loud, 'A calendar of the diplomas of the Norman Princes of Capua', *PBSR* 44 (1981), pp. 125–6 no. 33.

[74] I. Di Resta, *Capua (Le città nella storia d'Italia)* (Rome and Bari, 1985), pp. 27–30.

[75] *Annales Ceccanenses*, ed. G. H. Pertz, *MGH SS* XIX (Hanover, 1866), p. 281; *Annales Cavenses*, ed. G. H. Pertz, *MGH SS* III (Hanover, 1839), p. 190.

[76] *Regesto di S. Angelo in Formis,* ed. M. Inguanez (Montecassino, 1925), pp. 84–6 no. 28; Loud, 'Calendar', p.127 no. 49; *Malaterra*, Bk IV.26–8, pp. 104–6.

[77] *Diplomi inediti dei principi normanni di Capua, conti di Aversa*, ed. M. Inguanez, *Miscellanea Cassinese* III (Montecassino, 1926), pp. 18–20 no. 7. In 1093 Richard offered recompense to the monastery of S. Angelo in Formis 'on account of the devastation' inflicted on its property as a result of his siege of Capua, *Regesto di S. Angelo in Formis*, pp. 84–6 no. 28.

[78] *Regesto di S. Angelo in Formis*, pp. 47–50 no. 17; Loud, *Church and Society*, p. 90.

citizens' right to rebel was not denied outright). The rebellion has been depicted in ethnic terms as a Lombard revolt against the Normans. While this may have been an element, and indeed the Montecassino Chronicle states that 'all the Normans were driven out of the city', the fact that the Capuans were willing to accept Roger Borsa and, particularly, Roger of Sicily as their lord complicates matters.[79] We must remain aware of the potency of civic consciousness, and the desire for greater self-government, that was emerging in the urban populations of southern Italy at this time.

Similar and almost contemporary events were unfolding at Benevento. While the city's government maintained a strong Lombard character, transitions were taking place. In 1090, following the death of his colleague Stephen Sculdascio in the previous year, Dacomarius appears with the title of rector (which he may have already carried earlier).[80] Vehse and Girgensohn both agree that the rector enjoyed far-reaching responsibilities in Benevento as the general governor of the city, collector of papal revenues, leader of the urban militia and supervisor of the judicial system.[81] But it is likely that around 1100 the office was still in an embryonic stage and took time to evolve into its twelfth-century format. This is suggested by the initial arrangement of two closely associated officials, which seems for some reason to have been disbanded after Stephen's death. Urban II visited Benevento seven times in his eleven years as pope and seems to have been nominally recognised as the city's lord until his death in 1099.[82] However, as will become more evident in the twelfth century, the city's inhabitants often wanted the prestigious benefits of a papal overlord without his rule limiting their bitterly preserved independence. A combination of all these factors may explain why the city became increasingly, if not irreparably, distanced from the pope's rule as early as 1085, when Beneventan charters ceased recognising a papal overlord.[83]

At a time when the pope had to manage the early crusading movement as well as the continuing rift with the empire it is understandable that he could lose influence in the city at a local level. By the 1090s, as sole rector, Dacomarius had benefited from this, but his increased power

[79] *Chronicon Monasterii Casinensis*, Bk IV.10, p. 474; *Malaterra*, Bk IV.26, p. 104 also noted 'the deception of the Lombards' in the uprising.

[80] *Chron. S. Sophiae*, ii. 744–7 no. vi.24; *Cattedrale di Benevento*, pp. 154–5 no. 50.

[81] O. Vehse, 'Benevent als Territorium des Kirchenstaates bis zum Beginn der avignonesischen Epoche. II. Tiel', *QF* 23 (1932), pp. 82–7; D. Girgensohn, 'Documenti beneventani inediti del secolo XII', *Samnium* 40 (1967), p. 272.

[82] Houben, 'Urbano II e i normanni', in *Mezzogiorno normanno-svevo*, pp. 115–43.

[83] *Montevergine*, i. 319–20 no. 81.

probably had a popular basis supported by his links to the city's urban aristocracy.[84] A document of 1090 describing Dacomarius as 'rector to all the Beneventan people' again emphasises his connections to the citizenry, while it shows his association with Benevento's Archbishop Roffred I and one of the city's leading judges John the *gastald*.[85] Moreover, Dacomarius appears to have established a religious dimension to his authority. A Beneventan hagiographical text, possibly composed around 1090, claiming that St Nicholas had transferred from Bari to Benevento, presented Dacomarius acting with prudence and spiritual awareness in the formative development of the cult.[86] Anso succeeded his father Dacomarius after his death in 1097, demonstrating how far the latter had controlled internal affairs in the city.[87] It was a *fait accompli* tolerated by Urban II, who, in November 1098, in asking Anso to arbitrate in a dispute between the monasteries of Montecassino and S. Sofia of Benevento, called him 'lord of the Beneventans' and 'an extremely dear son'.[88] Anso maintained his father's style of government, continuing to consult 'suitable men' and consolidating relations with the archbishop of Benevento. He undoubtedly benefited from having seven brothers in the city and in association with them in July 1098 donated a church to Montecassino.[89] By 1100, with the pontificate of Paschal II barely a year old, Anso had ceased recognising papal rule; a document from June of that year is dated as the second year of the principate of the 'glorious Prince Anso'.[90] By also associating his son John as co-prince Anso was renewing the old Lombard style of princely rule and stating his intent to establish a dynasty. Yet there is little evidence that the population opposed this local and wealthy figure or considered him a 'tyrannus' as the *Annales Beneventani* did.[91] Anso, supported by his kin-group, certainly seems to have been an active ruler if we consider the restorations of 'usurped' property that the papacy made in the early 1100s.[92] Nevertheless his rule was short, the city was excommunicated in October 1100 by the pope and a year later, assisted by Roger Borsa, it was back under direct papal rule, with Anso forced into exile.[93] If anything, the last decade of the eleventh century showed, in the rise of

---

[84] See the earlier act of 1082 involving Dacomarius and Stephen Sculdascio, above p. 25.

[85] *Cattedrale di Benevento*, pp. 154–5 no. 50. This Lombard title was gradually replaced by the term *iudex* in the early decades of the twelfth century.

[86] G. Cangiano, 'L'Adventus Sancti Nycolai in Beneventum', *Atti della societa storica del Sannio* 2 (1924), pp. 150–2.

[87] Girgensohn, 'Documenti beneventani', pp. 267–8.

[88] *Chron. S. Sophiae*, i. 105–6 no. 5.   [89] *Chronicon Monasterii Casinensis*, Bk IV.19, p. 488.

[90] *Cattedrale di Benevento*, pp. 159–62 no. 52.   [91] Bertolini, 'Gli *Annales Beneventani*', p. 151.

[92] *Chron. S. Sophiae*, ii. 751–4 no. vi.26; *Montevergine*, ii. 71–4 no. 117.

[93] Bertolini, 'Gli *Annales Beneventani*', p. 151.

Dacomarius's kin-group, the capabilities of the Beneventan community to govern its city. This tendency was to have important repercussions for the city's government during the next thirty years.

Events developed at Benevento and Bari, after 1101 and 1111 respectively, in a new and unique way in the ensuing decades, and we shall focus specifically on these shortly. The nature of the government of these two cities changed rapidly, whereas elsewhere, despite the diversity of urban authorities, whether seemingly self-governing at Troia or effectively independent at Trani, developments were more gradual. The difference may be accentuated by the richer source material available at Benevento and Bari, but we must not overlook the fact that both cities were major agglomerations, traditionally important political centres of the highest rank and possessed increasingly strong civic identities which were being just as increasingly threatened by unruly Norman lords based in their hinterlands. Capua in 1098 could certainly be considered as a city set for a similar phase of transition. But the prince of Capua managed to reassert his dominion over the city and did so without having to install any novel governing institutions to supervise the population. Although a constable (by 1096) and *yconomus* (by 1105) had been added to the prince's administrative staff, urban government in Capua after 1098 changed little from what it had been before 1091.[94] Richard II certainly punished some rebels like a Pandulf *ministerialis*, whose confiscated lands were donated to the abbey of S. Biagio in Aversa in 1098 because he had 'exited from our [Richard's] loyalty and allied with enemies'.[95] There is also an emergence of new city judges at Capua after 1098, distinct from their long-serving palatine counterparts. Also, if only in the short term, Norman barons became more prominent at the prince's court. But the prince's weakening position in the principality as a whole prevented a wide purge. Loud has shown that in the early twelfth century there was 'a veritable civil war', particularly in the north of the principality and within the princely family itself. Robert I, who succeeded his brother Richard II, had been at war with the latter and required some eighteen months before cementing his position as prince in the summer of 1107. Robert's subsequent excursions north into papal lands at Ceprano and Anagni do not conceal the fact that under his successor Jordan II (1120–7) the prince's direct rule was confined to the Capuan plain.[96] In view of this and a lack of later rebellions,

[94] R. Piattoli, 'Miscellanea Diplomata (III)', *BISME* 57 (1941), pp. 155–7; Loud, 'Calendar', p. 133 no. 80.

[95] *CDNA*, pp. 403–7 no. 56.

[96] Loud, *Church and Society*, pp. 91–5; in 1106 Robert 'invaded Capua, and part of it was burned', *Annales Cavenses*, p. 191; *Annales Ceccanenses*, p. 282.

it seems that Capua's citizens, following their experience in the 1090s, were allowed at least a limited participation in government. Indeed in 1120 it was they who 'constituted' as Prince Richard III, the short-lived successor of Prince Robert. Their role here was purely formulaic but nevertheless was clearly recognised.[97]

A more detailed impression of civic government at Capua is confused by the uncertain jurisdictional boundaries with nearby Aversa and the generally rudimentary style of administration. Aversa was the traditional Norman centre of Campania and displayed Normanno-French-influenced social and legal structures which were quite distinct from those of Lombard Capua. However, with Aversa the prince's second city and one in which he resided almost as often as Capua there was considerable overlap between the settlements. The key officials of the prince were therefore found in both cities, and their offices were never specifically attached to either settlement, with the exception in 1119 of a Pantasia 'viscount of the city of Aversa'.[98] Some of these members of the prince's administration can be connected with a particular city, such as the long-serving chamberlain Odoaldus (1107–32?), who lived in Capua.[99] But the purely local apparatus of civic government which operated in either city while these princely officials were elsewhere remains elusive. The only identifiable urban officials of Capua and Aversa, the judges, are not found acting outside the sphere of private law and low-level justice. This is complicated by the likelihood that Aversa was supervised, in the absence of the prince and his officials, by a collection of men who mostly carried no official administrative titles. This group of men had at its core a 'noble' and knightly element of Normanno-French origin, many of whose ancestors were the first settlers at Aversa and later displaced the highest rank of the Lombard urban class at Capua too.[100] Indeed the first Norman prince of Capua, Richard, was from this social group and was originally the count of Aversa. Subsequently, it was the most prominent part of this group of men that the Norman princes of Capua grafted onto the existing Lombard administration and which formed the princely entourage. Among them were powerful kin-groups, such as the Musca, de Peroleo, Argentia and Lupini.[101] Their official governing responsibilities or jurisdictions are unknown,

---

[97] *Falco*, p. 54.   [98] *CDNA*, pp. 355–6 no. 28.

[99] *Le pergamene di Capua*, 3 vols., ed. J. Mazzoleni (Naples, 1957–8), i. 74–9 no. 31.

[100] See G. A. Loud, 'Nunneries, nobles and women in the Norman principality of Capua', in *Annali canossani 1* (Reggio Emilia, 1981), pp. 49–50 [reprinted in G. A. Loud, *Conquerors and Churchmen in Norman Italy* (Aldershot, 1999)]; A. Gallo, *Aversa normanna* (Naples, 1938), pp. 117–20.

[101] *Diplomi inediti dei principi normanni di Capua*, pp. 26–8 no. 11 offers a typical example of the prince's entourage from 1108.

but they drew their influence primarily from landed wealth and not from administrative titles, although some like Hugh de Apolita, the prince's *yconomus* in the 1120s, did have official labels.[102] This 'landed noble' urban class was much more distinct than any other in southern Italy, and most of the prince of Capua's decisions were taken through their counsel and 'intervention'. In 1116 Prince Robert I actually made a donation to a local abbey from the house in Aversa of the baron Richard Musca.[103] Aversa remained a stable city throughout the period and one that maintained its loyalty, notably in the 1090s, to the prince of Capua.

There was undoubtedly much continuity at Capua (the 1090s aside) and Aversa with the era before Prince Jordan I's death. Only indirect evidence suggests that the people of Capua increased their role in government after 1098. At Aversa, the urban 'aristocracy' may have largely influenced government, but whether this unique class represented the interests of the citizens over the prince is difficult to confirm. There are indications that Aversa's population had formed into designated communities (inhabitants defined themselves in charters as *barones*, *milites* or *burgenses*) perhaps for administrative ordering; but the likelihood is that these categories were rather fluid and arbitrary.[104] Unfortunately, it is unclear to what extent the archbishop of Capua or the bishop of Aversa assisted in government. Considering the interactions with the prince of Capua, and their increasing urban patrimonies, it would be reasonable to think that they participated in local government.[105] It is, however, worth noting that in the principality of Capua there was a clear and prominent example of a developed popular-based urban government. The city of Gaeta on the Tyrrhenian coast had been nominally subject to the prince of Capua since the 1060s and displayed signs of communal activity as early as the 1040s.[106] Its distance from the political centre of the principality and its Mediterranean trade links undoubtedly increased aspirations for autonomy, and the city (like Capua) rebelled in the 1090s. Thereafter the prince of Capua allowed the Gaetans a free hand in their internal affairs, although his position hardly gave him a choice. Gaeta had developed by the 1120s into what Skinner calls a proto-commune, governed by a consulate (the first in southern Italy) of four to six consuls. They were drawn predominantly from the city's newly risen urban aristocracy and enjoyed various public powers concerning finance,

---

[102] Loud, 'Calendar', p. 140 no. 133. [103] *CDNA*, p. 362 no. 32.
[104] For example *CDNA*, pp. 29–33 nos. 20, 21; *Pergamene di Capua*, i. 25–6 no. 10.
[105] See *Diplomi inediti dei principi normanni di Capua*, pp. 6–8 no. 2, pp. 14–28 nos. 5–11, pp. 30–2 no. 13; Loud, *Church and Society*, pp. 102–12.
[106] Loud, *Age of Robert Guiscard*, pp. 102–3.

commerce, building regulations and even external affairs.[107] The city, situated just south of the papal territories, was clearly influenced by its strong connections with Rome and northern Italy and even had its own coinage modelled on that found in the latter region.[108]

This advanced form of self-government had certain parallels with those at Bari and Benevento, to which we now return. As both progressed into the twelfth century their structures of urban government experienced profound and often disruptive changes. Bohemond had been largely absent from Bari in his later years, and with the city's archbishopric vacant from 1105 until the appointment of Riso in 1112 there was a dearth of guiding figures. It may be that the reported concession by Bohemond's widow, Constance, of a quarter of the city of Bari to Tancred, the son of the late Count Geoffrey of Conversano, was an attempt to fill this void.[109] Whatever the flashpoint was, the citizens of Bari, increasingly accustomed to a high level of autonomy, rose against Constance and had expelled her and the young Bohemond II by early 1113. The consequences of this drew the count of Conversano and collateral branches of his family into the city's affairs, and the next five years saw Bari involved in a network of changing alliances and wars with these Norman barons in the Terra di Bari. The leading citizens of Bohemond I's reign must have governed the city, and it was perhaps they who advised the populace in 1113 to appoint Archbishop Riso 'as their leader and master' in order 'to wage war'.[110] A rare charter from Bari in the same year demonstrates that the city had communal structures of government and real political independence. In the document, Riso, seeing the city threatened by its enemies, disposed of public money in order to fund a civic militia. Also for a fee, which would presumably contribute to the city's defence, the archbishop liberated from public servitude a man who would henceforth be 'free among [his] fellow citizens'. All decisions were taken 'with the advice of the whole city' and were 'decreed with the assent of [the] citizens of the commune'.[111]

It was clearly a period in which the city's power structure, social composition and classification of citizenship were undergoing a rapid transition. The re-emergence of factional conflict in the city serves as an

---

[107] Skinner, *Family Power in Southern Italy*, pp. 198–202. *Codex Diplomaticus Caietanus*, 2 vols. (Montecassino, 1887–92), ii. nos. 301–2, 305, 308, 311.

[108] G. A. Loud, 'Coinage, wealth and plunder in the age of Robert Guiscard', *English Historical Review 114* (1999), p. 821.

[109] G. Cioffari, *Storia della basilica di S. Nicola di Bari. I. L'epoca normanno sveva* (Bari, 1984), pp. 118–22; G. Musca and P. Corsi, 'Da Melo al regno normanno', in *Storia di Bari dalla conquista normanna al ducato sforzesco*, ed. F. Tateo (Bari, 1990), pp. 41–5.

[110] *Romuald*, p. 206.

[111] *CDBV*, no. 59; Martin, 'Les Communautés d'habitants de la Pouille', pp. 73–98.

adequate measure both of this and the breakdown of effective central authority. In 1115 one particular faction stormed a rival's tower, partly destroying it and killing a guard. The anonymous author of the Bari Chronicle states that 'many wars were engaged in between the citizens ... in which several young men were killed.' Two years later more fighting led to a tower collapsing on one of the mob's leaders and a band (*manus*) of 'noble' citizens. As ambitious men jostled for power the city was gripped by increasingly dangerous revenge strikes. The archbishop, unable to control them, was drawn into the factional strife and in 1117 was ambushed and murdered by Argiro, the leader of an apparently anti-Norman party dissatisfied at Riso's rapprochement with Constance and Tancred in 1115.[112] In the chaos, Constance and Bohemond were briefly able, in 1118 to 1119, to reaffirm their claims over Bari, as a document dated by the former's years of rule and the mention of judicial courts of 'the most glorious Bohemond' testify.[113] But the developments hinted at in the document of 1113 had not been annulled, as these courts referred to the participation of many 'noblemen' of the city and at one held in 1119 six judges appear, a notable development when the previous norm had been one or two. However, real power in Bari by this stage was held by a citizen called Grimoald Alfaranites, a beneficiary of the culling of many of Bari's urban elite in the recent mob fighting. He first appeared in 1117, was an ally of Archbishop Riso and by August 1119 had imprisoned Constance.[114] The latter was only released the following year on the plea of Pope Calixtus II and in return for the renunciation of her son's rights in Bari.[115] Grimoald became the highest authority in an effectively independent city and in a charter of June 1123 he claimed to be in his fifth year of rule as the 'Prince of Bari'.[116] He was therefore already prominent in Bari before June 1118 and perhaps had some (short-lived) arrangement with Constance over the city's government. The nature of Grimoald's rule seems to have been based on popular support and relied on a mixture of his own wealth, the maintenance of the city's established administrative structure and the use of civic propaganda.

Grimoald may have been a member of a prominent family that can be traced back through the previous century. Within this kin-group were holders of imperial titles and relations of another key Barese family, the *de Argiro*.[117] In 1119 we hear of a quarter in Bari called 'de Alfaranitis',

---

[112] *Anonymi Barensis Chronicon*, pp. 155–6; *Falco*, p. 34.   [113] *CDBI*, nos. 39, 40.

[114] See above n. 112; *Romuald*, p. 210.

[115] Musca and Corsi, 'Da Melo al regno normanno', p. 44.   [116] *CDBV*, no. 69.

[117] P. Skinner, 'Room for tension: Urban life in Apulia in the eleventh and twelfth centuries', *PBSR* 66 (1998), pp. 171–4.

perhaps part of Grimoald's family's urban patrimony.[118] The officials and governing structures of Grimoald's reign displayed continuity and probably operated in a manner similar to that shown in 1113. When Grimoald disposed of things pertaining to the *publicum* he did so with the counsel of the city's 'noble' men and through officials like the judge Michael, who had served under Constance.[119] It was in Bari in the 1120s that the preacher St John of Matera was accused of being a 'heretic and blasphemer'. The charge was put first before the archbishop, then the *primarii civitatis* and finally, through the aid of *sapientes*, was settled in John's favour by Prince Grimoald. The source must be used cautiously, but it quite probably offers an accurate reflection of the way the city's governing hierarchies were interlinked.[120] Grimoald could also rely on his local roots, possessing close links with the late Archbishop Riso's family and undoubtedly many other leading kin-groups; Nicholas Melipezzi, the wealthy judge active during the city's rule by Roger Borsa and Bohemond I, was still involved in civic affairs in 1120.[121] Falco of Benevento described Grimoald as 'a man of most admirable and warlike spirit', and indeed his policies were shrewd and revealed the city's political autonomy.[122] In 1122 a security pact was signed with the Venetian doge, while Grimoald also became a close ally of the pope after his visit to Bari in 1120.[123] This latter relationship enhanced the prince's prestige, something which his internal civic policies equally aimed at. Grimoald was a generous donor to local religious institutions, especially the basilica of S. Nicola and the monastery of Ognissanti of Cuti.[124] There was great political mileage to be gained from the association with the immensely popular patron saint of Bari. Grimoald called himself 'gratia dei et beati Nikolai barensis princeps', placing the city under the saint's protection, while one of the many hagiographic tales concerning St Nicholas depicted Grimoald and a band of his soldiers playing a key role in capturing a thief who had stolen the saint's arm.[125] This concern to appeal to the sentiment of the people of Bari is indirect testament to the influence that they could exert on the city's government. By 1127 Bari was a politically independent city governed on a 'communal' basis which developed out of the events of 1113 and which in turn had earlier antecedents in the freedom of action granted by Robert Guiscard's successors. The city's government was directed by a leading body of urban

---

[118] *CDBI*, no. 40.   [119] See above n. 113; *CDBV*, nos. 67, 72, 74.
[120] *Vita S. Iohannis a Mathera*, in *Acta Sanctorum*, June v (Paris, 1867), cols. 38–9.
[121] See above pp. 34–5; *CDBI*, no. 41.   [122] *Falco*, p. 120.
[123] *CDBV*, no. 68.   [124] *CDBV*, nos. 69, 71.
[125] A. Poncelet, 'Miracula Sancti Nicolai a Monacho Beccensi', in *Catalogus Codicum Hagiographicorum Latinorum Bibliotheca Nationali Parisiensi*, vol. 2 (1890), p. 426; Cioffari, *Storia*, p. 128.

'noble' families, at the top of which was Prince Grimoald, a local and seemingly popular ruler.

There are clear comparisons between the emergence of this independent principate at Bari and the earlier more rudimentary form that developed at Benevento in the 1090s under Dacomarius and his heirs. The key difference was that Benevento had an overlord, the pope, who was able to act with sufficient haste before such developments were irreversible. After 1101 the pope's control of Benevento aimed at being more active and visible through his increased visits and more importantly through the actions of the papal rector. It was from this point that the office started to evolve towards the form identified by Vehse and was henceforth occupied by senior clergy, usually, in the first half of the twelfth century, cardinals, who were dependent on Rome.[126] Of the seven men who can be definitely identified as rectors before 1127 only one, John de Cito, seems not to have been an ecclesiastic.[127] The remaining six included a monk, a deacon, a cardinal deacon, a cardinal bishop and two cardinal priests. The pope clearly wanted to prevent another urban family from attaining such a dangerous position. Yet after 1101 the rector's authority was not absolute, and his tenure of office remained unstable. The rector's powers seem to have immediately passed over to the pope and his entourage whenever they were in the city, they rarely held office for long and there also seem to have been periods of vacancies.[128] Only Peter, cardinal bishop of Porto, and Stephen the deacon would appear to have been rectors for more than four years, with the average being around two. Twice the pope had to create a supplementary office to that of rector in order to bolster papal rule in the city. In 1113 with 'the city of Benevento oppressed by strife on all sides', mostly from the depredations of local Norman barons, the pope appointed Landulf de Graeca 'an experienced and skilful knight as constable'.[129] Despite being primarily a military official required to organise the defence of the city, Landulf, who was from nearby Montefusco, was heavily involved in the city's internal government. He headed an anti-Norman faction, for which he was temporarily exiled from the city in 1114 and ultimately deposed from his position in 1117/18; however, he was allowed to reside again in Benevento by 1120.[130] The other official sent to Benevento was the Cardinal priest Hugh, who

[126] See above p. 41.

[127] For the biographical details of these papal rectors see G. A. Loud, 'A provisional list of the papal rectors of Benevento, 1101–1227', in *Montecassino and Benevento in the Middle Ages* (Aldershot, 2000), pp. 1–11.

[128] Girgensohn, 'Documenti beneventani', pp. 264–72.   [129] *Falco*, p. 6.

[130] *Falco*, pp. 22, 30, 38, 44, 56.

would appear to have been in the city sometime during the troubled years 1118–20. Hugh was described variously as *custos* of the city and also *provisor Beneventi curiae*, suggesting that he was the highest papal representative in Benevento, to whom the rector was subordinated.[131]

The most significant indication of the weakness of the rector's office, and therefore the pope's limited practical as opposed to theoretical control of Benevento, is found in the growing power which the citizens and local officials, both lay and religious, enjoyed in the city's affairs. The rector John de Cito was ejected from Benevento in 1102 by the citizens who feared that his enmity towards Roger Borsa was endangering the city.[132] John's apparently temporary successor Peter, cardinal bishop of Porto, amidst factional fighting in the city, was also compelled to leave by the distrust of the citizens in the same year. But before his departure he promised to beseech the pope that their next rector should be Rossemanus, who had already held the office – presumably sometime after October 1101.[133] The community's response to the new 'foreign' rectors is illuminating. There is no evidence for the pope's reaction to any of these events, but it seems acquiescence was his only option. This early reference to factional warfare in the city also highlights the fragility of the pope's hold over it, and the disorder intensified acutely after 1112. In this year it was the citizens themselves, desirous of peace, who actually informed the pope of the 'many violent animosities' in the city which had arisen between two parties contending to appoint their own rector from among the city's leading men. The pope, mindful of earlier precedents, rushed to the city and suppressed the faction that supported a certain Landulf Burellus. The people of Benevento clearly felt that the pope still carried authority, which was indeed verified by their overlord's response. But the crucial role played by the city's inhabitants and the pope's reliance on them was striking. Paschal II 'ordered the citizens to be called so that it could be decided how to deal with such a serious and important matter'. When Landulf Burellus' party subsequently seized some towers, they were restored to St Peter by 'the many loyal Beneventans who were of a sounder disposition', and it was the citizens again who asked the pope to constitute the court which led to the expulsion of the perpetrators.[134] As the attacks of local Norman barons placed Benevento under grave pressure, the city appears to have slipped completely out of the pope's control in 1113–14. The papal constable Landulf de Graeca's aggressive policy against the Normans saw the latter respond

---

[131] *Falco*, p. 60; Loud, 'A provisional list', p. 2.
[132] *Chronicon Ignoti Monachi Cisterciensis Sanctae Mariae de Ferraria*, p. 15.
[133] *Falco*, p. 2.   [134] *Falco*, p. 6.

with revenge attacks in the Beneventan hinterland. The result was the formation of a faction, led by the city's Archbishop Landulf, which advocated a peace settlement with the Normans and demanded the resignation of the constable Landulf. In 1114, as Falco of Benevento lamented, 'civil war commenced' between the two parties and drew in the wider population.[135] There is no reference to a rector in the city at this point, and the pope could only listen to the citizens' pleas and send two cardinals, who were 'unable to calm the revolt of the people'. It was only after the 'enraged populace' had forced Landulf to lay down the constableship later in 1114 that the pope finally seems to have grasped the gravity of the situation. But once again the papal response was dictated by, and was sympathetic to, the Beneventan people. Two more cardinals were dispatched to discover 'what the people of Benevento actually wanted', and a meeting 'of all the Beneventans' was held in the sacred Beneventan palace to recount 'the origin of the [civil] war'.[136] At the papal council of Ceprano, held in 1114, the pope deposed Archbishop Landulf, who was popular with the citizens, for his role in the factional strife. However, the archbishop was restored to his see within two years, while the largely unpopular Landulf de Graeca, having regained the constableship, had been again forced out of the city before 1117.[137]

The wider population was then increasingly active in the city's affairs, especially political ones. As the factional fighting shows, they were often led by a group of 'leading' citizens who acted for them and their city. We may see them in the 'hundred noble and good men' who were sent by the citizens in 1102 to supplicate the pope for a pastor-elect, or in the 'more noble Beneventan citizens' who went to the Lateran to represent the monastery of S. Sofia in 1123.[138] It is particularly significant that the party which opposed Landulf Burellus in 1112 wanted to make a certain Anso the rector. This may well have been the son of Dacomarius who had attempted to create an independent principate in the city and was expelled in 1101.[139] We know that the pope had been reconciled with one of Anso's brothers by October 1107, and it seems that the family soon regained its position in Benevento.[140] Anso's return to political activity in 1112 is testament to his popularity and the weak position of the pope. That Anso headed an anti-Norman faction may also throw light on his rise to power in the late 1090s and may explain why he escaped unpunished for his actions in 1112, for in 1118/19 he was still in

[135] *Falco*, pp. 12–4. [136] *Falco*, pp. 14–22.
[137] *Falco*, pp. 24–8, 38; *Chronicon Monasterii Casinensis*, Bk IV.61, p. 524.
[138] *Falco*, p. 2; *Chron. S. Sophiae*, ii. 786–8 no. vi.37. [139] See above pp. 41–3.
[140] Girgensohn, 'Documenti beneventani', pp. 282–8 nos. 1–3.

the city, selling two mills that Paschal II had restored to him.[141] The influence of city judges also seemed to be increasing.[142] Judge John was dispatched with Archbishop Landulf to Rome in 1112 to seek help for the city.[143] Significantly he and his fellow judge Persicus were specific targets of the pro-Norman party; both were forced to take an oath in 1114 against Landulf de Graeca, while Persicus' house had earlier been destroyed in the civil disturbances.[144] In 1120 both John and Persicus were among the select few chosen to lead Pope Calixtus II's horse through the city during his visit.[145] A year earlier the death of judge Alferius of *Porta Aurea* (a city quarter) was important enough to be recorded in Falco's chronicle.[146] This judge of *Porta Aurea* could suggest that urban government had officials assigned to individual urban districts.

The chaotic events of the 1110s demonstrate that the city's archbishop had also attained a dominant role at Benevento. Archbishop Landulf had been sent by the citizens in 1112 and 1114 to inform the pope of the city's 'calamities'.[147] On returning from the latter mission he exceeded his brief by deposing the constable Landulf and informing 'many of the citizens', who had gathered in the cathedral, that he had been given control of peace negotiations with the Normans; this disregard for the pope's instructions reveals the archbishop's strong position within the city. Landulf's *conjuratio* gained the support of the majority of the city and the accusations levelled at him during his deposition may show the basis of his power. Among other things, he was charged with usurping 'the regalia of St Peter', of holding the keys to the city's gates and of wearing 'the helmet and shield'; in other words that he controlled the civic treasury and fortifications, and could employ military force.[148] After being reinstated in August 1116 the archbishop continued to cultivate his relationship with the population and was by now surely more influential than the rector. In 1119 it was Landulf who informed the citizens of the election of the new pope, Calixtus II, and exhorted them 'to preserve their fealty' to St Peter.[149] A year later, 'seeing the city beset and ravaged on every side by various afflictions' (the continued Norman attacks), the archbishop held a synod to discuss the problems, and shortly afterwards, with Cardinal Hugh (the papal guardian of the city) and some Beneventan citizens, witnessed a truce between two warring Norman barons.[150] Landulf's successor Roffred helped compose a similar agreement in 1120, between Benevento and Count Rainulf of Caiazzo, and was probably involved in the peace pact that was sworn

---

[141] *Chron. S. Sophiae*, ii. 647–8 no. v.7.   [142] Vehse, 'Benevent', part 2, p. 88.
[143] *Falco*, pp. 4–6.   [144] *Falco*, pp. 16, 22.   [145] *Falco*, pp. 54–6.   [146] *Falco*, p. 52.
[147] *Falco*, pp. 4–6, 12.   [148] *Falco*, pp. 28–30.   [149] *Falco*, p. 42.   [150] *Falco*, p. 44.

between the Beneventans and Duke William of Apulia in 1122.[151] The archbishops also drew great influence from their spiritual roles. In 1119, when Landulf exhibited the bodies of some civic saints that had been exhumed, the whole city was united in celebration, and, according to Falco, nobody 'could remember when the city had been so entirely joyful'. Again, in 1124, during Roffred's translation of the body of Bishop Barbatus, 'the whole city crowded round' and a part of their sins was pardoned.[152]

The regular participation of the citizens of Benevento in civic government, the growing status of the archbishop and the relatively minor role played by papal officials suggest that the city was largely self-governing, particularly by the 1120s. Civic disturbances centred on the 'Norman' problem and kin-group rivalries – they were not yet aimed directly against papal rule. The popes could never permanently reside in Benevento, but when present, they mostly dealt effectively with civic matters in accord with the population's wishes. Private charters repeatedly refer to the 'law and custom of the city'. While this remained the case, the citizens of Benevento seemed to show a genuine deference to the pope and to appreciate the standing he brought to the city. This is evident in the joyous reception given by the citizens to Calixtus II on his entry into Benevento in 1120.[153]

There are notable parallels here with the experiences of northern and central Italian urban communities during the same period, except that the backdrop was different. Imperial rule was crumbling, and the often extensive civic powers of bishops were going through a transitional phase. Urban communities filled the void; they did not create it through revolt. They began to articulate their solidarity more clearly, stimulated by rapid demographic growth and inspired by the increased religious fervour of Church reform.[154] A great deal of early 'communal' formation is shrouded in obscurity, where we find the informality of language and structures so familiar in the South. The use of the term 'commune' only truly replaced that of *civitas* in the 1150s, despite suggestive signs of communal forms stretching back in some places to the second half of the eleventh century.[155] Consular officials also only appeared intermittently before *c.* 1150, and when identified they often hailed from old, established kin-groups. There seems to have been much compromise with

[151] *Falco*, pp. 54, 70.   [152] *Falco*, pp. 48, 74–6.   [153] *Falco*, p. 56.
[154] R. Bordone, ' "Civitas Nobilis et Antiqua". Per una storia delle origini del movimento comunale in Piemonte', in *Piemonte medievale. Forme del potere e della società. Studi per Giovanni Tabacco* (Turin, 1985), pp. 29–61.
[155] E. Coleman, 'The Italian communes. Recent work and current trends', *JMH* 25 (1999), pp. 381–3.

the old power-holders, in some cases with the city's bishop, who had previously ruled the city. There was definite continuity in the shift from pre-communal to communal governments. It was a slow and uneven process, during which urban elites, with the support of large sections of the community, obtained *de facto* rule. Men like Flaiperto Donadei, an imperial *missus*, who effectively governed Lucca in the 1080s–1100s, look very similar to Anso at Benevento and Grimoald at Bari.[156]

The period 1085–1127 saw a general weakening of central authority in the south Italian peninsula which created a variety of urban governments structured by local influences, and all of which had differing levels of popular participation. Salerno, Capua (1091–8 aside), Aversa and Conversano co-existed with their lords in a seemingly harmonious fashion. So too did Amalfi (after the 1090s), Troia and Bari (before 1111), although with much greater degrees of autonomy. Some, like the Apulian coastal cities of Trani and Monopoli, slipped peaceably into effective independence. Others like Bari (after 1111), Benevento (from *c.* 1100) and Gaeta developed, often violently, new styles of government which were more thoroughly representative of the urban population. All presuppose at least some forms of rudimentary communal institutions. Pressure for greater representation may also be linked with the increased size, and therefore power, of urban communities. At Capua a suburb had developed on the opposite bank of the Volturno by 1102, at Aversa an extramural settlement was emerging around the monastery of S. Biagio in the early 1100s, with more to follow later. Charters from Bari, which refer to trivial boundary disputes, disclose a high density of urban dwellings.[157] Southern Italy had a political environment conducive to the nascent aspirations of its growing civic populations. The death of Duke William of Apulia in June 1127 threatened to dramatically alter that environment and was to unite the fortunes of the peninsula's cities in an unprecedented manner.

---

[156] C. Wickham, *Courts and Conflict in Twelfth-Century Tuscany* (Oxford, 2003), pp. 21–2.

[157] Capua: *Le pergamene normanne della Mater Ecclesia capuana (1091–1197)*, ed. G. Bova (Naples, 1996), no. 4; Aversa: *CDNA*, pp. 355–6 no. 28, pp. 376–9 no. 39; Bari: *CDBV*, nos. 28, 33, 60, 67; *CDBI*, no. 35. See also below p. 166.

Chapter 3

CIVIL WAR AND UNIFICATION (1127–1139)

Duke William's death in June 1127, without a direct heir, left confusion over his succession and a power vacuum. The duke's uncle, Count Roger II of Sicily, was the best placed of a host of potential aspirants to fulfil his claims to the duchy.[1] Roger immediately faced a coalition comprising the pope, the prince of Capua and other South Italian nobles and cities, who all feared the prospect of the count attaining an over-whelming power base on the mainland to which he would import a more authoritarian style of government.[2] It was not until August 1128, after repeated campaigns, that Roger was invested as duke of Apulia by the reluctant Pope Honorius II. But the new duke's lands were far from being subdued, and his rule was only grudgingly acknowledged by the prince of Capua and others. In addition, the struggle took on international dimensions. Roger raised the status of his territories to a kingdom when he was crowned king in Palermo on Christmas Day of 1130.

This move, aimed at unifying the disparate lands of southern Italy, caused further alarm and especially threatened the hitherto independent prince of Capua, whose principality was indeed absorbed into the kingdom in 1135, and the duchy of Naples, which finally fell in 1139. The years from 1130–9 were ones of recurring revolts against Roger's rule by the region's leading men and cities. The new monarchy also found itself at the centre of the papal schism that lasted from 1130–8, as

---

[1] Other candidates included the pope and Bohemond II of Antioch; William of Tyre, *A History of Deeds Done Beyond the Sea*, ed. E. A. Babcock and A. C. Krey, 2 vols. (New York, 1976), ii. 32; Walter of Thérouanne, *Vita Karoli Comitis Flandriae*, ed. R. Köpke, *MGH SS* XII (Hanover, 1856), p. 540; H. Houben, *Roger II of Sicily. A Ruler between East and West* (Cambridge, 2002), pp. 41–4.

[2] Detailed discussion of the campaigns and revolts of the years 1127–39 is not necessary here and has been covered by Chalandon, *Histoire de la domination normande*, i. 380–404, ii. 1–97; Matthew, *Norman Kingdom*, pp. 31–53; Houben, *Roger II*, pp. 41–73.

one of the papal claimants, Anacletus II, had sponsored Roger's promotion to royalty in return for his backing. The ultimately successful
candidate, Innocent II, looked for support from the German emperor,
Lothar III. Both men opposed the new South Italian kingdom as an
encroachment upon their ancient rights in the region and led an ineffective invasion in 1137, during which they elected King Roger's
rebellious brother-in-law, Count Rainulf of Caiazzo, as duke of Apulia.
Despite this, the continued opposition of many cities and the death of
Anacletus early in 1138, Roger and the kingdom survived. Following
the sudden death of Rainulf in the spring of 1139 and Innocent's capture
by royal troops in the summer, the new king and his creation were
formally recognised by the pope in July, with Benevento remaining
a papal enclave. With the remaining pockets of resistance removed by
the end of 1139, the whole of southern Italy, stretching from the
Abruzzi to Sicily, formed part of a unified kingdom centred at Palermo.

The actions of some of southern Italy's cities, amidst the confusion
resulting from Duke William's death and the emergence of Roger's
mainland ambitions, provide a retrospective insight into their internal
developments in the preceding period of political fragmentation.
According to the chronicler Alexander of Telese, a panegyrist of Roger
II, on the death of William:

it happened that of the ducal cities such as Salerno, Troia, Melfi, Venosa and
the rest, which were left without duke or lord, some were seized by someone's
tyrannical ambition. Some persons who were pleasing to their eyes were able
to do as they liked without hindrance.[3]

This passage may well refer to those cities, noted in the previous
chapter, which were self-governing and had achieved a *modus vivendi*
with their superior, leaving the cities' leading men in effective charge.
The latter, ranging perhaps from bishops to urban 'nobles' of the same
kind as a Grimoald Alfaranites, were indeed pleasing to the eyes of their
fellow citizens and would have found the transition to autonomous
rule, after William's death, both seamless and born of expediency rather
than 'tyrannical ambition'. Once again Troia offers a particularly visible
example of this development. The city was afforded a charter of privileges
in December 1127 from Honorius II, at the height of the pope's efforts
to create a coalition against Roger II. Certainly this charter of privileges,
which effectively confirmed the city as an autonomous papal ally, is
quite problematic.[4] The document was drafted by the papal curia and
its vocabulary may well be influenced by central and northern Italian

---

[3] *Alex. Tel.*, Bk 1.1, p.6.   [4] *Troia*, no. 50.

terminology. It was also unlikely to have been issued primarily as a working statute, and its vocabulary is often ambiguous and must be treated with caution.[5] In sum, it remains difficult to know how much of this charter represents actual conditions at Troia, and how much was embellished or manufactured. Yet, if read critically, it would seem that the charter must have reflected some aspects of real, contemporary circumstances to maintain any hidden agenda within it. It is also noticeable that the tone of the document does not imply that great structural changes were required in the city in order to implement many of its clauses. The charter does not state how the council implied in clause 7 was to be constituted, the number of its members or its actual jurisdiction, which may suggest that such a body previously existed. Indeed the city judge and four 'distinguished men' from Troia, whom King Roger executed in 1133, may have been representatives of this municipal council.[6] Such a situation may indicate that Troia already enjoyed semi-autonomy brought about by a gradual appropriation of rights, the slowness of which had kept the city's inhabitants on good terms with its superior. The charter gives the impression that the city had a strong sense of identity, with a tradition of acting as a community. Clause 35 sanctions all the good customs which could be remembered by the city's *boni homines*, men who often appeared in local charters with somewhat elusive positions of responsibility, again perhaps representing the municipal body intimated in clause 7.[7] Several clauses hint at governing organs.[8] Clause 5 stipulates that a governor (*rector*) of the city should be appointed with the consent of the citizens. Perhaps papal and Beneventan influences were responsible for the appearance of this title of rector. Clause 7 refers to both the advice of the 'better part' (*senior pars*) of the citizens and to campaigns conducted in the civic interest, while clause 19 ensures that judges were to be natives. Further clauses allude to legal decisions imposed by a *curia*, to the inhabitants living under one law, to the banning of the ordeal (symbolic of independent status) and to control of the *contado*.[9] Significantly, a private charter of December 1127 was dated by the twenty-second year of the reign of Troia's Bishop William II, who styled himself, in an inscription on the cathedral doors, 'Liberator Patriae'.[10] Furthermore, the two judges acting in the above deed had dropped their ducal epithets and were simply entitled 'Troiani

[5] Martin, *Pouille*, p. 744.   [6] *Falco*, p. 154.   [7] Calasso, *La legislazione statutaria*, pp. 40–3.
[8] L. Zdekauer, 'Le franchigie concesse da Onorio II alla citta di Troia (1127)', *Rivista italiana per le scienze giuridiche* 25 (1898), pp. 242–57.
[9] *Troia*, no. 50 clauses 2, 12, 15, 19, 25; R. Bartlett, *Trial by Fire and Water: The Medieval Judicial Order* (Oxford, 1986), pp. 53–62.
[10] *Troia*, no. 51; Carabellese, *L'Apulia*, p. 413 n. 2.

iudices'; the city appeared to have created an autonomous government, guided by its bishop, built upon the foundations of the previous half-century.

Almost contemporaneously, in August 1127, Roger II of Sicily initiated the first phase of his attempt to become duke by composing an agreement with the citizens of Salerno to recognise his lordship. The inhabitants were active participants in the negotiations and obtained an accord which must have reflected their status under Duke William. Alexander of Telese's account depicts the Salernitans' initial refusal to accept Roger for fear that he would repeat the 'many evils' committed by Duke William and his predecessor. This supposed attitude was in stark contrast to other evidence on William's reign and Falco himself, no great friend of Roger, portrays the same events of 1127 as a smooth take-over. Perhaps this was Alexander's attempt to downplay the perception, being fanned by Roger's numerous detractors, that he was a tyrannical ruler.[11] By creating a picture of earlier oppression he could insinuate that resistance to Roger was due to bad experiences under previous despots. There is no contemporary surviving written form of the settlement, and the sources refer to only certain of the stipulations agreed: the Salernitans were to keep control of their citadel, were not to be imprisoned without proper trial or forced into any military campaign lasting more than two days.[12] Romuald of Salerno added that Roger confirmed the citizens' 'tenements, possessions and ancient customs'.[13] However, Matthew has demonstrated that a more comprehensive form of the agreement has survived in a document issued to the Salernitans in the fifteenth century by the Aragonese king Alfonso I. From this it is clear that the citizens also had control of public revenues ('administrationem publici peculii'), were free from servile obligations and were to have a *strategotus*, probably chosen by the inhabitants, residing in the city. Roger II 'had been required to confirm traditional customs, not offer novel concessions', and in doing so validated the city's pre-existing independence.[14]

It is also significant that, alongside Troia's customs, the only two other extant charters of privileges surviving from this period are those of Bari and Trani, two of southern Italy's most important and independent cities prior to 1127. In both cases the charters were granted by King Roger (in June 1132 to Bari and in June 1139 to Trani; however, this

---

[11] H. Wieruszowski, 'Roger II of Sicily, *Rex Tyrannus*, in twelfth-century political thought', *Speculum* 38 (1963), pp. 46–78.

[12] *Falco*, pp. 86, 88; *Alex. Tel.* Bk I.4–6, pp. 8–9.   [13] *Romuald*, p. 214.

[14] Matthew, 'Semper fideles', in *Salerno nel XII secolo*, pp. 29–32; the 1127 charter is edited in *Storia documentata della scuola medica di Salerno*, ed. S. De Renzi (Naples, 1857), pp. lxxii–lxxvi no. 177.

was to confirm a document already drafted in 1133) and unsurprisingly are more limited than the example from Troia.[15] They both largely recognise each city's civic customs, an important concession, however, given the extent to which these local usages permeated urban society in both settlements; Besta noted the first unambiguous mention of Barese customs in 1012, while a charter from 1131, in referring to the civil law and customs of Trani, at a time when the city was still effectively independent, must give added importance to their employment.[16] The Bari charter of 1132 is particularly concerned with the integrity of its ecclesiastical institutions, especially the basilica of S. Nicola, but also provides exemption from certain taxes and military service, while both privileges allow for native judges and certain judicial liberties. Martin correctly asserts that neither of these charters suggests a confirmation of autonomy as such but rather a guarantee of peace.[17] However, what the charters do reveal is that both cities previously enjoyed a wide measure of independence, and that King Roger saw the necessity of forging a compromise that would incorporate both cities into his vision of royal government. Moreover, the rather vague vocabulary of both documents, the *leges et consuetudines* referred to at Bari and the *conventiones* at Trani, implies that a wider body of unspecified privileges remained in force.

Events at Benevento immediately after 1127 also show the potent developments that had previously taken place within the city and its government. Civic discord continued to pivot ostensibly around the 'Norman' problem, which became more acute when Roger's mainland ambitions inevitably drew Benevento into a civil war concerning a kingdom of which it would not technically be a part. To threaten Benevento was an effective way for Roger to pressure a recalcitrant pope, while after 1130 the city became a battleground between the pro-royal Anacletans and the pro-imperial Innocentians. In September 1128, shortly after Roger's ducal investiture outside the city, a group of Beneventans murdered the papal rector William, and the *populus* organised a 'commune' ('communitate intra se ordinata').[18] It appears to have been a move aimed not at papal rule, nor determined exclusively by the

---

[15] Bari: *Rogerii II Regis Diplomata Latina* (Codex Diplomaticus Regni Siciliae, Ser. I.ii (1)), ed. C-R. Bruhl (Cologne, 1987), pp. 54–6 no. 20; Trani: *Trani*, no. 37.

[16] *CDBIV*, no. 12; E. Besta, 'Il diritto consuetudinario di Bari e la sua genesi', *Rivista italiana per le scienze giuridiche* 36 (1903), pp. 3–113; *Trani*, no. 33.

[17] Martin, 'Les Communautés d'habitants de la Pouille', pp. 73–98.

[18] *Falco*, p. 104; some of the men who were exiled by those who formed the commune included three judges, a doctor and another prominent citizen, Poto Spitameta.

external war, but one influenced by internal familial rivalries.[19] It is clear that the increased role that the populace played in its government in the preceding decades influenced the momentous events of 1128 and even more so that Pope Honorius II and his representative the rector, like many of his predecessors, could exert little authority over them. The pope, aware that he 'was unable to harm those who had killed his rector', simply accepted the feeble explanation for the murder which was presented by a civic delegation and in August 1129 hurried to Benevento, where he unsuccessfully 'begged the Beneventans who had made the commune' ('communitatem fecerant') to reinstate the exiles. Honorius' authority was so ineffective that he even appealed for the duke of Apulia, in a repeat of 1101, to 'exact vengeance on the citizens of Benevento'.[20] When Anacletus II had established his position in Benevento he too faced the same continuing problem; his attempts to dissolve the commune required the military aid of the prince of Capua in 1130 and led to grave factional fighting. The city had spiralled out of papal control by the end of 1132, with the chronicler Falco, an eye-witness to many of the events he recorded, referring to 'discord', 'conspiracies', 'flames of poison' and 'old enmities'.[21]

It is useful to briefly add here the case of Naples, the only city not to have experienced a regime change in the late eleventh century. In doing so, Naples maintained itself as an independent duchy, albeit one limited virtually to the city itself. The duke of Naples's recognition of a *societas* for the city's inhabitants in 1129–30 showed, however, that, in the preceding period, the city was subject to similar trends found elsewhere on the mainland – the consequences of Norman pressure mixed with a movement towards greater popular participation in civic government. The duke's *promissio* provided the citizens, although through the intervention of the *nobiliores*, with some influence over their own affairs. The urban community was guaranteed at least some role in the regulation of the financial system, the administration of justice and the right to provide counsel on matters concerning war, peace and new customs.[22] According to Cassandro, the duke's grant confirmed informal developments long since set in motion.[23]

In short, these most prominent examples alone make it clear why many of the region's cities reacted in the manner in which they did in

[19] Loud, 'Politics, piety and ecclesiastical patronage', pp. 286–7.
[20] *Falco*, pp. 104, 108.   [21] *Falco*, pp. 107, 112, 114, 116, 118.
[22] G. Cassandro, 'La *Promissio* del duca Sergio e la *Societas* napoletana', *Archivio storico italiano* 100 (1942), pp. 133–45; M. Schipa, 'Nobili e popolani in Napoli nel Medioevo in rapporto all'amministrazione municipale', *Archivio storico italiano* 83 (1925), pp. 3–44.
[23] G. Cassandro, 'La fine del ducato', *Storia di Napoli* (Naples, 1969), vol. II (i), pp. 331–7.

this period; they had undoubted privileged positions worth defending from external and, in Benevento, internal threats. As we shall see, for unique reasons, Salerno represented one of the only examples of a city that early on saw no contradiction in maintaining its urban liberties under Roger II. The city subsequently remained almost steadfastly loyal to the Sicilian. Elsewhere, however, this was not the case, as emphasised by the general theme in this tumultuous era, recurrent in the sources, hailing the virtue of liberty (*libertas*) and the need for the population to preserve it.[24] An inscription on the exterior of the cathedral of Troia, referring to the events of 1127, reads, 'the people [of Troia], in order to secure liberty, destroyed their citadel and fortified the city with walls.'[25] Prince Robert of Capua, in 1132, when addressing the anti-Rogerian coalition, announced that 'we are willing to shed our blood to defend our liberty and avoid falling into the hands of strangers.'[26] A year later, the people of Venosa, in resisting King Roger, 'welcomed the much desired liberation of their city' by accepting the rule of the rebel Tancred of Conversano 'of their own free will'.[27] The charter of customs at Trani granted to the people an 'honourable liberty', and it was in the same year of 1133 that the citizens of Benevento, fearing King Roger's designs, appealed to Pope Innocent II and Emperor Lothar III to restore to them 'the liberty which had been so deeply and long desired'. Falco of Benevento later talked of his city's 'jealously guarded liberty' and the hope 'that unhappy Apulia' would be 'restored to a glorious position'. Similarly, in 1136, the duke of Naples and his *fideles*, in opposing Roger, 'watched over the city's freedom [and] followed the virtuous tradition of their ancestors'.[28] At the same time Roger was increasingly being portrayed by his opponents as a *rex tyrannus*.[29] We must be aware that much, but by no means all, of this stress on civic liberties derives from Falco's chronicle and may reflect his personal view. Yet, as the author of a rich source and a member of the civic elite (as a notary and then judge), Falco's judgements are undoubtedly significant.[30] The confused history of this period in which many cities repeatedly, and often unexplainably, switched allegiance was really a series of tactical gambles taken by citizens hoping to follow the most likely path towards 'freedom'. The fight to preserve their 'liberty' testifies to the measure of self-government within many of the cities, a level of organisation that alone can explain the manner in which citizens

[24] Calasso, *La legislazione statutaria*, pp. 48–9. [25] See above n. 10. [26] *Falco*, p. 124.
[27] *Falco*, p. 148. [28] *Falco*, pp. 148, 164, 176. [29] See above n. 11.
[30] D. Foote, 'How the past becomes a rumor: the notarialization of historical consciousness in medieval Orvieto', *Speculum* 75 (2000), p. 815, notes 'the significance of the legal-notarial class as custodians of civic historical consciousness'.

throughout the peninsula acted as a body to fight on their city walls, to sign peace treaties, dispose of common funds and make alliances, all in the name of the *patria*.[31] This was a development in keeping with the Ciceronian ideal that 'when the liberty of the citizens is at stake, nobody can remain a private person.'[32]

King Roger's attempts to restructure this 'liberty' and consolidate his rule brought obvious disruption to the region's urban societies and its burgeoning civic governments. Many urban communities had obtained a role in self-government which at first glance appeared incongruous with the structures of a new monarchy. It was the cities of Apulia and Lucania which initially bore the brunt of the conflict, certainly up to 1133. Bari, led by Prince Grimoald, was prominent within the rebel coalition until the city was blockaded by Roger's Sicilian fleet in June 1129 and forced to submit. Roger's clemency in allowing Grimoald to retain his title and rule over Bari did not dissuade the prince from revolting again in 1131. The inevitable response the following year, a siege by royal forces, resulted in another surrender and the end of Grimoald's reign.[33] In July 1132 the citizens of Bari rose against the Muslim troops who had been sent by Roger and prevented them from constructing a fortress outside the city. The king, in a parlous position on the mainland at that time, 'was unwilling for the moment further to annoy the people of Bari . . . and left them for the time being in peace'. However, 1133 saw a hardening in Roger's previously lenient attitude towards the repeatedly rebellious cities, and he ordered that work on the citadel should resume.[34] Again in 1137, another siege, this time by the invading forces of Emperor Lothar and Pope Innocent, wrested the city from Roger's control after 'heavy casualties on both sides' and the massacre of the royal garrison.[35] Bari would remain as the last outpost of resistance to Roger until a destructive two-month siege in the summer of 1139 induced famine and 'sedition' in a population previously 'proud of spirit and puffed up with pride'. Further bloodshed followed the city's final submission when King Roger, exploiting a legal loophole, reneged on his surrender terms with Bari's recently risen Prince Jaquintus and executed him and other rebel leaders.[36]

Troia, perhaps the most persistently rebellious and challenging obstacle to Roger's rule, endured an equally turbulent time. In 1128, Troia

---

[31] F. Calasso, 'La città nell'Italia meridionale durante l'età normanna', *Archivio storico Pugliese* 12 (1959), pp. 18–34.

[32] Cicero, *De republica*, II, xxv, 46.   [33] *Alex. Tel.*, Bk II.20, p. 32; *Falco*, p. 120.

[34] *Alex. Tel.*, Bk II.34, p. 39, Bk II.49, p. 47.

[35] *Annalista Saxo*, ed. L. C. Bethman, *MGH SS* VI (Hanover, 1844), p. 774.

[36] *Falco*, pp. 228, 230.

was effectively the last city opposing Roger and was so well fortified that the duke 'could do nothing to capture it'.[37] It was not until 1129, after failed attempts to earn the support of the prince of Capua and Count Rainulf of Caiazzo, that Troia finally fell.[38] With the city's castle rebuilt, Troia appears to have remained subdued, although it would seem that (the now) King Roger distrusted the city. In 1133, possibly fuelled by rumours of concord with Rainulf and the prince of Capua, and despite the attempt of Troia's bishop to maintain the citizens' loyalty, the king levelled the city, hanging leading inhabitants and dispersing the population around the *contado*. Falco lamented that Roger ordered 'the houses and goods of the Troians to be destroyed by fire and sword. Oh what a wailing of women and children arose over the whole city'.[39] However, the city was repopulated sometime before 1137, for in this year Troia was plundered by an imperial force.[40] From this point the city appears once more to have turned against Roger, and, despite a charter of 1138 invoking the king's name, it became by 1139 one of the last rebel bulwarks, where Rainulf of Caiazzo died.[41] Roger's refusal to enter the city until Rainulf's body had been exhumed and thrown into a ditch showed his anger towards both parties.[42] In fact the king, at last victorious, still did not set foot in Troia.

On the capture of Trani in 1133 all the city's towers were demolished on Roger's orders and, even though shortly afterwards the city received its charter of customs, its inhabitants, in 1137, welcomed the approaching Emperor Lothar 'joyfully' and destroyed the royal citadel.[43] The redrafting of Trani's privileges in 1139 makes it clear that the citizens suffered in the conflicts, as a large section of the document deals with the return of prisoners of war 'who had been captured since the Germans arrived in these regions'. Melfi fell to Roger in 1128, and there the following year he promulgated a general peace as a demonstration of his power. In 1130 the citizens were ordered to rebuild the fortress that had been dismantled during Duke William's reign, and having rebelled once more Melfi was stormed by Roger in 1133.[44] Melfi appeared to maintain its loyalty, and in 1137 the citizens fought bravely, losing over 300 men, against an imperial force which eventually took the city.[45] Yet later the same year the people of Melfi, Bari, Troia and Trani helped the new duke Rainulf defeat King Roger in battle and from the captured booty 'returned to their homes rich men'.[46] We know little of the fate

---

[37] *Alex. Tel.*, Bk I.15, p. 15.   [38] *Alex. Tel.*, Bk I.18, Bk I.19, pp. 17–18.
[39] *Falco*, pp. 150, 154; *Alex. Tel.* Bk I.49, p. 47.   [40] *Annalista Saxo*, p. 773.
[41] *Troia*, no. 61.   [42] *Falco*, p. 224.   [43] *Alex. Tel.*, Bk II.49, p. 47; *Annalista Saxo*, p. 773.
[44] *Alex. Tel.*, Bk I.24, p. 20; *Falco*, p. 154.   [45] *Annalista Saxo*, p. 773.
[46] *Falco*, pp. 196, 198.

of Conversano in the conflict other than that King Roger had deposed the disobedient Count Alexander and imprisoned his brother Tancred in 1133.[47] The county was then conferred on Roger's brother-in-law Robert Basunville around 1134, but in a much reduced form.[48] The cycle of almost seasonal revolts and reprisals was repeated throughout Apulia and Lucania and undoubtedly drew in many more cities than the sources mention.

A similar pattern emerged in the principality of Capua but not really until 1134, even though its prince and many of the region's nobles and citizens had been openly opposed to Roger since 1132. It was only when the king felt sufficiently secure in Apulia (although this view soon proved optimistic) that he could focus his energy elsewhere. In 1134, with Prince Robert at Pisa attempting to find allies, King Roger arrived at Capua and 'received the surrender of its citizens and of all the magnates' of the surrounding region.[49] The city was furnished with a royal garrison which proved instrumental in maintaining order when false rumours of Roger's death in 1135 threatened to spark an uprising. In 1137 Capua did briefly pass back into the hands of its prince, who had bought off the German force that was besieging the city during Emperor Lothar III's expedition.[50] Yet within months, immediately following Lothar's departure from southern Italy, King Roger appeared before the city 'and stormed it furiously, devastating it with fire and sword. He ordered all the valuables and wealth of the city to be consigned to the flames or destroyed' and plundered Capua's churches.[51] Aversa suffered a similar fate. It fell to royal forces soon after Capua in 1134, but a year later, despite the warnings of two of Roger's key officials stationed in the region, the citizens, believing the monarch to be dead, 'threw off their obedience to the king and ... submitted to the prince [of Capua]'.[52] Aversa became for a while the military centre for the resistance, until in June 1135 the 'furious' king attacked the city, expelled its population and laid waste to the city, its suburbs and all the land as far as Naples so that 'the whole region was left a desert'. However, shortly afterwards, Roger realised the strategic importance of the city and rebuilt and repopulated it in order to 'restrain the pride of rebel Naples', where most of the insurgents had taken refuge.[53]

Even Salerno, despite its consistent loyalty towards Roger, did not avoid conflict. It seems that Roger, having decided to gain control of

---

[47] *Falco*, pp. 152, 154.   [48] Martin, *Pouille*, p. 775.
[49] *Alex. Tel.*, Bk II.66–7, pp. 55–6; *Falco*, p. 172
[50] *Alex. Tel.*, Bk III.7, p. 63; *Annalista Saxo*, p. 773.   [51] *Falco*, p. 196.
[52] *Alex. Tel.*, Bk III.6, p. 62.   [53] *Alex. Tel.*, Bk III.12–13, pp. 66–7, 22, p. 71.

Salerno's fortifications, which had been left in the citizens' hands in 1127, had to blockade the city in 1130.[54] The city appears to have unfairly fallen under suspicion in 1133 and only narrowly avoided punishment from Roger.[55] The imperial expedition of 1137, however, caused real damage. Salerno put up a valiant resistance to the combined forces of the emperor, the pope, the prince of Capua and the Pisans, but eventually surrendered after many casualties. After the capitulation, the Pisans even attacked the Salernitans, who responded in like fashion.[56] Within weeks, however, the city had welcomed back King Roger and received a valuable charter of privileges.[57]

Finally, Benevento, permeated with a unique concoction of inter-linking rivalries (between urban kin-groups, Norman barons, schismatic popes, a German emperor and Sicilian king), experienced extreme disorder. Following the violent dissolution of the city's commune in 1130 there was further civil dissension in 1132. This time it was a treaty signed by a civic faction with King Roger, and supported by the rector Crescentius, that caused conflict for, as Falco tells us, 'a terrible rumour ran round the city of Benevento and tongues wagged freely' that the pact would place the city under Roger's power and that the Beneventan delegates had been bribed. The majority of the citizenry took up arms, forced Crescentius out of the city and came to an agreement instead with the prince of Capua and Rainulf of Caiazzo that Benevento would remain neutral.[58]

Roger's reaction was to systematically ravage the city's surrounding lands, destroying harvests and taking captives. In response, the citizens of Benevento turned to Roger's enemy, Pope Innocent, whose party gained the ascendancy over Anacletus' in the city. A new rector, Cardinal priest Gerard, was installed to replace the Anacletan Crescentius, and the office of constable revived in the person of Rolpoto of S. Eustasio, who was henceforth 'active in the city's war'. Throughout 1133, led by Rolpoto, the citizens participated in repeated skirmishes with local barons who supported King Roger, while Crescentius and other Beneventan exiles plotted the constable's assassination and 'an armed take-over of the city squares'. The coup failed largely because of the 'sense of loyalty [in] the whole populace of Benevento' and many of the 'traitors' were executed.[59] But in 1134, after Count Rainulf's (temporary) submission to Roger, Anacletus' party 'through the king's power obtained command' over Benevento, and Rolpoto along with

---

[54] *Alex. Tel.*, Bk I.22, pp. 19–20.   [55] *Falco*, p. 158
[56] *Falco*, pp. 186, 188; *Romuald*, p. 223; *Annalista Saxo*, pp. 774–5.   [57] See below n. 72.
[58] *Falco*, pp. 128, 130.   [59] *Falco*, pp. 144, 146, 160, 164, 166.

more than 1,000 Beneventans (including the chronicler Falco) fled to Naples.[60] With the imperial expedition of 1137, Innocent once again, after further bloodshed, regained control of the city, enabling many Beneventan exiles (again including Falco) to return 'to their homeland'. It was at this point that the emperor freed 'the Beneventans from an old affliction' – the payment of various *fidantiae* (dues) which the local Norman barons had exacted from them.[61] Before the year was out, with Lothar having departed, Benevento had allied again 'in love and fealty' with Roger, who confirmed the emperor's earlier grant to the citizens. Following the death of Anacletus in January 1138 and Roger's recognition of Innocent (though this was not reciprocated by the pope for another eighteen months) this turbulent period for Benevento began to calm. Late in 1138 and again in 1139 King Roger even made respectful visits to the city and its religious shrines. After Roger and Innocent had come to terms over the question of the kingdom, and recognised the city's theoretical autonomy, the pope set about reorganising Benevento, 'he quashed every ordination' made by Anacletus and appointed a new rector.[62]

This extended roll-call of destruction underlines the chaotic impact of the civil war on southern Italy's urban governments and their communities. The disruption was significant, and many citizens must have died.[63] Private charters from this period provide a conflicting picture; many concern prosaic land sales or marriage agreements and give no sense of disturbance. Yet in most cities there are gaps in this documentation that correlate with spells of recorded disorder – thus charters are lacking at Troia and Aversa from 1132–8, at Trani from 1131–7, at Conversano from 1128–33, and at Bari from 1132–4. It is much easier to trace damage at the higher levels of civic government. Capua, Aversa, Conversano, Naples and Bari lost their native rulers, and all cities were deprived of any previous political independence. Yet, although Roger wanted to restructure the way southern Italy's cities were governed, this did not mean that he actively aimed to destabilise them and discard all previous traditions of rule. Roger kept the territorial divisions of southern Italy's previous polities as governmental districts.[64] The king's sons, Roger, Anfusus and Tancred, were installed in the 1130s as duke of Apulia, prince of Capua and prince of Bari (later Taranto) respectively,

---

[60] *Falco*, p. 172.   [61] *Falco*, p. 184, 192; *Annalista Saxo*, p. 773.

[62] *Falco*, pp. 202, 214, 224, 226.

[63] *CDNA*, pp. 52–4 no. 32, dated September 1132 at Aversa, mentions the death of many men at the Battle of Nocera in July of that year, a battle in which King Roger's forces had been defeated by a coalition led by the prince of Capua, *Alex. Tel.*, Bk II.29–32, pp. 36–8; *Falco*, pp. 134, 136, 138.

[64] H. Takayama, *The Administration of the Norman Kingdom of Sicily* (New York, 1993), p. 64.

although the latter two were too young to govern. Salerno was to remain, as it had under ducal rule, the mainland capital. According to the 1127 *pacta*, Roger agreed to conserve the city as 'caput [head] totius Principatus, nec non totius Apuliae et Calabriae'.[65] In doing so Roger showed sensitivity towards Salerno's traditional political sensibilities and ensured the citizens' enduring loyalty. The city had grown accustomed to its position as a seat of government, with all the rewards that this entailed, and Roger immediately made it clear that this would continue.[66] His immediate dash to Salerno on the death of Duke William showed an awareness of the symbolic importance of the city for gaining control on the peninsula. According to Romuald of Salerno, Roger was anointed as prince in the city in 1127. It was also near the city, in 1130, that Roger convoked a distinguished council to discuss his elevation to king.[67] Roger began and ended almost every campaigning season with a triumphant sojourn in the city. The duke of Naples offered his submission in Salerno in 1131, high-profile political prisoners were detained there and the king held a prestigious council in the city in 1137 to decide upon the papal schism.[68] Roger was not insincere when, in 1127, he stated to the Salernitans that under his rule they would 'achieve greater prosperity and the riches which, once upon a time, [they] had'.[69] For the most part the citizens responded positively. When Roger fled to Salerno, following a disastrous defeat at Nocera in 1132, rather than seeing an opportunity for gain, the citizens welcomed him warmly.[70] After the king suffered a similar reverse in 1137, the inhabitants, 'as was their custom, received him dutifully'. Only a few months earlier, on regaining Salerno from imperial control, Roger had been greeted by the Salernitans 'with the utmost devotion'.[71] The preamble to the charter of privileges that Roger awarded to the city, after its brave fight against his opponents in 1137, sums up the prudence in allowing the city's traditional role to continue:

We [the king] have decided to honour and raise up the people of Salerno, our *fideles*, because they have always been loyal to Robert Guiscard, and to Dukes Roger and William, our predecessors, as well as to us too, especially at this time at which Lothar with his *Teutones* entered into Apulia because of the treachery of our betrayers, and at a time when almost the entire land was stained with the mark of disloyalty, alone in Italy the city of Salerno maintained its loyalty unblemished.[72]

[65] *Storia documentata della scuola medica*, lxxiii no. 177.
[66] See above pp. 30–1; Matthew, 'Semper fideles', pp. 32–4.
[67] *Romuald*, p. 214; *Alex. Tel.*, Bk II.2, pp. 23–5.
[68] *Alex. Tel.*, Bk II.12, pp. 28–9; *Falco*, pp. 150, 202, 204.   [69] *Falco*, p. 88.
[70] *Falco*, p. 138.   [71] *Romuald*, p. 224.   [72] *Rogerii II Regis Diplomata Latina*, pp. 129–31 no. 46.

Indeed Roger was always reluctant to make wholesale changes and, for instance, showed respect for the princely title of Grimoald up until 1132. It must have been with Roger's acquiescence that Pope Anacletus, in November 1130, granted Bari's archbishop the right of consecrating the prince or his heirs – a remarkable recognition of Grimoald's position and its hereditary status. Only when Grimoald had rebelled one too many times did he lose his office.[73] It seems that Roger had been equally reluctant to depose the prince of Capua. Bishop William II of Troia, who had been a key figure within the autonomous city in 1127, received confirmation of his church's privileges from Roger shortly after the city had submitted in 1129, and he retained his office and influential position throughout the civil war.[74] A few new high-ranking royal officials were provisionally installed in the principality of Capua from 1134, such as the chancellor Guarin, the admiral John and in 1137 Robert of Selby.[75] But equally, William the archbishop-elect of Capua and Aimo of Argentia, an Aversan baron who had witnessed charters of the prince of Capua as late as 1132, were promoted to a rudimentary office of royal justiciar in 1135.[76] At the same time, the previous princely chamberlain Joscelin became the region's first royal chamberlain and was, by 1136, placed in charge of Capua.[77] Intriguing information on the situation at Trani also appears. Little is known of the city's governing structures in the preceding half-century and especially so in the years 1127–33, except that it must have enjoyed a wide-ranging independence. What then are we to make of the sudden appearance in 1136 of a certain Urso Trabalia, who claimed in a charter to have been committed with the maintenance of justice by royal power ('regia potestate'), and who was given, from King Roger, the privileged title of *tranensium dominator*?[78] Was Urso an outside royal appointment or, more tantalisingly, had he been established in the city for some years and risen from the urban aristocracy in the same way that Grimoald had at Bari? It would certainly seem that Urso was both local and wealthy; a document from 1138 shows that he possessed vines near Trani and he may have been related to Boamund Travallie, who later held a royal fief in Corato, as well as to a notary called Peter Traballus and a knight named Roger of Trani *qui et Trabalia*,

[73] *CDBI*, no. 42.   [74] *Troia*, no. 53.
[75] *Alex. Tel.*, Bk III.3, pp. 60–1; Takayama, *Administration of the Norman Kingdom*, pp. 61–4.
[76] Loud, *Church and Society*, pp. 163–4.
[77] *Alex. Tel.*, Bk III.32, p. 77; G. A. Loud, 'Continuity and change in Norman Italy: the Campania during the eleventh and twelfth centuries', *JMH* 22 (1996), pp. 336–7; *Chronicon Monasterii Casinensis*, Bk VI.98, p. 558.
[78] Jamison, 'Norman administration', cal. doc. no. 5.

who both appear in the 1190s.[79] It is quite remarkable that King Roger allowed a local individual to attain such a position in such an important city, and it is unfortunate that we do not know how long he retained his office. Perhaps if Prince Grimoald had been less intransigent he too would have been given a similar position in the new monarchy's hierarchy.

Alongside these surprising allusions to continuity at the higher levels of urban government and society, there were also those at the lower end. In Salerno, where Roger's presence was strongest, the officials and their titles displayed a recognisable continuity with the ducal era. One of Duke William's chamberlains in the Salerno region, Hugh Mansellus, continued in the same office under the king. Hugh's brother-in-law, Atenulf, became a royal chamberlain in the region in the 1140s and later was an important figure at the royal court in Palermo.[80] The official post of *strategotus*, introduced into Salerno in the ducal period, remained important and appears as the king's main representative in the city in the 1130s, seemingly in charge of supervising all urban property and revenues due to Roger.[81] Its importance is underlined by the prominence of its incumbents. Under Duke William, the city's *strategotus* had been held by a member of the Guarna family, the notable kin-group whose fortunes continued to rise thereafter.[82] In the 1130s the office was occupied by Sergius, from the local Caputus family. Sergius' brothers were active in civic affairs and his son and another relative became *strategoti* themselves in the 1150s and 60s.[83] The local elite survived and the example of the wealthy Guaiferius, the son of a ducal judge of Salerno, John, himself the son of a former Lombard count of the palace, is commonplace.[84] As we will see later, one of the city's administrative centres would remain in the old Lombard palace. At Troia the probable disappearance of certain individuals and the emergence of some new members of the civic elite can be discerned, but at this early stage it does not seem that the king greatly altered the city's ruling hierarchy. Aside from the sudden appearance of a *strategotus* in the first Troian charter issued under the new king, there is little evidence of royal officials being appointed from above.[85] Moreover, this *strategotus*, Amicus of Melfi

[79] *Trani*, no. 36; *Le Pergamene di Barletta. Archivio Capitolare (897–1285)*, ed. F. Nitti de Vito, *Codice diplomatico barese* VIII (Bari, 1914), no. 173; *Catalogus Baronum*, ed. E. M. Jamison, *FSI* CI (Rome, 1972), p.10 no. 47.

[80] Cava, Arm. Mag. (1125) F.34; *Necrologio del Liber Confratrum*, p. 34 col. 22, p. 353; Loud, *Age of Robert Guiscard*, p. 283.

[81] *Montevergine*, iii. 10–3 no. 204.   [82] See below p. 193.

[83] For the Caputus see below pp. 98, 196.

[84] *Documenti per la storia di Eboli*, p. 68 nos. 140–4; *Necrologio del Liber Confratrum*, p. 343.

[85] *Troia*, no. 56.

(clearly an outside appointment), does not appear again, having been most likely expelled soon afterwards. Falco does tell us that in 1133 Roger's razing of the city also included the hanging of a judge Robert and 'four other distinguished men' of Troia. A judge Robert was attested in Troia from 1129 to 1132, and one can only speculate on the particular nature of his, and the other men's, activities that drew this draconian response. In contrast to Robert's fate, the two other city judges of Troia, Secundinus and Iannucius, who were recorded during this period, seem to have survived the king's wrath. Indeed, both these judges retained their positions and enjoyed long careers, Secundinus from 1125–69 and Iannucius from 1127–44, with only simple changes to their titles (ducal, Troian, royal) to correlate with whoever ruled the city at that time.[86] The judges' position in the local hierarchy was firmly entrenched, and new regimes must have considered them indispensable.

The few charters that survive from Trani during this period betray little of the external instability raging throughout southern Italy. From 1130 these documents were no longer dated by the ruling years of the Byzantine empire and did not recognise any superior authority until the insertion of King Roger's name in 1139. But, as at Troia, no new officials or governing institutions appeared, aside from the puzzling figure of Urso Trabalia. The judge Silitto, who signed a document in 1138 when the city opposed the king, witnessed another in 1141 in Roger's name.[87] Although the copy of Trani's charter of privileges made in 1139 shows that many citizens had been taken prisoner, that document also provided for their return and that of their property. There seems to have been even less transition at Conversano, despite the arrival of a new royally appointed count in 1134. One of Count Robert's first acts in 1134 was to make a donation of urban property to the monastery of S. Benedetto – a policy of patronage identical to that of his comital predecessors.[88] The same civic officials remained in the same offices. The only exception was a certain Lizza, who was given a newly created office of *strategotus* in 1128 and was last testified in 1133, just before the new count's arrival.[89] Many men, however, survived the regime change, such as the judges Nicholas (1124–40) and Maio (1114?–44) and the notary Eustasius (1128–48).[90]

---

[86] Secundinus: *Troia*, nos. 49, 51, 52, 54, 66, 67, 76, 83; *Rogerii II Regis Diplomata Latina*, pp. 259–61 no. 1; Secundinus the judge was probably the same person as the notary Secundinus, son of Lawrence, found at Troia in 1122, *Colonie cassinensi*, no. 25; Iannucius: *Troia*, nos. 51, 59, 61, 65, 67.

[87] *Trani*, nos. 36, 39.   [88] *Conversano*, no. 8; and see above p. 38.

[89] *Conversano*, nos. 44, 78, 80.

[90] Nicholas: *Conversano*, nos. 76–8, 80, 85, 86, 88–90; Maio: *Conversano*, nos. 66–70, 90; Eustasius: *Conversano*, nos. 78, 87, 89, 99.

Private charters made no reference to the rule of the king, and the above officials were not designated as royal.

The impact of the civil war had a more visible effect on Bari, which permanently lost the rule of a native prince. The city hosted a royal garrison of Muslim soldiers from 1133 until their massacre by an imperial force in 1137, and private charters intermittently recognised Roger's rule from 1135. But there was as yet no sign of new royal institutions or officials in Bari. The city's charter of customs of 1132 referred to a royal court (*regis curia*), yet the privileges were not to be implemented by royal officials but by the Apulian counts of Conversano, Catanzaro and Gravina. In the power vacuum it is clear that Bari's urban elite maintained an influential place in the city's government despite it suffering two distinct purges: in 1132, when Roger dispatched 'Prince Grimoald and the wealthy and noble citizens who had opposed him' to a Sicilian prison, and again in 1139, when 'the king promptly ordered the prince [Jaquintus], the men named [the prince's counsellors] and ten others to be hanged, ten others to be blinded and mutilated and other prominent citizens to be arrested.'[91] However, many leading men, like the judge Leo de Rayza, displayed remarkable endurance throughout this period. Leo, the father of the later, influential admiral Maio of Bari, first appeared in 1119, when Grimoald dominated Bari, and was present in a *curia principis* of 1130, where he was termed a curial judge.[92] In 1135, in two documents dated by the king's regnal years, Leo carried the neutral title of judge of the Baresi (*barensium iudex*), but in documents of 1140 and 1141 he was named as a *regalis critis* (it is interesting to note the continued use of the Greek word *critis* for judge) and was still active in 1147.[93] In 1135 we have mention of a Basil Melipezzi, a probable member of the same family that produced the judge Nicholas Melipezzi, who was active under the reigns of Bohemond and Grimoald, while in 1144 Melia, the son of Stephen Sclavus, one of Bari's wealthiest men in the early 1100s, had inherited his father's patrimony and proclivity for lending money.[94] The emergence of the previously unrecorded Jaquintus as prince, probably sometime in 1137, demonstrates the vitality of the city's urban aristocracy.

Capua also lost its native prince, saw some of his partisans in the city deported to Salerno in 1135 and from this year sheltered a formidable royal garrison, but the limited information available suggests that the

---

[91] *Romuald*, p. 219; *Falco*, pp. 228, 230.   [92] *CDBI*, no. 40; *CDBV*, no. 79.
[93] Cava, *Arca* xxv.2; *CDBV*, nos. 84, 86, 94.
[94] Basil: *CDBV*, no. 84; Melia: *CDBV*, nos. 96, 97; see above pp. 34, 35, 48 and below
   p. 256.

city's governing hierarchy was not completely displaced.[95] Before the city's capture in 1134 the prince's administrative personnel remained virtually the same as before 1127, although a *strategotus* appeared briefly in the early 1130s; the same officer emerged almost at the same time at Conversano and Troia and perhaps was endowed with emergency military functions on account of the ominous political climate.[96] Even after 1134, and the relatively limited initial administrative restructuring of the principality, lower officials who served under the prince's government still did so under the king's rule. The judges Peter (1124–59?), and Tolomei (1132–55), for example, continued their activities.[97] These developments were paralleled at Aversa, with officials like the judge Herbert (1131–41) and the notary William (1111–44) continuing to serve under King Roger.[98] Aversa's leading landed urban kin-groups also mostly managed to survive the civil war; the Peroleo and Pinzoni survived the regime change, and some, like the already mentioned Aimo of Argentia, who became a royal justiciar, made astute moves to the royal side.[99]

It is quite befitting that such a confused period should leave an equally confused picture of how urban governments exactly functioned; the disruption of warfare, changing regimes and the removal of leading men is counterbalanced by the stability of long-serving officials, the endurance of the citizenry, the flexibility of the influential upper urban class and even the maintenance of some high-ranking officials. It is certain, however, that the movement for popular participation in the region's urban governments, which had burgeoned at different rates in the earlier decades, now matured out of expediency to fill, in conjunction with long-established civic officials, the power vacuum within many cities. As already noted, the theme of liberty, which appears in the source material for this period, most likely concealed the privileged position of many cities in which the citizenry, through rudimentary communal institutions, assisted increasingly in government. This development would

---

[95] *Alex. Tel.*, Bk III.7, p. 63.

[96] *CDNA*, pp. 41–2 no. 27; Loud, 'Calendar', p. 142 nos. 144, 145.

[97] Peter: *Pergamene di Capua*, i. 41–3 no. 19, pp. 63–9 nos. 25–7, pp. 70–1 no. 29, pp. 74–9 no. 31; ii. 16–8 no. 8; *CDNA*, pp. 60–3 no 36; *Pergamene normanne*, no. 11; Tolomei: *Pergamene di Capua*, i. 70–4 nos. 29–30, pp. 79–80 no. 32; ii. 18–22 nos. 9–10; *CDNA*, pp. 307–9 no. 1, pp. 342–4 no. 20; *Montevergine*, iii. 48–51 no. 213; *Regesto di S. Angelo in Formis*, pp. 207–12 no. 73.

[98] Herbert: *CDNA*, pp. 52–4 no. 32, pp. 68–71 nos. 40–1, pp. 74–5 no. 43, pp. 313–5 no. 4, pp. 376–81 nos. 39–40; William: *CDNA*, pp. 29–33 nos. 20–1, pp. 41–2 no. 27, pp. 46–54 nos. 30–2, pp. 68–71 nos. 40–1, pp. 74–5 no. 43, pp. 80–1 no. 46, pp. 83–6 nos. 48–9, pp. 309–11 no. 2, pp. 315–25 nos. 5–8, pp. 363–8 nos. 33–4, pp. 373–5 no. 37, pp. 376–81 nos. 39–40.

[99] See above p. 44; Peroleo: *CDNA*, pp. 44–6 no. 29, pp. 330–1 no. 13; Pinzoni: pp. 66–8 no. 39, pp. 111–2 no. 64, pp. 309–11 no. 2, pp. 323–5 no. 8: de Argentia: pp. 82–3 no. 47, pp. 379–81 no. 40.

seem to have reached its apogee in the 1130s; however, it was especially potent in Apulia and Benevento by the 1120s. Thus we see citizens repeatedly acting as a body in political contexts. The citizens of Salerno and Amalfi negotiated peace terms with Roger II over control of their city fortifications in 1127, and in the same year, as a prelude to receiving their civic customs, those of Troia invited the pope to receive their homage.[100] In 1132, following their rising against Muslim troops in the city, the inhabitants of Bari presented 'petitions' to King Roger.[101] Strategic alliances were composed by the citizen body: in 1129, and perhaps again by 1133, the Troians agreed a pact with Rainulf of Caiazzo and the prince of Capua, in 1133 the Venosans accepted the lordship of Tancred of Conversano and in 1135 'the leaders and people of Aversa' decided to support the prince of Capua.[102] Numerous examples also demonstrate that the *populus* could operate effectively in military matters both defensive and offensive. At Troia the inhabitants fortified their city in the late 1120s, in 1137 those at Bari successfully stormed the royal citadel and then with 'the people of other nearby towns [went] to rescue Monopoli' from Roger.[103] Again, in 1137, the people of Trani, Troia and Melfi assisted in the defeat of the king in pitched battle, while citizens also made tactical surrenders, like the 'city elders' who handed Salerno over to Lothar III in 1137.[104] Similarly, processions outside the city walls were made by the inhabitants of Troia (1133), Capua (1134 and 1135) and Salerno (1135) to prove to King Roger the authenticity of their submissions.[105] The demonstration of 1135 at Capua was particularly important because it represented the citizens' formal recognition of their archbishop-elect, whom the year before they had assisted in choosing, and also of Anfusus, 'the new prince' of Capua. More significantly it was the inhabitants of Bari who handed over their Prince Grimoald to Roger in 1132, and who again in 1139 forced Jaquintus to submit, showing a greater desire to protect their city than their leader.[106] Indeed at Bari, in 1139, peace was made 'with the agreement of the people'. It would seem that many urban populations were now acquiring a political authority to match their cognisance of political affairs. The appearance of factions within cities emphasises this; they were a concoction of political debate, social discord and local rivalry. Civic factions are alluded to in virtually every city: Bari was prominent

---

[100] *Alex. Tel.*, Bk I.5–7, pp. 8–10. [101] *Alex. Tel.*, Bk II.34, p. 39.
[102] *Falco*, p. 148, 150; *Alex. Tel.*, Bk I.18–19, pp. 16–8, Bk III.6, p. 62.
[103] See above n. 10; *Annalista Saxo*, p. 773–4. [104] *Falco*, p. 188.
[105] Troia: *Falco*, p. 154; Capua: *Alex. Tel.*, Bk II.67, p. 55, Bk III.32 p. 77; Salerno: *Alex. Tel.*, Bk III.9, p. 64.
[106] *Falco*, pp. 120, 228.

but so too was Capua, where, according to Alexander of Telese, there were those 'who more than others loved the prince [of Capua]'.[107]

Once the final conquest of the kingdom was complete, Roger did not completely truncate this broad movement and was willing to allow the cities a wide measure of self-government in return for their recognition of his rule. This 'bargain', what Martin called a 'circumscribed liberty', could not have been otherwise, seeing that there would be insufficient royal governing structures on the mainland until the 1150s.[108] The king's major concern, as Alexander of Telese records, was rather the institution of a 'continuous peace', hence his determination to garrison urban citadels. But provided a city upheld law and order then it would enjoy a certain semi-autonomy guided by local civic officials. Moreover, this very custom and law was not newly imposed by the king but was that which had been current in the cities before 1127. Royal legislation, probably of the early 1140s, stated clearly that 'because of the variety of people subject to our rule, the usages, customs and laws which have existed among them up to now are not annulled', unless they openly contradicted certain royal edicts.[109] With this in mind, returning to the charter of privileges given to Troia, Bari, Trani and Salerno, it is plausible, once the troubled 1130s had passed, that Roger was willing to allow large parts of them to remain in force. In the document for Troia some clauses must have been repealed. The inhabitants would not have been allowed to decide under what circumstances the city went to war (clause 7), it is unlikely that they were freed from all services (clauses 8, 9 and 31) and clause 6, forbidding the construction of a citadel at Troia, had long been void. But the majority of the clauses dealing with the justice system and lesser local customs may have remained intact, with the compromise solution of their supervision by 'royal'-titled officials of local origin. It seems that clause 19, guaranteeing that Troia had native judges, was maintained. The civic councils implied in clauses 5 and 7 were probably also continued, with lesser urban officials and prominent kin-groups forming its core under the sympathetic supervision of higher 'royal', but native, officials. Troia's charter of 1127 was not, as Carabellese called it, 'the song of a dying swan', but rather the basis of later urban government.[110] It was perhaps similar at Trani, where the charter of privileges granted to the city promised not to 'interfere with their [the

---

[107] *Alex. Tel.*, Bk III.7, p. 63.
[108] Martin, 'Les Communautés d'habitants de la Pouille', pp. 73–98; Takayama, *Administration of the Norman Kingdom*, pp. 73–8.
[109] G. M. Monti, *Lo stato normanno svevo. Lineamenti e ricerche* (Trani, 1945), p. 116 article I (Roger's legislation is edited within at pp. 83–184).
[110] Carabellese, *L'Apulia*, p. 442.

citizens'] laws and customs', and again we know that the stipulation providing for native judges and notaries was observed. At Bari the city's rebellion after the receipt of its privileges from Roger invalidated the agreement. But there is no reason to suppose that parts of it, particularly the clauses providing for the appointment of native ecclesiastical and civic officials and those concerning judicial, fiscal and property rights, were not revived after 1139 in some form. This is suggested by Roger's treatment of Jaquintus, the prince of Bari, on the city's capture in 1139. Roger clearly wanted rid of Jaquintus, yet he was ostensibly executed not for his previous opposition to the king but because his blinding of a local knight had broken *native* custom. To give additional legality to the act Roger appointed judges from Troia and Trani, conversant with local Apulian law, to rule on the matter. Evidence from the city's customs, which were compiled around the year 1200, suggests that the citizens' exemption from military expeditions by land or sea had been revoked. However, the wider continuance of Bari's customs is inferred in the prologue to the city's customs. Here it states that 'the divine [King] Roger, having captured the city by his most powerful arms and over-thrown its walls, both praised these customs [*sanctiones*] and maintained them undamaged.' A clause in these customs adds that 'in accordance with ancient custom ... we hold in perpetuity [the right] that no tax, service, gift or assistance may be exacted from the people of Bari, and that they are excused from all burdens, except for service on the galleys.'[111]

As a result of Salerno's loyalty, the provisions contained within Roger's two agreements (1127 and 1137) with its citizens certainly remained in force after 1139. Indeed, the 1127 settlement, which according to one scholar confirmed the city as 'a self regulating republic', was reissued in a fifteenth-century charter.[112] The document in question states that Salerno's privileges had remained inviolate until Frederick II's reign. The only known exception was control over the city's fortifications, which Roger annulled in 1130. A charter from 1128, referring to the use of the 'lex et consuetudo' of Salerno, shows that Roger had been as good as his word.[113] The grant of 1137, addressed to the faithful *Salernitani*, dealt more with financial matters rather than governing ones.[114] The citizens were exempted from certain customary payments, given the market taxes on certain imports, and their trading rights in Alexandria were placed on a par with those of the Sicilians. That Roger's reward did not cover any institutional arrangements may well suggest that the

---

[111] G. Petroni, *Della storia di Bari dagli antichi tempi sino all'anno 1856*, 2 vols. (Naples, 1857–8), ii. 432, 438 Rubric II.1 .
[112] Matthew, 'Semper fideles', p. 32.   [113] Cava, *Arca* xxii.52.   [114] See above n. 72.

city already boasted a substantial freedom in this area, perhaps guaranteed since 1127. It can be understood, from the document of 1133, that the citizens had power over local taxes, and that civic officials, rather than new royal appointees, comprised the main governing apparatus. Any royal rights, officials or institutions in Salerno are clearly played down, and all this in the mainland capital of the new kingdom.

Just how far King Roger (and his successors) allowed governing structures, which had developed prior to 1127, to continue after 1139 will become apparent in the following chapter. Even more openly 'communal' forms of government may have survived, especially at Naples and Gaeta.[115] In Naples, between the death of Duke Sergius in 1137 and the city's final, official submission in 1140, urban government was directed by *nobiles* who had public functions covering particular urban quarters. They supervised minors and oversaw the provision of advocates.[116] The subsequent history of the city in the kingdom is obscure, but, though hypothesis, it may well be that these communal bodies of regional 'nobles' continued under the direction of a leading royal official (*compalatius*). The same can be more safely posited for the consuls at Gaeta under the direction of a *baiulus*. Traces of such 'communal' types of government are hinted at under the monarchy and were recognised by the charter of privileges given by King Tancred to Naples in 1190 and to Gaeta in 1191.[117] In both it appears that many of the consular governing arrangements referred to had earlier foundations that survived in the kingdom. Indeed, Tancred's grant to Gaeta claimed to confirm 'all the practices and usages' which the citizens 'have had from ancient times and from the time of King Roger, our grandfather of happy memory, until now'.

Within many of the charters of privileges throughout the twelfth century, besides those written down, there are customs and usages which are referred to but not defined further. While some of these may not have survived, perhaps others had been preserved orally in what was still a semi-literate society, in which 'the oral, ritualistic and the symbolic' persisted.[118] The written word was still distrusted, and it was from

---

[115] J-M. Martin, 'Les Communes en Italie méridionale aux XII et XIII siècles', in *Villes, bonnes villes, cités et capitales: mélanges offerts à Bernard Chevalier* (Tours, 1989), pp. 203–5; Skinner, *Family Power in Southern Italy*, pp. 197–209.

[116] *Monumenta ad Neapolitani Ducatus Historiam Pertinentia*, 2 vols., ed. B. Capasso (Naples, 1885), ii (i). 432–5 nos. 680–1, which refer to the 'nobiles homines de regione S. Pauli maiori' and 'de regione Nilo' respectively; Cassandro, 'La fine del ducato', p. 380.

[117] *Tancredi et Willelmi III Regum Diplomata*, ed. H. Zielinski (Codex Diplomaticus Regni Sicilae, Ser. I.v) (Cologne, 1982), pp. 15–8 no. 6, pp. 43–5 no. 18; see below pp. 125–6, 128–9.

[118] B. Stock, *The Implications of Literacy: Written Language and Models of Interpretation in the Eleventh and Twelfth Centuries* (Princeton, 1983), p. 71.

the elders' wisdom and not textual accounts that much information was drawn. Evidence suggests that non-written remembrance, in this case certain local customs, constantly mutates so as to be valid for a given society at a given time. Therefore the description in the twelfth-century documents of the customs as 'ancient' may be objectively misleading in that those practised at that time may have been rather different from those a century earlier. However, as each successive generation was unaware of the extent of these largely unconscious and gradual changes, the customs represented, for them, an unbroken tradition and *were* therefore ancient.[119] As Stock noted, 'the single great storehouse of meaning is memory', and memory is both selective and continually mutable.[120]

Benevento, of course, never fell under royal control, but the developments that took place in other cities of southern Italy found their parallels here too, often in a more extreme format. The city's government was destabilised internally by the machinations of the competing papal parties and externally by the conflict between Roger II and his opponents. From 1127 to 1139 Benevento had no less than five different rectors, two of whom, the Innocentian Cardinal Gerard and the Anacletan Cardinal priest Crescentius, seem to have been competitors for the office, and as a result both suffered periods of exile.[121] Girgensohn emphasised the importance of the papal chamberlain but only one appeared in Benevento during this period and that was in November 1127.[122] Other temporary officials were often dispatched, by whichever pope ruled the city, to assist the rector; a sign, already visible in the preceding decades, that the rectorship was not all-powerful. In 1127/8 Pope Honorius sent Walter, archbishop of Taranto, to Benevento 'to deal with matters concerning the city, and lend his assistance to its protection'.[123] The rector was ordered 'to hand over money from the regalian revenues to the archbishop [of Taranto], from which the knights of the city might be armed', suggesting that Walter was in command of civic defence. It is interesting that the reason given by the citizens for the formation of the commune later in 1128 was the 'oppressions' and 'damage' which the subsequently murdered rector William heaped on the city; perhaps indicating that William had dared to be more rigorous

---

[119] See the important works of M. T. Clanchy, *From Memory to Written Record. England 1066–1307*, 2nd edn (Oxford, 1993) and 'Remembering the past and the good old law', *History* 55 (1970), pp. 165–76. More widely, in relation to non-written records, the word 'ancient' represents less a conception of a particular time and more something that is held in high esteem. Thus it was hugely important for such customs to be confirmed, F. Kern, *Kingship and Law in the Middle Ages* (Oxford, 1968), p. 156.

[120] Stock, *The Implications of Literacy*, p. 15.   [121] Loud, 'A provisional list', pp. 3–4.

[122] Girgensohn, 'Documenti beneventani', p. 272 and pp. 296–8 no. 6.   [123] *Falco*, p. 100.

than his rather passive predecessors.[124] Mention of a rector from 1128 until 1131, a period of acute disorder, is significantly absent. When the rector Crescentius appeared in January 1131 his inability to control the civic factions led to his exile and, in November 1132, the selection of Gerard. But the new rector was weak; he owed his position to a party within the city and needed to revive the office of constable. The man entrusted with this function was, remarkably, Rolpoto of S. Eustasio, who had been described in 1128 as 'the most ardent supporter of the commune'. The constable was to help 'to direct the affairs of the court and energetically to dispense justice to all'. Until Anacletus regained control of Benevento in 1134, forcing Rolpoto's flight, it was the constable, not the rector, who appeared to be the leading man in the city.[125] Rolpoto's military successes earned him a position in the city almost identical to that of the Constable Landulf de Graeca some twenty years earlier, and which was perhaps not wholly dissimilar to the part played by Grimoald Alfaranites and Urso Trabalia. Finally, in 1137, Innocent II seems to have temporarily appointed two rectors when he assigned the subdeacon Octavian 'to rule the city along with' the previous rector, Gerard.[126]

The weakness of the rector reflected that of the pope's control over the city, and the presence of two warring apostolic candidates allowed the citizens greater freedom in their own affairs. We have already discussed the city's commune and how it emerged from the increased participation of the populace in government. It is frustrating that we do not know more about its composition or institutions, and it therefore appears as a rather rudimentary organisation without the full backing of the citizenry.[127] However, the alarmed reaction of Popes Honorius and Anacletus, as well as of one civic faction, suggests it represented a clear threat that included two respected city judges and the later constable Rolpoto of S. Eustasio among its members. Falco of Benevento, in excusing his short account of these events, seems to refer to lost written sources when he states that 'it has indeed very frequently been related how the commune had been created', which in turn suggests that it was significant enough to attract the attention of various contemporary commentators.[128] It is certain that some sort of communal organisation continued in the city but, as before 1128, without an official title. Indeed, Innocent II may have countenanced some sort of restructured

---

[124] *Falco*, p. 102.   [125] *Falco*, p. 110, 144.
[126] Octavian was probably the later anti-pope Victor IV; *Falco*, p. 186.
[127] Martin, 'Les Communes en Italie méridionale', p. 205.
[128] *Falco*, p. 108; Loud, 'Genesis and context', p. 182.

communal arrangement in the city in 1132 in order to win support for his rule; hence the reappearance of Rolpoto of S. Eustasio.[129] Thus the commune's official dissolution in 1130 did not affect the influence that the populace could exert. The proposed alliance with King Roger in 1132 was negotiated by the city's archbishop, its judges and 'thirty other trusted men'. When the pact failed the Beneventans came to an agreement with Roger's opponents even though it was 'displeasing' to the rector Crescentius.[130] In 1133 the rector Gerard went to Rome with 'some of the more responsible Beneventan citizens' to appeal for Innocent's aid, and later the same year appointed the chronicler Falco as a city judge following the advice of Rolpoto the constable 'and other wiser citizens'.[131] Sometime between 1135 and 1137 the settlement of a dispute between Pope Anacletus and the monastery of S. Sofia was only attained 'with the agreement and consent of almost all the greater and more noble men of the city'.[132] In 1137, with Innocent II and the imperial army outside Benevento, the pope sent the aforesaid Gerard to the city 'to ask the inhabitants whether they wished to conclude a peace treaty', and, after a few skirmishes, 'some of the wise and sensible citizens' concluded a pact. Significantly, when Innocent entered Benevento he asked the citizens 'to maintain peace and justice' among themselves and quickly departed.[133] In the same year the populace gave their assent to the election of Archbishop Gregory, and shortly afterwards 'the judges and wise men of the city' asked the pope to intercede with the emperor to free them from the payment of local dues. Only a few months later 'the judges of the city of Benevento went with other citizens to the king [Roger] and made an alliance with him.'[134] Further examples could be cited to show the citizens' collective activity and power, especially in terms of military organisation. At the forefront of all this was a group of leading local figures, the wiser or more noble citizens. Among these, the city judges were prominent and were regularly involved in delegations, peace negotiations and civic factions. The judges John, Guistitius and Dauferius were exiled by the commune leaders in 1128 and were important enough for Pope Honorius to personally request their return. On the other hand the commune itself 'had for a long time been governed' by the advice of the judges Persicus and Roffred.[135] In 1132 the judges John, Persicus, Dauferius, Benedict and Roffred were described as being at the 'head' of the citizens.[136] The chronicler Falco's promotion to the judiciary in 1133 was significant

---

[129] *Falco*, pp. 144, 146.   [130] *Falco*, pp. 126, 128, 130.   [131] *Falco*, p. 148.
[132] *Chron. S. Sophiae*, ii. 662–6 no. v.12.   [133] *Falco*, pp. 180, 184.
[134] *Falco*, pp. 190, 192, 198.   [135] *Falco*, p. 110.   [136] *Falco*, p. 128.

enough to be relayed to Innocent for his personal confirmation, while in 1137 a judge Landulf, along with a doctor and abbot, conducted negotiations to surrender the city to the pope.[137] As in other cities in southern Italy, the judge occupied a fundamental position that far transcended his judicial functions.

Benevento's archbishop also played a significant role in secular civic matters. It was before Archbishop Landulf III, in 1132, that the citizens of Benevento swore an alliance with the prince of Capua and Rainulf of Caiazzo.[138] However, after Landulf's death later in 1132 the city had two rival archbishops, Gregory (1133/7–42), who was appointed by Innocent, and Rossemanus (1136–9), who was Anacletus' choice. The authority of the city's archbishop was clearly weakened. But, according to Falco, Rossemanus was 'in command' of Benevento in 1137 and 'persuaded almost all the citizens to rise up' against Innocent II. The Anacletan archbishop had apparently 'held the city by violence', though this may be a slur by the pro-Innocentian Falco. Indeed, after a brief exile we find Rossemanus, who was eventually deposed in 1139, acting in concert with the citizenry and judges to consolidate good relations with King Roger.[139]

The city suffered hugely during these years, and Falco's chronicle refers to over 1,000 exiled citizens and an unquantifiable number of imprisonments and deaths. But there is little sign that governmental structures, aside from the years 1128–30, were significantly different from those earlier in the century. Indeed the formation of civic factions (which could number hundreds of members) and rivalries in the 1130s, while pivoting around wider issues, may still have reflected underlying local familial enmities that had dogged the city in the previous forty years. Papal officials remained relatively weak in comparison to the strong roles enjoyed by local figures; the civic judges, the archbishop, the *populus* and the wiser citizens. Zazo has traced the survival after 1139 of almost every judge who appeared in Falco's chronicle in the years of civil war, as well as some prominent urban kin-groups such as the Spitameta – a pattern confirmed in other cities.[140] Falco himself, active as notary and judge from at least 1107–43, including a period of exile (1134–7), is proof both of the central role that civic officials enjoyed and the capacity for human survival in the most anarchic of periods.[141]

---

[137] *Falco*, p. 148, 180.   [138] *Falco*, p. 100, 130.   [139] *Falco*, pp. 180, 182, 184, 202, 224.
[140] A. Zazo, 'Professioni, arti e mestieri in Benevento nei secoli XII–XIV', *Samnium* 32 (1959), pp. 121–77.
[141] Loud, 'Genesis and context', pp. 183–5.

The twelve years of conflict after 1127 did not lead to an immediate major dislocation with the preceding era and the complete suppression of previous structures of civic government in southern Italy. From 1139 South Italian cities within the kingdom would be deprived of any external political power. However, we may question the significance of this apparent loss for the urban community and its internal functioning. Indeed, according to one scholar we 'should temper our perception of communal government as one which could only flourish in an independence movement'.[142] The same cities were at least to some degree able to retain their consultative role, preserve their own customs, keep the same local civic officials and enjoy a freedom of action in internal government under a nominal superior authority, and it was this that really mattered to the urban population. Moreover, before the 1130s the style of autonomy within many of the cities had been based upon 'traditions of vertical hierarchy' which were conducive to being incorporated into a hierarchical kingdom. These cities had developed urban governments which had a 'communal' basis formed in stages of graduated authority, with an oligarchy at the top often focused around one man, rather than a non-stratified 'horizontal' governing arrangement.[143] In some cases this format had worked under the nominal one-man rule of a duke, as at Salerno, Troia and Naples, or prince, as at Capua and Aversa. In other, more independent cases, at Bari and perhaps Trani, the highest stage in the hierarchy had been replaced by a local ruler, but the governing structure remained similar. At Gaeta and Benevento the more innovative arrangements still mostly fitted into a nominal structure with a ruling oligarchy recognising an overlord. In the latter city, the rise of Dacomarius' kin-group and the later prominence of Landulf de Graeca and Rolpoto of S. Eustasio likewise show tendencies among the populace towards favouring a structured hierarchic autonomy. Even the city's 'commune' certainly existed in some sense before and after 1128–30 within the bounds of papal rule. In most instances, the king simply took his place at the top of the ruling pyramid, the previous ruling elite remained, often as royal officials, and the wider community still had a role. Thus, the initial and understandable resistance of most of southern Italy's cities towards a man who was widely denigrated as a *tyrannus* was, to a certain extent, misplaced.

---

[142] Skinner, *Family Power in Southern Italy*, p. 299.
[143] Wickham, 'City society in twelfth-century Italy', pp. 21–3.

Chapter 4

THE NORMAN KINGDOM OF SICILY
(1139–1189)

Southern Italy emerged from a decade of civil war, in 1140, as a unified kingdom; a monumental development within the peninsula's fractious history. It is, therefore, especially lamentable that for the ensuing half-century fewer narrative sources survive to provide the intensity of coverage in the way that Alexander of Telese and Falco of Benevento had done for the preceding decades.[1] However, scraps of valuable information can be found in a wider range of sources, the focus of which is not always the south Italian mainland. An abundance of charter material, which steadily increases with the approach of the thirteenth century, is also available. By combining the two it is possible to uncover how urban government evolved within the structure of a new kingdom.

Roger II's agenda for the mainland cities was largely based on a compromise that did not suppress traditional forms of civic rule. It has been shown that during the 1130s the king provided for the continued functioning of local customs, officials and government, and that evidence from after 1190 confirms their sustained operation in some form within the intervening period in the kingdom. During the early years of the kingdom, Roger issued a collection of laws in which the maintenance of local 'usages, customs and law' is confirmed.[2] However, the other side of the compromise required the restructuring of any liberties within a more efficient superstructure guided by central government. The first step had been to maintain order, and for this purpose the cities

---

[1] See above p. 12 (and n. 32).

[2] According to *Romuald*, p. 226, Roger 'promulgated laws which he had newly drafted and removed evil customs'. For the legislation see above p. 74 n. 109. Many scholars date these assizes to the 1140s. For discussion of the latest findings see Houben, *Roger II of Sicily*, pp. 135–47, which considerably modifies L-R. Ménager, 'La Legislation sud-italienne sous la domination normande', in *Settimane di studio del Centro italiano di studi sull'Alto Medioevo xvi, Spoleto 1968* (Spoleto, 1969), pp. 465–95 [reprinted in L-R. Ménager, *Hommes et institutions de l'Italie normande* (London, 1981)].

had been deprived of their military power in the 1130s. This was followed by initiating a process of administrative reform which would bring the diverse territories of the mainland, and their revenues, into a closer relationship with the new royal authority based at Palermo.

According to Romuald of Salerno, at an undetermined date, probably about 1140, royal chamberlains and justiciars were instituted throughout the land.[3] These higher officials had already appeared in the 1130s as part of the temporary royal administration, grafted onto existing urban governments. But following the civil war they began to be systematically installed in and around important towns and became the populace's first real point of contact with central authority. Royal justiciars, whose main functions were in the judicial sphere, dealing with particularly important criminal cases, appeared in pairs from the 1140s. They did not seem to be permanently stationed in one place but initially operated throughout the traditional provinces – the principality of Capua (which came to be known as the Terra di Lavoro), the principality of Salerno and the Terra di Bari. Chamberlains, primarily responsible for royal fiscal rights, managing revenues and grants and determining demesne boundaries, at first mainly functioned in the two former principalities. They also supervised the local civic officials and bridged local and central government. Constables also appeared, primarily as military officials in garrison towns. Soon their tasks became increasingly administrative, with the same official often carrying the dual title of justiciar and constable. At the same time the apparatus of central government at Palermo itself was reformed.[4]

After Roger's death in 1154, the reigns of his son King William I (1154–66) and grandson King William II (1166–89) saw continued refinement of the royal administrative network on the mainland. A widespread revolt against King William I in 1155–6 may have prompted further reorganisation, with the appearance of two master captains of Apulia and the Terra di Lavoro. In 1157 a new office of master chamberlain emerged for the same region. Both formalised growing layers to the administrative hierarchy, with local justiciars and chamberlains subordinate to them, but equally both offices soon disappeared – master captains were not found from 1172 to 1191 and master chamberlains in Apulia were missing between 1167 and 1198.[5] From 1171 a new

---

[3] *Romuald*, p. 226.

[4] This discussion on the kingdom's administration follows the excellent works by Jamison, 'The Norman administration' and Takayama, *Administration of the Norman Kingdom*; see also J-M. Martin, 'L'Administration du royaume entre Normands et Souabes', in *Die Staufer im Süden. Sizilien und das Reich*, ed. T. Kölzer (Sigmaringen, 1996), pp. 113–40.

[5] With the possible exception of Tasselgardus 'royal chamberlain of all Apulia' attested 1180–2, *Trani*, nos. 70–1; *Pergamene di Barletta. Archivio Capitolare*, no. 138.

official emerged, the master constable and justiciar of Apulia and Terra di Lavoro, which probably superseded the functions of the earlier master captain. The master constables, of which two operated at the same time, were in effect the highest royal authority on the mainland and this was reflected by the status of some of the known incumbents.[6] This suggests an additional restructuring at the start of King William II's rule, and around 1168 an office called the *duana baronum* emerged on the mainland based at Salerno. The formation of this office was most likely linked to the revision of the Catalogue of Barons, a royal register initially compiled in the 1150s which detailed the military service owed to the crown on the mainland. Indeed the *duana baronum* appears to have been the mainland branch of the kingdom's central government. From 1174 the office of *magister duana baronum* is attested on the peninsula and was perhaps the replacement for that of the defunct master chamberlain.[7] This office had a wide range of responsibilities, including the supervision of royal lands, the transmission of royal edicts, the control of officials and the holding of courts. All the while local justiciars, chamberlains and constables continued to operate over increasingly wide territorial units of the kingdom.[8]

A uniform royal government thus steadily increased its presence on the mainland. This impacted upon the cities of the realm, particularly as most of them remained under the direct control of the crown. The list included Aversa, Barletta, Bari, Brindisi, Capua, Monopoli, Naples, Otranto, Salerno, Taranto, Trani and Troia. Other, usually lesser agglomerations were often placed under the immediate direction of a count, such as Conversano, Gravina and Lecce, but here also the same royal

---

[6] Including Counts Tancred of Lecce, Robert of Caserta, Roger of Andria and Richard of Gravina.

[7] E. Jamison, *Admiral Eugenius. His Life and Work and the Authorship of the Epistola ad Petrum and the Historia Hugonis Falcandi Siculi* (London, 1957), p. 53.

[8] According to Jamison and Takayama the basic administrative units of the kingdom within which the local justiciars, chamberlains and constables operated were roughly as follows: the principality of Capua, which seems to have been split into two main units, perhaps with one justiciar each, comprising the northern and southern parts (the Terra di Lavoro, which was equivalent to the old Lombard principality). It included the cities of Capua, Aversa and Naples; the principality of Salerno within which, during William II's reign, the duchy of Amalfi seemed to become a separate unit; the duchy of Apulia, which by William II's reign had split into various ill-defined components. These included a northern part (including the Abruzzi), a central region which became known as the Capitanata and included the cities of Troia and Lucera, the Honour of Monte S. Angelo (essentially the Gargano peninsula), the principality of Taranto incorporating the Salento peninsula and parts of Lucania, and which in the 1150s seems to have merged into a province called the Terra di Otranto, and finally the Terra di Bari. In the latter region were found the cities of Bari, Brindisi, Trani, Monopoli and Barletta. These units within the duchy of Apulia all perhaps had two local justiciars and a chamberlain each by 1189. Calabria was slightly distinct from the rest of the mainland and had closer administrative links with Sicily.

administrative system was largely employed.[9] There was a royal presence in every city even at the lowest levels. This was first and foremost a physical presence through the royal castle and its garrison, as well as in the obligation placed upon the citizens to provide some military service. Little is known about urban military forces and their contribution to the kingdom's defence.[10] But, as the Catalogue of Barons suggests, the king was aware of and keen to order such obligations more clearly. The grants in some of the civic customs in the 1120s and 1130s, which limited or exempted the urban community from military service, were soon afterwards almost certainly revoked. Later military exemptions and privileges in the period 1190–1220 (for Naples, Gaeta, Trani) suggest that military service, in particular galley service, had previously been required, and was burdensome. In 1132 the Beneventans had denounced, not without grounds it seems, a treaty contracted with Roger II because they were unwilling 'to wear [themselves] out on his expeditions and to pant under the sun with the Sicilians, Calabrians and Apulians'.[11] A later document from Frederick II's reign charged communities with the task of maintaining fortifications, which were usually, but not always, those of their own settlement, and this practice may well have begun in Roger II's era.[12] But since the turmoil from the mid-eleventh century, the urban communities would have been well accustomed to contributing to military defence. On the one hand they were now to do so less freely in the name of a wider polity and could even be required to serve outside southern Italy; on the other hand the kingdom was, aside from the major revolts, internally more peaceful for longer periods.

Importantly the king had access to the city's fiscal apparatus. This included customary rents and payments, market and customs duties, tolls, profits of justice and monopolies on activities such as dyeing. Aside from one-off general levies, the monarchy did not impose a new direct taxation system and continued the tradition of indirect taxes (such as the *plateaticum* raised on commercial transactions) used by its predecessors in the South.[13] However, the citizens had always been accustomed to paying various taxes, and their main concern was the amount and equitable nature of these taxes, not necessarily who the recipient might

---

[9] Fasoli, 'Città e ceti urbani', pp. 152–3.
[10] There are scattered references to individuals participating in the royal army; a document from Troia in 1154 reveals that a certain Coffus Storlatus served in the royal fleet, *Troia*, no. 72.
[11] *Falco*, p. 130.
[12] *Acta Imperii Inedita Saeculi XIII et XIV*, 2 vols., ed. E. Winkelmann (Innsbruck, 1880–5), i. 768–80 no. 1005; Fasoli, 'Città e ceti urbani', pp. 155–6; Martin, 'L'Empreinte de Byzance', p. 750.
[13] Martin, 'L' Empreinte de Byzance', pp. 750–1.

be.[14] Indeed, Roger's law code attempted to protect all citizens from overzealous tax collectors.[15] In any case these revenues, as before 1139, were collected by local men, although perhaps now with more regularity. The taxes and dues claimed by the monarch were essentially those that were traditional and long-standing, and based upon bargaining between ruler and subject.[16] Importantly the monarchy often exempted certain groups from taxes and service or allowed a local institution to collect and keep the proceeds. This mitigated the likelihood of a distant authority based at Palermo having too intrusive an influence on mainland civic life. In 1127 the Salernitans had been assured by Roger II that their tax contribution would be the same as in the preceding century, that public revenues would remain under their control and that any services required of them would be in accordance with local custom.[17] It is worth recalling the clause in the Barese customs of *c.* 1200 that 'in accordance with ancient custom . . . we hold in perpetuity [the right] that no tax, service, gift or assistance may be exacted from the people of Bari, and that they are excused from all burdens, except for service on the galleys.'[18] During the reign of King William II, the canons of Troia cathedral complained to the monarch that the exemptions from various *collecta*, granted by William I, to the citizens of Troia had contributed to their poverty.[19] King William had established that the archbishoprics of Salerno and Taranto should receive a tenth of the royal revenues from their respective cities, a portion from those of its dyeworks and, in the latter city, part of the proceeds from the *bucheria*.[20] There was also the introduction in 1140 of a new simplified coinage, aimed at unifying to some extent the pre-existing, divergent monetary systems. Coinage was certainly an important vehicle through which to communicate authority.[21] However, the currency reforms changed little in reality, and local mints continued to produce variant coinages at Amalfi and Salerno.

Most significantly the monarchy had a symbolic presence. This was clearly recognised in Apulia, where private documents at Bari, Monopoli, Trani and Troia were dated by the monarch's ruling years. City judges at Troia and Bari consistently employed the 'royal' epithet in their titles from 1139 onwards, although at Trani (not until the 1170s) and Monopoli (1180s) this was not immediately standard practice.

---

[14] S. Reynolds, *Kingdoms and Communities in Western Europe 900–1300* (Oxford, 1997), p. 211.

[15] Monti, *Stato normanno svevo*, pp. 117–8 article III.

[16] Matthew, *Norman Kingdom*, pp. 235–8.   [17] See above p. 58 n. 14.

[18] Petroni, *Storia di Bari*, ii. 438 Rubric II.1   [19] *Troia*, no. 87.

[20] *Tancredi et Willelmi III Regum Diplomata*, pp. 10–5 nos. 4–5, pp. 20–3 nos. 7–8; Jamison, *Admiral Eugenius*, appendix I, pp. 323–32 no. 4; *Taranto*, nos. 16–8, 22, 26.

[21] For more on currency see below pp. 116, 118, 128, 240, 260–1; *Falco*, p. 238.

Conversano, as a city under the immediate control of a count, represented a different case. Private documents do not refer to the king until 1154 and the probable inception of Robert II of Loritello's countship. When Robert was exiled in 1156, for his part in a mainland revolt, the city was incorporated into the royal demesne until the count was restored to favour in 1169. After Robert's death in 1182, the city once again reverted to direct royal control until 1190.[22] Thus traces of royal influence appear strongest in the years 1156–69 and 1182–90, and in the 1160s a judge and *catepan* carry the royal title for the first time.[23] It is notable, however, that in Campania such traces are less common. In Aversa, Capua and Salerno, charters showed the kings' ruling year but local officials did not call themselves royal.

Crucially, the kings were primarily based on the island of Sicily and thus were not often able to reinforce their theoretical presence on the mainland with a physical one. It is rather problematic to identify when, where and for how long the monarchs appeared on the mainland; but it is clear they were only intermittent visitors. An outline survey records Roger at Capua in 1140 and 1143 and at Salerno also in 1140, 1143, 1147, perhaps 1149 and 1150. William I was on the mainland at Salerno in 1155 and also in 1156. William II was in Salerno, Taranto, Barletta and perhaps Capua in 1172, Bari and Barletta in 1182, Capua again in 1183 and Brindisi in 1185.[24] Roger had set up his sons on the mainland in the 1130s – Roger as duke of Apulia, Anfusus as prince of Capua and Tancred (then William after 1138) as prince of Taranto – probably to counter the problem of a king who was absent for long periods. While these princes were royal representatives on the peninsula they had no defined functions, even though Anfusus' name was regularly included alongside his father's in charters within the principality of Capua, and he may have had his own body of officials.[25] Anfusus and Roger, especially, spent most of their time away from their ascribed regions on military excursions in the north of the kingdom or at Palermo.[26] Only Duke Roger showed limited signs of any judicial activity.[27] In any case by 1149, of all these siblings, only William was still alive, and by 1151 he

[22] *Conversano*, introduction pp. 50–2.   [23] *Conversano*, nos. 111, 113.

[24] For records of some of these visits, *Falco*, pp. 232–4; *Rogerii II Regis Diplomata Latina*, pp. 209–11 no. 73; *Annales Casinenses*, ed. G. H. Pertz, *MGH SS* XIX (Hanover, 1846), pp. 312–13. see also H. Enzensberger, 'Chanceries, charters and administration in Norman Italy', in *The Society of Norman Italy*, ed. G.A. Loud and A. J. Metcalfe (Leiden, 2002), pp. 124–5; see also below p. 89.

[25] Jamison, 'Norman administration', pp. 273–82; of the many charters dated by Anfusus' rule at Capua and, after his death in 1144, by William's see *Regesto di S. Angelo in Formis*, pp. 183–212 nos. 64–72; *Pergamene di Capua*, i. 69–71 nos. 28–9; *CDNA*, pp. 83–95 nos. 48–54.

[26] *Falco*, pp. 232, 234.

[27] Roger held a court perhaps near Troia in 1147, *Colonie cassinensi*, no. 27.

was associated as co-king. The position of the later dukes and princes, the sons of William I, became entirely nominal, owing to their young age and a more refined administrative network.

The diverse component parts of the new kingdom were reflected by the title of the monarch himself as 'King of Sicily, of the duchy of Apulia and of the principality of Capua', which acknowledged the region's traditional divisions. It was also echoed in the titles given to the royal heirs, and, even though after 1172 these positions were no longer filled, a royal grant to Gaeta in 1191 envisaged the future appointment of a prince of Capua.[28] With the kings effectively ruling as absentee monarchs on the mainland, great consequence was placed on the efficiency of the royal administrative network to pull all the regions into a coherent, working kingdom and to attempt to foster a common identity. Therefore in order to establish an accurate interpretation of the extent of the new royal presence within the cities we must search deeper and first explore the activities of the higher royal officials (justiciars, chamberlains and constables of varying grades). As they represented the main bridge between the local urban authorities and the central government it is essential to ascertain how often they were physically present within the cities.[29] At Bari the first reference to these royal functionaries does not occur until 1155, when the royal justiciars William de Tivilla and Robert Seneschal held a court which reinstated lands to the monastery of Ognissanti of Cuti. The document was also witnessed by the royal constable Iudex Maior.[30] From the same year, a court case held at Barletta referred to a previous hearing, concerning the monastery of Montesacro, which had been held before the justiciar Robert Seneschal and some judges of Bari.[31] Iudex Maior appeared again at Bari in 1174, this time as a justiciar alongside a colleague, Nicholas de Canusio, both of whom were in the city 'pro regis agendis'.[32] Two years later, Count Tancred of Lecce, the master constable and justiciar of Apulia and Terra di Lavoro, was at Bari to resolve a quarrel between two ecclesiastical establishments.[33] Also present were two royal justiciars and a royal chamberlain. In 1181 Tancred was again in the city to hear an appeal from the church

---

[28] *Tancredi et Willelmi III Regum Diplomata*, pp. 42–6 no. 18.

[29] As the distinction between acting as a private or public person was especially ambiguous in the medieval period the following survey concerns any reference to a figure recorded *in* a city *and* carrying a royal title. Thus, for example, the private dispute involving Lucas Guarna himself at Salerno in 1176 has been included because he is recorded with his royal title, whereas other 'private' charters involving the same man, but without his official designation, are not considered.

[30] *CDBV*, no. 112; Iudex Maior appears to have been a personal name and not a title.

[31] *Pergamene di Barletta. Archivio Capitolare*, no. 72.   [32] *CDBV*, no. 133.

[33] L-R. Ménager 'Les Fondations monastiques de Robert Guiscard, duc de Pouille et de Calabre', *QF* 39 (1958), pp. 113–14 app. no. 42.

of S. Nicola of Bari, alongside two other royal justiciars of the Terra di Bari, Bernaldus de Fontanella and John Amerusius.[34] It was not until 1164 that higher royal officials are recorded in Trani, when Bersacius the master chamberlain presided over a royal court with John the chamberlain of the Terra di Bari.[35] King William II made a general plea in 1170 to unnamed chamberlains and justiciars of the diocese of Trani. Later still we find the royal chamberlain Tasselgardus in the city in 1180 and the following year his son Peter, also a chamberlain, receiving a donation from the archbishop of Trani.[36]

A justiciar, Guimund of Montilari, was in the city of Troia in 1148 attempting to settle a dispute between a local baron and Montecassino. Another royal justiciar, Rao de Rocca, appeared there in 1159, as an advocate for a local monastery.[37] In *c.* 1170 Rao's son Lucas de Rocca was in the city with the title royal justiciar and *catepan*.[38] Royal chamberlains were also recorded at Troia: Mathew de Calvello in 1144 observed an accord between the city's bishop and the lord of Biccari, while in 1156 Leo of Foggia witnessed the conclusion to the disagreement which Guimund of Montilari had officiated on eight years earlier.[39] In 1177 a royal constable witnessed a judgement in the city.[40] Only once at Conversano are higher officials attested in the city. In 1188 Robert de Baro, the royal chamberlain of the count of Conversano, and another Robert, chamberlain of the honour of Montescaglioso, witnessed a donation by the lord of Turi.[41]

On the other side of the peninsula King Roger himself visited the key centre of Capua in 1143. In his entourage on that occasion were the known justiciar Aimo of Argentia (although without his title here) and Roger filius Boni, who seems to have also been some sort of justiciar (*iustificator curialis*).[42] In 1149 the chamberlain Ebulus de Magliano convened a court in the city.[43] Florius of Camerota and Aimeric of Montemorone, both royal justiciars, assembled in the castle at Capua in 1158 to deal with a complaint brought by the abbot of S. Sofia of Benevento.[44] Three years later in the same city we find a certain Marino the royal chamberlain.[45] In 1171 Count Robert of Caserta, the master constable and justiciar of Apulia and Terra di Lavoro, had convened a *curia* in Capua alongside a royal justiciar and was present in the city in 1173, with two royal justiciars and a chamberlain, to settle a case

[34] *CDBV*, no. 145.   [35] *CDBV*, no. 121.   [36] *Trani*, nos. 61, 69–71.   [37] *Troia*, no. 76.
[38] *Troia*, no. 87.   [39] *Troia*, no. 67; *Colonie cassinesi*, no. 30.   [40] *Troia*, no. 94.
[41] *Conversano*, no. 138.   [42] *Rogerii II Regis Diplomata Latina*, pp. 166–9 no. 59.
[43] Jamison, 'Norman administration', cal. doc. no. 29; *Regesto di S. Angelo in Formis*, pp. 207–12 no. 73.
[44] Pergamene Aldobrandini (formerly of the Biblioteca Apostolica Vaticano), II. 13.
[45] *Pergamene di Capua*, i. 83–4 no. 34.

concerning S. Sofia of Benevento.[46] Robert, with his chief colleague Tancred of Lecce, was present at another assembly in the city in 1182.[47] At Aversa there is an ambiguous reference to a possible chamberlain in the city in *c.* 1150.[48] More clearly, in *c.* 1166 three royal justiciars, the aforementioned Florius of Camerota, Matthew de Venabulo and John de Valle, adjudicated on the restoration of two mills to the bishop of Aversa. These officials professed to be 'performing the role of the lord king' in a 'plenariam et sollempnem curia' and also present were the archbishop of Capua and Nicholas, a chamberlain, who was said to be at that time staying in the city.[49] In 1171 a court was convened in the city in which the aforesaid justiciars Matthew and John were present with the master constable, Count Robert of Caserta.[50] Tancred of Lecce assembled a court in the city's episcopal palace in 1180 with the justiciar Robert de Molino.[51] The following year Count Robert of Caserta was again in Aversa to witness a sentence, while in 1182 William Russus, the royal chamberlain of the Terra di Lavoro, appears to have been in the city.[52]

Salerno continued to develop as the mainland capital. From 1168 Salerno hosted the office of *duana baronum* – the presence of central government therefore was certainly strongest there. Between 1141 and 1143 the city's Archbishop William and Lampus de Fasanella, described as 'regie iusticie iustificatores', held a court in Salerno.[53] In 1144 and 1146 Atenolf the royal chamberlain was in the city.[54] In 1150, before King Roger, and in 1151 the royal justiciars Florius of Camerota and Lampus de Fasanella, as well as the chamberlain Alfanus, held a court in the city.[55] From the Terracina palace in 1155 King William I and his royal entourage, including admiral Maio of Bari and chancellor Aschettin, judged the alleged misdemeanours of a local justiciar.[56] In

---

[46] Cava, *Arca* xxxiii.91 (edited in G. Tescione, *Caserta Medievale e i suoi conti e signori* (Caserta, 1990), pp. 160–2 no. 2); Pergamene Aldobrandini, II.27.

[47] *Catalogus Baronum commentario*, art. 964.   [48] *CDNA*, pp. 99–101 no. 50.

[49] *CDNA*, p. 121 no. 70; for the date emendation from 1158 to *c.* 1166 see Loud, *Church and Society*, p. 187.

[50] *Catalogus Baronum commentario*, art. 815.

[51] G. A. Loud, 'A Lombard abbey in a Norman world; St. Sophia, Benevento, 1050–1200', in *Anglo-Norman Studies 19. Proceedings of the Battle Conference 1996*, ed. C. Harper-Bill (Woodbridge, 1997), appendix, pp. 304–5 no. 7.

[52] *Catalogus Baronum commentario* art. 964; *CDNA*, pp. 222–6 nos. 119–20.

[53] Cava, *Arca.* xxv.3, xxv.38, xxv.40; C. H. Haskins, 'England and Sicily in the twelfth century', *English Historical Review* 26 (1911), p. 643.

[54] Jamison, 'Norman administration', cal doc. nos. 14, 20 (Cava, *Arca.* xxv.117).

[55] *Rogerii II Regis Diplomata Latina*, pp. 274–6 no. 7 (Jamison, 'Norman administration', appendix, no. 9).

[56] *Guillelmi I Regis Diplomata*, ed. H. Enzensberger (Codex Diplomaticus Regni Siciliae, Ser. I.iii) (Cologne, 1996) pp. 16–19 no. 6.

May 1163 a royal chamberlain, Mario Rubeus, witnessed the election of the abbess of S. Giorgio in Salerno, and in June of the same year a master chamberlain Bersacius granted some land just outside the city.[57] The royal justiciars Florius of Camerota and Lucas Guarna were in Salerno in 1172.[58] In 1174 Eugenius, master of the *duana baronum*, assembled a court to hear a case brought by the city *strategotus*.[59] Lucas Guarna, carrying the title of royal justiciar, was recorded in Salerno in 1176 owing to a dispute over water running from his own lands to those of the city's archbishopric.[60] In 1178 the prominent official Walter de Moac, elsewhere entitled *regii fortunati stolii amiratus et magister regie duane de secretis et duane baronum*, was in Salerno to address the grievances of some imperial envoys.[61] Eugenius was in the city again in 1178, as were the justiciars Florius of Camerota and Lucas Guarna to deal with the murder of a local abbot.[62] The latter justiciar was again in the city in 1182 and in 1184, when he acted alongside William of S. Severino, a royal constable and justiciar.[63] Finally, a court was held in Salerno in 1185 in the presence of two justiciars, Godfrey of Marturano and Santoro, who were representatives of the *magna regia curia*.[64]

Of course this survey cannot be an exhaustive catalogue of these officials' activities within these mainland cities, and the survival rate of medieval documentation means that their presence was undoubtedly more frequent. The intention is to offer a representative sample of the greater part of our current state of knowledge. It must also be noted that at times civic and ecclesiastical officials, and citizens, attended courts held by higher royal officials in the territory of a city rather than in the city itself. For example, in 1151 the justiciar Guimund of Montilari assembled a court in the *contado* of Troia which was attended by two leading men of the city, along with a city judge and castellan.[65] In 1172, the justiciar Lucas Guarna was present at a court in Eboli with three judges of Salerno.[66] Moreover, inhabitants of some cities travelled further afield to meet with, and appeal to, royal officials. In 1184, delegations

---

[57] Jamison, 'Norman administration', cal. doc. nos. 56, 57; *Italia Sacra*, vii. 402.

[58] Haskins, 'England and Sicily', p. 649.

[59] Jamison, *Admiral Eugenius*, cal. doc. no. 2 (Cava, *Arca* xxxiv.106); *Il Codice Perris. Cartulario amalfitano. Sec. X–XV*, 3 vols., ed. J. Mazzoleni and R. Orefice (Amalfi, 1985), pp. 291–3 no. 155.

[60] *Italia Sacra*, vii. 404.

[61] Takayama, *Administration of the Norman Kingdom*, p. 152; *Romuald*, p. 296; L-R. Ménager, *Amiratus – Ἀμηρᾶς – L'émirat et les origines de l'amirauté XI–XIII siècles)* (Paris, 1960), pp. 95–6.

[62] Jamison, *Admiral Eugenius*, cal. doc. no. 7; *Romuald*, p. 296.

[63] K. A. Kehr, *Die Urkunden der Normannisch-Sizilischen Könige – eine diplomatische Untersuchung* (Innsbruck, 1902), pp. 448–52 no. 26; Jamison, 'Norman administration', p. 368.

[64] *Documenti per la storia di Eboli*, p. 163 no. 345.

[65] Jamison, 'Norman administration', cal. doc. no. 31.   [66] Cava, *Arca* xxxiv.15.

from Troia and Ascoli Satriano journeyed to Barletta to settle a dispute before two master constables of Apulia and Terra di Lavoro.[67] A survey of the careers of many of the mainland's higher royal officials shows that the majority of them held office for a long time, and that they usually focused their activities in certain regions.[68] Yet, it remains far from easy to establish these higher royal officials' actual influence on daily civic, as opposed to regional, affairs, or to know how permanent their presence was in the cities.

Part of the problem lies in the uncertainty of the geographic jurisdictions of many of the royal officials. For the highest officials, the master captains and later master constables, it is clear that they were almost continually travelling around the kingdom. But what of the local justiciars and chamberlains who seemed to occupy an intermediate position between central and local urban government? The example of a man like Turgisius de Campora, a chamberlain for the Terra di Lavoro in the late 1160s and early 1170s, is indicative.[69] In the documents analysed for this study Turgisius is not specifically attested in Capua or Aversa and thus does not enter in the above survey.[70] It is highly unlikely that he did not spend any time within the main cities that fell under his jurisdiction, and the survival rate of charters is to blame. But may we also hypothesise that a limited amount of time actually spent on urban visitations, and/or a low profile when doing so, contributed as well to the paucity of evidence? Much of the day-to-day legal and customary functioning of a city simply did not require these officials' intervention, and their limited numbers, combined with the geographic extent of their jurisdiction, made it equally impractical. In the Terra di Bari, the chamberlain Tasselgardus (1177–86) fits this pattern, being attested at Trani and Bari but also on the opposite side of the Adriatic. Tasselgardus is found in a court at Ragusa in 1186 acting on behalf of King William II, who seems to have held a protectorate over this part of the Dalmatian coast.[71] The case of Bernaldus de Fontanella, a justiciar

---

[67] *Troia*, no. 102.

[68] See generally Takayama, *Administration of the Norman Kingdom*; Jamison, 'Norman administration'.

[69] *Acta Imperii Inedita*, i. 217–18 no. 235; See Jamison, 'Norman administration', p. 397.

[70] It is possible that Turgisius is the chamberlain referred to by Falcandus in 1168 as chamberlain of the Capitanata. If so, Turgisius must soon after have transferred to the Terra di Lavoro or even combined the two. Regardless of his identity, it is notable from our point of view that Falcandus' Turgisius was at Palermo in 1168 and absent from his chamberlainship, *Falcandus*, pp. 192–3 and n. 225.

[71] See above p. 89 n. 36; *Acta et Diplomata Ragusina*, ed. J. Radonić (Belgrade, 1934), no. 5; D. Abulafia, 'Dalmatian Ragusa and the Norman kingdom of Sicily', *The Slavonic and East European Review* 54 (1976), pp. 425–6.

for the Terra di Bari, is equally indicative. He was attested between
1176 and 1189 but only in three records, two of which place him at
Bari itself in 1176 and 1181, the other at nearby Bitonto in 1189.[72] This
period is a reasonably well-documented one for the Bari region and
suggests that Bernaldus' intervention was not frequently required. In
addition, higher royal officials may have opted to hold courts in smaller
rural settlements (for which the documentation is especially sparse)
rather than in Bari or Trani, where urban liberties blurred their jurisdictional competence. Even in the principalities of Salerno and Capua
we see a relatively high number of courts held by higher royal officials
in lesser settlements of the region, such as at Nocera, Sarno and perhaps
Auletta, rather than at Salerno, and at Maddaloni, Sora and Teano,
rather than at Capua.[73]

Florius of Camerota, attested from 1150 to 1189, provides a more
high-profile case. This justiciar for the principality of Salerno appeared
in cities within different territorial jurisdictions, for example at Capua
and Aversa in 1158. But Florius also operated in the highest political
circles and for some unknown reason was forced, around 1165, into
political exile at Jerusalem. In response Pope Alexander III intervened
on Florius' behalf, appealing to the king of France to intercede with
King William II and then, should this fail, to request the Byzantine
emperor to offer him support.[74] By 1168, having been restored to favour
with King William II, he was found at an important royal court at
Messina in Sicily and had accrued responsibilities additional to his local
justiciarate.[75] Indeed in 1176 he was sent as envoy to the king of England
to contract a marriage for the Sicilian monarch.[76] Florius remained
active in the region of Salerno, where he was found in 1172 and 1178,
but his appearances there were undoubtedly limited, and by the 1180s
he seems to have acquired official responsibilities in Calabria.[77] Another
example is offered by Cioffus, a chamberlain of Salerno, who was unable
to adjudicate on a dispute in 1184 because he had gone to the royal

---

[72] *CDBV*, nos. 145, 153; Ménager, 'Les Fondations monastiques', pp. 113–14 app. no. 42; Martin,
Pouille, p. 802.

[73] See tables in Jamison, 'Norman administration', pp. 394–5, 397; it is worth highlighting the
references here to chamberlains, possibly at Auletta, called Alfanus, Cioffus the notary of Salerno
and judge Rao, and the ambiguity of the territorial designations attached to their titles in the
respective documents, *Syllabus Graecarum Membranarum*, ed. F. Trinchera (Naples, 1865), nos.
148, 191, 195, 207–8, 210; L. Feller, 'The northern frontier of Norman Italy, 1060–1140', in *The
Society of Norman Italy*, p. 69, suggests that the Abruzzi settlements such as Teramo and Sulmona
were used as the chief centres for royal administration exactly because they had been relatively
insignificant beforehand and not associated with earlier local counts or bishops.

[74] *PL*, 200 no. 303, cols. 332–3.   [75] *Falcandus*, p. 193.   [76] *Romuald*, p. 268.

[77] See above p. 91 n. 62; *Catalogus Baronum commentario*, art. 454; F. Schneider, 'Neue Dokumente
vornehmlich aus Süditalien', *QF* 16 (1914), p. 30 no. 9.

court at Palermo.[78] Equally interesting, the court at which Cioffus was
expected to attend had been convened by two master justiciars at
Barletta in Apulia. The case involved the men of Ascoli Satriano, a city
on the extreme eastern boundary of Cioffus' jurisdiction and some
85 km from Salerno. In fact Cioffus may well have been in Ascoli in
1182.[79] It is clear that this chamberlain, like other royal officials, was
accustomed to spells away from his main jurisdictional region and thus
the key cities within them. Given that as a rule there seems to have been
only a pair of local justiciars and one chamberlain assigned to each region
at any one time, their often lengthy absences have significant implications for the intensity of central government on the mainland. Indeed,
in 1184 Cioffus had to rely on two men, with no official titles, one of
whom was his nephew, to act at Barletta on his behalf; the superstructure of central authority could be rather thin in places.

On balance, and even including Salerno, it would seem that the new
royal officials were a consistent, but not overwhelming presence in the
major cities. More importantly, and perhaps irrespective of the frequency of their appearances, the actual nature of their presence was not
overly intrusive for the urban population. There are two main reasons
for this – the origins of these officials and their activities within the cities.

Firstly, a large proportion of the local justiciars, chamberlains and
constables were not outsiders imposed upon the region. Many were
drawn not from Sicily, or even a distant part of the mainland, but from
the upper classes of the very region in which they were primarily to
operate. Having local backgrounds, these officials were surely imbued
with an awareness of their native traditions and an understanding of
the practical functioning of local government. They were likely to be
more sensitive to local interests, which surely encouraged local adher-
ence. As such, their presence should not always be seen as an obstacle to
self-governance and the influence of the local community. There are
innumerable examples of the local origins of these officials.

The earliest proto-justiciars of the 1130s, Urso Trabalia, Aimo of
Argentia and William, the archbishop-elect of Capua, all had strong
links with the regions placed under their jurisdiction. The latter two can
still be found in this office in the 1140s.[80] In the principality of Capua,
the justiciar Henry of Bolita held fiefs in Aversa and Sessa and was a
descendant of a family which had enjoyed close relations with the
Norman princes of Capua.[81] The justiciar John de Valle held land at

---

[78] *Troia*, no. 102. [79] *Montevergine*, viii. no. 723.
[80] William had been transferred in 1137 to the archbishopric of Salerno.
[81] *Catalogus Baronum commentario*, art. 867.

Aversa, as did his colleagues Matthew de Venabulo and Robert de Molino, who were both from leading families of the city and its locality.[82] In the principality of Salerno, Lampus de Fasanella held land throughout the area and within Salerno itself. He was lord of Fasanella by 1128 and was descended from a Lombard family related to Prince Guaimar IV of Salerno and also the Norman counts of the Principate.[83] Florius of Camerota was also, as his surname informs us, of local origin. As well as holding various lands in the principality he was the nephew of Archbishop Alfanus of Capua.[84] The justiciar Lucas Guarna was from an important urban kin-group in Salerno which produced local judges, ducal officials and Archbishop Romuald II. The royal chamberlain Marius Russus was his brother-in-law.[85] Some of the chamberlains of the principality descended from Lombard comital kin-groups and were closely linked to Salerno's administrative elite. One chamberlain, Philip, was the nephew of Peter the *protoiudex* of Salerno and was also the cousin of fellow Salernitan Matthew, the royal vice-chancellor.[86] The chamberlain Atenulf, attested in the mid-1140s, had a significant quantity of property in Salerno to suggest his local importance.[87] In the 1180s the office of chamberlain was occupied by Rao, a city judge, Cioffus, a city notary, and two men from leading Salernitan families: William Butrumiles and Alfanus Ioncata.[88]

In the Terra di Bari, the justiciar Robert Seneschal had land at Bitonto and Barletta, while his colleague William of Tivilla held fiefs at Noa, Bitonto and Rutigiliano (as well as in the principalities of Salerno and Taranto).[89] The later justiciar Iudex Maior was from Bitonto, and John Amerusius was a member of a prominent family from Bari: he was lord of Triviano and was related to a Barese judge, a justiciar and a chamberlain.[90] The chamberlains Tasselgardus (1177–86) and his son

[82] *Catalogus Baronum commentario*, arts. 866, 849, 962.

[83] Jamison, 'Norman administration', p. 310.

[84] *Catalogus Baronum commentario*, art. 454. Loud, 'Royal control of the Church', p. 158.

[85] *Catalogus Baronum commentario*, art. 520; *Italia Sacra*, vii. 404; see below p. 193 for the Guarna.

[86] *Catalogus Baronum commentario*, art. 610; *Italia Sacra*, vii. 403.

[87] Jamison, 'Norman administration', pp. 391–2. Atenulf was later a chamberlain of the royal palace at Palermo and was with Maio of Bari when he was ambushed in 1160, *Falcandus*, pp. 96–7 and n. 68.

[88] Takayama, *Administration of the Norman Kingdom*, p. 160; Jamison, 'Norman administration' pp. 393–5; other individuals appear in Salernitan documents with the Butrumiles surname, though it is not possible to establish if they all were related. A Landulf donated a door to the city cathedral (see below p. 240) and in 1190 a Roger was a city *strategotus* (see below p. 130); various sources show other Butrumiles as a judge, cleric and active in the property market, for example Cava, *Arca* xvi.118, xvii.5, xvii.4, xvii.77, xx.75, xxiv.44, xxxv.81; For William Butrumiles see Cava, *Arca* xxxvii.34; for Butrumiles and Ioncata names see *Necrologio del Liber Confratrum*, pp. 337, 346, 354, 359, 361, 368–9; For another Ioncata, *Nuove pergamene*, pp. 70–2 no. 29.

[89] Jamison, 'Norman administration', pp. 308–9.   [90] *CDBI*, no. 94

Peter (attested in 1180) were both from Trani. In central Apulia one justiciar, Guimund, hailed from the local settlement of Montilari, while two later justiciars, Rao and his son Lucas, were members of the de Rocca kin-group of Troia.

Thus many of these royal officials were local men with strong local ties. The justiciars were, according to Jamison, mostly 'counts or smaller tenants-in-chief' of the crown.[91] Others, particularly the chamberlains, rose from the urban local elite. Moreover, most of these figures seemed to enjoy extended tenures in their office and usually were active for around a decade. Some, like Florius of Camerota, in varying capacities (1150–89), and Lucas Guarna (1172–1189) served for even longer. They were a force for continuity. Only in the principality of Salerno in the 1180s do we have evidence suggesting that the office of chamberlain was alternated on a yearly basis.[92] Overall, through these royal officials, 'a definite scheme of enlisting the greatest weight of local support on the king's side' was established.[93]

The second factor demonstrating the non-intrusive position of the higher royal officials upon urban communities concerns the nature of their activities. We have already alluded to the likelihood that these officials were rarely required to intervene in daily civic affairs. Moreover, when they did intercede, their role was often limited by the authority of local urban officials, the power of local communities and the liberties that both of these groups could utilise. In theory, the most powerful local urban official after 1139 was the chief city magistrate, who was, again in theory, a royal representative. In Campania this figure usually carried the title of *strategotus*, while in Apulia he was often called *catepan* – both offices boasted a long tradition in urban government.[94] This official functioned in a supervisory position over civic affairs and was responsible for the city's public property (*res publica*). However, other local officials, particularly judges, continued to enjoy a preponderant influence over urban affairs. These figures were all supposed to represent the monarchy, yet inevitably their primary concern often lay with local urban interests. Moreover, the leading men (*boni seu probi homines*) of the city still had a role in important civic affairs.

Again, numerous examples can be provided for the limited and often supplementary role played by higher royal officials in relation to their local counterparts. At Bari, in 1155, when two royal justiciars reinstated lands to the monastery of Ognissanti of Cuti they were in fact reiterating

---

[91] Jamison, 'Norman administration', p. 314.   [92] See above p. 95 n. 88.
[93] Jamison, 'Norman administration', p. 315.
[94] See above p. 18; in Naples this official was called the *compalacius*.

the previous judgement of the Barese judge Leo de Rayza.[95] In 1174 the justiciar Iudex Maior de Bitonto restored ownership of a church to S. Nicola of Bari only after receiving counsel from a curia, at which four Barese judges and a local castellan played a key part.[96] Four judges of Bari acted similarly in a court, held by Tancred of Lecce in 1181, which was attended by two royal justiciars and a host of royal barons.[97] At the royal court held at Trani in 1164, besides a master chamberlain and local chamberlain, three judges of Trani and a leading citizen named Tasselgardus were present.[98] In 1151, at a court gathered in the *contado* of Troia, the Troian judge Roger oversaw, on an equal footing with a royal justiciar, an agreement between the abbeys of Cava and S. Maria of Bolfannana, before two royal barons, two judges of Foggia and a Troian castellan.[99] In 1156 two more judges from Troia underwrote, on a par with a royal baron and a chamberlain, the conclusion of a long-running dispute between the baron John de Boccio and Montecassino.[100] There are further examples of local judges operating in these more elevated circles and not being overtly hindered by the presence of superior functionaries. In 1159, five of Troia's judges settled an important case concerning the bishop of Troia and a local monastery, with the presence of the justiciar, Rao de Rocca, limited to the role of the latter's advocate.[101] Finally, in a dispute of 1177 between the lord of Biccari and the bishop of Troia, heard before various knights, judges from Biccari, a Troian constable, a Troian *catepan* and involving the recital of royal mandates sent by two justiciars, five local judges chaired the proceedings and seemingly held supreme authority in the council.[102]

In Campania, at Capua the royal chamberlain Ebolus convened a curia in 1149 before the barons, *probi homines* and judges of Capua. The latter, although ordered by Ebolus to make sentence on a long-running land dispute, did so independently after consultation with local men.[103] In 1161 a complaint made by the *strategotus* of Capua was heard before two city judges. The role of Marino the royal chamberlain, who was 'residing on that day' in the curia, appears entirely incidental to the proceedings.[104] At Aversa, in 1158, a mill was restored to the city's bishopric after a series of hearings in which not only three royal justiciars and a chamberlain participated, but also a *strategotus* and judges from Salerno, Capua and Aversa.[105] At Salerno, in 1146, the chamberlain

[95] *CDBV*, no. 112.   [96] *CDBV*, no. 133.   [97] *CDBV*, no. 145.   [98] *CDBV*, no. 121.

[99] Jamison, 'Norman administration', cal. doc. no. 31.   [100] *Colonie cassinesi*, no. 30.

[101] *Troia*, no. 76.   [102] *Troia*, no. 94.

[103] *Regesto di S. Angelo in Formis*, pp. 207–12 no. 73 (Jamison, 'Norman administration', cal. doc. no. 29).

[104] *Pergamene di Capua*, i. 83–4 no. 34.   [105] *CDNA*, p. 121 no. 70.

Atenolf appears merely to have been in attendance at a court comprising the *strategotus* of Salerno, *idonei homines* and two city judges.[106] Eugenius, the *magister regie duana baronum*, initiated a series of courts in Salerno in 1174 to investigate a complaint brought by the city's *strategotus*. However, in each of the assemblies it was the six judges of Salerno who directed proceedings and produced a settlement.[107] The same Eugenius gathered three Salernitan judges in 1178 to examine an important and long-standing dispute between the men of Amalfi and Ravello.[108] At the same assembly the Salernitan judge Matthew even acted as advocate for the Amalfitan delegation.[109] Finally, in 1182 the *strategotus* of Salerno convened a court, composed of six city judges and *viri prudentes*, in order to adjudicate on the claims of the abbey of Cava over the nearby port of Vietri. Royal letters were recited and almost as an afterthought we are informed that the justiciar, Lucas Guarna, was present and that he played a discreet role in proceedings.[110]

Thus in a sizeable proportion of the limited occasions on which higher royal officials are attested in cities they appear in a circumspect, supervisory role, which is fully integrated with the workings of the local urban hierarchy. Royal rule was slowly and discreetly grafted onto a well-established civic administration. This meant that local officials still participated fully in important matters and were figures of consequence. The city *strategotus* was a significant figure, especially in Salerno, where he acted in a number of important ways. He held his own courts, received letters direct from the king and obtained loans from the *duana baronum*. The *strategotus* of Salerno acted on behalf of the public interest of the city (*pro parte rei publice civitatis*), as for example in 1174 when he protested about buildings encroaching upon public land.[111] But, as in a dispute with Cava in 1178, this official also acknowledged his royal mandate.[112] After Salerno had rebelled in 1162 King William I entrusted the '*strategotus* and the magistrates [judges]' to capture any remaining conspirators in the city.[113] The same official often held the post for some time, and in Salerno it was regularly occupied by the Caputus family. Sergius Caputus was *strategotus* from 1134 to 1146 and was succeeded by his son Ursus. Landulf, a nephew of Sergius, is attested in the office from 1166 to 1174, while his son attained the position in 1182. The *strategotus* was almost certainly chosen by the city and his election merely ratified

---

[106] Jamison, 'Norman administration', cal. doc. no. 20 (Cava, *Arca* xxv.117).
[107] *Codice Perris*, pp. 291–3 no. 155.   [108] Jamison, *Admiral Eugenius*, cal. doc. nos. 7, 8.
[109] Jamison, *Admiral Eugenius*, cal. doc. no. 7.
[110] Kehr, *Urkunden*, pp. 448–52 no. 26 (Jamison, *Admiral Eugenius*, cal. doc. no. 2).
[111] See above n. 107.   [112] *Documenti per la storia di Eboli*, pp. 140–1 no. 291.
[113] *Falcandus*, p.132.

by the king.[114] The special position of this official is emphasised in Frederick II's 'Constitutions' of 1231. Here the *compalacii* of Naples and the *strategoti* of Salerno and Messina are singled out for being given 'cognisance even of criminal cases [which] is deigned to have been granted by special and ancient prerogative'.[115] At Naples the *compalacius* was introduced after the city's incorporation into the city and was, it seems, equivalent to the *strategotus*.

The chief magistrates of Naples and especially of Salerno may well have held a more prominent position than their counterparts in other cities. Although it may be chance, the documentation on the *strategoti* of Salerno surpasses that for the chief magistrates in most other places. Only in 1161 is a *strategotus* recorded at Capua, attempting to claim property erected on public land which should be used 'ad opus curie'.[116] But nothing more is given on his duties or status. At Aversa the *strategotus* is an especially confusing figure. There are nine references to the official, but eight of these fall into the period 1149–58 which saw six different holders of the title.[117] In each case the *strategotus* is attested as simply being present at a court or acting as a witness. It is tempting to think that the office was rotated on a yearly basis at Aversa. In 1149 its incumbent was called Alexander, in 1150 John Cutina, in 1151 Clement Tallapetra, in 1154 Dominic, in 1155 Peter Servati, in 1156 Dominic again, while in 1158 Robert de Conte appeared as a former *strategotus*.[118] Moreover, when Peter Servati was attested in 1155 one of his predecessors, Clement Tallapetra, acted as a witness in the same document. While Clement appeared in March 1151 as *strategotus*, he did not employ, or have, the title in July 1151, when he received some land and described himself as 'unus ex burgensibus civitatis Aversae'. As their other charter appearances without their official title suggest, men like Clement and Peter, were important members of the community.[119]

---

[114] For the Caputus family see above p. 69 and below p. 196; see also Matthew, 'Semper fideles', in *Salerno nel XII secolo*, p. 43 n. 37 and pp. 34–6 for a good discussion on the *strategotus* of Salerno.

[115] *The Liber Augustalis or Constitutions of Melfi Promulgated by the Emperor Frederick II for the Kingdom of Sicily in 1231*, trans. J. M. Powell (New York, 1971), p. 40 Bk I Title lxxi (49).

[116] *Pergamene di Capua*, i. 83–4 no. 34. However, in 1140 there was a Peter, *strategotus* of Capua and *compalacius* of Naples, who was found at Aversa; clearly a transitional phase in administrative structures after the war, *CDNA*, pp. 70–1 no. 41.

[117] A William Bairus is attested in 1165 as a *strategotus*, but not specifically of Aversa. The following year he appeared with the title of *vicecomes*, *CDNA*, pp. 153–7 nos. 87–8. The ninth reference is to a Nicholas Fruncus, *strategotus* of Aversa, who signed a document in 1182, *CDNA*, p. 224 no. 119.

[118] *CDNA*, pp. 99–101 no. 57, pp. 102–3 no. 59, pp. 117–19 no. 68, pp. 120–1 no. 70, pp. 329–30 no. 12, pp. 333–5 no. 15, pp. 339–40 no. 18.

[119] For Clement and Peter: *CDNA*, pp. 99–101 no. 57, pp. 105–7 no. 61, pp. 113–17 nos. 65–8, pp. 129–30 no. 74; for Peter's son Jacob, pp. 176–9 no. 99, pp. 185–7 no. 102, pp. 226–9 no. 121.

The equivalent of the *strategotus* in Apulia, the *catepan* (or more rarely *turmarch*), was attested even more intermittently. The Englishman John of Salisbury, however, does refer to the *catepans* in his *Historia Pontificalis* as 'powerful officials who exercise the authority of the princes [the king?] in the cities and castles'.[120] At Troia there are only three references to such an official: in 1144 the *catepan* Nicholas son of Peter de Sparano witnessed a sale of land, around 1170 Lucas de Rocca, carrying the title of royal justiciar and *catepan*, attested an agreement between the bishop of Troia and his canons, and finally in 1177 a certain *catepan* named Solomon helped resolve a dispute between the city's bishopric and the lord of Biccari.[121] Nothing more can be gleaned from these appearances, other than that Lucas de Rocca (and possibly Nicholas) was from an important local family. At Trani there is no indication of any such chief city magistrate; however, its charter of liberties of 1139 had referred to the possibility of establishing a *strategotus* or *baiulus* over the citizens.[122] At Conversano only one *catepan*, named Sclavus, is known. He is attested in office from 1148 to 1165, but his activities are limited to court attendance or acting as an advocate for the monastery of S. Benedetto of Conversano.[123] Likewise, at Monopoli a certain Alexander *catepanus et miles*, found giving counsel at a court held in the city's episcopal palace in 1154, provides the sole example of the office's existence there.[124] The greater evidence for their activities comes from Bari, where the *catepan* had been a key figure under Bohemond I.[125] But most of this evidence is found after 1189, and in the earlier period only one *catepan* of Bari can be identified by name – Bisantius Quatrainfussa, who in 1157 held a *curia* outside the city at Ceglie.[126] Earlier there is, however, mention of *turmarchi*. Two royal *turmarchi* 'of the Baresi' witnessed a sale in 1146, and then in 1174 a protonotary, John Horebone, took the same title when witnessing a high-profile agreement between a royal baron and the church of S. Nicola of Bari.[127] It may be from the later part of the period covered here that the office of *catepan* developed into that format which emerged after 1200: sometimes more than one *catepan* operating, with a host of bailiffs below. By that point the *catepan* retained some judicial functions and could act as a *mundoald* for women, but at the same time the office's fiscal responsibilities, especially in collecting public revenues, were highly apparent. An inquest of 1223 referred to a *catepan* of Bari in the period of King William (II?) who dealt

---

[120] *The Historia Pontificalis of John Salisbury*, ed. and trans. M. Chibnall (Oxford, 1986), p. 80.
[121] *Troia*, nos. 65, 87, 94.   [122] *Trani*, no. 37.   [123] *Conversano*, nos. 99, 106, 111, 113.
[124] *CDBI*, appendix III, p. 220 no. 1.   [125] See above p. 34.
[126] *CDBV*, no. 115; for Bisantius see also *CDBV*, no. 128.
[127] *CDBV*, nos. 99, 134, 135. In 1181 John was simply titled 'protonotary', *CDBV*, no. 145.

with the receipt of the city's *plateaticum*.[128] By the late twelfth century there was increasing overlap between the terms *catepan* and *baiulus*.

As the twelfth century progressed a growing complexity developed in the layers of local urban government. In particular, the term *baiulus* appears more frequently in the sources, but in a bewildering mix of guises. It could denote a high-ranking and powerful official like the bailiff grafted onto the more atypical local government at Gaeta, or which was envisaged in Trani's privileges of 1139.[129] More commonly, *baiulus* appears to have been a generic term for any low-level official who was primarily responsible for collecting public revenues within a certain jurisdiction (*baiulatio*), which could also include areas outside a city.[130] In 1174 Eugenius, master of the *duana baronum*, had been dispatched by the king to Salerno 'for the purpose of exacting accounts from the bailiffs of that district'.[131] However, some *baiuli* accrued judicial functions and attended court. In 1170 King William II ordered the *baiuli* to assist the archbishop of Trani in preventing the judgement of clerical misdemeanours or cases concerning adultery from passing to a secular court.[132] The *baiuli* appear to have been directly subordinate to, and worked closely with, the city *strategotus* or *catepan*. On some occasions they may even have been the same official. By the 1170s it is clear that the *strategotus* of Salerno had several *baiuli* assisting him in civic administration.[133] One of the *baiulus'* tasks at Bari, Salerno and Taranto was to collect customs and port dues. In 1180 those in the principality of Salerno received a royal order to allow the church of Cefalù exemption from such taxes in the area.[134] It appears that in some cities a fiscal institution/treasury, called the *dohana*, was established to supervise the local financial apparatus.[135]

An inquest of 1247 into Cava's rights to market dues at Salerno shows that under King William II the *baiuli* supervised the *plateaticum*. It also refers to the *baiuli* and 'other men of Salerno' 'qui emebant ipsas plateas', which suggests that part of the office's duties were being farmed.[136] Another investigation of 1247 suggests that the revenues of the *bucheria* at Taranto were sold with the *baiulatio* of that city, perhaps as far back as William II's reign.[137] Such 'farming' was certainly the case at Barletta in 1179 and at Bari in the 1190s, if not before.[138] Often complaints about

---

[128] *CDBVI*, no. 42.   [129] See below p. 115.   [130] Martin, *Pouille*, pp. 820–3.
[131] Jamison, *Admiral Eugenius*, cal. doc. no. 2 (Cava, *Arca* xxxiv.106); *Codice Perris*, pp. 291–3 no. 155.
[132] *Trani*, no. 61.   [133] Cava, *Arca* xxxiii.100; Kehr, *Urkunden*, pp. 448–52 no. 26.
[134] *I diplomi greci ed arabi di Sicilia*, ed. S. Cusa (Palermo, 1868–82), pp. 489–90 no. 7.
[135] Martin, 'L'Administration du royaume', p. 118.   [136] *CDS*, pp. 227–30 no. 125.
[137] *Taranto*, pp. 75–85 no. 22, pp. 90–1 no. 24, pp. 94–101 no. 26.
[138] *Pergamene di Barletta del Reale Archivio di Napoli (1075–1309)*, ed. R. Filangieri di Candida, *Codice diplomatico barese* X (Bari, 1927), no. 30.

an abuse of the system were directed against *bauili* either as the perpetrators of, or the ones entrusted with rectifying, wrongdoings. In
1182, a royal chamberlain decreed that the monastery of S. Severino of
Naples should no longer suffer aggravation from the *baiuli* of Aversa and
Somma over the possession of some nearby lands.[139] The move towards
leasing out the *baiulatio* for a set fee made political and fiscal sense for
the monarchy. It tied further the already wealthy and the aspirational to
the crown and was likely to guarantee more consistent revenue collection. On the other hand, it inevitably created opportunities for corruption which could be a contributing factor to certain discords recorded
within cities.

An investigation carried out at Taranto in 1231 throws light on the
running of the *baiulatio* and the nature of its officials in the preceding
century.[140] A group of men were brought forward to testify that
Taranto's archbishopric had received the tithe of the city's *baiulatio*, and
some of them identified this right as going back to the time of King
William II. The evidence provided shows that the leading men of the
city effectively controlled this organ of local government and that it was
occupied by several men simultaneously, who were often succeeded,
after a designated term in office, by their relations. Simon de Falco
testified that his uncle, Tafurus, had been a *baiulus* at the time of King
William II and that he had seen him paying over the tithe. Simon also
said that he himself had attained the office under Henry VI. Further
evidence demonstrated that Tafurus was assisted by at least three other
baiuli, also called his associates (*socii*). Segnorus de Archonta similarly
witnessed the payment of the tithe by his father and uncle, who were
both *baiuli*. Other witnesses, one a judge, identified themselves as former
baiuli; however, in these cases it is doubtful that they could have been
active much before 1189. These former *baiuli* disclosed how long they
had held the office – varying between two, three, six and ten years.
Two of them qualified the duration of their time as *baiulus* with the
phrase 'per diversa tempora', which may indicate that they did not hold
the office in one continuous term but at different points. The ambiguity
that existed between the office of *baiulus* and *catepan* is confirmed by the
testimony of a certain Pancalus, who saw two men, *comitus* Melis and
the notary Leo, 'who were at that time *catepans*', assigning the tithe to
the archbishopric.

The increasing number of urban officials may well link to the
emergence of a more complex taxation system and the monarchy's
efforts to exact revenue more effectively from the cities. Other local

[139] *CDNA*, pp. 224–6 no. 120.   [140] *Taranto*, pp. 60–9 nos. 16–18.

officials, whose competences were rather specialised, also begin to emerge, though only very rarely. Most of the major cities housed a royal garrison, usually in a castle, in or near the settlement, hence the appearance of castellans to manage the castle. At Bari the castellan Julian is referred to, in 1166 and 1174, as an advocate and witness respectively, while an unnamed castellan is alluded to in a document of 1188.[141] A castellan of Troia witnessed an important accord in the city's *contado* in 1151.[142] New officials appear in port cities, again in Apulia. A captain of the naval fleet (*comes galee*) can be found at Monopoli, maritime judges are referred to at Trani in 1169 and customs officials (*regius potortius/portulanus*) are mentioned at Bari and Salerno.[143] The old office of *vicecomes* lingered on, particularly at Aversa, while at Trani there is evidence for a *comes curtis*. However, their duties are obscure and they became increasingly rare after the 1160s.[144]

Local urban government always depended heavily upon another key civic official – the city judge. Falco of Benevento, a notary and judge, demonstrated in his chronicle the great esteem in which these figures were held and the power they could attain. The local judge enjoyed an exceptionally wide-ranging influence. His most basic responsibilities placed him in the closest relationship with daily city life, judging upon, witnessing and authenticating various types of private and public sales, donations and agreements. It was the judge who gave authorization, following Lombard law, for a woman to fulfil a legal transaction and who assigned *boni homines* to, for example, assess and alleviate cases of poverty or to delineate a disputed territory. Yet, on the other hand, as we have seen, this official regularly operated in more elevated circles, often outside the city itself, and could count archbishops, *strategoti* and the highest-ranking royal officials among his peers.[145] During this period most cities usually had between two and six judges. In Campania, in particular, the city's judicial body had a clear hierarchy with a chief judge; in Salerno we see a *protoiudex* from around the 1150s, and a *magister iudex* at Capua.[146] The charters of privileges of Bari, Trani, Troia and Salerno legislated for the local origin of city judges, who,

---

[141] *CDBI*, no. 61. [142] Jamison, 'Norman administration', cal. doc. no. 31.

[143] *Conversano*, nos. 115, 141; *CDBV*, no. 127; see also above p. 101 n. 134.

[144] For example *CDNA*, pp. 70–1 no. 41, pp. 80–1 no. 46, pp. 85–6 no. 49, pp. 92–3 no. 53, pp. 126–9 no. 73, pp. 155–7 no. 88; *Pergamene di Barletta del Reale Archivio*, nos. 22, 23.

[145] Of the many examples of judges (and notaries) acting outside their city see Salernitan judges at Eboli: Cava, *Arca* xxxiv.15; Nocera: B. Ruggiero, 'Per una storia della pieve rurale nel Mezzogiorno medievale', *Studi Medievali* 16 (1975), pp. 611–25, appendix no. 2; also on judges see below pp. 190–1.

[146] For example: Cava, *Arca* xxix.70, xxx.12; *Nuove pergamene*, pp. 34–7 no. 14; *Pergamene di Capua*, i. 83–6 nos. 34–35; Pergamene Aldobrandini, II. 27, and possibly *CDNA*, pp. 99–101 no. 57.

being most responsible for the practical operation of cherished local customs, undoubtedly acquired a symbolic importance for the populace. It is entirely understandable why so many examples exist of a judge's long tenure in office. At Troia, judges like Secundinus (1125–69), Urso (1154–98) and Antonius de Guinde Sonoro (1169–99?) survived in their offices through periods of political upheaval and regime change.[147] The major impact of external politics seems to have been in the mere nominal change of the judge's title to synchronise with whoever was the city's current superior. Thus a man like Secundinus was called a ducal judge in 1125, a Troian judge during the city's period of autonomy, ducal again from 1128–30 and thereafter royal until 1169. At Bari similar examples are provided by judges Melipezze (1151–67), who survived the city's demolition in 1156, Ameruzius (1167–85) and Petracca Buffus (1174–1202).[148] From Trani we can add judges such as Ameruzius (1160–72) and Trasagustus (1160–72), from Capua Leo (1181–92) and from Aversa judges Alexander (1144–68) and Roger (1174–1206).[149] At Salerno a large body of judges can be found, though many carried the same forename, making the exact length of their careers difficult to ascertain. Galante has demonstrated 'the complete detachment of the judicial authority [in Salerno] from the political powers and, there-fore, the definitive independence' of the city's judges. Accordingly the Salernitan judges were powerful people within their community.[150] A certain *protoiudex*, Peter, the son of another judge, was related to Matthew, the vice-chancellor of the kingdom, had a royal chamberlain for a nephew and received land at Montecorvino direct from the king.[151]

---

[147] Secundinus: see above p. 70 n. 86; Urso: *Troia*, nos. 70, 93, 94, 100, 118, 121; *Montevergine*, vi. no. 568, x. nos. 942, 974; Antonius: *Troia*, nos. 84, 88, 94, 100, 102, 103, 108; *Montevergine*, xi. no. 1061.

[148] Melipezze, had already been witnessing charters in the 1140s and was himself the son of a judge (*critis*); Petracca: *CDBV*, nos. 95, 96, 112, 117, 119, 120, 124, 125, frag. 17–18; *CDBI*, nos. 48, 50; Ameruzius: *CDBV*, nos. 120, 125, 128, 131, 133, 134, 140, 142, 145, frag. 16; *Pergamene di Barletta del Reale Archivio*, no. 32; *Pergamene di Barletta. Archivio Capitolare*, no. 109. Petracca was also the son of a judge John attested in 1155: *CDBV*, nos. 110, 130, 131, 133, 145, 148, 150, 154, 156–8, 161, 163, 164; *CDBI*, nos. 70, 71, 82, 94; *CDVI*, nos. 4–6, 11, 13, 24, 50.

[149] Amoruzius: *Trani*, nos. 49, 63 (and possibly no. 40 from 1142); Trasagustus: *Trani*, nos. 48, 54, 64; *Pergamene di Barletta del Reale Archivio*, nos. 22, 23; Leo: *Pergamene normanne*, nos. 22–4, 26, 34 and *Parte seconda, regesti e transunti di Gabrielle Ianelli*, nos. 113, 120, 138, 143; Alexander: *CDNA*, p. 88 no. 50, pp. 99–101 no. 57, pp. 102–7 nos. 59–61, pp. 111–14 nos. 64–5, pp. 115–19 nos. 67–8, pp. 120–1 no. 70, pp. 129–30 no. 74, pp. 135–6 no. 77, pp. 150–60 nos. 85–9, pp. 332–5 nos. 14–5, pp. 339–42 nos. 18–19; Roger: *CDNA*, pp. 174–6 no. 98, pp. 180–2 no. 100, pp. 187–92 nos. 103–4, pp. 194–6 no. 106, pp. 199–201 no. 98, pp. 208–0 no. 112, pp. 211–13 no. 114, pp. 222–4 no. 119, pp. 236–8 no. 127, pp. 248–9 no. 132, pp. 251–3 no. 134, pp. 264–5 no. 140, pp. 297–300 no. 105; *CDSA*, pp. 19–22 nos. 9–10, pp. 32–3 no. 16, pp. 49–53 nos. 24–5, pp. 66–9 nos. 32–3, pp. 85–7 no. 42, pp. 90–4 nos. 44–5, pp. 99–100 no. 48.

[150] M. Galante, 'Il giudice a Salerno in età normanna', in *Salerno nel XII secolo*, pp. 49, 54.

[151] *Italia Sacra*, vii. 403.

Similarly, at Bari the judge Leo de Rayza (1119–47) was the father of the powerful royal admiral Maio.[152] Indeed, the city judge was at the very heart of the urban elite and indispensable to the monarchy. Many leading families were defined by boasting a member in the judiciary, which brought prestige and wealth. Often sons followed their father's footsteps into the judiciary. Among the many examples are judge Petracca Buffus, son of judge John Buffus, at Bari, and judge Leo, son of judge Leo, at Capua.[153]

This network of local officials governed through the traditional customs familiar to them and had responsibility in civil and low criminal justice. However, the important cases of treason (*proditio*) or high crime (*magnum maleficium*) were beyond their jurisdiction. It is clear that some of the legislation promulgated by Roger II in the 1140s was put into effect, and this has been verified by Houben, who noted two documents from the Bari region to support this.[154] However, this royal legislation was mostly a supplement to, rather than a substitute for the local customs, which were allowed to continue. Numerous private documents refer to local custom. Like those charters of customs that survive in written form from places such as Bari, Trani and Gaeta, they give only tantalising hints at the real depth and complexity of what is undoubtedly a larger body of (probably in large part unwritten) customs.[155] At Salerno a long-running dispute over some property in the city was determined in 1176 'secundum usum et consuetudinem civitatis Salerni'. Salernitan charters also often refer to the *lex et consuetudo de obligatis et thingatis*, a law usually concerned with the leasing of property.[156] In 1154 the boundaries of land near Capua were measured according to that city's customs.[157] In 1168 and 1175 some plots of land, with basic tenements near Aversa, were conceded to the city's cathedral, along with the annual rent due from them, which was to be paid 'according to the use and custom' of Aversa.[158] At Monopoli in 1154 two city judges ordered the transcription of an earlier document of donation 'in accordance with the usage of the whole region and our civil custom'.[159] At Trani in 1163 a woman drew up a will 'de iure civili tranensi', while in 1165 the mediators and the oath required to fulfil payment of a dowry

---

[152] For more see below pp. 194–5.   [153] Petracca: see above n. 148; Leo: see above n. 149.

[154] Houben, *Roger II*, pp. 135–47; *CDBI*, no. 50; *I documenti storici di Corato (1046–1327)*, ed. G. Beltrani, *Codice diplomatico barese* IX (Bari, 1923), no. 63.

[155] See also above pp. 76–7.

[156] *Codice Perris*, p. 304 no. 160; *Pergamene di S. Nicola di Gallucanta*, no. 138; G. Abignente, 'Le consuetudine inedite di Salerno', in *Studi e documenti di storia e diritto*, 9 fasc. 4 (Rome, 1888), pp. 305–87.

[157] *Montevergine*, iv. no. 320.   [158] *CDNA*, pp. 157–60 no. 89, pp. 176–9 no. 99.

[159] *CDBI*, appendix III, p. 220 no. 1.

were established in agreement with 'the civil usage of the *Tranensi*'.[160] It is from Bari that most references to civic custom can be found. Among the various combinations are *secundum nostrum civilem consuetudinem, iuxta morem barensium, secundum barensem consuetudinem, ut barensis mos est* and *ut usus Bari est*.[161] Most of these dealt with matters concerning women: marriage contracts, dowries and the giving of the *morgincaph*.[162] But some concerned building regulations, the transmission of legal documents, the renewal of charters and the execution of wills.[163] It is also interesting to find former Barese citizens invoking their civic customs in Monopoli and Palermo.[164] On the other hand it is rather surprising that, apart from the 1127 charter of privileges, the abundant documentation from Troia provides only one unambiguous reference to civic customs, dating from 1202.[165]

Local custom was a powerful weapon for the community, and once again it is from Bari and its code of customs that this is most obvious. Here it states that:

no person of Bari is to be dragged away by counts, justiciars or any magistrate at all from our city, or is to be taken to other places against his will to be judged; but he must be brought before a judge within his own *patria* and convicted, so that due honour may be kept also for the city, and that the citizens and the civil law may not be able to be harmed through ignorance.[166]

A dispute between the people of Amalfi and Ravello, heard at Salerno and then at Minori in 1178, further proves the vigour of local custom. The Amalfitans had complained of violent incursions on the settlement of Forcella by the Ravellesi. After an initial attempt by the royal officials to assist the Amalfitans, both of these parties were forced to back down as the Ravellesi invoked their ancient custom, which recognised only the testimony of fellow citizens. Thus the court at Minori issued a confirmation of this custom of Ravello, and Amalfi lost its claims to compensation and also ownership of the disputed land.[167] In addition there was no established royal system for holding local courts: rather their location was dictated on an *ad hoc* basis and by local circumstances. At times, courts were called 'royal' and the Terracina palace in Salerno certainly constituted a centre for higher-profile hearings. But often a court's venue is not recorded and when it is a variety of sites were used.

---

[160] *Trani*, no. 54; *Pergamene di Barletta del Reale Archivio*, nos. 22.
[161] *CDBI*, nos. 48, 57, 61; *CDBV*, nos. 107, 144.
[162] *CDBI*, no. 57; *CDBV*, nos. 107, 108, 131, 142, frag. no. 16.
[163] *CDBI*, nos. 48, 61; *CDBV*, nos. 140, 144.   [164] *CDBI*, no. 57; *CDBV*, no. 107.
[165] *Montevergine*, xii. no. 1173.   [166] Petroni, *Storia di Bari*, ii. 440 Rubric II.7.
[167] Jamison, *Admiral Eugenius*, cal. doc. nos. 7, 8.

In Salerno cases were also heard at the old Lombard *sacrum palatium* or even in places like the nunnery of S. Giorgio.[168] In Capua it is likely that the city's Lombard palace was similarly used but so was the castle.[169] More regularly the bishop's palace, as at Salerno (1152) Monopoli (1154), Troia (1177) and Aversa (1180), or the city cathedral, again at Aversa (1158), were employed.[170] Likewise in northern Italy, communes did not have their own recognised seats of government until the late twelfth-century construction of communal *palazzi* (buildings which had no evident parallels in the South at this point). Prior to this, communal business, elections and legal enactments were usually carried out either in or before the city cathedral, or via the open forum of a political assembly.[171]

In short, as before 1139, the day-to-day organisation of the city remained in the hands of a body of local officials composed primarily of a chief city magistrate and civic judges. They were drawn from the native population, who almost certainly chose them with the king's subsequent ratification. These local officials played significant roles in local government, which limited the urban community's interaction with the more transient higher royal officials and the monarchy that they represented. It is, however, essential at this point to reiterate the need to detach any modern structured sense from the words 'government' and 'administration' when using them in a medieval context. There was huge informality in medieval governing structures, and jurisdictions were at best indistinct and regularly overlapped. The unstructured nature of governing systems required a role to be played by the urban populace itself. Although this role was not endowed with defined functions or even a title, like all facets of medieval urban government the absence of a 'technical' vocabulary should not be taken to imply non-existence. The experiences of the previous half-century had instilled in the South Italian urban community an awareness of its potential political power and the desire to use it to protect its interests. Now incorporated within a kingdom, the *populus* continued to enjoy leverage in local government. This gave cities the power still to operate independently when necessary. Much can be deduced about the populace's position, and the relationship between monarch and city, from the widespread revolts during King William I's reign in 1155–6 and 1160–2. The first uprising

---

[168] Jamison, 'Norman administration', pp. 456–7 appendix no. 3; *Nuove pergamene*, pp. 34–7 no. 15; Matthew, 'Semper fideles', pp. 35–6

[169] *Pergamene Aldabrandini*, II. nos. 13, 27.

[170] *Pergamene di Barletta del Reale Archivio*, no. 131; *Troia*, no. 94; *CDBI*, appendix III, p. 220 no. 1; *CDNA*, pp. 120–1 no. 70; Loud, 'A Lombard abbey', appendix I, pp. 304–5 no. 7.

[171] E. Coleman, 'Representative assemblies in communal Italy', in *Political Assemblies in the Earlier Middle Ages*, ed. P. Barnwell and M. Mostert (Turnhout, 2003), pp. 193–210.

was directed by a coalition of parties dissatisfied with the creation of the Sicilian kingdom, and the policies of Roger II, rather than with his unfortunate son, William.[172] Roger's death in 1154 provided the opportunity for a Byzantine military expedition primarily in Apulia, a papal-sponsored attack in the north of the kingdom, led by exiles such as the deposed Prince Robert of Capua, and the rumour of an assault by Frederick Barbarossa (which in the end did not materialise). By the end of 1155 most of the mainland was in the hands of the Byzantines and rebel counts, while the unrest had spread to Sicily. According to Falcandus, only a handful of cities remained loyal to the king – Naples, Amalfi, Salerno, Troia and Melfi.[173] The defection of other cities, however, need not have been due wholly to any latent dissatisfaction with their lot under the monarchy, but a short-term calculation made on the basis of the immediate parlous political climate.

According to Otto of Freising, Prince Robert of Capua and the other exiles 'received back without opposition the cities, castles and other possessions which they once had, the inhabitants supposing that the emperor [Frederick Barbarossa] would follow them'.[174] The last clause of the statement is revealing, and the presumption must be that in Capua and Aversa local officials and the populace made a political calculation as a collectivity. In Apulia the same commentator reveals similar developments. Most of the coastal cities surrendered to a Byzantine invasion force; however, we must treat with suspicion the claim that 'practically all the inhabitants of the cities and towns supported them [the Byzantines], because they had for so long been oppressed by the tyranny of [the Sicilian kings] . . . and longed to be freed from so heavy a yoke.'[175] There may indeed have been some impulsive desire to throw off the mild royal influence, mixed with some residual atavistic longing for an earlier era. Falcandus inveighed against the 'people of Apulia [who] are utterly disloyal, and vainly hope to win their independence'. But this was perhaps based upon a literary myth arising from events of an earlier period.[176] From what is known of the true nature of urban

---

[172] G. A. Loud, 'William the Bad or William the Unlucky? Kingship in Sicily – 1155–1166', *The Haskins Society Journal* 8 (1996), pp. 99–113.

[173] *Falcandus*, p. 223.

[174] *The Deeds of Frederick Barbarossa, by Otto of Freising and His Continuator Rahewin*, trans. C. C. Mierow (New York, 1966), Bk II, pp. 154–5; a charter from Aversa in May 1156 was dated in the twenty-ninth year of the rule of Robert II, Prince of Capua and Count of Aversa, *Montevergine*, iv. no. 348.

[175] *Deeds of Frederick Barbarossa*, Bk II, pp. 165–6.

[176] See above p. 39 n. 69; *Falcandus*, p. 66 and also D. Matthew, 'Maio of Bari's commentary on the Lord's prayer', in *Intellectual Life in the Middle Ages. Essays Presented to Margaret Gibson*, ed. C. Smith and B. Ward (London, 1992), pp. 122–3.

Order ID: 026-1561891-1561922

Thank you for buying from David's-Cambridge on Amazon Marketplace.

Delivery address:
Mrs K Rajput
Loughborough Grammar School
Burton Walks
LOUGHBOROUGH
Leics
LE11 2DU
United Kingdom

Order Date: 6 Feb 2015
Delivery Service: Standard
Buyer Name: Kiran Rajput
Seller Name: David's-Cambridge

Quantity	Product Details
1	**Sanctity and Pilgrimage in Medieval Southern Italy, 1000-1200 [Hardcover] [2014] Oldfield, Paul** **SKU:** 3D-8BCU-0VB0 **ASIN:** 1107000289 **Listing ID:** 0128PBIP1RG **Order Item ID:** 63636151135491 **Condition:** Used - Good **Comments:** Ex-review copy. Would have been listed as 'like new' but for slight scuffing/bruising to top, front edge corners(really only affecting the d.w.) C.U.P.2014. ~ i.e. - NOT...ex-library, scored, highlighted or print-on -demand).

Thanks for buying on Amazon Marketplace. To provide feedback for the seller please visit www.amazon.co.uk/feedback. To contact the seller, go to Your Orders in Your Account. Click the seller's name under the appropriate product. Then, in the "Further Information" section, click "Contact the Seller."

government in the kingdom, it is misleading to speak of oppression in the way Otto of Freising does. The 'tyrant' label was used widely by opponents (usually foreign) of the Sicilian monarchy, and Otto may be closer to the citizens' real motives when he referred to the Byzantines' use of bribery.[177] This is supported by Falcandus, who adduces additional reasons for the revolt. These ranged from 'pure capriciousness', 'hope of plunder' and, more interestingly, to avenge King William, who was falsely rumoured to be dead.[178] Yet there is no mention of monarchic repression. Moreover, the cities showed a remarkable reluctance to capitulate. At Trani the citizens refused to surrender and displayed a prescient knowledge of the region's political geography, for they knew 'it would be impossible for [the Byzantine force] to take Trani if [it] had not first occupied Bari.' At Bari the Byzantine force was met by the strong resistance of 500 Baresi on the city's battlements. However, part of the citizenry was bribed, and the chronicler John Kinnamos pointedly remarked that 'nothing is more deceitful for men than golden bait.' When the remaining faction of citizens rushed to defend themselves in the citadel, John mused that 'it was something really worthy of wonder, to see those lately united in race and purpose today sundered by gold as if by a wall.' The city was finally stormed after seven further days of stout resistance. The report that some of the citizens wished to destroy the captured citadel out of hatred for King Roger is the only sign, and a dubious one at that, of any anti-royal protest in Bari. Instead the strongest motive throughout, for most of the citizens, was financial opportunism. On the fall of Bari the people of Trani duly made a treaty with the invading force. However, the Byzantine garrison installed in the city was left 'in great dread' over the loyalty of the inhabitants of a city that had once been the most Grecophile in southern Italy.[179]

The fall of Monopoli is even more revealing. A citizen militia composed of over 200 knights, more than 1,000 infantry and an 'innumerable crowd of slingers' tenaciously resisted the Byzantine army. Although despairing of their fate, the citizens refused an outright surrender and instead agreed a month's armistice in the hope that a royal force would relieve the city. However, the Byzantines soon attacked again, forcing the people of Monopoli to bravely defend themselves 'in a violent struggle'. Seeing no royal assistance on its way, the Monopolitans, through an embassy, agreed to the establishment of a Greek garrison in the city. In opposition to this, 'some of the citizen body of Monopoli'

[177] See above n. 175; Wieruszowski, 'Roger II of Sicily', pp. 46–78.   [178] *Falcandus*, p. 66.
[179] *Deeds of John and Manuel Comnenus by John Cinnamus*, trans. C. M. Brand (New York, 1976), Bk IV.3, 4, pp. 108–10.

planned a nocturnal uprising, but when this reached the ears of the Byzantine commander another group of citizens 'sent and invited the general to the city again, ascribing the problem to others, who had rashly done the present deed without *common consent*'. Only then did the city finally capitulate.[180] It has been suggested that the Apulians were enchanted with the prospect of restoring distant Byzantine rule, and that the invasion failed largely because of luck, military factors and the desertion of South Italian rebel leaders. However, the above evidence indicates that Apulian communities were broadly reluctant to accept the Byzantines, and that this played an important role in their defeat.[181] Moreover, recent research suggests that the Byzantine expedition was never intended as a territorial conquest but was a calculated strike forming part of Manuel I's wider defensive strategy. It may well be that many Apulian cities also perceived the uncertain and temporary nature of the Byzantine incursion, which is only likely to have strengthened attachments to the Sicilian monarchy and further encouraged resistance to the Byzantines.[182]

In all these cases the garrison provides the only reference to a royal presence in a city. If local officials were conspicuous as royal representatives then certainly mention might have been made of them, instead the sources consider them to be part of the civic body. The impression, supported by the varied actions of the citizenry, is that these cities were self-sufficient units capable, despite inevitable factions, of making important political decisions. This presupposes the existence of civic councils. At Taranto, after the news of the fall of Massafra to a Greek force, 'the men of Taranto gathered by guilds and neighbourhoods' to reprimand a royal count whom they held responsible for the defeat.[183] The word 'guild' here is unusual, but perhaps the sense is the general one of groups associated for mutual aid. As at Monopoli, a certain attachment to the status quo is discernible. King William eventually appeared on the mainland in 1156 and took the two key centres of Byzantine operations, Brindisi and Bari. William, needing to make a forceful political statement, severely punished the two cities for not opposing the Byzantines more vigorously, even though many in Bari had put up resistance. Brindisi was depopulated, while at Bari the pleas of the entire population did not assuage the king's anger at the demolition

---

[180] *Deeds of John and Manuel Comnenus*, Bk IV.5, 8–9, pp. 113–14, 119–22.
[181] P. Magdalino, *The Empire of Manuel I Komnenos, 1143–1180* (Cambridge, 1993), pp. 59–60.
[182] D. N. Tolstoy-Miloslavsky, 'Manuel I Komnenos and Italy: Byzantine Foreign Policy, 1135–1180' (Unpublished PhD thesis, Royal Holloway, University of London, 2008); I would like to thank the author for kindly allowing me to view this work.
[183] *Deeds of John and Manuel Comnenus*, Bk IV. 8, p. 119.

of the royal citadel.[184] The king gave the inhabitants two days to leave Bari with their property, and 'the destruction of the entire city followed'. Thereafter, 'the towns of all Apulia' quickly went over to the king, which suggests that many of them at no point throughout the rebellion acted with any great conviction. It is especially interesting that Prince Robert of Capua, on hearing news of the king's appearance in Apulia, did not trust the loyalty of the inhabitants of the Terra di Lavoro and chose to flee southern Italy.[185] The rebellion fell apart with remarkable speed. Bari itself began to be slowly repopulated within a few years and many important local officials of the city remained in their offices after 1156. It is likely that some of the city's privileges were revoked only to be restored, probably by King William II, after 1166, and by the late twelfth century they appear to be in force again. Interestingly, there is some muddled news of an uprising at Naples in 1156. The city's *mediani* destroyed the old pacts of agreement that had been contracted with the city's *nobiles*. The revolt was put down by the latter and should not be seen as a movement against the monarchy. It appears to have been stimulated by local social tension within the city and focused on internal government.[186] Indeed, Falcandus named the city as one that had remained loyal to the king in that year. Thus we should avoid the temptation of seeing the widespread 'uprising' of 1155–6 as an inevitable clash between a centralising monarchy and self-governing cities. There was not an underlying friction between the positions of the two, and a monarchy that left local government mostly in the hands of local people could still function effectively.

The continued rumblings of discontent on the mainland in the years following 1156 do not contradict this interpretation, rather they support it. Rumours began to grow that King William's chief adviser, admiral Maio of Bari, was actually governing the kingdom and even plotting to assassinate the monarch. Falcandus informs us that 'the disgrace of the thing [the rumour] turned the minds of all against Maio', that 'Apulia was in turmoil' and that a coalition of leading men and 'many cities' formed to depose the admiral. Even 'the majority of the citizens' of traditionally loyal Salerno joined the movement.[187] Maio's response was to send letters to several cities to ignore 'the false insinuations'. However, 'things had got to such a point that no one gave recognition to the royal letters; it was said that they were issued by a traitor's hand, and that

---

[184] Brindisi's fate is documented in *Guillelmi I Regis Diplomata*, pp. 42–4 no. 15.
[185] *Falcandus*, pp. 73–4.
[186] *Guillelmi I Regis Diplomata*, p. 37 no. 13; Schipa, 'Nobili e popolani in Napoli', pp. 13–14.
[187] *Falcandus*, pp. 82–4.

it was Maio's policy, not the king's'.[188] The chain of events culminated in Maio's murder in Palermo in November 1160 and King William's temporary imprisonment in March 1161. Three key observations can be drawn from this series of episodes. Firstly, that various cities were involved in the disturbances not as a protest against the monarchy but rather the corruption of it. Secondly, the dissemination of wild rumours throughout the mainland, and Maio's makeshift attempts to counter them, highlight the logistical problems of communication and hence the limitations of the monarchy's administrative network. Where were the higher royal officials within the cities to provide the inhabitants with legitimate information? Once again, the local government and community had to make its own decisions. Thirdly, it seems that at the root of the anti-Maio feelings were the admiral's attempts to further reform and improve central administration. Although these reforms may not have been aimed directly at local urban government, any miscommunication of such plans, which there clearly was, may have threatened the cities and the 'compromise' established after the 1130s.[189]

The royal response to the events of 1160 to 1162 provides more significant insights. While King William had been detained in Palermo, the exiled Count Robert of Loritello had made gains on the mainland by taking a number of cities in Apulia and the Terra di Lavoro. But on hearing of the king's release and arrival on the mainland in early 1162 Robert refused a head-on clash 'because he mistrusted the divided loyalties of the South Italians'. The king speedily regained the captured cities – at Taranto, for example, the citizens assisted in their city's fall by handing over one of Count Robert's knights. As in 1156, it is clear that many cities acted spontaneously, quickly submitting to the nearest armed force, and were not motivated by any long-term plan. Falcandus captures this mood perfectly when speaking of the region's people who 'now rushed to join him [the king] with a fickleness as great as the foolishness with which they had previously rebelled against him'.[190] Significantly, King William's retribution on the 'rebellious' cities reflected this ambiguity, as 'he decided to impose a stated quantity of money as a redemption fine on all those cities and towns which had accepted the count of Loritello or had seemed to any extent to have supported him, wishing to make up for what his treasury had lost with this money.' The

---

[188] *Falcandus*, p. 85; *Romuald*, p. 245 (English translation in 'additional texts section' of *Falcandus*, p. 228), speaks of 'great war and faction in all of Apulia'.

[189] Indeed Maio, a member of a leading Barese family, may have naturally looked to enhance the powers of local urban authorities. There does not seem to be any conclusive evidence for the 'anti-municipal policy' attributed to Maio by Jamison, 'Norman administration', pp. 259–60.

[190] *Falcandus*, p.128.

last phrase suggests that the citizens were literally paying for a rebellion that was not entirely of their making. Moreover, William recognised that some people had undertaken, under duress, obligations to the rebels concerning their property, yet the king still 'forced [them] to redeem that property by a small fine.'[191]

Punishments were arbitrary, often imposed on the innocent and influenced by financial gain. The monarch's attempt to demolish Salerno supports this. With the main rebel leaders having fled, the citizens provided the only targets. Romuald, perhaps predictably, informs us that the Salernitans had refused to participate in Count Robert's rebellion and 'remained faithful to the king as was their custom.'[192] Falcandus, however, suggests that at least a faction of the citizens, called the *capiturinos*, had allied with the rebels. The city's *maiores* attempted, unsuccessfully, to prove Salerno's loyalty to the king. These two sources hereafter confusedly overlap.[193] Romuald suggests that William used the indiscretions of a few to extort money from the citizens. Falcandus shows the royal *familiaris* Matthew attempting to save his home-city by enlisting the support of his high-ranking colleagues to argue that 'the people as a whole should not suffer punishment undeservedly because of the crimes of others.' In both versions the king's decision to demolish Salerno was considered an injustice. William did eventually spare the city; according to Falcandus, he was dissuaded by his officials' cogent appeals, while Romuald put the king's change of mind down to a fearsome storm brewed up by Salerno's patron saint, Matthew. In both accounts the citizens, as a body, act assertively, and in Falcandus the city *strategotus* and the magistrates, the local authorities, were given the task of identifying the conspirators. Almost the first act in 1166 of the new king, William II, and his mother, Margaret, as co-ruler, suggests that many unjust punishments had been previously inflicted upon the inhabitants of the kingdom. Prisoners were released, and it was decreed that 'the unbearable burden of redemption fees, which had shaken the whole of Apulia and the Terra di Lavoro with utter despair, should be entirely abolished, and she [Margaret] wrote to the master chamberlains that they should not demand redemption fees again from anyone on any grounds.'[194]

The relationship between monarchy and city, especially in King William I's reign, was often confused by misinformation, tainted by financial opportunity and dictated by the king's need to be seen to be in

---

[191] *Falcandus*, p.129.   [192] *Romuald*, p. 249 (English translation in *Falcandus*, p. 232).
[193] *Falcandus*, pp. 13–33; *Romuald*, p. 251 (English translation in *Falcandus*, pp. 235–6).
[194] *Falcandus*, p. 139.

control. Yet there was no deliberate plan to repress civic liberties and no calculated policy of the cities to break away from royal rule. The city was often the unfortunate vehicle for the rebellion of external parties. Fasoli has emphasised this: the cities were not the 'natural antagonists' of the monarchy. Many communities in the thirteenth century attempted to restore customs that had been current under the Norman kings, notably King Roger II and King William II. The monarchs, suspicious of many South Italian counts and aware of Frederick Barbarossa's problems with the Lombard cities, were keen to pacify their own urban communities by providing the stability that they desired. This meant the continued operation of traditional liberties, while the very payment of the *redemptio* may provide further evidence that the cities controlled a financial administration that operated below the royal one.[195] Indeed 'it was the abuse, not the structure' of the governing system that brought complaints from the citizenry. The consultative role of the population in organising its own affairs was never in doubt.[196] This is evident in the charter material, on a more prosaic basis, represented in the *boni homines* and *viri prudentes* who gave counsel on a wide range of matters and stood as witnesses. In 1146 the *strategotus* of Salerno, with *sapientes viri* and advocates, helped compose an out-of-court settlement between two monasteries.[197] In 1148, in the presence of a justiciar, John de Boccio of Troia settled his differences with the abbot of Montecassino, through 'interventu Troianorum, parentum et amicorum'.[198] Numerous private charters from Aversa contain long witness lists carrying the names of artisans and *burgenses*, who were clearly assisting in local government. At Taranto, in 1156, the citizens were grouped by 'guilds' and neighbourhoods. In that same year some citizens of Monopoli denounced the attempts of others in the city to break the surrender pact with the Byzantines, saying that they had acted without 'common consent'.[199] The unrest at Naples, also of 1156, suggests the community had a role within government and that it was guided by the city *nobiles*.[200] Again in Monopoli, in the 1160s transactions are, on occasion, accomplished without a city judge and instead are completed in the presence of citizens, some of whom carry the title of *negotiator* and *nauclerius*.[201] The references to the *maiores* of Salerno may well conceal an urban council.[202]

---

[195] Fasoli, 'Città e ceti urbani', pp. 150–1, 165–71.
[196] Reynolds, *Kingdoms and Communities*, p. 211.
[197] Cava, *Arca* xxv.115.   [198] *Colonie cassinensi*, no. 28.   [199] See above p. 110.
[200] M. Fuiano, 'Napoli normanna e sveva', in *Storia di Napoli* (Naples, 1969), vol. II (i), pp. 424–32.
[201] *Conversano*, nos. 115, 118; see also below pp. 199–200, 254–5.
[202] See above pp. 73 n. 104, 113 n. 193.

According to Calasso, civic councils did exist under the monarchy, but they were neither political in character nor true institutions of civic organisation.[203] Here it must once again be asked how important control over an abstract notion of political power was to the medieval urban community, while at the same time emphasising that the informality of any governing structure should not minimise its significance. The citizens were able to act collectively in political affairs when they wanted, but otherwise were more concerned with their economic and judicial position. However, there are hints that a more formally ordered communal-style government may well have endured in a restructured format, perhaps at Naples and particularly at Gaeta. In Gaeta, consuls were last referred to in 1135 before the city's capitulation to Roger II. The city's government in the kingdom remains obscure, and in the late 1140s there is curious mention of a John Senior *dominator* of the city and also a 'Bonus Gaitanus consul and bailiff of the most powerful king'.[204] Interestingly, a royal privilege of 1187 refers to a Richard the bailiff as well as to consuls of Gaeta.[205] Tancred's privilege to the city of 1191 further suggests that the nascent commune and civic consulate of the 1120s still existed in some form after its incorporation into the kingdom in the late 1130s.[206] Both it and the same king's earlier grant to Naples in 1190 show communal and consular urban governments which surely blossomed from earlier structures that survived under the monarchy.

An interesting comparative model for the cities within the kingdom in this period is offered by Benevento. The Treaty of Mignano of July 1139 had preserved the city under papal rule, meaning it was not theoretically part of the new kingdom. However, the reality was entirely different. Benevento was encircled by the kingdom and inevitably enjoyed strong political, social and economic links with it. Benevento's religious establishments, notably the archbishopric and the monasteries of S. Sofia and S. Modesto, had extensive patrimonies in the peninsula that drew them into the realm's legal and administrative orbit.[207] Even before Mignano, in March 1139, we find S. Modesto reaching agreement before the royal chamberlain Hugo Mansellus over lands near Montesarchio, 15 km from Benevento.[208] Representatives of S. Sofia appeared before royal justiciars and chamberlains in 1158 at Capua, in 1164 at Lesina and in 1173 at Alife and Capua again.[209] Judges from Benevento also appeared in the cities of the kingdom. In 1147, at a court

[203] Calasso, *La legislazione statutaria*, pp. 75–6.   [204] *Cod. Dip. Caietanus*, ii. 273–5 nos. 339–40.
[205] *Le pergamene di Gaeta. Archivio storico comunale 1187–1440*, ed. P. Corbo (Gaeta, 1997), no. 1.
[206] See above p. 76 and see below pp. 125–6, 128–9.
[207] Loud, 'A Lombard abbey', pp. 289–95.   [208] *S. Modesto*, no. 8.
[209] Pergamene Aldobrandini, II nos. 13, 15, 27.

in the Capitanata, we find the judge Roffred of Benevento, alongside various noblemen, the archbishop-elect of Palermo, the bishop-elect of Troia and Duke Roger of Apulia, to witness a case that had no ostensible link to Beneventan affairs.[210] In 1152 at Salerno, the archbishop of that city and the abbot of Cava judged a dispute between S. Sofia and SS. Trinità of Venosa over land near Ascoli and were assisted by three Salernitan and three Beneventan judges.[211] In the 1180s the Beneventan judge Lucas twice crossed into the kingdom to witness, at Montesarchio, donations made to S. Modesto of Benevento.[212] The Beneventan judge John travelled further, to Capua and Lesina, to represent the monastery of S. Sofia before higher royal officials and barons.[213] Many citizens also held land outside the city's territory. Herein lay the significance of King Roger's privilege of 1137 which exempted the Beneventans from the usual dues exacted in this surrounding region. In 1144, Roger II sent his chancellor, Robert of Selby, to Benevento and revoked these privileges, which left the citizens 'troubled, distressed and afraid'.[214] These privileges had been restored by 1172, but there are still references to Beneventans having to pay these dues (*fidantiae*) on lands held outside the city after this date.[215] It is also interesting that the Beneventans still recognised in the 1180s as 'Normans' those who received the *fidantiae*. Moreover, the citizens were keen to ensure that the settlement of any disputes over these lands should be settled within the city of Benevento and not in the kingdom.[216] However, these legal and fiscal concerns merely emphasise the daily interaction between the two. Indeed, despite having to pay taxes on lands within the kingdom, the Beneventans, and in particular their religious establishments, clearly benefited from the protection provided by royal justice.[217] There were many other links. From a document of 1153 we see that certain customs had been established between 'the citizens of Benevento and the barons of Montefusco', a settlement in the kingdom.[218] In addition, in 1140, Roger even attempted to introduce a new coinage into Benevento, to the indignation of the pope and Falco of Benevento.[219] A colony of Amalfitans and Ravellesi, men from the kingdom, seemed to have played an important role in the city's commerce.[220]

---

[210] *Colonie cassinensi*, no. 27.   [211] *Pergamene di Barletta del Reale Archivio*, no. 131.

[212] *S. Modesto*, nos. 20–1.   [213] Pergamene Aldabrandini, II. 13, 15.

[214] *Chronicon Ignoti Monachi Cisterciensis Sanctae Mariae de Ferraria*, p. 27.

[215] *Italia Pontificia*, ix. 42 no. 106; *Montevergine*, vii. nos. 682–3.

[216] Girgensohn, 'Documenti beneventani', pp. 305–6 no. 10; *Montevergine*, vi. no. 682.

[217] See above n. 207.   [218] *Montevergine*, iv. no. 315.   [219] *Falco*, p. 238.

[220] S. Borgia, *Memorie istoriche della pontificia città di Benevento dal secolo VIII al secolo XVIII*, 3 vols. (Rome, 1763–9), iii, pp. 163–6.

Indeed, Benevento was located on an important communication path running through the kingdom. Thus Benevento was very much within the kingdom's sphere of interest. This was most apparent when political calculations were to be made. Just as in the 1130s the city could be targeted in order to affect a change in papal policy. As early as the 1140s the papacy was again reluctant to recognise Roger's new kingdom while his sons were conducting incursions towards papal territory. Roger strove to force a papal recognition 'not by soothing prayers but compelled by necessity, and he hoped to disloyally achieve this through the Beneventans', who were harassed by nearby royal barons and had their immunities of 1137 revoked.[221] It was much the same in 1155, when a royal army besieged the city 'for quite some time and set fire to its suburbs'.[222] King William I aimed on this occasion to persuade Pope Adrian IV to acknowledge his royal status. However, the resistance of the Beneventans, and desertion on the royal side, led to the raising of the siege.[223] The pope responded by joining the growing coalition that would cause havoc in southern Italy for the next year. King William's successful second attack on Benevento in the summer of 1156 marked the end of the whole uprising. It also produced the Treaty of Benevento, in which the pope recognised William's royal title and the territorial integrity of the kingdom, as well as settling the nature of royal control over ecclesiastical affairs in the realm.[224] Thereafter the pope and, by association, Benevento remained on good terms with the kings of Sicily, largely because of the spectre of Frederick Barbarossa. It may even be that the kings enjoyed some sort of protectorate over the city.[225] Loud perfectly sums up the position of Benevento in relation to the kingdom: 'independent it might be, separate it was not'.[226]

The city had certain fundamental similarities with those found in the kingdom on the mainland. In both cases they had distant rulers who were often occupied with more pressing affairs at Palermo and Rome respectively. The pope did not visit Benevento between 1139 and 1155, when Adrian IV spent nine months in the city. Alexander III did take refuge there from 1167 to 1171 during the papal schism under Frederick Barbarossa, but after his short visits in 1176 and 1177, to and from the peace conference at Venice, a pope did not stay in Benevento again in

---

[221] *Chronicon Ignoti Monachi Cisterciensis Sanctae Mariae de Ferraria*, p. 27.
[222] Boso's *Life of Pope Adrian IV*, translated in 'additional texts' of *Falcandus*, p. 244.
[223] *Romuald*, p. 238 (English translation in *Falcandus*, p. 222).
[224] The Treaty of Benevento of 1156 is translated in 'additional texts' of *Falcandus*, pp. 248–52 and also in *Guillelmi I Regis Diplomata*, pp. 34–5 no. 12.
[225] Vehse, 'Benevent', part 1, p. 154.
[226] Loud, 'Politics, piety and ecclesiastical patronage', p. 292.

the twelfth century.[227] The repercussions for local government are obvious. While the Sicilian monarchs left much of urban government untouched on the mainland they did at least set in place an administrative superstructure which aimed to bring ruler and ruled into a closer relationship. At Benevento one might have expected the pope to restructure civic government after the tumultuous 1130s. That no such reforms appear to have emerged is indicative of the pope's inability to intervene, as well as his more urgent international priorities. This was accentuated by the standing of the pope's main representative in the city – the rector. From its inception the office had been fraught with problems. After 1139 the authority of the rector showed little sign of development. The office, usually occupied by a cardinal, was often filled with men of lower rank, usually for a few years at most. Of the eleven rectors identified between 1139 and 1189 just three were cardinals and one of these, Guido, was in office only from the summer of 1139 until March 1140. The remainder included four subdeacons, three men without title and one former anti-pope.[228] This may have been improved slightly by the appointments, in 1171 and 1179, of cardinals to the post of city archbishop. A rector is specifically attested in the city for the following years: 1139, 1140, 1147, 1148, 1152, 1157, 1160, 1162, 1171, 1172, 1180 and 1184. From this it would appear that, just like the higher officials of the kingdom, the rector was not an overwhelming presence in Benevento. But this may partly reflect the limitations of the sources, and as the rector did not have a tour of duty he was surely more of a regular fixture in the city. We can see the rector acting in important matters. In 1140 King Roger came to Benevento and 'had a long and thorough conference' with the rector, John the subdeacon, 'about the peace and best interests of the city, and its fealty to the pope'. Later on that year it was to the same rector that the king directed a letter asking the city to accept the new royal coinage.[229] In 1175 the rector Peter received a papal request to guarantee the exemption of the monks of Montecassino from the city's market dues.[230] In 1184 the pope addressed a mandate to the rector Ayroldus to ensure that the customs of the city's colony of Amalfitans and Ravellesi were acknowledged.[231]

However, no other papal administrative officials were established in the city, and the one reference to a papal chamberlain of Benevento in 1168 is probably linked to Alexander III's extended domicile there.[232]

---

[227] Loud, 'Politics, piety and ecclesiastical patronage', pp. 287–8.
[228] Loud, 'A provisional list', pp. 4–6. The anti-pope was John of Struma, who had taken the name Calixtus III.
[229] *Falco*, pp. 232, 234, 238. [230] *Italia Pontificia*, ix. 43 no. 108.
[231] See above p. 116 n. 220. [232] Girgensohn, 'Documenti beneventani', pp. 305–6 no. 10.

Until the 1180s there were few 'formal' layers to local administration, which consisted essentially of the rector, judges and notaries. In the kingdom there were two basic tiers of higher officials: the master and local justiciars, alongside the chamberlains and constables, followed by a lower rung constituted by a chief city magistrate (*strategotus, catepan*), the civic judges and a host of other lesser officials (often called *baiulus*). The result in Benevento was that the rector was even more reliant upon the cooperation of the local governing hierarchy. A settlement reached in 1157 'per interlocutionem domini rectoris et iudicum' was typical.[233] On another occasion, in 1160, the rector ordered the suspension of some contested building works until the judge and some *probi viri* had inspected the site.[234] The majority of the rector's appearances were simply to witness, in the sacred Beneventan palace, private transactions. A group of four or six judges usually ran proceedings, according to civic custom and assisted by that enigmatic group, the *boni homines*. On occasion the parties to a dispute announced that legal proceedings had been avoided because they had reached 'a good conclusion and concord through the agreement of other good men, namely neighbours and friends'.[235] At other times we hear of agreements which were 'arbitrated by the commonly chosen (*communiter electi*) masters (*magistri*) and friends'.[236] Numerous documents refer to the continuance of a wide range of civic usages. Donations to minors, marriage agreements, a variety of matters relating to a woman's legal status, the renunciation and restoration of proprietorial rights, the assignment of patrons to a church and pledges against loans were all fulfilled *secundum legem et consuetudinem civitatis*.[237] Unfortunately Falco's chronicle, so useful to elucidate the informal role of the populace, which is otherwise concealed by the formulaic nature of charters, only extends to 1140, covering the rectorship of Guido and the first year of John's. Yet this limited coverage is enough to show that after the 1130s local elements were still as influential and the rector was not a dominant force. During Roger II's contacts with the rector John in 1140 the Beneventans were in both cases heavily involved. At the 'conference' Roger engaged in peace talks not only with the rector but also 'other Beneventans'. The later letter sent by the king, notifying an intended monetary change, was sent to the rector and the citizens, some of whom certainly provided the rector with subsequent 'counsel'. This role of the populace did not end at the

---

[233] *Cattedrale di Benevento*, no. 76.   [234] *Cattedrale di Benevento*, no. 81.
[235] *Montevergine*, iii. no. 276.   [236] *Montevergine*, vi. no. 524.
[237] *Montevergine*, iii. no. 291, iv. no. 383, vii. no. 626; Girgensohn, 'Documenti beneventani', pp. 310–13 no. 13; *Cattedrale di Benevento*, nos. 65, 79, 99, 100, 122.

same time as the extant version of Falco's chronicle. In the troubles of
1144 we hear nothing of a rector but instead are told that the Beneventans dispatched pleas to the king and that the archbishop attempted
to reach the pope only to be captured by a royal baron.[238] During the
royal siege of the city in 1155 the citizens offered notable resistance
and even 'killed their archbishop, Peter, whom they suspected of being
a royal partisan'.[239]

Here again one notes the similarity of the role enjoyed by the citizens
in Benevento with what obtained throughout southern Italy. An equal
likeness occurs in the importance of local civic officials, the way they
governed and the strong theme of underlying continuity. Mention
has already been made of the long career of the chronicler Falco of
Benevento as both notary and judge (1107–43) through a period of
huge political upheaval.[240] Falco's son, Trasemundus, also a notary, was
attested from 1137 to 1188.[241] The work of Zazo has uncovered
numerous further examples and notably identified the survival of many
judges (and their kin-groups) who were active in the 1120s and 30s
through to the 1140s and 50s.[242] To this can be added an especially
interesting example of a family maintaining its rank in society. In documents from 1133, 1149, 1159 and 1193 we see the descendants of Stephen
Sculdascio, the eleventh-century rector of Benevento.[243] Moreover,
Stephen's grandson Jacob, who inherited some of his property in the
platea maior, became a Beneventan consul only to be murdered sometime before December 1199.[244] Elsewhere, one particular city judge,
called Nicholas, was involved in a remarkable and diverse range of
affairs, which can only emphasise his standing. It seems that he was the
official who at some point before 1175, along with Pope Alexander III,
Hubald, the cardinal bishop of Ostia, and the archdeacon Rainulf, had
successfully entreated the archbishop of Benevento to transfer a church
in benefice.[245] In 1175 Count Roger of Andria donated territory to the
Beneventan nunnery of S. Maria de Porta Somma with the advice of
judge Nicholas.[246] In 1184 Nicholas authenticated the pope's confirmation

---

[238] *Chronicon Ignoti Monachi Cisterciensis Sanctae Mariae de Ferraria*, p. 27.
[239] *Romuald*, p. 238 (English translation in *Falcandus*, p. 222).
[240] See above p. 80.   [241] Loud, 'Genesis and context', p. 184 and n. 38.
[242] Zazo, 'Professioni, arti e mestieri in Benevento', pp. 149–66.
[243] *Montevergine*, iii. nos. 212, 291, iv. no. 375, ix. no. 897.
[244] *Die Register Innocenz III – 2. Pontifikatsjahr, 1199/1200*, ed. O. Hageneder, W. Maleckzek and
A. A. Strnad (Vienna, 1979), pp. 419–20 no. 216.
[245] *Cattedrale di Benevento*, no. 92.
[246] E. Jamison, 'The Abbess Bethlem of S. Maria di Porta Somma and the barons of the Terra
Beneventana', in *Oxford Essays in Medieval History Presented to Herbert Edward Salter* (Oxford,
1934), appendix, p. 64 no. 10.

of the customs of the Amalfitans and Ravellesi dwelling in the city.[247] It is likely that this was the same judge who signed the foundation charter in 1197 of the fraternity of S. Spirito of Benevento, a devotional association open to the whole lay population, and also the city's civic statutes of 1202.[248]

At some point, however, in the second half of the twelfth century a major development, not seen elsewhere in southern Italy other than at Gaeta and Naples, had occurred in the civic administration: the appearance of consuls. The shadowy emergence of a consulate warns us of the extent to which sources can give a falsely limited impression of urban activities. It is a caution that must be kept in mind for all cities. Indeed this first record of Beneventan consuls is frustratingly laconic – a papal mandate of 1184 addressed simply to the rector, judges and consuls. Further on in the document a witness testifies that the Amalfitans and Ravellesi, who lived in the city, had enjoyed their own customs 'from the time of the consulate in which Cratus was consul'. Other witnesses recognised the customs from the time of the rector William (murdered in 1128), from the time of Innocent II (1130–43), from the time of the fire (1141 or 1155), from the time of Adrian IV (1154–9) and some simply from twenty-four to thirty years ago. In short, there is no certain time reference into which Cratus' consulate can be fixed.[249] An order directed by Pope Alexander III to only the clergy, judges and people of Benevento in 1169 could suggest that at that point the consulate did not exist, but this is still far from conclusive proof.[250] Just as the process of their formation remains obscure so do the functions of the consuls at this early stage. After 1184 no further mention of consuls occurs until the 1190s, when such references increase. The city's statutes, recorded in 1202, reveal that the consulate was by that time a developed institution central to civic government.[251] It is difficult to estimate how far back we can project any of the findings provided from 1202. However, the consulate's complexity as portrayed in the document, and the appeal at its outset to respect the existing civic statutes as they had already been drafted, suggest that its origins are undoubtedly to be found in the period covered here (if not earlier) and that they may have been popular, rather than papal, in inspiration.

---

[247] Borgia, *Memorie istoriche*, iii. 163–6.
[248] Houben, 'Confraternite e religiosità nel Mezzogiorno medievale (secc. XII–XV)', in *Mezzogiorno normanno-svevo*, pp. 361–2, 374–5; see below pp. 157–8 for the city statutes.
[249] Borgia, *Memorie istoriche*, iii. 163–6.   [250] *Cattedrale di Benevento*, no. 89.
[251] See for example P. F. Kehr, 'Una bolla inedita di Papa Celestino III per la città di Benevento', *Samnium* 13 (1940), pp. 1–4 and below pp. 157–60.

By 1189 urban government in Benevento, as elsewhere on the mainland, was growing in complexity. But just as in the kingdom, this did not mean that the local community had less control over its affairs, rather the opposite. The Beneventans, through their 'independent' position, were able to develop self-government further. Yet the more explicit vocabulary for urban government at Benevento may mask only a difference in degree, not kind, from most other South Italian cities. We should not forget that Benevento owed this language and terminology to peculiar circumstances. It is the only South Italian city for which a highly detailed, urban-focused chronicle has survived from this period, and the only one to have been ruled by a power that had strong connections with central and northern Italy.

One might posit that the monarchs' 'bargain' with the cities was struck early enough to legitimise his position and the informal one of the communities and their customs, giving them the force of tradition. Southern Italy's urban communities did not need to articulate their position more clearly. The opposite seems to have occurred in northern Italy, where there was no single authority sufficiently powerful or acceptable from which the community's new position could be recognised permanently. Indeed, it has been argued that the development of communal government arose not from revolutionary impulses but was actually 'a conservative reaction to crisis'. In contrast to southern Italy, by the 1150s informal styles of government had to become more formalised and a more explicit vocabulary created, and out of this emerged a problem of legitimacy.[252] Frederick Barbarossa was not willing to give it, until forced to do so at Constance in 1183. By this time the communes of northern Italy were already creating their own traditions of legitimacy, although how successful they were is open to question. The maintenance of pre-communal structures such as the assembly and the sacralising of the commune, through association with the Church and local patron saints, were attempts to substitute imperial sanction.[253] The later codification of communal civic statutes may have been a response to a sense of external threat. South Italian urban communities may well have felt secure enough under royal rule not to need to establish similarly detailed written statutes.

The modern assumption that the Norman kingdom represented a unique authoritative and bureaucratic state has recently begun to be

---

[252] Wickham, *Courts and Conflict*, p. 19; R. Bordone, 'L'amministrazione del regno d'Italia', *BISME* 96 (1990), pp. 133–56.

[253] Coleman, 'Representative assemblies', p. 195; A. Thompson, *Cities of God. The Religion of the Italian Communes 1125–1325* (Pennsylvania, 2005), pp. 4, 114–15, 132–6.

questioned.[254] The corollary of this is a reassessment, attempted here, of royal relations with the mainland cities. Maturation rather than oppression of local government and urban society characterised the period 1139–89. It was actually assisted in this process by the protective guidance of the Norman monarchy. For most of the three decades after 1189, however, that secure superstructure would be lacking. The manner in which civic government still functioned in this later period was the result of over a century of often turbulent evolution. It proves that the cities had not grown dangerously dependent on the monarchy and had retained control of their own government to such an extent as to be able to operate effectively without it.

[254] Matthew, *Norman Kingdom*, pp. 165–9.

Chapter 5

FROM THE NORMANS TO THE STAUFEN
(1189–1220)

> The kingdom lies desolate,
> Destroyed and in confusion,
> And thus it must suffer
> The arrival of all its enemies;
> Because of this all should wail and lament.

So the chronicler Richard of S. Germano bemoaned the passing of William II in November 1189.[1] The king's death without direct heirs threatened to disrupt the balance that had developed between the region's cities and the public power.[2] There were two candidates for the throne: Count Tancred of Lecce, previously a master justiciar and illegitimate child of Roger II's eldest son, and Henry VI of Germany, the son of Emperor Frederick Barbarossa and husband since 1186 of Roger II's daughter Constance. The immediate momentum was with Tancred, who was native, present and familiar with the machinery of the kingdom's government. In January 1190 Tancred was crowned king in Palermo, but he had to contend with Henry's continuing claims and a small German force that briefly entered the kingdom that year. The dual claim for the throne left some confusion over who was in power. Not all cities openly supported Tancred. In documents at Capua and Aversa, in July and September 1190 respectively, local officials candidly stated that they did not know who was ruling.[3] Presumably, amidst

---

[1] *Rich. S. Germano*, p. 7 lines 30–5.

[2] Robert of Torigni claimed that William II had a son called Bohemond, and if correct the boy doubtless died young, *Roberti de Monte Cronica*, ed. L. C. Bethmann, *MGH* SS VI (Hanover, 1844), p. 532 a. 1182.

[3] *Montevergine*, ix. no. 839 from Capua says that 'after the death of King William II . . . the rule of the *regnum* was not generally arranged, therefore . . . at the start of this document we do not place the name of the king and the year of his rule'; *CDNA*, pp. 265–5 no. 140 from Aversa says, 'it is not known who should rule as *dominus* in this *regnum*, therefore his name and reigning date have not been placed in this document.'

the uncertainty, local government functioned in a quasi-independent manner. Richard of S. Germano mentions movements in favour of Henry in Campania and Apulia. The *Annales Casinenses* specifies that Aversa and Capua rebelled and that the latter only surrendered to Tancred's forces 'on imprudent advice, as was always the case'.[4] It is worth noting that Capua's archbishop, Matthew, resolutely supported Henry VI's claim and became a chief adviser to him.[5] At Troia, the city's bishop, Walter of Pagliaria, seems to have also immediately sided with the German candidate. On the other hand, Hugh, the dean of the cathedral of Troia (and later archbishop of Siponto), was a partisan of the king's.[6] A charter of 1190 from the city remains neutral, with no reference to any superior authority.[7] However, sometime in 1190 the bishop of Troia, its clergy and its people, alongside a major native rival of Tancred's, Count Roger of Andria, reportedly attacked Foggia, sacking three suburbs and various churches.[8] It seems Foggia was ostensibly targeted on account of its allegiance to Tancred. But this allegiance was very much set in a local context of rivalry between the neighbouring settlements. Tancred appeared willing to give the Foggians episcopal status, which would have diminished Troia's. Wider conflicts were masking local ones and the same would occur elsewhere.[9]

Tancred was an energetic campaigner, manoeuvring around the mainland. By the end of 1190 most, but not all, cities seem to have accepted Tancred.[10] However, in such a strained climate, it was inevitable that greater authority in urban government would devolve upon local officials and the community. Both had experienced an active role in local government under previous kings and must by now have acquired notable responsibilities. This was certainly the case at Naples. The decreased scope of royal government, the external threat and the already prominent position of native elements in civic government combine to explain Tancred's concession to that city in June 1190. The act confirmed the operation of a consulate and various other judicial, trading and financial rights.[11] Only the consuls and citizens of Naples could

---

[4] *Annales Casinenses*, p. 314.   [5] Loud, *Church and Society*, pp. 187–8.
[6] G. A Loud, 'The papacy and the rulers of southern Italy, 1058–1198', in *The Society of Norman Italy*, ed. G. A. Loud and A. J. Metcalfe (Leiden, 2002), p. 183 n. 118.
[7] *Montevergine*, ix. no. 840.   [8] *Troia*, no. 139, pp. 380–1.
[9] For example between Aversa and Naples, see below pp. 133, 144.
[10] *Rich. S. Germano*, p. 9.
[11] *Tancredi et Willelmi III Regum Diplomata*, pp. 15–18 no. 6 – the concession giving the city control over its own mint appears to be a later interpolation; see also pp. 3–5 no. 1, in which Tancred gave a charter of protection to Barletta in April 1190. It included judicial and financial privileges but disclosed nothing on urban government, aside from the possible presence of a royal bailiff in the city.

dispense justice, not royal justiciars. The citizens were also exempt from service in the royal fleet. The grant was made partly to win political support and may offer an atypical picture of civic government. However, like many politically motivated actions, a basis in reality must have existed for it to have carried any value. The consular officials represent an apparently new development. But it is likely, given the sudden and matter-of-fact nature of their appearance, that the consuls, and most of the governing arrangements found in the concession, had either functioned beforehand or developed from earlier foundations. Indeed, the document confirmed certain *pacta* agreed *already* between the city's *nobiles* and the remainder of the *populus*. Moreover, these pacts were described as 'in scriptis autenticis'; that is they had a written and not only oral tradition.[12] In fact, in the previous month the Neapolitans, or more accurately 'Aligernus Cotunus, consuls, constables, knights and the whole populace', made an important public grant to Amalfitans in the city.[13] The document was signed by twenty-one consuls and Aligernus Cotunus, who, untraceable before 1190, appears to preside over the consulate. Aligernus' role may have evolved from the earlier one of *compalatius*, and, if so, he may in essence still have been a representative of the king.[14] The text was drawn up by the notary of the city's archbishop, which suggests the tacit support of the Neapolitan Church, and ratified 'by the common counsel and will of the city'. There is no reference to royal authority. It is possible that similar conditions were current in other cities, if not quite to the same extent as at Naples.

When Henry VI, recently crowned emperor, finally crossed into the kingdom in April 1191, the uncertainty intensified. As in the 1130s, it is clear that urban communities had to make their own independent decisions. Inevitably, factions arose within cities, with all that this implies for the committed role of the community in its own affairs. Various counts from the kingdom's northern provinces sided with Henry.[15] The main thrust of the attack centred on the Terra di Lavoro, where most of the region, including Aversa and Capua, fell to the emperor; but not Naples. Peter of Eboli's poem informs us of the chaotic atmosphere within two cities, Salerno and Capua, during Henry's expedition. Putting aside Peter's pro-imperial biases, strained metaphors and literary

---

[12] C. Vetere, *Le consuetudini di Napoli – Il testo e la tradizione* (Salerno, 1999), pp. 17–18 n. 8.

[13] R. Filangieri, 'Note al *Privilegium Libertatis* concesso dai Napoletani agli Amalfitani in 1190', *PBSR* 24 (1956), pp. 107–16.

[14] Fuiano, 'Napoli normanna e sveva', p. 446.

[15] Such as the counts of Molise, Fondi and Caserta, *Rich. S. Germano*, p. 12. See also for example D. R. Clementi, 'Calendar of the diplomas of the Hohenstaufen Emperor Henry VI concerning the kingdom of Sicily', *QF* 35 (1955), pp. 99–101 no. 4.

constructions, it is possible to find value in his account. While Henry was besieging Naples, a leading Salernitan approached the imperial camp and requested that Constance enter Salerno, 'the city of her father', where there was a 'wavering loyalty'.[16] Constance's subsequent arrival in the city was met by a perfumed, celebratory welcoming procession. Yet almost immediately, Peter informs us, Constance 'perceives the loyalty to Tancred in the city': 'many people, in groups, whisper quietly, [and] talk to each other of the changed prospects' and combat erupts.[17] At the same time a legate of Henry VI chose, presumably pro-imperial, 'men from the many distinguished people' at Salerno to go to the imperial camp outside Naples for discussions with Henry, who had contracted tertian fever.[18] Meanwhile, in Salerno, Count Richard of Acerra, Tancred's leading commander, and the city's archbishop, Nicholas, rallied the citizens against Henry. Peter of Eboli suggests their successes against the emperor were assisted by gold and royal gifts – so much so that Henry's leading generals 'were awash with bronze' and his men were 'belching with gold'. As Henry, sick, withdrew from the siege of Naples and, by September, the kingdom, Tancred's followers filled Salerno with various conflicting rumours on the emperor's health – just as 'the harsh buzzing of the bees sounds angrily in a smoky cave'. Finally, 'the savage people of Salerno, incited by bad advice' taunted Constance, while she sheltered in the Terracina palace.[19] The queen was captured and dispatched to Sicily to secure Tancred's favour.[20] Peter of Eboli also offers a lively account of the climate within Capua, while Tancred's troops were attempting to retake that city from imperial control. With Henry retreating to Germany, Peter tells of a desperate rallying speech by the German commander, Conrad Muscancervello, to his men in Capua. Conrad shouts 'there is no hope of flight, because an enemy besieges us outside [and] an enemy is within, no house is without an enemy.' The citizens were again likened to a swarm of bees protecting their honey as 'the whole city [became] roused up by the Germans . . . crying out

---

[16] *Peter of Eboli*, p. 35 Bk I.XV lines 396–9 and n. 1 suggest that the Salernitan envoy was called an 'archoticon', meaning one of the *ottimati* (elite), and was a certain John Princeps – a relation of the Guarna family. The illustration of this event (tav. 16, p. 129) names the Salernitan messengers as John Princeps, Romuald and Cioffus. For a more recent edition of Peter of Eboli, *Liber ad honorem Augusti sive de rebus Siculis: Codex 120 II der Bürgerbibliothek Bern*, ed. T. Kölzer and M. Stähli (Sigmaringen, 1994).

[17] *Peter of Eboli*, pp. 36–9 Bk I.XV–XVI.

[18] *Peter of Eboli*, pp. 39–40 Bk I.XVII. There is some confusion over the identity of these leading men. Peter mentions an Alfanides Princeps and an Aldrisio the archdeacon (who may be the same person), alongside a Romuald, called 'the scales of justice' (a judge?). It has been suggested that these individuals were linked to the Guarna, some of whom seem to have favoured Henry, Jamison, *Admiral Eugenius*, p. 81 n. 2. See also above n. 16 for the earlier envoys from Salerno.

[19] *Peter of Eboli*, pp. 41–6 Bk I.XX.   [20] *Rich. S. Germano*, p. 13.

that it acknowledged as king none other than Tancred.' The result was 'the unspeakable horror of civil war' inside Capua.[21] The city was indeed recaptured, evidently with inside assistance, by royal forces, and some 'nobiles Capuae' were imprisoned.[22]

The leading protagonists are citizens, both lay and ecclesiastic, acting individually or as a collective. The emphasis is on rapidly changing attitudes, the process by which these can be altered by rumour and money and above all the emergence of rival groups. It is clear that we should not deduce too much from the apparent position or policy of a city in relation to who ostensibly controlled it. Power fluctuated swiftly between different factions within the city walls. Attitudes were influenced primarily by calculations of immediate gain or security, and not by high-minded conceptual debates on which candidate had the best dynastic claim or whether their prospects were better served in a monarchy or an empire. Capua had shown no signs of supporting Tancred in 1190, its archbishop was a staunch imperialist and it apparently fell to Henry without resistance in 1191.[23] Yet Peter's account, though embroidered, implies that the Capuans eagerly sided with Tancred, a move corroborated by the *Annales Casinenses*. It could be that the majority of the civic community had got wind of Henry VI's setbacks and, perhaps with some disenchantment with the close German presence in the city, simply tried the alternative option.

At the same time during Henry's invasion, and surely in response to it, Tancred issued another wide-ranging grant, this time to Gaeta, which illustrates a more formal and extensive recognition of the hands-on governing role which urban communities were adopting at this point.[24] The document, which referred to a civic 'commune', allowed the city the freedom to select its own consuls, monopolies over dyeing and minting, wide judicial exemptions and the continued operation of local customs, supervised by local judges who were chosen by the Gaetans. This 'communal' government was still connected to the wider royal network. It might have been an empty exercise, but the judges still had to receive royal approval after being selected by the inhabitants and were 'to keep all the laws of the king and of you [the Gaetans]'. Criminal cases, and those concerning treason, were still to be dealt with by the

---

[21] *Peter of Eboli*, pp. 60–3 Bk I.XXVI.
[22] *Annales Casinenses*, p. 315 says that Count Richard of Acerra 'marched out with an army and with the people of Naples, and took Capua through the betrayal of its citizens, where many Germans perished by the sword'.
[23] The first extant document from Capua recognising Tancred is not until April 1191, *Montevergine*, ix. no. 856.
[24] *Tancredi et Willelmi III Regum Diplomata*, pp. 42–6 no. 18.

magna curia at Palermo.[25] The office of *baiulus*, which before 1189 had been akin to the *strategotus* and seemed to be high-ranking, was maintained. But the *baiulus* had to be an inhabitant of Gaeta and was not to be simultaneously a consul or *consiliarius*. The latter title appears to be a new one. Like its Neapolitan precursor, the content of the grant depicts a type of urban government that already had roots. Indeed, Tancred's grant to Gaeta claimed to be a confirmation 'of all the practices and usages' which the citizens 'have had from ancient times and from the time of King Roger, our grandfather of happy memory, until now'.

Although Henry had left the kingdom, German garrisons remained in some frontier posts in the Abruzzi and the Terra di Lavoro. Sporadic raids continued and contributed to the instability. In Aversa, for example, documents were dated by the reign of Henry VI from August 1191 into 1192. Thereafter no charters survive from the city during the remainder of Tancred's rule, and the king retook Aversa in 1193.[26] Tancred's reign was one of continuing uncertainty, and he was forced to undertake a programme of fortifying and garrisoning key cities and strategic points. A royal presence was thus maintained in many mainland cities. Tancred himself was occasionally found in some of the major cities, visiting Barletta, Salerno and Brindisi between January and August 1192.[27] Until Tancred's death in February 1194 there are some signs that central administration had not entirely collapsed and was still connected to the cities. For what it is worth, documents did at least carry Tancred's name at Conversano, Bari, Monopoli and Taranto, and in the latter three cities judges were still called 'royal'.[28] From the Salerno region, the Cava archives contain documents consistently bearing Tancred's name from as early as January 1190.[29] Even at Capua, charters sporadically recognise Tancred, and seemingly also at Troia – both cities with prelates who vigorously backed Henry.[30] Urban government showed little sign of notable change. The same local officials appeared mostly in the same positions, and in places they were linked in to the central administration, which appeared to survive, if in a reduced form. At

---

[25] However, the document envisages that when a Prince of Capua will have been appointed, these cases will be transferred to his court instead; an interesting allusion to the possible revival of the principality as a territorial unit.

[26] *CDNA*, pp. 268–9 nos. 141–2, pp. 272–4 no. 144; *Montevergine* ix. no. 887; *Annales Casinenses*, p. 317.

[27] *Tancredi et Willelmi III Regum Diplomata*, pp. 54–8 nos. 23–4, pp. 66–7 no. 27.

[28] *Conversano*, nos. 141–2; *CDBV*, nos. 155–9.   [29] *Cava*, *Arca* xiii.57.

[30] Capua: *Pergamene di Capua*, ii.i 44–6 no. 6; *Montevergine*, ix. no. 856; *Pergamene normanne*, nos. 35–6; Troia: *Montevergine*, x. no. 924, the document dated 21 February 1194 recognises Queen Constance. It appears that Constance's name replaced that of Tancred and/or William III when the charter was renewed under Frederick II.

Salerno, from June to November 1190, Tancred was in touch with Darius *palatinus camerarius et magister doane baronum*, head of the royal financial administration for the mainland provinces, over the concession of the revenues of the city's dyeworks to the archbishop. Roger Butrumiles, *strategotus* of Salerno, who appears to have been from a leading urban kin-group, was also involved in the correspondence.[31] A document from Ascoli Satriano, near Troia, shows that the master captains and justiciars of Apulia and Terra di Lavoro, Berard Gentilis, count of Lesina, and Hugh Lupin, count of Conversano, dealt with the fortification of the settlement.[32] Both of these officials were active in William II's reign.[33] In May 1191 Tancred restored to the *fideles cives* of Trani any possessions that they had lost. The following year Pope Celestine III confirmed to Samarus, archbishop of Trani, 'the tithe of the royal revenues at Trani and Barletta' which had already been donated by Tancred.[34] In November 1191 'sacred royal letters' were shown by the abbot of S. Lorenzo of Aversa to the judges and *catepan* of Foggia concerning disputed land.[35] In 1192 Tancred confirmed King William II's grant to the monastery of S. Gregorio Armeno of Naples. It included exemption from mill taxes, on the royal mills in the region of Capua, and a portion of the royal revenues from the salt-works in Naples.[36] But few higher royal officials appear in the charter documentation for the cities during Tancred's reign.[37] A master chamberlain called Peter appeared at Brindisi in 1192.[38] Darius was still attested in the Salerno region in July 1193 with the title *privatus palatinus camerarius et magister regie duane baronum*.[39] At Taranto, in October 1193, the city's archbishop restored some revenues to the canons and clerics of the cathedral, and did so before John de Butrinio, justiciar and castellan of Taranto, as well as a proto-judge and two royal judges.[40] But for most cities only a handful of charters survive for this period. In fact, only a few justiciars are known at all for Tancred's reign, such as Robert de Venusio, who appeared in 1192.[41] Jamison noted a slight restructuring

---

[31] *Tancredi et Willelmi III Regum Diplomata*, pp. 10–5 nos. 4–5, pp. 20–3 nos. 7–8; see above p. 95 n. 88 for the Butrumiles family.
[32] *Montevergine*, ix. no. 847.
[33] D. R. Clementi, 'An administrative document of 1190 from Apulia', *PBSR* 24 (1956), pp. 101–6.
[34] *Trani*, nos. 81–2 (*Tancredi et Willelmi III Regum Diplomata*, pp. 28–9 no. 11).
[35] *CDNA*, pp. 270–2 no. 143.
[36] *Le pergamene di San Gregorio Armeno (1141–1198)*, ed. R. Pilone (Salerno, 1996), no. 44.
[37] Jamison, *Admiral Eugenius*, p. 87.
[38] *Codice diplomatico brindisino*, vol. I, 492–1299, ed. G-M. Monti (Bari, 1977), no. 28.
[39] Jamison, *Admiral Eugenius*, p. 98; Cava, *Arca* xliii.83.   [40] *Taranto*, pp. 39–45 no. 11.
[41] Jamison, *Admiral Eugenius*, pp. 147–8 n. 5; E. Cuozzo, 'Corona, contee e nobiltà feudale nel regno di Sicilia. All'indomani dell'elezione di re Tancredi d'Altavilla', in *Medioevo Mezzogiorno*

of higher royal officials under Tancred, with counts Hugh Lupin of Conversano, Berard Gentilis of Lesina and Richard of Carinola all assuming the 'captain' title in one format or another. Others, like Robert de Venusio, adopted 'constable' within their labels. Perhaps, in the circumstances, these offices developed a more conspicuous military role, and as a result their duties may have been less concerned with urban government. Conversano, which had been part of the royal demesne in the late 1180s, had been given to the aforesaid Hugh Lupin in 1190. Yet Hugh's additional administrative role took him away from Conversano, and the vacancy again must have been filled by local figures.

The little that is known on the way urban government functioned in the years 1189 to 1194 – and it is only little – suggests that the cities had already been accustomed, under the Norman monarchy, to some freedom of action within their internal affairs. Tancred's policies did not alter this. He had to act pragmatically and recognise the limited scope of royal authority that he could hope to exercise vis-à-vis the cities. The provincial royal administrative structures must have been disrupted. In line with this he also had to be generous to gain their support: hence the king's benevolent attitude towards Naples, Gaeta and others. Many of Tancred's grants provided fiscal exemptions and financial rewards. But it seems that Tancred was doing little more than confirming the status quo and giving open recognition to styles of urban government that had tacitly functioned under his predecessors. This candid admission was where the novelty of Tancred's policy towards the kingdom's cities lay.

Tancred's sudden death in February 1194 left his wife, Sibylla, as regent for their young son, William III. Where charters survive it appears that some cities recognised the boy-king as ruler.[42] The only charter from Aversa in this period notably does not carry the name of any authority, while for other cities, like Conversano and Trani, there are simply no suitable documents.[43] Evidence indicates the maintenance of at least a façade of a royal governing framework.[44] However, by August, Henry VI had re-entered the kingdom. Learning from the 1191 expedition, he avoided costly sieges and bypassed the main urban centres and fortresses.[45] It seems that central government all but ceased on the

---

Mediterraneo – studi in onore di Mario Del Treppo, ed. G. Rossetti and G. Vitolo (Naples, 2000), pp. 254–5.

[42] Cava charters carry William's name from April 1194 (Cava, *Arca* xliii.106); at Bari in April (*CDBV*, no. 163); Monopoli in May (*CDNA*, pp. 277–8 no. 146); at Troia in June (*Montevergine*, x. no. 935).

[43] *Montevergine*, x. no. 927.

[44] See for example *Tancredi et Willelmi III Regum Diplomata*, pp. 93–4 no. 2.

[45] D. R. Clementi, 'Some unnoticed aspects of the Emperor Henry VI's conquest of the Norman kingdom of Sicily', *Bulletin of the John Rylands Library* 36 (1953–4), pp. 328–59.

mainland. Moreover, the royal fleet, so vital in the defence of 1191, was inactive. The Genoese and Pisan allies of Henry were able to proceed unhindered along the south Italian coastline. The cities of southern Italy were left to take their own path. According to the *Annales Casinenses*, Naples agreed with the Pisans to surrender in advance. The Genoese Annals simply state that the city and Count Aligern (very likely the aforementioned Aligernus Cotunus, who appears therefore to have retained his pre-eminence in the city from 1190), came to an agreement with the combined fleet from Pisa and Genoa. Just prior to this, the fleet had received the surrender of Gaeta and 'oaths of fealty from the bishop, consuls and people of the city'.[46] Henry did stop at one main centre – Salerno – the scene of his wife's capture in 1191. Peter of Eboli described the emotional plea of the city's archdeacon to the citizens to surrender to the approaching emperor. Interestingly a Guarna, Philip, was also at the archdeacon's side.[47] But the city, having opted to resist, was stormed and then devastated.[48] The narrative sources then relate Apulia's fall seemingly without resistance.[49] This confirmed the fears of an anonymous author who had penned an impassioned letter to Peter, the treasurer of Palermo. The letter, written probably either in the spring of 1190 or 1194, envisaged the damage of 'the blast of enemy invasion' on the kingdom.[50] The author states 'I do not think any hope of reliance ought to be placed in the Apulians, who constantly plot revolution because of the pleasure they take in novelty.'[51] This was a somewhat unfair assessment, and such widespread defection had not materialised in the 1191 invasion. That it appears to have done so in 1194 reflected the need for expediency in the face of collapsing royal authority, and not inherent duplicity. This too was no different from events in some Campanian cities like Naples and Gaeta. In November,

---

[46] *Annales Casinenses*, p. 317; Jamison, *Admiral Eugenius*, p. 112; *Annali genovesi di Caffaro e de' suoi continuatori*, 5 vols., ed. L. T. Belgrano, *FSI* XI, XII, XIII, XIV, XIV (ii) (Genoa, 1890–1901, Rome 1923–9), ii, pp. 46–7. For Aligernus and his kin see below p. 192 n. 52.

[47] *Peter of Eboli*, pp. 82–3 Bk II.

[48] Roger of Howden, who was reasonably well informed on southern Italy, says that the more powerful (*potentiores*) citizens were either put to death or exiled and their wives and daughters were exposed to the army, *Chronica*, 4 vols., ed. W. Stubbs (Rolls Series, 1868–71), iii, p. 269.

[49] *Rich. S. Germano*, pp. 16–17 and *Annales Casinenses*, p. 317. Soon after 30 September Henry VI informed the Pisans, who were in advance of him, that he was proceeding quickly from Salerno and that Melfi (?), Potenza, Barletta, Bari, Molfetta, Giovinazzo, Siponto, Trani and others had fallen. The emperor expected the imminent capitulation of Brindisi and 'totius maritimae'; Clementi, 'Calendar', pp. 120–1 no. 24.

[50] Both dates are possible, although 1194 is perhaps more likely – see D. R. Clementi, 'The circumstances of Count Tancred's accession to the kingdom of Sicily, duchy of Apulia and the principality of Capua', in *Mélanges Antonio Marongiu – Studies Presented to the International Commission for the History of Representative and Parliamentary Institutions* 34 (Brussels, 1968), p. 72 n. 59.

[51] *Falcandus*, p. 254.

Henry had taken Palermo, William III and Tancred's widow, Sibylla, submitted, and he was crowned king on Christmas Day 1194. The kingdom of Sicily was now attached to the empire.

Many individuals gained or lost from Henry's victory, and others preserved their position by timely switches of allegiance. The Guarna family of Salerno, for instance, seemed to have generally favoured the imperial cause. Some members had attempted to negotiate the city's surrender to Henry. Most likely as reward, Philip Guarna (perhaps the same Philip mentioned by Peter of Eboli) was raised in 1195 to count of Marsico, and another relation, John Princeps, was briefly archbishop-elect of Salerno in 1195–6 (although he never obtained papal consecration), while Archbishop Nicholas was languishing in prison.[52] For the urban communities in general, after the initial chaos of the invasion, it is difficult to see how their positions changed. Henry VI issued a general *collecta* in 1197, but this expedient was not unknown to his Norman predecessors.[53] On the other hand, some cities received specific privileges in reward for their loyalty to the emperor. In March 1195 Henry VI recognised the fidelity of the *cives* of Gallipoli by confirming all liberties and customs held since King Roger II's reign. Incidentally this provides more evidence of Roger's policy of allowing civic customs to remain in operation.[54] In April, Aversa received a wide grant from Henry VI. The city was placed in the imperial demesne and had all the churches restored to it which Tancred had allegedly taken. The 'barons, knights and all citizens' were granted all the honours, usages and good customs in the time of both King Williams. The same groupings were also given freedom from particular duties and confirmation of all their holdings under the aforesaid kings. Only an Aversan could be appointed as judge or bailiff in the city. Possessions held by Neapolitans in the city were confiscated. Moreover any *Aversanus* who held property from a Neapolitan would henceforth hold it directly from the emperor. This was important, for there was continuing conflict between the two cities, which seems to have influenced their choice of candidate to support. In the 1190 privilege to Naples, Tancred had confirmed Neapolitan possessions in and around Aversa, some of which had been gained since King William II's death.[55] But some institutions within cities that had previously appeared to support Tancred also received privileges. The church of Trani, and its Archbishop Samarus, who had enjoyed good

---

[52] *Codice Perris*, p. 384 no. 196; N. Kamp, *Kirche und Monarchie im staufischen Königsreich Sizilien. 1. Prosoprographische Grundlegung. Bistümer unde Bischöfe des Königsreich 1194–1266*, 4 vols. (Munich, 1973–82), vol. I, pp. 432–5; see above p. 127 nn. 16, 18 and p. 132 n. 47.

[53] *Rich. S. Germano*, p. 18.   [54] Clementi, 'Calendar', pp. 150–1 no. 62.

[55] Clementi, 'Calendar', pp. 166–7 no. 79.

relations with Tancred, received imperial protection and the confirmation of all rights and customs since the time of King William (II?).[56]

The church of Taranto obtained a similar grant. Interestingly this particular award mentioned the annulment of some unspecified rights which Tancred had granted to all cities.[57] But, we might ask, what in practice could this annulment have entailed? Tancred does not appear to have issued any innovatory new privileges. He provided a more 'open' recognition of urban government as it stood under his predecessors, based on the current limitations of the royal administration. As we can see, Henry VI repeatedly issued confirmations of the situation as it existed in the time of King William II. His concern to stress his legitimacy and continuity with the earlier Norman kings was paramount to his ruling style. In real terms then, both Tancred and Henry's policies were essentially founded on the *status quo ante* November 1189. In the longer term, Henry surely envisaged reinstating closer royal supervision of the cities as it had been before that date. In doing so, the 'open' recognitions of Tancred's reign could be avoided, with the aim of reverting to the earlier royal tactic of a more tacit acknowledgement of urban freedoms wrapped up in a royal visage. If Naples's consulate disappears under Henry VI this may not need to be linked to the city's earlier opposition. Punishments were more likely to be immediate demonstrations of authority rather than major structural changes in urban government. Thus the consulate may have reverted to being a less conspicuously named city council that fitted with royal authority. Something similar may have occurred at Gaeta. The demolition of the city walls at Naples, Capua, Bari and Salerno may, however, have been one attempt at a wider reordering. These destructive acts seem to be more than simple reprisals and would probably have occurred sooner than 1195–6 if that was their sole purpose. Moreover, Bari had surrendered without a fight, while Aversa, despite its loyalty to Henry, had to gain special permission to maintain its walls.[58]

As importantly, had Henry VI wished to diverge greatly from earlier royal policy on the cities he had little prospect of making such fundamental changes. His wider imperial duties, and crusading ambitions, pulled him in various directions. He conducted a rapid tour of Calabria and Apulia in the spring of 1195, visiting among other places Bari, Barletta and Trani, where privileges were issued, mostly to mainland

[56] *Trani*, nos. 88–9 (Clementi, 'Calendar', pp. 164–5 nos. 77–8).
[57] *Italia Sacra*, ix 131–2 (Clementi, 'Calendar', pp. 137–8 no. 45).
[58] *Rich. of S. Germano*, p. 18; *Chronicon Ignoti Monachi Cisterciensis Sanctae Mariae de Ferraria*, p. 32; Clementi, 'An administrative document of 1190', p. 104; Clementi, 'Calendar', p. 166 no. 79 for permission for Aversa to keep its fortifications.

ecclesiastical institutions.[59] By the end of April, Henry had left the kingdom and would not return until November 1196. In December 1196 he was at Capua, in January 1197 at Barletta and the next month at Taranto before crossing over to Sicily in March. It was on the island that the emperor fell ill and died in September 1197. Of Henry's short reign only a small proportion was spent in the southern Italian mainland. Moreover, much of it was devoted to repressing disaffection and not to restructuring. The sources, although ambiguous, suggest that there remained much unrest, and two major court conspiracies were unearthed during Henry's reign.[60] It was not until 1196 that Count Richard of Acerra, Tancred's leading ally, was captured and savagely executed at Capua. Henry's conquest was so rapid, bypassing whole regions, that it should not be surprising that some cities did not immediately recognise the emperor's rule. A document from Capua, in December 1194 still used the regnal years of King William III, even after his submission to Henry VI.[61] Furthermore, a declaration at the end of a charter of March 1195, again from Capua, states:

because formerly our master King William III, as it pleased the Lord, gave way before the force and imperial power and lost the sceptre of his rule, at a time when the city of Capua had not yet inclined towards the control of the emperor, for that reason in this document, the name of the ruling power and the duration of its rule has not been written at the beginning.[62]

If we follow the charters, most cities, at least ostensibly, accepted Henry's rule, and at Capua a document from May 1195 carried the emperor's name.[63] But there is little sign of organised central government to supervise the urban communities, or that the royal administration of an earlier period was fully reinstated. Some high-ranking positions were created and most were filled by foreigners. The master captains and justiciars of Tancred's era disappear; their duties seemingly divided into an essentially military role, assumed by Diepold of Schweinspeunt and Conrad of Lützelnhard, and a judicial and administrative one, which fell

---

[59] Clementi, 'Calendar', pp. 153–4 no. 66, pp. 155–6 no. 68, p. 159 no. 71, pp. 165–7 nos. 78–9.

[60] *Rich. S. Germano*, p. 18; Jamison, *Admiral Eugenius*, pp. 146, 152–3 identifies areas in the Terra di Bari, Terra di Lavoro and the region of Salerno; *Rich. of S. Germano*, p. 18. According to the Marburg Annals, in 1197, 'all the cities and castles in Apulia and Sicily' rose in revolt, *Die Chronik Ottos von St. Blasien und Die Marbacher Annalen*, ed. and trans. F-J. Schmale (Darmstadt, 1998), pp. 196–8.

[61] *Pergamene normanne*, no. 37. [62] *Montevergine*, x. no, 965.

[63] *Pergamene normanne*, no. 38. From the region of Salerno, Cava charters carry Henry's name from October 1194 and in the same month also at Troia, Cava, *Arca* xliii.120; see also *Pergamene del monastero benedettino di S. Giorgio (1038–1698)*, ed. L. Cassese (Salerno, 1950), nos. 13–14; *Montevergine*, x. no. 942.

to Conrad of Querfurt, bishop-elect of Hildesheim. Conrad was also imperial chancellor and *legatus totius Italie et Sicilie*. Frederick of Hohenstadt was given the position of master chamberlain and Conrad, duke of Spoleto, that of *vicarius regni Sicilie*.[64] Some natives did obtain high positions: Walter of Pagliaria, bishop of Troia, became chancellor of the kingdom of Sicily and Matthew, archbishop of Capua, was an imperial *familiaris*.

But more important for the cities, in terms of their integration into the central administration, was the position of the lower-ranking royal officials. Significantly, only a few regional justiciars and chamberlains are recorded in this period and when they are they appear still to be from the kingdom.[65] Robert de Venusio, who was attested in Tancred's reign as justiciar and constable, had previously been a justiciar under William II and was so still under Henry VI.[66] In October 1196 Conrad of Querfurt was found at Brindisi, alongside Robert and Count Roger of Balvano, both called 'imperial justiciars', restoring lands.[67] In December of the same year, in the region of Bari, a John de Fraxineto, imperial justiciar, presided over a dispute between the monastery of S. Lorenzo of Aversa and Atto, an imperial *miles*. John was also lord of Turi, like his father, the royal baron Thomas de Fraxineto, who was attested in Barese charters in the 1170s, and was the great-grandson of Count Robert I of Conversano.[68] Finally, Eugenius son of John the admiral appeared at a court at Bari in August 1196, described as *familiaris* of Conrad of Querfurt.[69] Following the detective work of Jamison, this Eugenius would be the former royal admiral and master of the *duana baronum* at Salerno in the 1170s, who was attested from *c.* 1158 to 1202.[70] At the hearing in Bari, Eugenius' judgement in favour of S. Nicola of Bari was based on the latter's production of an earlier ruling, from the reign of William II, by Count Tancred of Lecce. The need for continuity with the past allowed for this reference to a man who had been Henry's rival for the throne.

None of this should detract from the disruption and bloodshed that characterised the years from 1189 to 1197. For most cities, the charter

---

[64] For these administrative posts see Jamison, *Admiral Eugenius*, pp. 146–8.
[65] For a complete list of the justiciars recorded in Apulia at this period see Martin, *Pouille*, pp. 802–4.
[66] See above p. 130 n. 41. [67] *Cod. dip. Brindisi*, no. 33.
[68] *CDBV*, nos. 133–5; Martin, *Pouille*, p. 860: In June 1197 both Robert de Venusio and John de Fraxineto, called imperial justiciars for Terra di Bari, were found at a court near Gravina, D. R. Clementi, 'Further documents concerning the administration of the province of *Apulia et Terra Laboris* during the reign of the Emperor Henry VI', *PBSR* 27 (1959), pp. 176–82 no. 4.
[69] Eugenius, though not present, was also referred to in a case of May 1197 at Bari as receiving letters from Conrad of Querfurt, who had been at Barletta, *CDBVI*, no. 4.
[70] Jamison, *Admiral Eugenius*, cal doc. nos. 1–40.

material deals with prosaic urban affairs and does not reveal to what extent the fundamental structures of urban life and government were altered. The recognition of Henry VI's rule in many documents represents the only discernible change, although at Bari and Trani judges were called imperial rather than royal.[71] There was the very occasional appearance of higher officials, but mostly these were long-serving figures with roots in the kingdom. Bari is one of the few cities where the sources allow reasonably detailed insight into the state of urban government. In doing so they also reveal that amidst the undoubted chaos of the 1190s there were at least some perceptible and continuing links with the pre-1189 period. In November 1195 Queen Constance confirmed to the church of Bari the city's tithe, just as it had been previously given by King William II to Tasselgardus, who had then been chamberlain.[72] Moreover, the archbishop of Bari could establish his own men to work alongside the *catepans* and bailiffs of the city in order to collect the revenues. The document also refers to the bailiffs' duty of receiving the *plateaticum* and *ancoraticum* in the port. From Barletta, in 1197 Conrad of Querfurt ordered the 'catepanii, iudices, petegarii et universis homines Bari' to follow old custom and not compel men of the church of S. Nicola of Bari to undertake galley service.[73] In the same year the master chamberlain Frederick of Hohenstadt presided over a court at Bari which restored some goods to a certain Alfarana.[74] Present were six imperial judges of Bari, including Petracca Buffus (attested in office from 1174 to 1202) and Richard of Barletta, *curator mortizii Bari* (guardian of the goods of the deceased people of Bari).[75] More revealingly the *curia* was held in the house of Roger de Amirato. Clearly an important figure, this Roger may be the Roger son of Maio the great admiral (the leading court official under King William I) who witnessed a document in the city later on in the year.[76] Another Bari charter of 1197 shows a local judge presiding over an 'imperial curia of our lord emperor'.[77] But this was very much a traditional city court. Also present at the court were 'certain *sapientes* of our city', while the dowry in question had been set 'iuxta morem barensium'.[78] Finally, Bartholomew de Simbulo, *catepan* of Bari, sold the *baiulatio* of Bari, and some of its

---

[71] *CDBI*, no. 66; *CDBVI*, nos. 4–7; *Trani*, nos. 85 (where one of the judges is called imperial *and* royal), 86, 87, 88; *Pergamene di Barletta. Archivio Capitolare*, no. 228.

[72] *CDBI*, no. 65.   [73] *CDBVI*, no. 3.   [74] *CDBVI*, no. 4.

[75] Petracca appeared in other charters of this period, *CDBVI*, nos. 5, 6. For more on the local importance of Petracca see above p. 104 n. 148 and below p. 191.

[76] *CDBVI*, no. 5 and see below pp. 194–5.   [77] *CDBVI*, no. 7.

[78] *CDBVI*, no. 6 refers to 'civilem barensium consuetudinem' and *CDBI*, no. 66 speaks simply of a 'barensis curia' in 1196.

surrounding territories, for the period from 1 May 1196 to 30 April 1197, at the huge price of 660 ounces of gold. The four men who purchased the *baiulatio* were 'omnes barenses'.[79] The *baiulatio* was run by local men and by being farmed out was detached further from central administration. In theory those purchasing the *baiulatio* could administer it independently, providing the annual fee was met.

In most cities searching for continuity of local officials in this era yields mixed results. Some disappear (or have seemingly short careers) and others emerge at times which coincide with great disruption.[80] But this does not necessarily reveal a great deal. Death, natural or otherwise, dismissal, promotion, retirement, the nature of the surviving documentation, could all be explanations that might be linked to the political upheaval and just as likely might not be. On the other hand there are various officials who do survive such periods, which, along with the type of evidence found at Bari, suggests that urban society had a core resilience in the face of disorder raging in its midst.[81]

---

[79] *CDBVI*, no. 29; the annual sum was split into sevenths, which may suggest seven individuals in total.

[80] For example at Capua, a man with the distinctive name Gilius was attested as a notary from 1183 to 1185, and it could be that this Gilius was the same as the later judge recorded in the city from 1189 to 1191. *Pergamene di Capua*, i. 96–7 no. 41, ii. 42–4 no. 5; *Pergamene normanne*, nos. 27, no. 30, *Parte seconda*, no. 139; *Montevergine*, ix. nos. 839, 856. This seems confirmed by a document of 1202 in which a charter was handed over which had been written by Gilius the judge 'who was then a notary', *Le pergamene sveve della Mater Ecclesia capuana*, 2 vols., ed. G. Bova (Naples, 1998–9), i. no. 5. The documents in which Gilius the judge appears show the general confusion. One of December 1189 carries King William II's name, while another of the same month does not, saying that the king's death had left 'the kingdom as if vacant'. Gilius appears in a document of 1190 without a ruler's name, because, it says, 'the rule of the kingdom was not arranged'. His final record is in a charter of April 1191 carrying Tancred's name. To what extent was Gilius' subsequent disappearance from the documentation linked to the turbulent events in Capua?

[81] At Bari the protonotary Ravellensis was recorded from 1155 to 1199: *CDBI*, nos. 58, 61, 84; *CDBV*, nos. 113, 161–62, frag. 21–22; *CDBVI*, nos. 2, 5; *Pergamene di Barletta del Reale Archivio*, no. 32; at Troia, the judge Nicholas de Sperano was attested from November 1189, just before King William's death, to 1235: *Troia*, nos. 109, 121, 129, 133, 141, 143, 149, 151; *Le Cartulaire de S.Matteo di Sculgola en Capitanate (registri d'istrumenti di S.Maria del Gualdo) (1177–1239)*, 2 vols., ed. J-M. Martin (Bari, 1987), ii, pp. 479–82 no. 275 and possibly 466–9 no. 269; at Aversa a judge Roger is attested from 1174 to 1206 (see above p. 104); still in Aversa, a notary Jacob is recorded in 1173, 1182 and 1187, *Montevergine*, vi. no. 567; *CDNA*, pp. 220–2 no. 118, 250–1 no. 133; a judge of the same name is then documented in the city from 1191 to 1217 – the references are too numerous to record in their entirety but include: *Montevergine*, vol. ix. no. 887, x. no. 927, xi. nos. 1017, 1037; *CDNA*, pp. 266–7 no. 141, pp. 272–4 no. 144, pp. 286–90 nos. 151–2; *CDSA*, pp. 6–10 nos. 3–4, pp. 13–15 no. 6, pp. 17–19 no. 8, pp. 22–8 no. 11–13 , pp. 100–2 no. 49, pp. 135–7 no. 67, pp. 177–9 no. 87. We cannot, however, be certain that we are dealing with only one Roger and Jacob throughout. If it was the same Jacob, should we attach any significance to his promotion to judge occurring between 1187 to 1191? Is his position linked to a regime? It is difficult to answer in the affirmative to either of these, especially when officials like Petracca Buffus could appear in documents recognising William II, Tancred, Henry VI and Frederick II: see above p. 104 n. 148.

Resilience was certainly needed. On Henry VI's death, his heir Frederick II was not yet three years old. Although Frederick was immediately elected king of the Romans, his claims to the empire were overlooked. Henry's brother Philip, having tried to gain support for Frederick, was himself elected king, in Germany, in March 1198. Frederick in turn was crowned king of Sicily in May 1198, and his earlier title dropped. Constance took over the reins of government in southern Italy as regent. Perhaps in line with general resentment at the foreign element in the kingdom, she appears to have distanced herself from her husband's German followers. Markward of Anweiler, Henry's seneschal, and others were forced out of the kingdom, and Constance turned more to the native nobility.[82] There was, however, no apparent restoration for those who had previously adhered to Tancred. Constance died in November 1198, and the meagre material available for her short reign does not offer much on urban government. While Constance does not seem to have ventured to the mainland, the cities there appear to have accepted her as regent. At least a veneer of central administration seemed to continue. In July 1198 the long-serving Eugenius appeared with the title of master chamberlain of Apulia and Terra di Lavoro. The revival of this office, not seen since 1168, suggests that at some point after 1190 the *duana baronum* had collapsed, and by extension shows the problems on the mainland. Eugenius received letters from Constance and her son in which he was ordered to assign land, from the imperial demesne near Aversa, to the monastery of Fossanova. The size of the land was calculated by some Aversans, and Eugenius ordered John Bassus, the chamberlain of Aversa, to complete the transfer. The document also mentioned Leo, chamberlain of Terra di Lavoro.[83] John Bassus, chamberlain of Aversa, was also recorded witnessing two charters in the city in February 1198.[84] Elsewhere, Constance wrote in September 1198 to the chamberlains and bailiffs of Trani and Barletta confirming to the archbishop of Trani the tithe of those cities.[85] Bailiffs were referred to at Taranto, with the task of gathering royal revenues, as were *griparii*, who had been mentioned in

---

[82] *Rich. S. Germano*, p. 19.

[83] Jamison, *Admiral Eugenius*, cal. doc. nos. 29, 30; Clementi suggests that Constance reunited, at least for financial administration, the provinces of Apulia and Terra di Lavoro, which might have been separated since the early 1190s, Clementi, 'An administrative document of 1190', p. 102; Martin, 'L'Administration du royaume', p. 123.

[84] *CDSA*, pp. 3–8 nos. 2–3. A John Bassi held a fief in Aversa according to the *Catalogus Baronum*, art. 858.

[85] *Trani*, no. 89.

an earlier grant by William III.[86] At Gioia, in the vicinity of Bari, an imperial justiciar of the Terra di Bari, Roger de Binetto, is recorded in September 1198.[87] The court was held in a hospital/hostel, where Roger, 'for imperial services', was to examine a land dispute. The investigation also involved the archbishop of Bari, a judge of Bari, some citizens, a Barese *catepan* and two former *foresterii* of the *baiulatio* of Bari in the time of King William (II?). Local governing structures seem to be intact. The one document surviving from Constance's reign at Troia sees the long-serving judge Urso *Troianus* (1154–98) and the notary Baresanus (1170–98) establish a guardian, 'on behalf of the royal court', for some minor siblings.[88]

Constance's death heralded a new period of instability. She had named Pope Innocent III as the kingdom's regent and Frederick's custodian until the boy came of age.[89] The papacy keenly accepted the chance to keep southern Italy and the empire detached, and thus prevent Rome being squeezed in an imperial vice. A power struggle to retain the independence of the kingdom and Frederick's kingship was initiated against those who wanted to restore the imperial unity of Henry's reign. Markward of Anweiler was among these and claimed to have himself received the right to be Frederick's regent. It is important to note, however, that the wider conflict was not simply between an external 'German' party and a native, papal-backed one. Many indigenous counts and cities blurred the boundaries by flitting between both sides, often in relation to local, and not kingdom-wide, considerations. Even without such conflict, the pope could never have been in a position to govern the kingdom in the way it had been previously. The kingdom had to be run under papal aegis by a council of mostly native *familiares* at Palermo – the composition of which constantly fluctuated. In addition, Innocent III employed papal legates in the south, often cardinals such as Gerard of S. Adriano, apostolic vicar of the kingdom (1203–8). Yet some were from southern Italy, like the archbishops of Taranto and Naples, who, according to one papal letter, 'recognised fully the constitutions and customs of the kingdom'.[90] But the pope's

---

[86] This is known from a grant by Constance, which reconfirmed an earlier one of Henry VI, *Constantiae Imperatricis et Reginae Siciliae Diplomata*, pp. 159–66 no. 44.

[87] *CDBI*, no. 67, the date of the document follows Martin, *Pouille*, p. 802.

[88] *Troia*, no. 121; for Urso and Baresanus: *Troia*, nos. 70, 93, 94, 100, 118, 121; *Montevergine*, vi. no. 568, x. no. 942, xi. no. 974.

[89] *Rich. S. Germano*, p. 19; useful works include D. Abulafia, *Frederick II. A Medieval Emperor*, 2nd edn (London, 2002); F. Baethgen, *Die Regentschaft Papst Innocenz III. im Königreich Sizilien* (Heidelberg, 1914); W. Stürner, *Friedrich II. Teil 1. Die Königsherrschaft in Sizilien und Deutschland 1194–1220* (Darmstadt, 1992).

[90] *PL* 214, col. 806 no. 245.

agenda often clashed with that of the *familiares* and created mutual suspicion. Only the briefest outline must suffice of the endless attacks and counter-attacks which engulfed the kingdom, and the incessant jostling for power and control of Frederick II in Sicily.[91] Markward and his German followers re-entered southern Italy in 1198, and a period of near-guerilla warfare ensued. After a brief truce with the papacy collapsed, open war recommenced, and Markward established himself in Sicily until his death in 1202.[92] In the meantime, Innocent had sought the help of Tancred's son-in-law, the Frenchman Walter of Brienne, to provide an effective military presence in the South. Brienne's potential to be a claimant for the throne itself aroused distrust among some South Italians, not least Walter of Pagliaria. The bishop of Troia (until his deposition from that see in 1201), had become a force in his own right as a *familiaris* and royal chancellor. Pagliaria was able to manoeuvre between opposing factions and had briefly allied with some German and native leaders, to no success, against Brienne on the mainland in 1202.[93] Brienne seemed to hold an ascendant position in the mainland from 1201 to 1205 on Innocent's behalf. However, in 1205 he was captured during a skirmish with the German Diepold of Acerra and died soon afterwards in prison. At varying points control of Frederick had passed between Markward, Pagliaria's brother Gentilis, Diepold and another German called William of Capparone. Innocent did not actually enter the kingdom until 1208 – the year in which Frederick II came of age.

Developments in Germany immediately came to the fore. Otto IV, a Welf and old rival of Frederick II's Staufen family, had obtained the upper hand in the contest for the imperial throne following the murder of the king, Philip of Swabia, in 1208. Indeed, Innocent III crowned Otto as emperor in 1209 and hoped the separation of the empire and the kingdom would be preserved. Otto subsequently disregarded this and in October/November 1210 launched an invasion of southern Italy – large areas of Campania and Apulia submitted and recognised his rule. Frederick remained in Sicily, but as Otto was preparing to cross to the island he was forced to return to Germany late in 1211. Nevertheless, many cities continued to acknowledge Otto's rule for some years after.[94] In light of Otto's actions, Innocent decided to accept Frederick's claims

---

[91] See Matthew, *Norman Kingdom*, pp. 298–306.

[92] *Rich. S. Germano*, pp. 20–1, notes Markward's activities in Apulia, Molise and Terra di Lavoro; also T. C. van Cleve, *Markward of Anweiler and the Sicilian Regency* (Princeton, 1937); E. Kennan, 'Innocent III and the first political crusade', *Traditio* 27 (1971), pp. 231–49.

[93] Brienne defeated this coalition at Canne in Apulia, *Rich. S. Germano*, p. 23.

[94] P. Oldfield, 'Otto IV and southern Italy', *Archivio normanno-svevo* 1 (forthcoming); B-U. Hucker, *Kaiser Otto IV* (Hanover, 1990), pp. 142–55; See below pp. 144–5, 149–50.

in Germany, in return for the continued separation of empire and kingdom. This was made possible by the birth in 1211 of Frederick's son Henry, who was to succeed to the Sicilian throne when his father had obtained the imperial one. All in all this was a potentially hazardous move by the pope. Frederick left the kingdom in spring 1212, passing briefly through Campania, his first visit to the mainland. He was elected king in Germany in December 1212, but he was not in a position to be officially crowned until 1215, after Otto's disastrous defeat at the Battle of Bouvines the year before. The deaths of Innocent III in 1216 and Otto in 1218 strengthened Frederick's position. It also made it increasingly unlikely that Frederick would separate the two crowns, if indeed he had ever intended to. Already in 1216 he had brought his son Henry to Germany and in 1220 had him elected as king of the Romans. Frederick himself received the imperial coronation in November 1220 and showed no sign of relinquishing the South Italian throne. He immediately returned to the kingdom, where in December 1220 he issued the Assizes of Capua and the promulgation of an extensive plan to reform government and to revive royal authority. From 1212 to 1220, therefore, Frederick was entirely absent from southern Italy.

The anarchic conditions hit the high provincial administrative structures on the mainland, and the urban communities were left, in effect, politically autonomous. Royal chamberlains and justiciars feature only infrequently. When they do, their powers appear decentralised; their circumscriptions seem limited to a city, and no longer to a province, and titles are largely held by local elites. Master chamberlains and master justiciars (sometimes also called captains) are still attested. Among the men to hold the position of master justiciar of Apulia and Terra di Lavoro after 1198 were 'outsiders' like Walter of Brienne, Innocent III's cousin Jacob and Diepold (who also held the county of Acerra).[95] But there were also 'native' men such as the counts Berard of Loreto and Conversano, Peter of Celano and Richard of Fondi.[96] While many new counties were created in this period, most likely unofficially, the holders of them were still keen to legitimise their holding of public powers by adopting traditional royal titles such as master justiciar.[97] As a result, a façade of continuity was retained for Frederick II to revive after 1220. Eugenius, very likely the long-serving former admiral, was still attested in royal service as a master chamberlain of Apulia and Terra di Lavoro.

---

[95] *PL* 215, cols. 209–11 no. 191, col. 409 no. 124; Diepold appeared at Salerno with the title of captain and master justiciar, *Montevergine*, xiii. no. 1276.

[96] Berard: *PL* 214 , col. 754 no. 205; Peter: *PL* 215, col. 1031 no. 195; Richard: *PL* 215, col. 1449 no. 133.

[97] Martin, 'L'Administration du royaume', pp. 113–40.

A papal letter addressed to him and two other colleagues in 1202 ordered the officials to hand over revenues from the chamberlainship to assist Brienne's campaign against Markward. However, the content of the letter suggests the difficulty of actually obtaining these revenues. These problems may explain why after 1202, until Frederick II's return, royal chamberlains disappear on the mainland, although seigneurial chamberlains can still be found.[98] There was, moreover, much inconsistency, and the functions of higher royal offices were continually mutating in the face of rapidly changing circumstances. When Innocent III intervened in the kingdom's affairs he often appeared to bypass royal officials, while the presence within the cities of what remained of the higher royal officials is difficult to precisely establish.[99]

Although there was much continuity for the cities and local government, in the years from 1189 to 1198, it had still been somewhat of a transitional phase. The disruption required that the cities developed those liberties enjoyed under the Norman monarchy into a more open and wide-ranging role in self-government. In this sense the ground was prepared for the chaos after 1198. Some of the charter documentation reveals the effects of war. One from Salerno of 1206 refers to a house, 'like many others', which had been damaged 'propter afflictionem seu contrictionem Salerni'.[100] Another of 1212 saw the fraternity of the cathedral of Salerno complaining of diminished revenues, and blamed this on the 'wickedness of the time'.[101] At Aversa in 1203 Richard Villanus was compelled to sell land because he was not able to pay the debt which had arisen 'for redeeming my person from the hands of the Germans'. In the same city a charter of 1206 stipulated that an annual census was to be paid whether it will have been 'a time of peace or war'.[102] At Capua in 1202 a family had been forced to sell land because they were 'weighed down by very severe pressure of hunger arising from the upheavals of war'.[103] Richard of S. Germano provides a small, but valuable, snapshot of conditions in Campania and the Terra di Lavoro in the early phase of Frederick's minority. His work records the political instability in the region and offers some insight into the position that the urban communities found themselves in.[104] According

---

[98] Jamison, *Admiral Eugenius*, cal. doc. no. 38 and also nos. 31–7; *PL* 214, col. 974 no. 22, cols. 1072–3 nos. 86–7; Martin, 'L'Administration du royaume', pp. 132–3; see below p. 150 for a chamberlain at Conversano.

[99] J-M. Martin, 'Le città demaniali', in *Federico II e le città italiane*, ed. P. Toubert and A. Paravicini Bagliani (Palermo, 1994), p. 181; Jamison, *Admiral Eugenius*, pp. 164, 169–71.

[100] *CDS*, pp. 60–1 no. 11.   [101] *CDS*, pp. 99–101 no. 37.

[102] *CDSA*, pp. 69–71 no. 34; *CDSA*, pp. 100–2 no. 49; see also *CDSA*, pp. 59–61 no. 29.

[103] *Pergamene sveve*, i. no. 5.   [104] *Rich. S. Germano*, pp. 21–34.

to Richard, in 1199 Salerno was loyal to Diepold, a leading supporter of Markward, who subsequently 'marched all through the kingdom committing innumerable evils'. Diepold's rampaging was later checked by Walter of Brienne at Capua in 1201. The *Gesta Innocenti III* says that the Capuans did not allow Brienne to enter their city, but Walter seems to have at least briefly held it.[105] By 1204 he had also taken the Terracina fortress at Salerno and, after enduring a siege from Diepold and the citizens of Salerno, was able to drive the German out. Yet the following year Brienne's death allowed Diepold to regain Salerno, where 'he arrested many people . . . and punished them as traitors.' It was via Salerno that Diepold launched an attack, in 1207, on the Neapolitans, 'inflicting great slaughter upon them', and capturing their captain Geoffrey of Montefuscolo. However, according to Richard of S. Germano, in 1208 Innocent III appointed counts Peter of Celano and Richard of Fondi as master captains 'in charge of all things from Salerno to Ceprano'. Peter was specifically nominated master justiciar of Apulia and Terra di Lavoro, while Richard was 'appointed as the special rector of the city of Naples', although both men seem to have held these positions before 1208. It was Richard who retook Capua from Diepold in that same year. Curiously it had been the Capuans who had 'summoned' Richard, 'because of their hatred for the count of Celano, whose son Rainald was the archbishop of that city'. In 1209 the count of Celano 'recovered the citadel of Capua' with the assistance of his son, the archbishop. But by 1210 Peter and Diepold had allied. They had also come to an agreement with Emperor Otto IV, who was preparing his invasion, to surrender Capua and Salerno to him. Otto entered Campania, where Naples surrendered 'because of its hatred for Aversa'. Then 'at the prompting of the Neapolitans [the emperor] besieged Aversa, which came to an agreement with him and remained unharmed.' Persistent local tensions once again permeated other conflicts. The *Annales Ceccanenses* offers a different version of events, in which Otto moved from Capua and 'besieged [Aversa] up to Christmas, and not being able to take it he returned to Capua and wintered there, constructing machines for taking cities which did not want to receive him'.[106] It reminds us that not all cities welcomed the newcomer. From Campania Otto moved into Apulia and took most of the region.

However, after Otto had been forced to return to Germany in 1211, we know very little as to how the emperor's rule came to be still recognised in the South, in some cases as late as early 1217.[107] The emperor

---

[105] *PL* 214, col. 254.   [106] *Annales Ceccanenses*, p. 300 a.1210.
[107] See Oldfield, 'Otto IV'.

could not have had the capability to exert any influence on the mainland cities during his absence, nor the time to initiate any real reforms. In the same way, little can be deduced on the process in which Frederick's party reasserted its authority within the mainland cities. We can glimpse a dizzying number of changed allegiances for what seems an equally dizzying and largely concealed number of reasons. Most cities did, at least in their charters, recognise the rule of Frederick II, aside from the period surrounding Otto's invasion. Surviving charters at Salerno (1211–14), Aversa (1212–15) and Capua (1211–17) show that Otto's rule was acknowledged for some time.[108] How urban government functioned throughout the turmoil of this entire period, and by whom it was supervised, is not easy to tell. The charters from Capua offer scant insight apart from one document of 1209. In it a certain Maczolinus, carrying the novel title of master judge of Capua and Terra di Lavoro, along with two judges of Capua, investigated a land dispute on the orders of Count Richard of Fondi, captain and master Justiciar of Apulia and Terra di Lavoro.[109] From Aversa little more can be deduced. The chamberlain of Aversa, John Bassus, is still found in the city in 1201, as was a Humphrey de Rebursa, constable of Aversa.[110] But both appear merely as witnesses to land transactions. Humphrey, still constable, offered land to the city cathedral in 1209. However, by 1217 he had died and his son Peter, in making a similar donation to the cathedral, was himself called constable of Aversa.[111] The de Rebursas had clearly been important local figures for some time. A Humphrey de Rebursa was recorded in the Catalogue of Barons as holding a fief in Aversa, and in 1156 a man of the same name, entitled a *miles* of Aversa, exchanged three pieces of land for some property.[112] This Humphrey was himself the son of a Humphrey de Rebursa, and his own sons were named as Robert and Humphrey (probably the constable of 1201, and an example of the confusing use of favoured lead-names among families).[113] In 1195 a Peter son of Humphrey de Rebursa received a fief from Henry VI.[114] A document of 1203 mentioned the land of the count of Aversa, Humphrey de Rebursa, while Peter was 'unus ex feudatis militibus Aversane civitatis',

[108] It is likely that Otto was acknowledged in many places for longer as it appears that his name was erased from many charters and replaced with Frederick's name following rulings issued at the Assizes of Capua of 1220 and the Constitutions of Melfi of 1231, *Liber Augustalis*, p. 87 title xxviii (28).

[109] *Pergamene sveve*, i. no. 9. Maczolinus appeared the year before in Capua with the same title, *Pergamene sveve*, i. *Seconda parte*, no. 36.

[110] See above p. 139; *CDSA*, pp. 40–2 no. 20, pp. 45–7 no. 22. This may well be the first reference to a constable in Aversa.

[111] *CDSA*, pp.112–14 no. 55, p. 170 no. 84.   [112] *Catalogus Baronum commentario*, arts. 883, 886.

[113] *CDNA*, pp. 117–19 no. 68.   [114] See above n. 55.

and his 1217 bequest was made for the soul of the deceased Bishop Gentile of Aversa.[115] Peter was still the city constable in 1231, when, described as a *vir nobilis*, he drew up a will ahead of a journey 'to regions across the sea [*partes transmarinas*] on imperial order'.[116] In the meantime, there is only the most fleeting allusion to royal authority in the city: in 1201 a land bequest was guaranteed against 'all parties, and especially and expressly [against] the royal curia', while in 1205 the revenue from some donated property was still to be paid to the royal court.[117]

At Salerno, in around 1212, a city *strategotus*, Petronus Domna saracena, assembled a curia of *viri prudentes*, a *protoiudex* and three other judges in the old sacred palace.[118] But little else can be deduced from this case on the position of the *strategotus*, in what is a very rare reference to the chief city official during the period.[119] From an inquest held in 1247 on Cava's rights to a share of the *plateaticum* of Salerno, it would seem that there was continuity in urban government at the lower levels. Witnesses recalled that the bailiffs of Salerno, from the time of King William II until that point, had been handing over the tithe to the monastery.[120] Elsewhere, one has to rely on rather unsatisfactory indirect references. In 1216, Frederick II's wife, Constance, rewarded the loyal archbishop of Salerno by offering revenues from Eboli to the Salernitan Church.[121] The donation was guaranteed against counts, barons, justiciars and bailiffs. Later in 1220, before his return to the kingdom, Frederick II gave the archbishop justiciar powers over the Church's lands and people. The grant was again safeguarded against a similar list of dignitaries. Another charter of Frederick's, concerning the Church of Salerno in 1220, was addressed to the '*strategoti*, judges, knights and the whole people of Salerno'.[122] Admittedly, these cases deal with formulaic lists and they are far from proving the maintenance of royal administration. But they suggest, at the least, the monarchy's hope, or expectation, that those structures were still in place. Yet the bottom line remains that the startlingly limited information on urban government is all the more conspicuous because, at Aversa and Salerno in particular, there is a wealth of charter material for this period.

---

[115] *CDSA*, pp. 66–7 no. 32. Another family member was a cathedral canon and administrator of the bishopric in 1226; Kamp, *Kirche und Monarchie*, i. 348–9.

[116] *CDSA*, pp. 293–5 no. 145, pp. 298–9 no. 147; perhaps the expedition was to the Holy Land, where Frederick II was also king of Jerusalem.

[117] *CDSA*, pp. 35–8 no. 18, pp. 94–6 no. 46.   [118] *CDS*, pp. 90–3 no. 32.

[119] See also *Historia Diplomatica Friderici Secundi*, 6 vols., ed. J. L. A. Huillard-Bréholles (Paris, 1852–61), i. 151–2 note 1.

[120] *CDS*, pp. 227–30 no. 125.   [121] *Acta Imperii Inedita*, i. 376–7 no. 443.

[122] *CDS*, pp. 124–5 no. 54, p. 128 no. 57.

Comparable gaps are also evident in our understanding of Gaeta and Naples. The limited documentation on urban life at Gaeta shows some royal presence. In 1202 a master justiciar of the royal court was in the city, while in 1208 Alexander, a royal chaplain and messenger, acknowledged the voluntary payment of 45,000 gold tari by the Gaetans.[123] More importantly, later charters show that the city had a consular government by 1214, and refer again to the 'commune of Gaeta'.[124] We do not know, however, whether this had been the case continuously since the consuls were last mentioned at the city's capture in 1194. Also, in another document of 1214, a new development in the city's urban government is apparent.[125] John of Ceccano acknowledged receipt of 150 ounces of gold, as agreed by the consuls and people of Gaeta, who had constituted him as *potestas* (podestà) of the city for the previous year. The annual appointment of a salaried external official over the 'commune' had clear parallels with northern Italy, where the podestà acted as an 'impartial' supervisor with administrative and judicial responsibilities, which lasted over a fixed term for which he was accountable afterwards. Further real political independence is suggested by the peace pact agreed, on the consuls' directions, between Gaeta and Pisa in 1214.[126] Another pact was signed with Marseilles in 1216.[127]

At Naples little certain evidence exists on the city's organisation after 1194. The consuls disappear, but civic administration seems to have been run by some sort of collegial group as it had probably been under the Norman kings. Also, it seems that the *nobiles* still retained their role, as witnessed in the late 1130s, in the administration of the city's *regiones*. Although not directly attested, it would seem that a figure similar to the earlier *compalacius* presided over this system. Aligernus Cotunus appeared to have this role in the early 1190s. Later, Godfrey of Montefuscolo, related by marriage to Aligernus' son Peter, had been appointed by the Neapolitans 'as their captain'. While Godfrey's office does not seem to be in the mould of the podestà, it may have been a hybridised form of Aligernus' position with more conspicuous military duties. In 1208, a year after Godfrey's capture by Diepold, Innocent III appointed Count Richard of Fondi 'as the special rector of the city of Naples, supervising those matters that pertain to the business of the city'.[128] Whether

[123] *Cod. Dip. Caietanus*, ii. 327–8 no. 370, 333–4 no. 373.
[124] *Cod. Dip. Caietanus*, ii. 323–5 no. 367 and 337–8 no. 377, where at the end the charter is transcribed into 'the red booklets of the commune of Gaeta'.
[125] *Cod. Dip. Caietanus*, ii. 339–40 no. 378.   [126] *Antiquitates Italicae Medii Aevi*, iv. 393–6.
[127] *Storia d'Italia*, vol. III, *Il Mezzogiorno dai Bizantini a Federico II*, ed. A. Guillou *et al.* (Turin, 1983), p. 662.
[128] *Rich. S. Germano*, p. 27.

Richard was able to exercise any real authority is unclear, especially after Otto's invasion of the kingdom. Indeed papal letters from the period reveal that the inhabitants of Naples, Sorrento and Melfi had chosen to recognise Otto.[129] One might note a dual process at Naples, and in most of the peninsula's cities, during this period: the further refinement of autonomous urban governments which in broad terms still recognised, and tried to work with, a higher royal authority.[130] After Frederick II's return to southern Italy, in 1220, the *compalacius* reappeared for certain.[131] An incidental reference in a papal letter further confirms the limitations of the documentary evidence available. In 1213 the archbishop of Sorrento was accused of simony and contriving to ally his city with Otto IV. The archbishop responded that the writ served against him was legally invalid as it did not 'contain the month [and the names of] the consuls under whom the crime is said to have been committed'. The local plaintiff replied that stating the month or year of the crime was not necessary for a number of reasons, and that appending the name of the consuls would not be of any use because 'the same person could have, as consul, carried out the function of the consulship on various occasions and in a number of years.'[132] Suddenly it emerges that poorly documented Sorrento appears to have had some sort of consulate.

In Apulia after 1198 less is known on the wider political environment, partly because our main source for this period, Richard of S. Germano, focuses more on his native Campania, but at the same time there are some interesting insights into local government. Most cities again acknowledged Frederick's rule either side of that period, generally briefer than for some cities of Campania, in which Otto was accepted. But this was not the same as openly welcoming those who were dispatched to rule in the young king's name. Consequently there was much unrest in the region. Fleeting references in the *Deeds of Pope Innocent III* show that Walter of Brienne's 'domination' was resisted in 1201 by, among others, Monopoli and Taranto. In 1203, apparently on the back of false rumours of Innocent III's death, Barletta and other cities rebelled against Brienne and Jacob, the master justiciar and cousin of the pope, who had earlier been sent to Apulia.[133] Indeed, in the same year, Innocent III scolded the archbishop of Brindisi, the abbot of S. Andrea, and the city's inhabitants for forming a conspiracy against Brienne, during which the latter's castellan was killed and the castle

---

[129] *PL* 214 no. 115 cols. 625–7; *PL* 216 no. 74 cols. 437–8, no. 139 cols. 928–30.
[130] Fuiano, 'Napoli normanna e sveva', p. 466.
[131] *Liber Augustalis*, p. 40 Bk I title lxxi (49); Fuiano, 'Napoli normanna e sveva', p. 476.
[132] *PL* 219, cols. 928–30 no. 139.   [133] *PL* 214, cols. 54, 66.

occupied.[134] An atmosphere of disorder can be detected behind Innocent's letter of November 1199 to the 'whole people of Bari', praising their loyalty to the king and exhorting them to persevere in it. Another papal letter of the following month to the 'royal bailiff, judges and people of Bari', ordering them to release a galley which was to be sent to the Holy Land and which they had seized, suggests that the pope had little actual control over events.[135] A notable document of 1201 relating an incident at the monastery of Ognissanti of Cuti, just outside Bari, confirms the picture of local disorder. In it the monastery's abbot acknowledged before city judges that:

> although the admission of the underwritten Baresi [of which around twenty-four were named] to our monastery seemed at first to be suspect and troublesome to us, we have however since clearly learnt that they entered the monastery out of enthusiasm for loyalty to the king and for the honour and comfort of the city of Bari and all its territory, and also particularly so that they might resist, with vigilant zeal, the plots of the enemies of the king and the kingdom.[136]

The abbot then allowed the named Baresi freedom thereafter to 'approach' the monastery. In the same year Innocent III assured a Roman merchant that he would be repaid the sum of money which he had loaned to two canons of S. Nicola of Bari. The canons had been 'held in chains by Germans', while on their way to the pope at Rome and had needed the money for their ransom.[137]

An investigation conducted in the 1220s on the episcopal rights of the city of Troia also provides insight into the later disturbance caused by Emperor Otto's invasion.[138] It shows that the populace of Troia, by accepting Otto, opted for a different position from that taken by their bishop. The pope threatened to transfer the city's bishopric to its nearby Foggian rivals if they did not resume their loyalty to Frederick. One witness said that when he had gone to Troia 'on business, he saw [Bishop] Philip of Troia before the pulpit of the cathedral ... preaching and warning the Troian people' to once again show fidelity to the king. The city did eventually recognise Frederick again, although whether it was due to Otto's weakening position, the bishop's pleas or the potential for their neighbours to obtain an episcopal see is not clear. The episode highlights the local rivalry that had steadily sharpened between Troia and Foggia since at least the 1190s and the potential for independent

---

[134] *PL* 214, cols. 209–11 no. 191. Another letter of 1203 spoke of revolts at, among others, Brindisi, Otranto and Gallipoli, *PL* 214, cols. 211–3 no. 192.
[135] *CDBVI*, nos. 8, 9.   [136] *CDBI*, no. 70.   [137] *CDBVI*, no. 12.   [138] *Troia*, no. 139.

action within the urban community. Similar conflicts no doubt emerged in other cities during Otto's venture into the South.[139]

In the light of external disruption and internal friction what more can we understand about how these cities were governed? At Bari, Monopoli, Taranto and Trani, judges continued to carry the royal title.[140] At Monopoli, besides a Formosus 'count of the galleys' who witnessed a charter of 1205, there are no other records of any officials with a rank higher than judge or notary.[141] At Troia there is only reference to a constable of the city, William de Ypolito, who also appears once in 1203 with the title of justiciar.[142] At Conversano there had been further changes in the comital ruling dynasty. In the late 1190s Berard, count of Loreto, also obtained the county of Conversano in succession to the Lupin family, which may have lost its position as a result of possible participation in the 1197 conspiracy against Henry VI.[143] Like his predecessors, Berard had other high-ranking duties: he was a royal justiciar and could only rarely have been at Conversano.[144] A charter of 1201 mentions a castellan of Count Berard, while in 1204, in a routine charter relating to the renting of a vineyard, some high-ranking officials appear: William de Basilio, chamberlain of the county of Conversano, and John de Fraxineto, royal justiciar (attested elsewhere in the late 1190s), are found alongside city judges and 'probi homines'.[145] Fortunately, the documentation from Bari is once again rich enough to offer clearer insight into urban government. The local bailiffs and *catepans* (titles which can seem interchangeable) still functioned. In 1210 and 1215 *catepans* are found acting as guardians to women on 'behalf of the king'.[146] As at Salerno, a later inquest also shows the continuance of these offices in an earlier period. In 1223 an investigation was conducted after an appeal by the church of S. Nicola of Bari, which claimed its right to a share of the city's *plateaticum* was being impeded by the *catepans*

---

[139] At Melfi for example, *PL* 214 no. 115 cols. 625–7.

[140] For example at Bari: *Montevergine*, xi. no. 1073; *CDBVI*, no. 68; Monopoli: *Conversano*: nos. 147, 148, 160, 166; Taranto: *Taranto*, pp. 49–54 no. 13; Trani: *Trani*, no. 97 where one judge is also called imperial, as is the case also in nos. 91, 95 and *Pergamene di Barletta del Reale Archivio*, no. 38. There was also a notary with the imperial title in Trani, *Pergamene di Barletta Archivio Capitolare*, no. 186.

[141] *Conversano*, no. 155.

[142] *Troia*, nos. 139, 141; Martin, 'L'Administration du royaume', p. 130.

[143] *Conversano*, introduction p. 52; Martin, *Pouille*, p. 776; Jamison, *Admiral Eugenius*, p. 159 n. 3.

[144] *Rich. S. Germano*, p. 19 says that Berard, and Count Peter of Celano, had in 1197 been entrusted by Constance to bring the young Frederick into the kingdom.

[145] *Conversano*, nos. 151, 154, another castellan is mentioned in 1217, no. 167.

[146] *CDBI*, no. 77; *CBVI*, no. 31.

of Bari.[147] S. Nicola claimed to have received these revenues continuously from the time of William I until Frederick II's reign. Two
current *catepans*, called to answer the case, deferred to the 'old bailiffs
of Bari who knew better the truth of this matter'. The bailiffs asserted
that two-thirds of the *plateaticum* used to go to the *catepans* and a third
to the church.

These local officials were drawn very much from leading circles. One
catepan was the son of the Barese judge John Pronti, the other was the
son of one of the men who had bought the *baiulatio* of Bari in 1196–7.
Among the four old bailiffs was the protonotary Silvester (attested 1197–
1223).[148] Stephen de Malecore, the *catepan* attested in 1215, was
recorded in Bari in 1191 and was still alive in the 1240s.[149] His grandfather had been a notary, while Stephen himself acted as a witness and
owned some notable real estate. Stephen only appeared once with the
catepan title, which could corroborate the supposition that this office was
held for relatively short fixed periods of time. Inquests from Taranto,
held in 1231 and 1247, show a similar continuity of the institution of the
baiulatio from the Norman period to Frederick's reign and its operation
by the local elite.[150] The *baiulatio* was able to survive the anarchic
conditions precisely because it had a solid social base, rooted in the
urban community.[151] As we have seen, by this point it would appear
that the *baiulatio* was being farmed out to influential local people.[152] In
doing so a still limited, but none the less widening, number of inhabitants were directly involved in urban government. While this practice
had its roots in the period before 1189 it had become more pronounced
by the turn of the century. It was a development in line with a growing
specialisation of urban government which saw more taxes and more
officials required to collect them. Officials such as the *potortius*, *griparius*
and *curator mortizii* suggest more efficient organisation, even at a time of
growing political disorder. At a more elevated status we find Garganus
de Corticio, who in 1201 was called justiciar of Bari, while part of a
Barese delegation that established a security pact with the Dalmatian
city of Ragusa.[153] This was the only time that Garganus appeared with

---

[147] *CDBVI*, no. 42. It is interesting to note that a document from Bari in 1199 refers to 'an
instrument of donation made by the lord Grimoald, former prince of Bari'. The Barese
principate had not been effaced from local memory, *CDBI*, no. 68.

[148] *CDBVI*, nos. 29, 32, 39, 42.

[149] *CDBI*, nos. 157, 159, *CDBVI*, nos. 22, 48, 69, 77, 81, 84, 85, frag. no. 1. See also Appendix,
'An example of a kin-group and its network of relationships', below.

[150] See above pp. 101–2.   [151] Martin, 'Le città demaniali', p. 194.

[152] The constitutions of Melfi show that the office of bailiff and also chamberlain could be farmed
by 1231, *Liber Augustalis*, pp. 37–8 Bk I title lx (45), p. 39 Bk I title lxxi.

[153] *Acta et Diplomata Ragusina*, no. 13.

the title; he was attested from 1194 to 1233 and witnessed charters in Bari, acted as an *epitropos* and owned lands.[154] Also at Bari there emerged a hybridised office similar to that held at Capua by Maczolinus. In 1202 a 'master Andrea, master justiciar of the great court and judge of the Baresi' witnessed a dispute involving the Church of Bari, for which Andrea also acted as advocate.[155] In 1209, either at Bari or Bitritto, we find William de Partenico and Andrea de Baro, both called master justiciar of the great royal court (*magna regia curia*).[156] Later, in 1219, another joint title was held by Grimoald, judge of the Baresi and justiciar of the Terra di Bari.[157]

At the same time we can see that civic custom remained at the heart of urban government and that the community played a role, however minor. In 1216 'many *nobiles*' attended a royal court at Bari where an old document was legally validated and copied according to 'our civil custom'.[158] An anonymous group of *cives* certified the value of oil in 1205, while at a court in 1214, assembled to authenticate a will, the presiding judge noted that he was sitting with his 'fellow citizens'.[159] These 'citizens' seem to be adopting semi-public functions, and we have discussed elsewhere the possible significance of a relationship with the *civis* label.[160] On a lower scale, in 1210 a land transaction took place 'through the agreement and arbitration of good men (*boni homines*) whom we [the two parties involved] jointly elected'.[161] In fact it is from this era that the Customs of Bari appear to have been compiled.[162] While they do not seem to be drawn from an earlier formal document, the city's customs may have existed in various unofficial written and oral versions since at least the late eleventh century.[163] The customs survive in two seemingly independent and unofficial compilations. It has been suggested that they were the works of the aforesaid judge Andrea and another Barese judge called Sparro.[164] The document's focus is largely on private and public legal procedure, showing Lombard and Roman influence. While it does provide useful insight into the city's social ordering and development of civic identity, there is little direct treatment of urban government. The significance of the *catepan* is confirmed by the clause that 'we [the Baresi] have not been used to, and are not

---

[154] *CDBV*, no. 162; *CDBVI*, no. 37, frag. no. 3; *CDBI*, nos. 68, 70, 77, 78, 97; *Montevergine*, xii. no. 1172; *Pergamene di Barletta. Archivio Capitolare*, no. 239.

[155] *CDBI*, no. 72.   [156] *CDBI*, no. 76.

[157] *CDBI*, no. 38. A judge Grimoald was attested at Bari throughout this period: *CDBVI*, nos. 2, 4. 16, 28, 29, 30, 39, 42, 50, 51, frag. no. 2; *CDBI*, nos. 70, 71, 77, 78, 83, 84, 94.

[158] *CDBI*, no. 84.   [159] *CDBVI*, nos. 16, 30.   [160] See below pp. 171–83.

[161] *CDBI*, no. 77.   [162] Petroni, *Storia di Bari*, ii. appendix.   [163] See above p. 59 n. 16.

[164] *CDBI*, nos. 66, 76; Besta, 'Il diritto consuetudinario di Bari', pp. 8–9, 13, 15–21.

obliged to have, a foreign *catepan* or judge.'[165] The people of Bari, in accordance with ancient custom, were to be exempt from taxes, services and all burdens. This stipulation must surely refer to *ad hoc* levies over and above normal taxes, and was not to imply a blanket exemption. Indeed, the inhabitants owed galley service, with the exception of those who were knights, judges and notaries. The people of Bari were only to be judged in their own *patria* and were not to be 'dragged away by counts, justiciars or any magistrate', while the 'odious' judicial duel (*monomachia*) was banned.[166]

Elsewhere in Apulia, a document of 1215 provides some detail for the city of Trani. In it, Liepold, bishop of Worms and legate for the kingdom of Sicily, confirmed, on behalf of Frederick II, the city's privileges and customs.[167] The confirmations were in return for Trani's loyalty to the king. Again the document is in no way a record of all civic custom and what is contained is presented in a disordered manner. In civil or criminal cases the inhabitants were to be judged by their own officials in their own city. The inhabitants were freed from the duel, except when charged with treason. The *Tranesi* were required only to give two galleys, when a general levy was called, and were not forced to go on an expedition by land to where they had never been accustomed to go. The inhabitants were freed from port taxes on the Apulian coast and from other payments. Provision was made for the *dohana* (on this occasion perhaps the civic treasury) to pay the person who drew the water from the public fountain, 'which is useful for everybody and is very necessary to provide a drink for thirsty horses'. Also the *dohana* was to pay, as accustomed, the city's judges. This payment was to be included in the accounts of the chamberlains and *dohanerii*. The inhabitants were not to receive any justiciar other than the one appointed in the province by the king. Perhaps individuals had been acting as justiciars without royal approval. Alongside the city judges' competence in criminal justice, this further suggests the decentralising of the justiciarate. The impression emerges of a functioning civic government, with a population which already enjoyed some important specified and unspecified privileges. The city's government was ostensibly linked to a provincial administration, but in reality the concession hints at the latter's virtual breakdown.

On top of this, there are clearer indications from around 1200 that some cities in Apulia were functioning with a degree of political independence. In 1199 at Brindisi a host of local officials, including a royal

---

[165] Petroni, *Storia di Bari*, ii. 440 Rubric II.4.
[166] Petroni, *Storia di Bari*, ii. 440, 442 Rubric II. 7, 10. [167] *Hist. Dip. Friderici Secundi*, i (ii). 375–7.

chamberlain, *catepans* and judges, alongside the whole populace, confirmed a peace pact with the leaders of the Venetian fleet which had arrived in the city port in pursuit of its Pisan enemies.[168] The document safeguarded the Venetians and it is significant that in several places the agreement was extended to include not just the inhabitants of Brindisi but also those of the entire kingdom. The Venetians were to be guaranteed, except for those 'who will harm the men of our city and of the kingdom'. In turn the Venetians swore 'not to offend the kingdom of Sicily and Apulia or the men of that kingdom, whether they be in the kingdom or outside it', and later to uphold the agreement with 'the *concives* of Brindisi and all the men of all the kingdom'. The pact was signed by thirty-four individuals, including a royal chamberlain, a former chamberlain, one *catepan*, seven judges (of whom one was a judge of the Ravellesi), a host of individuals with the label *comes*, three knights, a sailor and others. The document acknowledged Frederick II's position and involved low-level officials. At the same time it demonstrates a role for the wider urban community in formulating important political decisions, which normally would have been reserved for the highest royal officials. This strange element of respect for a light royal presence in a city which itself acts almost independently seems indicative of the way urban government had developed by this point.

There are further examples of 'independent' treaties with the Dalmatian city of Ragusa. These were essentially economic in content but their significance goes further. Pacts were made with Termoli (1203), Molfetta (in 1208, which was a renewal of an agreement of 1148) and Bisceglie (1211). Also, in 1201 Paganus, bishop of Monopoli, the *catepan*, judges, *camestres* (chamberlains?), knights and whole populace established a concord which gave the inhabitants of Ragusa security in the port and city of Monopoli. Significantly, the Monopolitans' pledge was conditional on the same friendship and security being shown to their consuls: perhaps commercial officials of Monopoli who were to be stationed in Ragusa.[169] Again, in 1201, Bari agreed a similar pact, lasting for twelve years, with Ragusa. The Bari delegation, led by Garganus de Corticio, called justiciar of Bari, Leo Mancinus, judge of Bari, Roger Madii, son of Ammirati, and Leo Batius acted 'by the will and mandate of all the people of Bari'.[170] We know from other evidence that these men were significant local figures, and, although otherwise unattested, this surely

---

[168] *Acta Imperii Inedita*, i. 470–1 no. 583.
[169] *Acta et Diplomata Ragusina*, nos. 12–16, similar consuls of Amalfi appeared at Naples and the Holy Land in the 1190s.
[170] *Acta et Diplomata Ragusina*, no. 13.

includes Leo Batius too.[171] While the agreement appears to have been an independent initiative on the part of the urban community, it is again striking that the observation of the pact respected 'the loyalty and arrangement of our lord King Frederick'. It must be noted that 1201 was also the year in which the disturbances took place at the monastery of Ognissanti of Cuti. In the document which related that episode the independent action of a group of Baresi was mixed into a strange cocktail of civic honour and loyalty to the king. Cities were becoming, to all intents and purposes, autonomous by fact and not revolutionary desire.

Benevento of course was not, in theory, subject to the same regime changes and political tribulations. Yet stimulated by the wars of the 1190s, like many of the region's cities, Benevento may well have developed its own factions. While Henry was undertaking the siege of Naples he issued a privilege to his *fideles* in Benevento in recognition of their loyalty. This was essentially a renewal of William II's privilege of *c.* 1171 and perhaps also of Lothar III's of 1137. The Beneventans were released from payment of the *fidantia* in their surrounding territory and ordered not to receive Henry's enemies within the city.[172] The important monastery of S. Sofia may have been more amenable to the imperial cause, and if so this decision must have carried influence within the city.[173] In 1193, in turn, Tancred issued a similar, but slightly extended, grant to the Beneventans.[174] A document from Benevento of 1205 shows that events in the kingdom impacted on the city at a lower level also. It records how a John Rascardo had been captured by Germans and subjected to injuries.[175] To obtain release John had paid 1.5 ounces of gold and gave his only daughter as hostage. To then be able to pay his daughter's ransom money John, in the present charter, sold land outside the city. As always the city was very much enmeshed in the wider events unfolding in the South.

The connections between the kingdom and Benevento were strengthened when Innocent III was *baiulus* of the former from 1198 to 1208. But this limited even further the amount of attention which could be devoted to Beneventan affairs. Innocent III, for example, did not

---

[171] For Roger and Garganus see above pp. 137, 151–2; Judge Leo Mancinus was attested at Bari from 1201–38 and was also present at two assemblies held at Barletta in 1205 and 1206, alongside a crowd of notables including Matthew Gentilis, count of Lesina and captain and master justiciar; *CDBI*, nos. 70, 71, 94; *CDBVI*, nos. 49, 52, 67, 69, frag. no. 4; *Pergamene di Barletta. Archivio Capitolare*, no. 239; Schneider, 'Neue Dokumente', pp. 33–6 nos. 12–13.

[172] Clementi, 'Calendar', pp. 106–7 no. 8.

[173] G. A. Loud, 'Monarchy and monastery in the Mezzogiorno: the abbey of St. Sophia, Benevento and the Staufen', *PBSR* 59 (1991), p. 286.

[174] *Tancredi et Willelmi III Regum Diplomata*, pp. 85–7 no. 35.

[175] *Montevergine*, xiii no. 1217.

venture to the South until 1208 and then only, it seems, briefly to S. Germano. After the mid-1190s few cardinals held the office of rector, and this has been connected to events in the kingdom after 1198. From this date, with the pope's new role in the kingdom, a cardinal was regularly in the South acting as legate there. Perhaps it was felt that there was no call for another cardinal to govern at Benevento, and the rectors were thereafter lower-ranking figures.[176] The cardinal-legate could not focus undivided attention on the city and, when necessary, bolster the position of the rector. While urban government displayed continuity and growing complexity, its links to the papal court were intermittent, largely as a result of the political chaos in the mainland. When the rectors are attested in Benevento they appear to work with, and not over, the local administration, at times on seemingly everyday cases. In 1193 two Beneventan judges, following *consilium* with the rector, transferred ownership of a house.[177] In 1215 the rector of Benevento was involved in a case relating to a monastery's exemption from the payment of an egg as *plateaticum* on some shops in the city.[178] At the same time, references to the rector often show the problems which faced the pope in effectively supervising the city. A rare notice to the rector Cencius emerges in 1199 from a letter of Innocent III about the murder of Jacob Sculdascio, a consul of Benevento. The rector was to prevent the culprit, and his accessories, from entering the city until they had presented themselves at Rome to explain events. The response displays the practical limitations of the pope in controlling internal Beneventan affairs, especially emphatic when the nature of the crime is considered.[179] A later chain of events, recorded in a document of June 1216, highlights this further. Before that year, the Beneventan judge Peter Malanima had been accused of repeatedly burdening a monastery in the city. The pope originally delegated the case to the bishop of Ariano before transferring it to the city rector, Gregory. However, Gregory could not pronounce a judgement because he had left to attend the Fourth Lateran Council, held in November 1215. It seems that Peter Malanima may have taken advantage of this delay to continue his conduct towards the monastery. In the course of the continuing dispute, Peter directed *infamosa verba* towards the new rector, Bishop Philip of Troia. It was not until October 1216 that the case was resolved, with Peter having admitted to his 'excesses and crimes'. But Philip was only one of several parties responsible for the resolution. The rector sat in the sacred

---

[176] Loud, 'A provisional list', p. 7.   [177] *Cattedrale di Benevento*, no. 124.
[178] *Abbazia di Montevergine*, p. 78 no. 1382.
[179] *Register Innocenz*, pp. 419–20 no. 216, see also above p. 120 and below p. 220.

Beneventan palace with 'judges and consuls to deal with the business of the city' and it had been Roger, the city's archbishop, and not he, who had already suspended Peter from office.[180] It seems, moreover, that the pope could not always restrain the rector himself. In 1217, Honorius III ordered the current city rector to investigate alienations of papal possessions in Benevento which had been made by a former papal chamberlain and former rectors, including Bishop Philip of Troia.[181]

At the same time, the city's consuls were becoming more conspicuous within the administration. In 1195 Pope Celestine III addressed the city's archbishop, churches, priests, clergy, judges, consuls and all of the people of Benevento when confirming the city's apostolic protection. The same document reveals that the papal concession was made at the request of the city's envoys – the city rector, the prior of S. Andrea and Serephinus the consul.[182] Letters of Innocent III and Honorius III to the city often addressed the consuls alongside the judges and Beneventan people.[183] In 1199, a Beneventan consul was murdered, while in 1200, before the city rector, the judge Nicholas redrafted a document in which a Zacharias, consul, appeared as a representative of the curia in a dispute over the *mundium* of a widow.[184] The resolution of the case, involving Peter Malanima in 1216, was witnessed by eleven consuls. It is possible that further investigation will bring to light more references to consuls and more insight into their roles. Consular government seems to have developed in the city in conjunction with the populace's growing need and desire for a more formalised associative role in government. This role had become increasingly necessary as papal rule grew ever more distant.

The city's statutes, compiled in 1202, provide a valuable, if brief, snapshot of the development of Benevento's urban government.[185] The statutes, split into two *constitutiones*, were confirmed by Innocent III in 1207 and ratified again in 1230. The prelude to the drafting of the

---

[180] Borgia, *Memorie istoriche*, iii. 178–87; *Abbazia di Montevergine*, pp. 82–3 no. 1398, p. 85 no. 1405.

[181] *Documenti tratti dai registri vaticani (da Innocenzo III a Nicola IV)*, ed. D. Vendola (Trani, 1940), p. 79 no. 82.

[182] Kehr, 'Una bolla inedita di Papa Celestino III', 1–4; a Serephinus is recorded in the *obituarium* of the church of S. Spirito at Benevento, *L'Obituarium S. Spiritus della biblioteca capitolare di Benevento (sec. XII–XIV)*, ed. A. Zazo (Naples, 1963), p. 132 c. 61a.

[183] *PL* 214, cols. 217–18 nos. 256–7; *Regesta Honorii Papae III*, 3 vols., ed. P. Presutti (Rome 1888–95), i. 29 no. 152, 112 no. 649, 216 no. 1304, 549 no. 3381.

[184] *Cattedrale di Benevento*, no. 135 and above n. 179.

[185] The statutes are in Borgia, *Memorie istoriche*, ii. 409–34, and in a modern edition by G. Intorcia, *Civitas beneventana, appendix, pp. 81–90. For useful coverage of the statutes see G. Verigineo, Storia di Benevento e dintorni, vol. I, Dalle origini mitiche agli statuti del 1230* (Rome, 1985), pp. 226–41.

1202 statutes consisted of a popular appeal through the *iurati*, who were the direct representatives of the populace by whom they were elected, to respect an arrangement of civic government that certainly already existed. The request was primarily directed at the rector and judges, but other officials were involved: consuls, advocates, notaries, *servientes curie* and *plazearii* (collectors of market taxes). The material of the first *constitutio* is presented in a disorganised way and deals with legal, judicial and administrative procedure. Judgements were to be made according to Lombard law, and in its absence then according to Roman law. The section emphasises the close relationship between the different groups of officials as well as their interaction with the community. At one point it is stated that 'the officials should honour and love the populace [and] the populace should love and honour the officials.' Elsewhere, the judges, consuls and rector should respect each other in all circumstances, while any new general prescription must be made with the counsel of the notables of each civic quarter ('potiorum de singulis portis consilio'). Judges were not to decide on notorious crimes ('notoriis maleficiis') without the consultation of the consuls. The second *constitutio* which follows is essentially public in character and repeats parts of the first *constitutio*. It again begins with a popular appeal presented by the 'wise and honourable' *iurati*. The petition was directed primarily to the rector and judges and concerned the conduct of the consuls. The people complained that 'to the disadvantage and burden of the citizens', the constitutions themselves 'were not being upheld as they had been drafted by the consuls'. In response, the consuls swore an oath to uphold them. When a consul left his office, presumably after one year, he was not to enter into the consulship again within the next five years, nor was his father, brother or son allowed to enter the ensuing consulship. The consul had to respond to any accusation of crimes committed during his tenure within a month of leaving the position. A consul was to be elected by three sworn persons who themselves had been chosen for the task by the rector, judges and consuls, with three *ministeriales* present. The *ministeriales*, a generic term for officers, emerge as a key component of civic administration and were 'to meet as a group in the interests of the city and for the honour of the curia, and for quelling disturbances'. Another set of officials, the *servientes curie*, were 'to faithfully carry out the orders' of the rectors, judges and consuls. The second *constitutio* further emphasises that the rector and consuls had an important judicial role.

We can identify some of the more important figures in Benevento's urban government at this point and gain some sense of the size of the administrative groupings. The first *constitutio* was signed by twenty-four *iurati* and twelve judges. Among the *iurati* were a notary, possibly a bell-ringer (*campanarus*), a goldsmith, perhaps a dyer (*tintunerius*) and a builder (*conciator*).[186] The judges included important long-serving figures such as Malfridus and Bartholomew Collivaccinus, Canterberius, Nicholas and Saductus Marci. The second *constitutio* was signed by (possibly) twelve consuls and the same twenty-four *iurati* and twelve judges as before. The consuls included a *vicecomes* and a goldsmith. The second *constitutio* is followed by Innocent III's approval of the statutes dated to 1207, and then by a list of twelve judges, twelve old consuls, twelve new consuls and seven individuals 'pro populo'. It would seem, however, that this list dates to the time when the statutes were recorded again in 1230. Some interesting names are found here. Among the judges is a Peter Malaina, likely to be he who had been suspended in 1216, and the renowned jurist Roffred Epiphanio, called here *civilis scientiae profexor*; among the old consuls are a knight, two sons of judges, a notary, a *comes*, a *compalatius* and even another possible dyer (*tintunerus*); among the individuals who swore 'pro populo' were a *comes*, a notary, a son of a judge and a Robert Malanox, while in the 1202 draft we find a Robert Malanox junior as a consul. In the 1216 ruling on Peter Malanima, among the consuls present were two *comites* and a certain John 'Bull's Eye' (*oculus bovis*). If John was the same man, with this distinctive name, who was later attested as a city notary, and who died shortly after August 1271, he must then have attained the consulship at a young age.[187]

Some individuals can possibly be traced as consuls in different periods. There is no indication of how long a consul could continuously serve, although one year is likely. They seem to be twelve in number and one wonders whether this was also the case in the later twelfth century. The Saraphinus of the 1202 list may be the same consul mentioned in 1195, and, if the statutes were being followed, this would fit with the necessary five-year moratorium.[188] In the document from 1216 the consuls included Alferius domni azonis and Dauferius *compalatius* (both of whom signed the statutes as old consuls in 1230), Malfridus Falconis the notary (consul in the 1202 list), and Zacharias (perhaps the man mentioned in 1200). The election process, as outlined in the statutes, involved a relatively closed and privileged circle, and it was likely, although not entirely inevitable, that the consul would therefore be drawn from a similar milieu. The fact that an individual had to wait five years before re-election to the consulship, and could not be succeeded by father,

---

[186] As always, the reservation surrounding the meanings of surnames must be maintained, see below pp. 203–4.
[187] *S. Modesto*, nos. 44, 58, 60, 76.   [188] See above p. 157 n. 182.

brother or son, need not have opened the office to a notably wider social platform.

The content of the document which relays the 1202 statutes is replete with difficulties and paradoxes. A popular protest against the 'establishment' lay behind the drafting of the statutes. But it was a protest that was seemingly peaceful and which was expected to be achieved through the 'establishment'. The statutes juxtapose respect for apostolic authority with a populace keen to be represented in urban government. The appeal over the conduct of the consuls shows that the correct functioning of that office was important to the community, but that by 1202 it was perceived as not adequately fulfilling its role, whatever that may be. The evidence is not sufficiently detailed, but the important role of the consuls at Benevento (and more so at Naples, Gaeta and Sorrento) never appears to have approached the wide powers of consulates in northern and central Italy.[189] The rector is presented as the supreme official, but it is hard to measure how real this was. The respective jurisdictions of rector, consul and judge are rarely delineated, and the way the latter two ranked in relation to each other is not clear. There is no unambiguous indication of the consuls' involvement in public policy or in the wider political process. The *ministeriales* and *servienties curie* could have placed more barriers between the community and the higher circles of government or alternatively offered more contact, depending on which way one views it. Either way, it is the *iurati* who appear to be the most direct *vox populi*, but there was also a role for leading figures within each city quarter. The apparent request for a confirmation of the statutes in 1207 suggests that the community was highly aware of what it expected of its government, and that it was still not satisfied with what it saw. Here an earlier letter of Innocent III in June 1198 to the consuls, judges and people of Benevento should be noted. It indicates that the inhabitants had shown a *scriptum* to the pope, and a request was made by the 'common assent' of all the Beneventans for certain articles (*capitula*) within the document to be confirmed. The *capitula* concerned the payments of judges and notaries, and this episode, both in the nature and subject matter of the plea, appears as a precedent to the events of 1202.[190]

The sum of the evidence from Benevento at this period would suggest growing layers to, and increased sophistication of, government

---

[189] Compare, for example, the powers of Genoese consuls, S. A. Epstein, *Genoa and the Genoese 958–1528* (North Carolina, 1996), pp. 34–49.
[190] *PL* 214, col. 218 no. 257.

which required the continued participation of the community.[191] At the same time, external links with the central papal court were becoming more irregular as a result of the political atmosphere. The city, in short, was becoming more of a self-sufficient organism while still, at least nominally, recognising a higher authority. This pattern is reflected in most mainland cities, but here the disruption and, by consequence, freedom of action from higher authority was even greater. Frederick II's Assizes of Capua, issued in late 1220, confirm this and suggest that in some cases urban communities had gone beyond the previously accepted royal governing framework. The aim to reinstate the *status quo* as it was before 1189 was a central theme of the Assizes: 'all the good usages and customs from the time of William II were to be observed.' Private war and feuds were prohibited, and the carrying of weapons inside and outside cities was banned, as it had been under William. Nobody was allowed to exercise the title of justiciar without royal mandate, and master justiciars and justiciars were to act 'without fraud'. Castles and walls built since 1189 were to be dismantled, and the actions of castellans were to be regulated. New markets were forbidden. New forms of taxation which had sprung up were abolished, and all taxes, revenues received by *baiuli* (as at the time of William) and demesne goods (including cities) were to be restored. Clause 13 is especially revealing:

we order that a *potestas* should not be chosen in any city, nor should they have a consul or rector, but a bailiff should be established through appointed chamberlains of the curia, and justice, through justiciars and people arranged by the curia, should be directed by the order of law, and the approved customs of the kingdom should be observed.[192]

Many of these themes were outlined emphatically in Frederick's Constitutions of Melfi in 1231, which continued the drive to re-establish order and efficient royal government. Here a similar rendition of the above clause 13 goes further and refers to the usurpation of offices 'by authority of some custom or by election of the people'.[193]

The picture painted by the Assizes is clear and in places complements what the sources for the period 1189–1220 tell us. Civil and criminal justice was dispensed, taxes and levies collected and defences organised, but control of this was less than ever in the hands of central authority and more so in those of the local government and community. One suspects that this was even more the case during politically disruptive

---

[191] For example a document of 1193 saw the transfer of a house carried out by a *catepan* (an office not normally associated with Benevento) and a *serviens curie*, after consultation between city judges and the rector, *Cattedrale di Benevento*, no. 124.

[192] *Rich S. Germano*, version A, pp. 88–91. [193] *Liber Augustalis*, pp. 48–9 Bk I title 1 [61].

periods when royal revenues, criminal cases and general inquiries about public policy could not be passed from the cities to the royal court. Indeed, a key theme of the period was the granting out of royal revenues to retain support; the effect was to decentralise government and financially exhaust royal authority. Some cities controlled their external trading and, by extension, political policies and enjoyed greater freedom in selecting their own officials. But the greater autonomy was born out of necessity not revolt – most cities generally continued to recognise the legitimacy and value of higher authority, working within its traditional framework. Thus at the same time there was evidence of continuity, without which Frederick II might not have restored royal power so effectively and curtailed what he considered excessive freedom in some cities. This may well throw some light on the diverse development of urban communities in the North in the early thirteenth century. For all their efforts to emphasise their historical continuity, the communes in the North, or the ruling classes within them, whether they were old noble consular families, the podestà and his associates or members of the newly risen *popolo*, appear to have faced increasing and repeated crises of legitimacy by *c.* 1200. From this came an inability to control dissent and factionalism within the community, which itself was accentuated by continued population expansion, rapid social changes and the fact that, in many cases, communal government was simply not as representative as it claimed to be. The result, according to Tabacco, was institutional instability and the fluid creation of new structures in order to synchronise political power with social transition.[194] Royal authority in southern Italy during this phase, by virtue of its paradoxical 'absent presence', provided a benign mechanism that was viewed as legitimate and neutral. Through it local urban power politics, communal functioning and social change could be stabilised and guided.

The greater role and representation of the urban community which emerged in the cities of southern Italy, and its increased freedom of action, was also the product of wider social and administrative developments which were being effected throughout Europe. The example from Benevento, and indeed elsewhere in the Norman kingdom before 1189, shows that arrangements which placed more emphasis on the role of the community were actually possible under the auspices of a higher authority. The extent to which these survived, and how urban government was reintegrated into the royal administrative network after 1220, takes us into yet another phase for the cities of southern Italy and one that cannot be explored here.

---

[194] Tabacco, *Struggle for Power*, pp. 228–9.

Part II

URBAN SOCIETY: COMMUNITY, IDENTITY AND WEALTH

Chapter 6

POPULATIONS, CULTURAL IDENTITY
AND CITIZENSHIP

The urban community played a significant role in civic government. In this function it emerges, for the most part, as a rather undefined whole concealing a more intricate, but largely unknown, organisation. Beyond this the urban populace's exact position in the governing framework is mostly indeterminate, and it may be that this reflected its unofficial nature. But away from a political context it is clear that the social ordering, inter-relationships and groupings that interlaced the communities themselves were far more complex. Population size, cultural identity and the concept of citizenship are fundamental to the shaping of any urban community and offer the best place to start an analysis.

POPULATION SIZE

Unfortunately, evaluating the size of the region's urban populations is extremely difficult. Medieval demographic patterns can only be general, and southern Italy offers no exception. While there is broad agreement upon widespread demographic growth from *c.* 1000, which reached its peak around three centuries later, findings on the rate of expansion and regional differences are extremely tentative and often contradictory.[1] For many regions the first usable statistical data are not available until the late thirteenth and early fourteenth centuries. In southern Italy this is provided by a survey of hearth taxes from the late thirteenth century which is highly problematic to interpret.[2] It has been roughly estimated that at the assumed peak of demographic growth (*c.* 1300) Naples was the only South Italian mainland city to rival in any way the largest

[1] N. J. G. Pounds, *An Economic History of Medieval Europe* (London, 1994), pp. 143–60.
[2] A. Filangieri, *Territorio e popolazione nell'Italia meridionale* (Naples, 1980), p. 128, which shows that estimates of late medieval populations for mainland southern Italy have varied from 2 to 3.4 million.

north and central Italian cities (Milan, Genoa, Venice, Florence), whose populations numbered *c.* 100,000.[3]

It is possible that, around 1300, southern Italy's main cities like Salerno and those on the Apulian coast, as well as some inland centres such as Benevento, had populations between 10,000 and 20,000.[4] Capua and Aversa probably fell within the mid to lower range in this grouping, while places like Troia and Conversano almost certainly had populations below 10,000. Attempts to project these rudimentary conclusions back to the period under study here can only be basic. It would seem, however, that whatever their population numbers, the relative difference in size between individual cities remained similar between 1100 and 1300, apart from some exceptions like Naples and Foggia, both of which grew exponentially from the late twelfth century. There is evidence from the late eleventh century of increasing urban populations. Suburbs emerged outside several cities, urban property was increasingly divided into smaller tenements, often with upper floors, while intricate boundary disputes suggest a growing density of buildings.[5] More rural land was being cultivated to provide for a rising demand. The Tavoliere plain near Troia was almost entirely reclaimed for cereal cultivation, and in its middle emerged the settlement of Foggia, which by the late twelfth century had probably surpassed nearby Troia in size.[6] However, the combination of a general population increase alongside clear evidence for the underlying continuity of urban traditions and kin-groups was balanced by the ever-present threat of war, epidemic and disaster (natural or otherwise).[7] An earthquake was recorded in 1094.[8] The chronicler Falco relayed the devastation wrought by yet another in his city in 1125.[9] The *Annales Cavenses* reports 'huge famine and death' (*fames et mortalitas maxima*) in 1085, extensive fatalities in 1180 'through the whole Terra di Lavoro so that the bodies of the dead were placed unburied in litters' and a famine the following year 'through the whole of Italy'.[10] In 1098 Troia was 'consumed by fire', while the *Annales Beneventani* details a number of potentially damaging sudden climatic changes around 1100, some of which resulted in famine and widespread death.[11]

---

[3] Nicholas, *The Growth of the Medieval City*, p. 178.
[4] Filangieri, *Territorio e popolazione,* pp. 129–30.
[5] See above p. 54; of the many examples, there was a suburb at Salerno in 1160 (*Nuove pergamene*, pp. 34–7 no. 15) and a 'burgo novo' at Trani in 1169 (*Trani* no. 59).
[6] See J-M. Martin, *Foggia nel Medioevo* (Rome, 1998); P. Oldfield, 'Rural settlement and economic development in southern Italy: Troia and its *contado*, c.1020–c.1230', *JMH* 31 (2005), pp. 327–45.
[7] Filangieri, *Territorio e popolazione,* pp. 73–6.   [8] Bertolini, 'Gli *Annales Beneventani*', p. 149.
[9] *Falco*, p. 82.   [10] *Annales Cavenses*, pp. 190, 193.
[11] *Romuald*, p. 201; Bertolini, 'Gli *Annales Beneventani*', pp. 145, 149, 150, 152, 154.

Thus, the overall rate of increase from the mid-eleventh to mid-thirteenth century seems to have been steady, rather than spectacular. This suggests that population sizes by the mid-twelfth century may not have been, apart from the case of Naples and a few places, dramatically lower than those around *c.* 1300. The general trend of long-term increase was unlikely to have been linear – it undoubtedly hit plateaux and suffered temporary downturns. Moreover, although everywhere the urban population seemed to be growing, it did so at a rate which certainly varied from city to city. Bari offers an interesting case. The translation of 1087 and the crusades turned this provincial capital into a booming international port, swelling the population, which, according to one scholar, stood at *c.* 35,000.[12] But in the twelfth century the troubles of the 1110s, and certainly the civil war, must have impacted on this growth. Falco of Benevento provides us with the exaggerated, but none the less interesting figure of 50,000 inhabitants at Bari in 1139.[13] The city was completely razed in 1156 and its full repopulation took some years. When Benjamin of Tudela, a Jewish merchant from Spain, visited southern Italy, probably in the 1160s, he noted that Bari still lay desolate, although charters were being redacted in the city as early as 1159, suggesting that urban life was reviving.[14] Thus, by 1200 Bari's urban population may not have attained its level of a century earlier and thereafter may have grown only marginally by 1300. Although not direct demographic evidence, the tax lists of 1276 placed Bari behind Barletta, Bitonto and Trani within the Terra di Bari.[15] Similarly, Troia (in 1133) and Aversa (in 1135) had been destroyed and their populations dispersed through the surrounding countryside – some of the Troians fled to Benevento. But both were soon rebuilt – King Roger permitted the inhabitants of Aversa to return to the city in the month following its destruction, while, according to the figures given by Falco of Benevento (to be treated with some caution), Troia, in 1139, sheltered 200 knights and 20,000 armed men within its walls.[16] These cities were rapidly repopulated, displayed great continuity with the pre-1130 era and showed

---

[12] Cioffari, *Storia della basilica di S. Nicola*, p. 28, rather higher than Pounds's estimate of 10–25,000 for the later period.

[13] Falco, p. 218; F. Porsia, 'Vita economica e sociale', in *Storia di Bari – dalla conquista normanna al ducato sforzesco*, ed. F. Tateo (Bari, 1990), pp. 201–7, wonders whether Falco's calculation may have included the inhabitants of the *contado* as well.

[14] *The Itinerary of Benjamin of Tudela*, ed. M. N. Adler (London, 1907), p. 9; *CDBV*, nos. 117–20. *CDBI*, no. 50, dated to 1167, has a cryptic reference to a 'restoration' made 'to all the citizens of Bari' by the 'kindness' of the king (William II).

[15] Porsia, 'Vita economica e sociale', p. 203.

[16] Aversa: *Alex. Tel.*, Bk III.12–3 pp. 66–7, 22 p. 71, Falco, pp. 172, 174; Troia: *Alex. Tel.*, Bk II.49, p. 47; Falco, pp. 154, 218.

signs of flourishing. But at what point their regenerated populations surpassed earlier levels is difficult to ascertain precisely. The same question can likewise be posed for Salerno after the siege of 1076/7 or the huge disruption suffered there in the late twelfth and early thirteenth centuries.

There are too many variables to trace more than the faintest profile of demographic patterns. Contemporary commentators provide inferential information that must only be used with great caution. Falco reports more numbers. In 1114 the Beneventan constable Landulf commanded a force of 'some 4,000 citizens' – presumably only those who supported Landulf's policies and were willing (and able) to fight for them. In 1127 at Capua, 5,000 people, including the pope, attended the anointing of Prince Robert II. In 1128 Roger II's ducal investiture outside Benevento was witnessed by nearly 20,000 people. In 1134 Falco himself was among over 1,000 Beneventans exiled from the city – a number which probably related only to the most politically active section within one civic faction. Later, in 1156, John Kinnamos estimated the civic militia of Monopoli alone, an average sized city, at more than 200 knights, 1,000 infantry and 'an innumerable crowd of slingers'.[17] The geographic survey of the kingdom conducted around 1150 by the Muslim scholar Muhammad al-Idrisi on behalf of King Roger offers plenty of topographical detail but nothing on population sizes. In it almost every mainland city is somehow described as 'populous', which at least shows medieval perceptions of what they considered a key characteristic of a city to be. It is also difficult to deduce much on population size from the survey of the region's urban Jewish communities, which was compiled by the already mentioned Benjamin of Tudela, most likely in the 1160s.[18] The investigation estimated the Jewish population to be about 300 at Capua, 500 at Naples, 600 at Salerno, 20 at Amalfi, 40 at Ascoli, 200 at Benevento, Melfi and Trani, 300 at Taranto, 10 at Brindisi and 500 at Otranto. It is clear that the size of the Jewish communities in relation to the overall population varied greatly and does not entirely reflect the relative size of cities. Traditional Jewish settlement patterns and the date of the survey must also be taken into account. The lack of any community at Bari, where Benjamin noted there had been one earlier, and perhaps the low number at Brindisi, is due to the events of 1156. Moreover, there is a possibility that Benjamin's numbers refer not to individuals but to *capifamiglie*, which would allow the figures to be multiplied

---

[17] *Deeds of John and Manuel Comnenus*, Bk IV.5 p. 113.
[18] *L'Italia descritta nel 'Libro del re Ruggero' compilato da Edrisi*, ed. and trans. M. Amari and C. Schiaparelli (Rome, 1883); *Itinerary Ben. Tudela*, pp. 7–9.

by five.[19] This would give an approximate Jewish population at Salerno of 3,000 and provides an interesting, but most likely inflated, guess at the city's total population. If one follows the estimation that the region's Jewish communities represented between 3 and 5 per cent of the whole, it would place Salerno's urban population at a rather unlikely *c.* 60,000.[20]

CULTURAL IDENTITY

The mainland urban populations of southern Italy consisted of a mosaic of cultural groups. In Campania, the Abruzzi and most of Apulia the majority of inhabitants were of Lombard descent, although the latter region was influenced by Byzantine culture, especially in coastal areas. The Tyrrhenian coastal cities of Amalfi, Gaeta and Naples had avoided Lombard rule and consequently any overt 'Lombardisation'. Here Roman, and not Lombard, law was prevalent and it was also appealed to, mostly by women, in the Salerno region despite that city's heritage. In Calabria there was a large Greek population, which by the time of the Norman arrival was spreading gradually northwards.[21] Greek communities were widespread in the Salento peninsula, southern parts of Apulia, in Lucania and also in and around Salerno. To take one example, illuminated by von Falkenhausen, the population of eleventh-century Taranto appears to have been part Lombard but predominantly Greek.[22] On the other hand, in the cities of central Apulia there were Greek signatures in private documents, but they were most often of Lombard names and documents actually in Greek were rare. Lombards in these regions clearly assimilated Greek cultural reference points, such as names and costume.[23] This cultural overlap, combined with the end of Byzantine rule, meant that by the twelfth century Greek communities were being gradually subsumed within the predominant Latin milieu; yet although dwindling in numbers they, and the Greek Christian rite, still maintained a significant presence into the thirteenth century.[24] Benjamin of Tudela considered Taranto's population as Greek, and from 981 to 1228 some seventy-six Greek documents have survived from

---

[19] A. Milano, *Storia degli ebrei in Italia* (Turin, 1963), p. 105; P. E. Fornaciari, 'Beniamino da Tudela in Italia', *Archivio storico italiano* 147 (1989), p. 416.

[20] H. Houben, 'Gli ebrei nell'Italia meridionale tra la metà dell'XI secolo e l'inizio del XIII secolo', in *Mezzogiorno normanno-svevo*, p. 204 and n. 57.

[21] Loud, *Age of Robert Guiscard*, pp. 54–9; J-M. Martin, 'L'Empreinte de Byzance', pp. 733–50.

[22] V. von Falkenhausen, 'Taranto in epoca bizantina', *Studi Medievali* 9 (1968), pp. 149–52.

[23] Von Falkenhausen, *La dominazione bizantina*, pp. 173–5.

[24] As recently demonstrated by G. A. Loud, *The Latin Church in Norman Italy* (Cambridge, 2007), pp. 494–520.

the city.[25] In addition, as we have already seen, Jewish communities were also found in most of the region's cities.[26] Through the course of the eleventh century a mixture of Normanno-French settlers were added to this. The quantitative and qualitative impact of the newcomers has been debated at length, with the only real certainty being that they were few in number, particularly within cities.[27] We have already seen the effect of this on the nature of urban government. The Norman rulers were sensitive to existing traditions; they maintained the native elites and administrative officials and adopted most indigenous governing models. The Norman importation of new forms of tenurial relationships was a gradual and uneven process. Nor should the impact of its later development in southern Italy be overestimated. Filangieri has shown that in the twelfth century approximately only one sixth of the region's total population may have been drawn into new types of land tenure, and that the major urban centres of Campania and Apulia were not enfeoffed.[28] There was much continuity and perhaps little perceptible change in daily life for the urban dweller. Lombard law functioned throughout the period, as did Roman law, particularly at Amalfi, Naples and also at Salerno. Salernitan and Amalfitan families continued to emphasise their ancient origin in family genealogies in the twelfth century and beyond. The foundations of local civic customs were preserved. Aversa may be the one settlement where the Normans were sufficient in number to introduce, still within a blend of local patterns, laws and customs with a more northern European flavour. Eleventh-century charters from Aversa speak of people who were French or Norman and mention 'the custom of the Franks' (*mos Francorum*), while the vocabulary and precision of the city's social groups (*burgenses, vavassores*) were both unique and reflective of French models.[29] However, the references to Normanno-French custom and descent tend to fade in the twelfth century.

For the most part, within cities, there was not a Lombard majority distinct and separate from a Norman minority. By the early twelfth

---

[25] *Itinerary Ben. Tudela*, p. 9; V. von Falkenhausen, 'Un inedito documento greco del monastero di S. Vito del Pizzo (Taranto)', *Cenacolo*, n. s. 7 (19) (1995), pp. 7–20; *Taranto*, pp. 10–12 no. 3 (a. 1113), pp. 23–5 no. 7 (a. 1157), pp. 31–4 no. 9 (a. 1175); C. D. Fonseca, 'La chiesa di Taranto tra il primo e il secundo millennio', *BISME* 81 (1969), pp. 105–13.

[26] For more discussion on these see pp. 209–14.

[27] See above pp. 23–4 and n. 34; Loud, *Age of Robert Guiscard*, pp. 278–90 also provides an excellent discussion on this subject.

[28] P. Skinner, 'When was southern Italy "feudal"?', in *Il feudalismo nell'Alto Medioevo, 8th–12th April 1999. Settimane di studio del Centro italiano di studi sull'Alto Medioevo* 47, (Spoleto, 2000), vol. I, pp. 309–40; A. Filangieri, 'La struttura degli insediamenti in Campania e in Puglia nei secoli XII–XIV', *Archivio storico per le provincie napoletane* 103 (1985), pp. 61–86.

[29] *CDNA*, pp. 386–7 no. 43, pp. 389–90 no. 45, pp. 393–4 no. 48 , pp. 396–7 no. 50, pp. 399–401 no. 53.

century the distinction between both 'groups' was becoming increasingly blurred.[30] Later references, such as in the 1180s, to 'Normans' receiving *fidantiae* from Beneventans in the vicinity of their city or at Salerno in 1185 to a woman living by Norman law, are very rare. At Benevento it may be the result of the continued use of a traditional terminology that was applied to those who exacted those payments in the eleventh century, rather than reflecting current attitudes on different ethnic groups.[31] Intermarriage, which occurred at all social levels, was key to the merging of identities. Normans took on Lombard customs such as the *morgengabe* and *mundium*, and Lombards in particular began to use Norman names. At Salerno the Norman arrival did little to alter 'family structure in terms of changing marriage customs or introducing new forms of patrimonial holding/inheritance'.[32] It should be noted that even in Falco of Benevento's important work 'it would seem that Lombard identity or solidarity was far less important . . . than being a citizen of Benevento.'[33] Likewise, the revolt in the 1090s at Capua may have partly been aimed against the Normans as a group, but civic pride may have played just as big a part.[34] Indeed the concept of *Normannitas* among the region's writers faded noticeably in the twelfth century, whereas in the preceding one the courage and audacity of the Norman *gens* was extolled by the likes of Amatus, Geoffrey Malaterra and William of Apulia. The emphasis of later twelfth-century writers like Hugo Falcandus and Romuald of Salerno was directed more to the monarchy.[35] By this point Norman and Lombard anthroponyms were no longer safe guides to identity, while the effects of acculturation presumably made it less relevant to emphasise Lombard or Norman descent at all.[36]

CITIZENSHIP

Often, and for simplicity, modern historians understandably interchange the word 'citizens' with 'populace', 'urban community', 'inhabitants' and

---

[30] Loud, 'Continuity and change', pp. 325–32. Drell argues that concepts of separate Norman and Lombard identities persisted in the principality of Salerno up to *c.* 1180, Drell, 'Cultural syncretism and ethnic identity', pp. 187–202.

[31] See above p. 116; Abignente, 'Le consuetudine inedite di Salerno', p. 384 no. 18.

[32] J. Drell, 'Family structure in Salernitan society', in *Salerno nel XII secolo*, ed. P. Delogu and P. Peduto (Salerno, 2004), pp. 111, 113.

[33] Loud, *Age of Robert Guiscard*, p. 285.   [34] See above pp. 40–1.

[35] T. S. Brown, 'The political use of the past in Norman Sicily', *The Perception of the Past in Twelfth-Century Europe*, ed. P. Magdalino (London, 1992), pp. 193–4.

[36] Loud, *Age of Robert Guiscard*, p. 288. As we have seen, Lombard customs continued in the twelfth century and beyond, and some inhabitants did still also identify themselves, if less conspicuously, as Lombards: a man from Bari in 1228 handed over a document of 'morgincaph', 'according to the usage of our Lombard people', *CDBVI*, no. 47.

the like. Yet it is far from certain whether 'citizens' in the medieval period were synonymous with any of these terms or even what citizenship meant. Attempting an explicit definition of citizenship at the outset is a difficult task, likely to produce conceptions which would be anachronistic for our period. All that can be safely concluded is that the title of citizen (*civis*) in its broadest sense carries the claim of membership within a particular community. Both that community and the individual *civis* confer advantage on each other. The *civis* label implies a relationship in theory different from that implied by other words such as *habitator* (inhabitant).

It seems that Roman urban traditions, and the idea of the city (*civitas*), survived far more in southern Italy and the rest of the peninsula into the medieval period than elsewhere. Many cities were located on, or near to, classical sites.[37] It has also been suggested that the peninsula enjoyed an uninterrupted tradition of the use of the word *civis* from Roman times.[38] In the Roman world, citizenship brought rights (*iura*) and duties (*munera*).[39] The *iura* were public (such as the right to vote in elections and on legislation, to stand for office) and private (the right to contract a marriage, to avoid arbitrary judgement, to enter into business contracts, to inherit). The important aspect of the private *iura* was that they conformed to Roman law and were therefore legally recognised. The *munera* above all entailed defending the state and perhaps the requirement to pay tax (although probably at a privileged rate). To be a citizen the individual had to be 'free' and could not be a slave. There were gradations of citizenship, and not all *iura* and *munera* were applied to all citizens. In southern Italy, even if the *civis* title did still persist, it is unclear to what extent the Roman concept of it was transmitted to the medieval period. By the eleventh century it would seem that the term was used primarily in narrative sources with a generic sense, and only rarely in charter documentation, where the relationship between an individual's legal and social status, and the terminology by which it is identified, is likely to carry more significance. When it is used in charters it may have conferred a specific meaning. It is by focusing on this latter body of evidence that we are best placed to explore the nature of citizenship.

---

[37] Jones, *Italian City-State*, pp. 74–85; for continuity and transition from the late Roman to early medieval periods see S. Gelichi, 'The cities', in *Italy in the Early Middle Ages*, ed. C. La Rocca (Oxford, 2002), pp. 168–88. The city of Troia, for instance, in northern Apulia, was founded in 1019. But it was located near to the abandoned classical settlement of Aecae, and evidence from Troia indicates some interest in its classical 'predecessor', Oldfield, 'Rural settlement', p. 332.

[38] Calasso, 'La città nell'Italia meridionale', pp. 268–9.

[39] The classic work remains A. N. Sherwin-White, *The Roman Citizenship* (Oxford, 1973); see also J. F. Gardner, *Being a Roman Citizen* (London, 1993); *The Oxford Classical Dictionary*, 3rd edn, ed. S. Hornblower and A. Spawforth (Oxford, 1996), pp. 334–5.

Populations, cultural identity and citizenship

In the eleventh and twelfth centuries, inhabitants were most regularly named after their city (*Barenses*, *Salernitani*) or were collectively termed *populus*, *cives* or *concives* (fellow citizens).[40] In certain cities the use of the word *civis* in the charter material is virtually non-existent throughout our period, although the term *civitas* always appears. At Capua, where there is only a single reference to a *civis* in 1229, inhabitants are simply called *habitator Capuane civitatis*.[41] Similarly at Conversano, aside from one reference to a *concivis* in 1099, most members of the urban community are defined as *de* or *ex civitate cupersanense*.[42] At Salerno *cives* do not seem to appear in charters much before the 1220s, yet narrative and other sources had applied this term to the Salernitans for some time.[43] However, in a semi-public document from Gaeta of 1125, Peter Sfagilla *civis salernitanus* gave security to the consuls and entire populace of Gaeta. The pledge was in relation to merchandise that had been confiscated amidst 'war' and 'enmity' between the *concives* of both cities.[44] In some urban centres, where the word does appear in the charter material it is more often in documents of a public nature. At Trani, in private, or semi-public, charters there are only a handful of references throughout our period to people identified as *cives*, one of whom, interestingly, is Jewish.[45] However, the city's charter of privileges, redrafted in 1139, while adopting a varied terminology for the Tranesi, does refer to *concives* in two clauses – one dealing with the restitution of prisoners and the other guaranteeing that only a *concivis* of Trani could be a city judge or notary.[46] Later, in 1191, King Tancred restored to the *cives Tranenses* any possessions lost amidst the recent conflict, while in 1195 Henry VI took the city's Jewish community under his protection and safeguarded

[40] At Monopoli in 1054 a role was confirmed for 'the monks and all *cives*' in the election of the *antistes* of the monastery of S. Nicola, *Syllabus Graecarum Membranarum*, pp. 53–5 no. 42.
[41] *Pergamene sveve*, ii. no. 3.   [42] *Conversano*, no. 60.
[43] *Nuove pergamene*, pp. 75–7 no. 31, pp. 97–9 no. 40; in 1219 Pope Honorius III confirmed a judgement to a John Buccamugellus *civis Salernitanus*, *Regesta Honorii Papae III*, i. 337–8 no. 2043. In an inscription made in 1180 in the cathedral of Salerno, the famous royal vice-chancellor Matthew was described as *magnus civis Salerni*, *Italia Sacra*, vii. 405; Salernitan *cives* are found in a variety of narrative sources including the eleventh-century poetical works of Archbishop Alfanus I of Salerno and William of Apulia, as well as that of Peter of Eboli for the late twelfth century. There are also references in the chronicle attributed to Archbishop Romuald II of Salerno and the twelfth-century work of the so-called Hugo Falcandus. The city's 1127 *pacta* with Roger II, which survives only in a fifteenth-century copy, repeatedly refers to *cives*. However the *pacta* are transcribed more as a report by fifteenth-century *Salernitani* than as a verbatim document. Thus, although its content appears to reflect twelfth-century conditions the same cannot be said as certainly for the language employed, see above p. 58 n. 14.
[44] *Cod. Dip. Caietanus*, ii. 227–8 no. 308.
[45] *Trani*, nos. 59, 69, 70. There are Trani *cives* in Barletta charters: *Pergamene di Barletta. Archivio Capitolare*, nos. 141, 228.
[46] *Trani*, no. 37.

them from any 'ecclesiastical or lay person or any *baiulus* of our court, judge or *civis*'.[47] In another public document, Frederick II's confirmation of all Trani's customs and privileges of 1215, the *cives* are referred to again. While most of the document uses the adjective *Tranenses*, one clause, perhaps significantly, adopts the *cives* usage and says that:

whatsoever stranger [*alienigenus*] who comes to Trani from wheresoever and howsoever, for the purpose of living, is to be assessed [*censeatur*] as a citizen of Trani [*Tranensis civis*] and is to gain all the privileges and civil usages of the city, and is not to be dragged against their will by anyone out of Trani.[48]

Are we dealing here with a loose employment of terms, or is the content of the clause, which refers to assessments, presumably fiscal, the enjoyment of all civic customs and legal status, specifically connected with the word *civis*?

Likewise at Bari, when the word appears it is mostly in narrative sources and public documents. It only sporadically enters later into private charters. In the eleventh century the inhabitants often referred to themselves as *de civitate Bari*. By the mid-twelfth century the most common practice was to use a simple appended *Barensis*. But shortly after 1100 more specific information emerges to throw some light on citizenship. In 1108 a man called Aldebertus, described as a *commorator* of Bari, asked the city *catepan* to be freed from the *affidatura publica*. *Affidati* appear to have been semi-free people who, usually after being settled from other areas, were under the authority of an institution (or even an individual) and were subject to certain payments or services (*affidatura*) connected to their status.[49] Aldebertus would, following a payment, thereafter be 'good and free' and released from all the requisitions associated with *affidatura*. Aldebertus' new condition allowed him legal control over his own affairs, to act according to Barese customs and seemed to include all his household.[50] Later, from an important document of 1113, the archbishop of Bari released a number of individuals from the *affidatio* in return for the usual payment, which would be used to protect the endangered city. From this we learn that the *affidati* paid an annual sum to the *res publica*; however, now they no longer had to pay this and were henceforth classed as 'liberi et absoluti inter concives' of the city. Interestingly the decision to release these *affidati* was reached with 'the assent of [the] citizens of the commune'.[51] Later in 1127 a dispute over whether a certain Lupo was of slave rank provides another reference.

---

[47] *Trani*, nos. 81, 84. [48] *Hist. Dip. Friderici Secundi*, i (i, ii). 375–7.
[49] N. Tamassia, '*Ius Affidandi*. Origine e svolgimento nell'Italia meridionale', *Atti del reale istituto veneto di scienze, lettere ed arti* 72 [part 2] (1912–13), pp. 343–90; Martin, *Pouille*, p. 313.
[50] *CDBV*, no. 51. [51] *CDBV*, no, 59.

Lupo argued that he was a freeman (*ingenuus*) because his mother was Bulgarian and that therefore he was not born from slaves. Witnesses were brought forward to attest this and the Bulgarian descent of Lupo's mother 'was known by many of our fellow citizens' (*concives*).[52] The city's charter of privileges of 1132 twice refers to the *cives* – first to guarantee their role in the election of important local religious officials and then to establish that only a *civis*, not an *extraneus*, will be appointed as a city judge. Interestingly, at the end of the document all the privileges are confirmed for an apparently wider body called, on this occasion, *habitatores civitatis Bari*. An additional qualification at this point excepting the *Amalfitani* and *affidati* from these guarantees suggests that these groups were normally considered as *habitatores*, if perhaps not *cives*.[53] References thereafter to 'citizens' are rare before 1200.[54] After this date *cives* appear to be linked more closely to semi-public functions. In a public document of 1201, the four delegates of Bari who, on behalf of their city, had signed a treaty with Ragusa, were called *cives*.[55] Later, in 1205, an unnamed group of *concives* certified the price of oil. In 1214 and 1230 similar groups of *concives* sat in court and assisted in cases concerning wills.[56]

It is also from *c.* 1200 that the Customs of Bari survive. While the customs quite regularly use the label *civis*, they only confuse an understanding of any separate identity attached to it. On the whole, when the customs employ the term it seems synonymous with its usage of *Barenses* and both appear in contexts which ostensibly deal with ideas of citizenship. We are told that whoever takes up domicile in Bari is immediately made a person of the city (*statim Barensis efficitur*) and shall live, and be judged, by civic law and custom.[57] In addition, *Barenses* are free from taxes and services, they are not to be taken from the city to be judged and the rank of knight (*miles*) is open to anybody born a *Barensis*.[58] Yet elsewhere it is stated that 'there never has been any difference between our knights (*milites*) and the *rest* of our citizens (*ceteros cives nostros*) but they have been equal and indistinct in all matters' – though confusingly certain differences of *gener* and *vita* were noted, and the

[52] *CDBV*, no. 74.   [53] *Rogerii II Regis Diplomata Latina*, pp. 54–6 no. 20.
[54] In 1177 *CDBI*, no. 53; and 1180 *CDBV*, no. 144; a fragmentary document of 1169, redacted in Trani, refers to a *concivis* of a person from Bari, *CDBV*, no. 127.
[55] *Acta et Diplomata Ragusina*, no. 13.
[56] *CDBVI*, nos. 16, 30, 50. For examples of more specifically identified *cives*: in 1216 a Malgerius de Comestabulo *asculensis* (Ascoli Satriano) *civis et barensis* appears. It is impossible to know whether we are dealing with dual citizenship or some form of surname, *CDBI*, no. 84. In 1205 John de Agralisto was described by the archbishop of Bari as *nobilis concivis noster*, *CDBI*, no. 73.
[57] Petroni, *Storia di Bari*, ii. 440 Rubric II. 8
[58] Petroni, *Storia di Bari*, ii. 438, 440 Rubric II. 1, 2, 7.

milites were exempt from galley service.[59] Another clause identifies four groups as owing galley service – *civis, incola Barensis* (inhabitant of Bari), *affidatus* and *indigena* (native) – suggesting that each had its own legal identity.[60] Again later, *Barensis* and *civis* seem to be used as synonyms in the clauses concerning the locations of courts and cases brought by men from Ravello who were living in Bari.[61] Finally, a foreign witness (*extraneus*) could not bring a case against a *civis*, although those 'who have their residence in Bari are not regarded as *extranei*'.[62]

The examples thus far suggest that the *civis* label was growing in use as the twelfth century progressed. When the word appears it does in some cases seem to be linked to particular rights and privileges: the right to hold public office, to have access to local custom and law and to be freed from certain payments. The *civis* title is often used where public duties are concerned, and it is also employed as a contrast to the *extraneus* (foreigner/outsider). But confusingly, and of huge significance, at other times different terminology is employed in the same contexts where the *civis* title had, or would have been expected to have, been used.

Evidence from elsewhere does not unfortunately clear up the ambiguity. But two further and very different cases, Benevento and Aversa, can at least verify the increased appearance of the word by the later twelfth century. Likewise they confirm the disparate contexts, and potential meanings, in which the 'citizen' title can appear. Usage of *civis* in the charter documentation at Benevento appears from the 1080s at least. Its precocious emergence may well be due to the fact that Benevento passed to papal rule in the 1070s, thus providing direct connections with the centre and north of the peninsula, where the language of citizenship was more prominent. Indeed, the use of the word *civis* appears only in public and semi-public documents, usually drafted by either the pope, the rector (his main representative in the city) or the city's archbishop. In contrast to other cities it did not infiltrate into private charters later on in our period; however, Falco repeatedly used the word in his chronicle which he compiled from the early 1120s to *c.* 1144. Most frequently the word was used for groups acting in some sort of consultative context: thus in 1082 Stephen Sculdascio, the rector, took the advice of certain *cives* over a concession made to S. Sofia; a document of 1123 tells of a delegation to the pope which consisted of

[59] Petroni, *Storia di Bari*, ii. 440 Rubric II. 3. D. Waley, *Siena and the Sienese in the Thirteenth Century* (Cambridge, 1991), 'The obligation of the wealthier citizens to serve in the community's cavalry force was common to all the independent Italian cities', p. 189.
[60] Petroni, *Storia di Bari*, ii. 440 Rubric II. 5.
[61] Petroni, *Storia di Bari*, ii. 440, 448 Rubric II. 7, III. 11.
[62] Petroni, *Storia di Bari*, ii. 444 Rubric III. 4.

'the more noble Beneventan citizens'; and in the mid-1130s Pope Anacletus restored two mills to S. Sofia with the consent of 'almost all the
greater and more noble citizens'.[63] Later on, in 1216, 'an abundant
multitude of Beneventan citizens' were present, with the rector, at a
court case.[64] In other charters the 'citizen' title is used in a wider sense.
In 1106 the city rector restored land that had been usurped in an earlier
rebellion and spoke of the injustice suffered by many citizens.[65] In 1153
an agreement upheld the (unspecified) customs in force between the
cives beneventani and the barons of nearby Montefusco, while the archbishop of Benevento declared in 1176 that, for a three-year period, no
civis of Benevento or an *extraneus* (foreigner/outsider) should be admitted
to the choir.[66] A papal decree of 1184 allowed the city's Amalfitan and
Ravellese communities to be judged by their own officials when action
was brought by a citizen of Benevento.[67] On only a few occasions were
individuals specifically named as citizens; for example, in 1128 the rector
of Benevento conceded the former property of an 'adversary of the city
of Benevento' to a Richard Paccone '*civis Beneventanus* and *fidelis* of
Blessed Peter', and in 1199 Pope Innocent III referred to a man charged
with murdering a city consul as Gerard, son of Roffred, *civis Beneventanus*.[68] That the *civis* title could be applied at Benevento to men in
such contrasting positions is notable.

The city's statutes of 1202 do refer to citizens, but like other records
of customs, the label is often interchangeable with other terms such as
populus. This double-usage occurs immediately in the document's preamble, written in 1230.[69] The subsequent copy of the 1202 statutes then
states that 'the *populus* [were] complaining that the constitutions were
not being upheld as they had been drafted' and that this was 'to the
disadvantage and burden of the *cives*' – surely here these groups are one
and the same. When *civis* is used in isolation in the document it concerns
intricate judicial matters. While the statutes are poorly ordered, with
little structure, one would have still expected such a source to provide

---

[63] *Chron. S. Sophiae*, ii. 662–6 no. v.12, 786–8 no. vi.37.
[64] Borgia, *Memorie istoriche*, iii. 185–7.
[65] *Chron. S. Sophiae*, ii. 744–7 no. vi.24; *Montevergine*, ii. no. 117.
[66] *Montevergine*, iv. no. 315; *Cattedrale di Benevento*, no. 97.
[67] Borgia, *Memorie istoriche*, iii. 163–6.
[68] *Montevergine*, ii. no. 169; *Register Innocenz III*, pp. 419–20 no. 216. For other individual references
to named *cives* (all post-1200) see *Montevergine*, xii. no. 1180; *Regesta Honorii Papae III*, i. 26 no.
139, 112 no. 649, 216 no. 1304 (the latter case was the famous jurist Roffred Epiphanio, see
below pp. 190–1); H. Houben, 'Urkunden zur italienischen Rechtsgeschichte. Abschriften aus
dem Staats-archiv Neapel im Nachlass Julius Ficker', *QF* 79 (1999), pp. 64–5 no. 12.
[69] See above p. 156 n. 179.

a clearer picture of citizenship.[70] A later letter of Pope Honorius III to the city in 1216 does, however, make an interesting allusion to citizenship. The pope established that free (*liber*) people who had chosen to live in Benevento, provided that they had taken an oath of loyalty to the papacy, 'ought to be counted in all respects as [if] a citizen', and were not to be forced to return to their former abodes.[71] A similar connection with residence was noted in the aforementioned Customs of Bari.

At Aversa, on the other hand, the first charter reference to *cives* occurs only in 1195 and thereafter its use proliferates. Before this the standard *de civitate Aversa* and *habitator civitatis Averse* abound. However, almost unique in southern Italy and another northern European influence on Aversa, some people in the community were also called *burgenses* and referred to themselves as *unus ex burgensibus civitatis Averse*. The meaning of the word is problematic. It may be that the term *burgensis* applied to an inhabitant of a suburb or was simply an ordinary freeman.[72] It certainly seems that at Aversa the *burgensis* had a much narrower significance than *civis*, as employed in other South Italian cities, and that as a group the *burgenses* formed only one subset of the wider community. This is supported by the way numerous other inhabitants identified themselves variously as *unus ex militibus*, *ex baronibus* or *de vavassoribus civitatis Averse*. Moreover, a strange document from 1150 seems to group fifty-six witnesses into the categories of *diaconi*, *Aversani*, *burgenses* and *Amalfitani*.[73] However, it is important to note that King Roger's legislation, applied generally to the kingdom, contained a clause referring to *cives*, *burgenses* and *rustici*, which suggests a distinction between the categories.[74] The term *burgensis* first appeared in 1109, when the prince of Capua conceded dyeing rights to two *burgenses et fideles* of Aversa.[75] From the further occasions in which the *burgenses* appear in private documents (1150?, 1151, 1153, 1155, 1160, 1168, 1194), one common theme emerges – most of those who carried the title were reasonably prominent local figures, with artisan connections and some land or property.[76] Of course many crafts developed in extramural settlements,

[70] Vergineo, *Storia di Benevento*, pp. 226–41.   [71] *Regesta Honorii Papae III*, i.25 no. 133.

[72] Jones, *Italian City-State*, p. 288; Martin, *Pouille*, p. 309; Fasoli, 'Città e ceti urbani', p. 162 suggests little difference between *burgenses* and *cives*.

[73] *CDNA*, pp. 99–101 no. 57.   [74] Monti, *Stato normanno svevo*, p. 118 article III.

[75] *Pergamene di Capua*, i. 25–6 no. 10.

[76] *CDNA*, pp. 99–101 no. 57, pp. 105–7 no. 61, pp. 113–14 no. 65, pp. 341–2 no. 19, pp. 135–6 no. 78, pp. 157–60 no. 89; *Montevergine*, x. no. 927. Some of these *burgenses* had surnames of professions which may have represented their present job, like Gilbert Parmentarius (tailor), who also received the dyeing rights in 1109, or which at least denoted their descent from an artisan family, like Clement Tallapetra (quarryman/sculptor), who was a *strategotus* of Aversa. Others were the sons of artisans, like Roger son of Pippin tanitor (tanner), while the deacon Robert de

and some of these *burgenses* may have lived within them, yet there are numerous examples of other people who expressly identified themselves only as *habitatores* while living in Aversa's various suburbs.[77] One of these *burgenses* of Aversa, Roger the son of Pippin the tanner, appeared four times between 1158 and 1168 and only once was called *burgensis*; interestingly this one occasion was the only occasion when Roger was the main participant in the charter and acted in the first person.[78] In short, how a person attained the status of *burgensis* and what it really denoted in Aversa is not known. Notably at Brindisi, in 1144, the city's *catepan* granted some land to be held 'moreque novorum burgensium' (by the custom of the new *burgenses*).[79]

Whatever its meaning, it appears that the word *burgensis* was increasingly dropping out of usage at Aversa by the last third of the twelfth century, especially as the final two references from private charters, in 1168 and 1194, are made by men whose fathers had been *burgenses* but who themselves were not.[80] The last (and anonymous) *burgensis* reference at Aversa would appear to be in Henry VI's confirmation of various privileges to the city in 1195.[81] Interestingly this document is also the first to mention citizens. In it, the *barones*, *milites* and *cives* of Aversa received ratification of all their good customs from the time of both King Williams. Further on, *omnes cives Aversani* had all their holdings at the time of the same kings safeguarded, while immediately afterwards in the grant the *burgenses ipsius civitatis* (are they also *cives*?) were to give homage only to Henry and his heirs. It seems significant that this document represents the last charter record of *burgenses* and the first of *cives* in the city – particularly when the decline in the use of the former occurred at roughly the same time (from *c.* 1170) as the rise in the use of the latter in other South Italian cities. From 1197 'citizens' appear increasingly in the private documentation for Aversa.[82] They appear

---

Sancto Paulo, not described as a *burgensis*, inherited shops from his father William, who had been one.

[77] *CDNA*, pp. 132–4 no. 76, pp. 180–8 no. 100, pp. 187–92 nos. 103–4, pp. 339–42 nos. 18–19; *CDSA*, pp. 28–30 no. 14, pp. 219–21 no. 109.

[78] See below p. 205.   [79] *Conversano*, no. 94.

[80] 'Robbertus de Sancto Paulo, filius olim Willelmi de Sancto Paulo, qui fuit unus ex burgiensibus Averse', *CDNA*, pp. 157–60 no. 89; 'Laurentius filius quondam Raonis Monsororii, qui fuit unus ex burgiensibus civitatis Averse', *Montevergine*, x. no. 927. The ambiguity of the Latin makes it difficult to know whether the *qui* clause refers to the father or the son, although the latter appears more likely in both cases.

[81] Clementi, 'Calendar', pp. 166–7 no. 79 (full text in P. Scheffer-Boichorst, 'Urkunden und Forschungen zu den Regesten der staufischen Periode', *Neues Archiv der Gesellschaft für ältere deutsche Geschichtskunde* 27 (1902), pp. 78–81).

[82] For example *Montevergine*, xi. no. 1037; *Pergamene sveve*, i. no. 17; *CDSA*, pp. 10–13 no. 5, pp. 24–6 no. 12, pp. 43–5 no. 21, pp. 152–5 no. 76, pp. 201–2 no. 99; Houben, 'Urkunden',

largely similar to the previous *burgenses* – some had artisan surnames, many were clearly important figures and most had landed wealth. But those carrying this *civis* title were more disparate, including religious and civic officials as well as *milites*. The label was often attached (as at Bari) to groups of people acting in the semi-public function of executing wills.[83] On other occasions the *civis* was someone who paid a census for property – perhaps showing a link between possession of property and citizenship (already noted at Trani).[84] It might be that the emergence of the *civis* title subsumed that of the *burgensis*, which may in turn suggest an equalising and a widening of the concept of the civic community. Nevertheless, it was the *burgensis* label and not *civis* which was used in the decrees issued in Frederick II's Constitutions of Melfi of 1231.[85]

Finally, material from Troia shows a similar chronology in the emergence of the *civis* label and perhaps provides one explanation for the usage and meaning of the 'citizen' title. Before 1170 the only reference to *civis* is found in the city's charter of privileges of 1127; a document drawn up by Pope Honorius II, who, it perhaps should be noted, was from Bologna. A variety of terms or groups – *Troianus habitator*, *Troiani*, *Troianus incola*, *extraneus* – are used, but also on three occasions so too is *civis*. The pope allowed the more respectable section of the citizens (*sanior pars civium*) to decide on military policy, undertook to protect the citizens from plunder or violence and acknowledged certain rights which were granted to him by them.[86] However, from 1170 onwards an upsurge occurs in the use of the word in private charters by a variety of people, including women and in one case a minor.[87] The circumstances in which people were adopting the civic designation do not conform to any apparent pattern and cover an array of ordinary land sales and legal transactions. It might be worth considering here the rise of nearby Foggia, a settlement within Troia's *contado*, as a possible reason for the rapid increase and arbitrary employment of the *civis* label. By the later twelfth century, Foggia's economic and physical expansion was

---

p. 76 no. 18. Though it is worth noting that in an Aversan charter of 1186 we do find the word used for a Ligorio *civis Neapolitano et baro civitatis Averse*, *CDNA*, p. 242 no. 130.

[83] *CDSA*, pp. 63–6 no. 31, pp. 142–3 no. 70, pp. 155–6 no. 77, pp. 175–7 no. 86, pp. 193–5 no. 95.

[84] *CDSA*, pp. 108–9 no. 53, pp. 142–3 no. 70, pp. 146–8 no. 72, pp. 155–6 no. 77, pp. 161–3 no. 80, pp. 168–70 no. 83, pp. 193–5 no. 95, pp. 197–9 no. 97, pp. 272–4 no. 136 (which sees a woman with the *civis* title).

[85] *Hist. Dip. Friderici Secundi*, iv (i). 123 Bk III title vi (58), 148–9 Bk III title xliii (22); Powell's English translation here reads 'townsman' for *burgensis*, *Liber Augustalis*, pp. 109, 129–30.

[86] *Troia*, no. 50 clauses 7, 8, 22.

[87] *Troia*, nos. 86, 92, 93, 100, 103, 121, 128, 129, 133, 139, 141–43, 158; *Colonie cassinesi*, nos. 38, 40; *Montevergine*, vi. no. 568, vii. nos. 606, 684, x. nos. 924, 935, xii. nos. 1144, 1161, 1173, xiii. no. 1243.

outstripping Troia and threatening its primacy in the region of the Tavoliere plain. Foggia's ecclesiastical dependence on the Church of Troia became more incongruous as the settlement, still called a *castrum*, now seemed a 'city' in all but name. The possession of its own bishopric, which in the tradition of ancient Christianity was usually a measure of civic status, would confirm Foggia's new position. The ramifications for Troia were obvious.[88] Indeed, in some charters of the 1190s Foggia was called a *civitas* and in the 1220s Foggians were identifying themselves as *cives*.[89] In the 1190s, and again in the 1210s, Foggia also seemed on the cusp of gaining episcopal rank. The appearance of the *Troiani cives* in private charters from the 1170s occurred almost at the same time as the first open discords between the two settlements.[90] This growing local tension, stimulated by civic pride, might well have influenced the people of Troia to assert their ascendancy more clearly by emphasising their citizen status. This in turn would imply that civic status was something worth having and brought advantage. As a term, one of its uses appears to be to define superiority and belonging and at the same time to identify otherness.

The notion of citizenship in twelfth-century southern Italy appears to have had a transient, uncertain quality and to lack any neat categories. There are no discernible patterns, except for a newly emergent awareness of it from the later twelfth century, and the fact that as a concept it was flexible. Citizenship in the South was largely described in the language and terminology of an earlier civilisation which had developed a sophisticated and influential concept of the *civis*. Yet despite the South's classical legacy, the Roman notion of citizenship may have played only a minor part here, as the most general of templates. The increasing emergence of the 'citizen' in medieval southern Italy, and the core of its meaning, was much more a result of the particular circumstances of the region's cities at that period. Even in northern Italy the question of citizenship appears more imprecise and less central to urban life than expected. Recent work has tended to emphasise the haphazard manner in which urban institutions and civic ordering developed there in the late eleventh and twelfth centuries.[91] Even for the later period Waley states that in Siena, in the thirteenth century, 'the question of citizenship arose quite rarely and its achievement was less significant than might

---

[88] Martin, *Foggia*, especially pp. 29–53.
[89] *CDNA*, pp. 270–2, no. 143; Houben, 'Urkunden', pp. 57–9 no. 8; *Colonie cassinesi*, nos. 36, 39.
[90] These discords had turned violent at least by the 1190s, for example *Troia*, pp. 114–15, no. 139; Oldfield, 'Rural settlement', 327–45.
[91] C. Wickham, 'The sense of the past in Italian communal narratives', in *The Perception of the Past in Twelfth-Century Europe*, ed. P. Magdalino (London, 1992), pp. 185–7.

be supposed', suggesting that it was not 'a coveted and all-important change of status'.[92] Bowsky's survey, from the same city in the period 1287–1355, highlights the problems of understanding citizenship, even with, by medieval standards, a wealth of source material.[93]

For the South one can only speculate on the reasons for the increasing use of the word. Growing, ever-mobile, urban populations and a more articulate civic consciousness could be part of the explanation, and in this context perhaps there is a link with the emerging references in the sources to civic rights (*iura civilia*) as opposed to local customs and usages (*consuetudines et usus*).[94] Indeed, the twelfth century saw a revived understanding of Roman law in places like Bologna, which may have brought a renewed interest in Roman models of citizenship. However, how far this legal revival affected the South remains uncertain, particularly as parts of the region were already familiar with its use, or forms of it, as a result of the Byzantine inheritance.[95] The requirements of more efficient and demanding governments could also be a factor. Linked to this could be the greater production, and therefore likely survival rate, of documentation from this later period. We cannot be sure that the word *civis*, in a non-narrative context, was not more widely used earlier. The lack of any real citizenship legislation, such as exists later in northern Italy, may result from the loss of such documentation. Or perhaps the scarcity of references is due to the likelihood that in earlier and different circumstances the need to clearly define civic status was not a relevant enough issue to require attention and record.

A rare reference to the *civis* title at Monopoli in 1181 encapsulates the dilemma. Peter Paulus, son of Silvester, of the city of Monopoli (*civitatis Monopoli*), established three *concives* as his mediators. They included Segnorus, son of Eustasius, Nicholas Longum of Monopoli (*de Monopoli*) and John of Massafra, inhabitant of the city of Monopoli (*de Massafro habitatorem civitatis Monopoli*). The last man was identified, at the same time, as from Massafra and as both a *habitator* and *concivis* of Monopoli.[96] Perhaps it was the public aspect of acting as mediator which was primarily responsible for the *concivis* label here. Most frequently the *civis* title does appear within a public context or is attributed to someone with public

[92] Waley, *Siena and the Sienese*, p. 72.
[93] W. M. Bowsky, 'Medieval citizenship: the individual and the state in the commune of Siena, 1287–1355', *Studies in Medieval and Renaissance History* 4 (1967), pp. 193–243.
[94] For civic identity see below pp. 241–5.
[95] In 1180 a notary from Bari was 'in Boloniam ad legendum', *CDBV*, no. 144; in 1199 an archdeacon of Otranto was 'in scolis apud Boloniam', *CDSA*, pp. 19–21 no. 9. The jurist Roffred de Epiphanio of Benevento also studied at Bologna, see below pp. 190–1.
[96] *CDBI*, no. 57.

responsibilities. Our body of evidence also suggests that social status, a level of personal freedom, residency and tax-paying/property ownership were all contexts in which the *civis* label was used. In some places it does seem that the *civis* title meant something specific, although we do not know what. In others, the suspicion arises that we are joining too directly the *civis* title with concepts that might not otherwise have been solely dependent on the word's use. As alluded to earlier, the authorship of documents referring to *cives* should also be taken into account. *Civis* may well have carried a vastly different core meaning depending on whether it appeared in a papal, episcopal, public or private charter.[97] Above all, can we make any firm deductions, given the inconsistency of terminology found in the source material? It may simply be that, as today, words were used loosely, that they carried inherent ambiguities and contradictions that were meant to be so. When the *civis* title was employed, did it denote any additional personal rights or political, social and economic advantages? Were the individuals who referred to themselves as a *habitator civitatis* or a *Salernitanus* not in practice also a *civis*, and was the 'citizen' title not an interchangeable one, only adopted in particular circumstances? Were those who lacked a variety of privileges, such as slaves/servants, *affidati*, religious minorities and foreigners, held to be citizens? Were perhaps the *affidati* unfree citizens? A charter from Barletta of 1183 reveals a Samuel *ebreus Tranensis civis* alongside non-Jews who were also sporting the *civis* label – does this mean that Jews were considered to be as much a part of the citizen body as Christians?[98] It could well be that different forms of citizenship functioned within the same city.[99] The number of unanswered questions and uncertainties seems almost infinite. Perhaps we should not attempt to fit such clearly fluctuating concepts into defined categories and meanings, while also acknowledging a flexibility that those in the medieval world seemed comfortable with.

---

[97] The influence of Christianity on the idea of *civis* and *civitas*, and especially St Augustine and his *The City of God*, could also offer an interesting route to explore.

[98] *Pergamene di Barletta. Archivio Capitolare*, no. 141, also see below pp. 209–14.

[99] J. Kirshner, 'Civitas sibi faciat civem; Bartolous of Sassoferato's doctrine on the making of a citizen', *Speculum* 48 (1973), pp. 694–713.

Chapter 7

THE COMMUNITY

It is perhaps significant that the uncertainties of citizenship reflected those of the social ordering of urban society. Whether all 'citizens' or not, the urban community was, on occasion, categorised into other rudimentary groups. One of the most common divisions was *maiores*, *mediocres* and *minores* or *clerici*, *milites*, and *universus populus*.[1] However, a whole range of other labels was employed, showing their artificial, arbitrary and subjective construction, as well as regional variations. A brief sample of the narrative sources reveals this variety, with a focus mostly on elite terminology. William of Apulia's account of the siege of Bari (1068–71) refers at different points to *primates urbis*, *maiores* and *minores* (but not to *mediocres*) and to 'those who form the most noble and powerful section of the city'.[2] Still in Bari, in the 1110s and 1120s we hear of *nobiles Barensium* (the noble men of Bari), *primarii civitatis* and *sapientes*.[3] When the city fell to Roger II in 1139 certain *prudentes cives* were arrested.[4] Likewise in Salerno we encounter groups called the *sapientes civitatis* (1137), the *Salernitanorum maiores* (1162) and the *nobiles viri* (1191).[5] Elsewhere, in 1099 Pope Urban II addressed the clergy, nobles (*nobiles*) and people (*plebs*) of Trani.[6] At Naples, Duke Sergius'

---

[1] Fasoli, 'Città e ceti urbani', pp. 161–3; Chalandon, *Histoire de la domination normande,* ii. 601–2. The latter set reflects the medieval literary perception that society had a tripartite ordering of those who prayed, those who fought and those who worked, A. Murray, *Reason and Society in the Middle Ages* (Oxford, 1978), p. 96; C. D. Fonseca, ' "*Ordines*" istituzionali e ruoli sociali', in *Condizione umana e ruoli sociali nel Mezzogiorno normanno-sveve. Atti delle none giornate normanno-sveve. Bari, 1989*, ed. G. Musca (Bari, 1991), pp. 9–18; letters from Innocent III to the cities of the South were often addressed 'episcopo, clero, militibus et populo', *Register Innocenz*, pp. 453–5 no. 236.

[2] *Will. Apulia,* Bk II pp. 158–62 lines 479–573, Bk III pp. 170–2 lines 111–66.

[3] *Anonymi Barensis Chronicon,* p. 154 a.1117; *Vita S. Iohannis a Mathera,* cols. 38–9. In Barese charters *plerique nobiles civitatis* were present at court cases, *CDBI*, no. 40; *CDBV*, no. 67.

[4] *Falco,* p. 230.

[5] 1137: *Falco,* p. 188; 1162: *Historia o Liber de regno,* p. 81 and in the English translation *Falcandus,* pp. 131–2; 1191: *Peter of Eboli,* p. 39 Bk I.XVII line 453.

[6] *Trani,* no. 25.

promissio of 1129/30 was made to 'all the noblemen, all the *mediani* and to all the inhabitants of Naples', while documents from Gaeta speak both of *maiores*, *mediocres* and *minores* and the *populus magnus vel parvus*.[7] We might note here the comparison with the tripartite ordering (*capitanei*, *valvassores* and *populus*) that apparently so shaped the social composition in some early communal regimes in northern and central Italy.[8]

A fundamental problem lies in the kaleidoscope of overlapping vertical and horizontal communities which operated in differing frameworks (social, geographic, familial, religious, ethnic, professional, economic, political) within the urban populace. Recent research emphasises the importance of viewing communities as networks of individuals.[9] It would have been (as it is today) impossible to create a conceptual vocabulary to represent the complexity of such continually mutable relationships. In deference to this, and for textual clarity, medieval commentators often employed catch-all terminology when discussing the urban community, and we should not apply a specificity to them which they were not intended to have. Aversa seems atypical, where inhabitants identified themselves as *milites*, *barones*, *vavassores* and *burgenses* – but these categories still present numerous ambiguities.[10] The idea that *nobiles* or *maiores* were a defined 'privileged class' of nobles and knights clearly separated from the *mediani*, who were themselves solely medium-sized landholders, officials and specialist artisans, in turn separated from the menial workers, the poor and the underprivileged who made up the *popolani*, is far too inflexible. Such categories were not intended to demarcate legal distinctions but were mutable, perceived and subjective classifications of people by their mode of living, wealth and influence.[11] Particularly in the twelfth century, southern Italy was subject to trends common throughout Europe that increased the amorphous nature of urban class structures: the steady revival of the economy, urbanisation, population growth and the influence of the twelfth-century cultural renaissance. These developments opened opportunities for social ascent (and descent) to an ever-widening circle of people. Trade, commerce and urban growth provided wealth for those who could not primarily rely on birth or a landed income, while slowly increasing literacy rates opened up public office to a wider circle of people at a time when government was becoming more complex. European-wide literary references to the social order of the eleventh and twelfth centuries

---

[7] Cassandro, 'La *Promissio*', appendix, p. 145; *Cod. Dip. Caietanus*, ii. nos. 301, 308.
[8] *Deeds of Frederick Barbarossa*, Bk II p. 127; Coleman, 'Italian communes', pp. 382–3.
[9] Lynch, *Individuals, Families, and Communities*, pp. 14–15.   [10] See above pp. 178–80.
[11] G. Fasoli, 'Governanti e governati nei comuni cittadini fra l'XI ed il XIII secolo', in *Scritti di storia medievale* (Bologna, 1974), pp. 205–6.

depict people rising from humble origins to a higher social status. The philosophical allegory of Fortune's Wheel, which emerged in the twelfth century, reflected the fluidity of social mobility.[12]

As a result, the margins between social groups were easily blurred, and an individual could be a member of different ones according to context and circumstance. Any understanding of them must be flexible and tentative. At the pinnacle of every medieval urban population was a solidarity grouping which attained (or maintained) that position through a combination of wealth (primarily landed), inheritance and/or public office.[13] As we have seen, it was this elite, or upper class, that most closely participated in urban government, with the support of the *populus*. It directed civic councils, and some of its members formed the higher circles of the city ruler's entourage (as at Aversa, Capua and Salerno) or, in his absence, actually governed the city itself (as at Bari under Grimoald and at Benevento in the 1090s and the 1120s–30s). After 1139 many of the urban elite maintained their influence (and wealth) by accepting royal offices. It was to this group that commentators attributed the epithets *nobiles*, *sapientes* and *maiores*. There is evidence that the term *nobiles* in some way represented a distinct solidarity, with a sense of a collective consciousness. The copy of Salerno's privileges of 1127 repeatedly distinguishes the *nobiles* from the rest of the community. One clause stipulates that Roger II was to prevent the '*nobiles* from integrating themselves with the populace and the populace from obtaining the privileges of the nobles [*munera nobilium*], let them be distinct as before and after the arrival of the Lombards, as has been practised and observed up to now'.[14] The sense of a separate group identity is especially apparent at Naples. It is evident in Duke Sergius' *promissio*, in the governing role of the *nobiles* in 1137–9 and in the rebellion of 1156 by the *mediani* in which the *nobiles* restored order. Later, in Tancred's grant to Naples and Naples's to Amalfi (both in 1190), references were made to agreements and pacts previously made between the *nobiles* and the *populus*.[15] This

---

[12] Murray, *Reason and Society*, pp. 97–101. The idea of Fortune's Wheel features in southern Italy in the work of Geoffrey Malaterra and especially in that of the so-called *Falcandus*, pp. 37–8 for a discussion.

[13] L. Genicot, 'Recent research on the medieval nobility', in *The Medieval Nobility*, ed. T. Reuter (Oxford, 1978), p. 18.

[14] *Storia documentata della scuola medica di Salerno*, lxxiii no. 177. Though as noted previously we must remain cautious around the language of this document, see above p. 173 n. 43.

[15] Cassandro, 'La *Promissio*', appendix, p. 145; Fuiano, 'Napoli normanna e sveva', pp. 430–2; *Tancredi et Willelmi III Regum Diplomata*, pp. 15–8 no. 6; Filangieri, 'Note al *Privilegium Libertatis*', pp. 107–16.

separate status was probably drawn above all from a shared identity derived from birth, landed power, which carried jurisdiction over those on the land, and wealth. The urban domicile of the nobility was relatively prevalent throughout Italy's cities in comparison with those of northern Europe. This was the case at Salerno, where the title of *comes* became an indicator of noble standing. To carry the comital title undoubtedly placed a person within the highest level of urban society, just below the prince. It was essentially an honorific office, and evidence for it conveying public and territorial power is slight. This distinction becomes more superfluous in the course of the eleventh century, as the title developed increasingly into a hereditary one and was restricted to a smaller social circle.[16] After the Norman take-over the comital title appears more infrequently. However, the title still retained a social cachet and in the thirteenth century families still traced their ancestry back to a *comes*.[17] The Guarna are a prime example of both this and of how such kin-groups maintained their position under Norman rule in a different guise. At Amalfi, leading families of the twelfth and thirteenth centuries also recorded their noble status by tracing unique genealogies that sometimes stretched back ten or eleven generations to a comital progenitor.[18] At Aversa, individuals clearly identified themselves as one of the barons ('unus ex baro') of the city or as holding a barony ('baroniam') there. Often these figures had both urban and rural property and interests alongside a lordship in the city's territory.[19]

The knights (*milites*), referred to as a grouping with increasing consistency from the twelfth century, were essentially a lesser element within this nobility. If the rank was primarily a Norman importation, it was not only they but also indigenous people who appear to have held it. Originally it may have represented a soldier profession, but gradually it seems to have developed into a marker of social status. Aside from numerous individual references in charters from many cities, *milites* not surprisingly appear repeatedly as an identifiable solidarity, especially at Aversa, but also at Naples, where there was in fact a pre-Norman tradition of the use of the word. Neapolitan *milites* feature in the surrender agreement with Roger II in 1140, in the rebellion of 1156 and also in the two important agreements in 1190 between Tancred and Naples and between Naples and the Amalfitans.[20] King Roger's legislation attempted to make the knightly class a closed one by forbidding entrance to

---

[16] V. Loré, 'L'aristocrazia salernitana nell'XI secolo', in *Salerno nel XII secolo*, pp. 61–102.
[17] See above p. 31 n. 10.
[18] M. Del Treppo and A. Leone, *Amalfi medioevale* (Naples, 1977), pp. 89–119.
[19] For example *CDNA*, pp. 279–81 no. 147, pp. 382–4 no. 41; *CDSA*, pp. 3–5 no. 2, pp. 22–4 no. 11.
[20] *Falco*, p. 236; Filangieri, 'Note al *Privilegium Libertatis*', pp. 107–16.

anyone not 'descended from the stock [*prosapia*] of a knightly family' or without royal approval.[21] However, numerous references to *milites* within cities as being the offspring of judges and artisans suggest that this was not rigorously enforced, and that knighthood was neither a closed nor consistent social grouping.[22] The terminology used by individuals was often vague, and in central Apulia, for example, the title of *sire* or *sere* might or might not at times have been its equivalent.[23] Tancred's grant to Naples in 1190 allowed any citizen of Naples who wished to be a *miles* to become one, although this appears to have been a late thirteenth-century interpolation. Frederick II's constitutions of 1231 reiterated Roger II's earlier decree but admitted that 'knights, who until now have obtained the knightly dignity contrary to the prohibition [of Roger II], should retain their dignity . . . as long as they live in a knightly manner.'[24] From the Bari customs (*c.* 1200) a contradictory classification emerges. Apparently in the city '*nobilitas* is general and open [*generosa*], so that whoever wishes may enroll himself in military service and be knighted, and no question is to be asked upon from what father or mother he has been born, provided he is only a Baresi by birth.' However, it goes on to state that 'there has never been any difference between our *milites* and *cives*', except for those in *gener et vita.*[25]

It certainly seems that there existed a traditional and 'legally privileged' noble group within South Italian cities. The Constitutions of Melfi stipulated different punishment for injuries 'according to the rank of men' – these included townsman (*burgensis*), countryman (*rusticus*) and even different grades within the knighthood and nobility. The judgements of nobles are also referred to, suggesting judicial privileges.[26] Yet the above evidence from Bari suggests it is important not to have too rigid a conception of those forming the urban upper class. The urban nobility was a fluid and open class constantly being reshaped and renewed. In fact, those we would consider to be nobles often appear to be very similar to those whom we would not. To further confuse matters the word *nobilis* can, for example, as Genicot notes, 'connote something individual, social, or legal; [it] can apply to people of great personal value,

---

[21] Monti, *Stato normanno svevo*, p. 131 article xix.

[22] At Aversa, for example, in 1182, the knight Lawrence was the *nepos* of Alexander the judge of Aversa, *CDNA*, pp. 220–2 no. 118; in 1205 we encounter a Robert de Iudice, son of judge Stephen, who was *unus ex feudatis militis* of Aversa and, in the same document, the Aversan knight Humphrey son of Rao the doctor, *CDSA*, pp. 94–6 no. 46. Furthermore, many children of knights did not enter knighthood, such as Ciprianus *nauclerius* (skipper/sailor), the son of a knight attested at Monopoli in 1168, *Conversano*, no. 118.

[23] Martin, *Pouille*, pp. 749–54.   [24] *Liber Augustalis*, p. 141 Bk III, title lix (1), lx (38).

[25] Petroni, *Storia di Bari*, ii. 438, 440 Rubric II.2, 3.

[26] *Liber Augustalis*, pp. 129–30 Bk III, title xliii.

to the members of a superior class, or to members of a legally privileged group'.[27] By the late eleventh century, owing largely to the trends already touched upon, the elites expanded beyond the traditional nobility to incorporate a much more diverse range of people. This becomes more apparent if the descriptive vocabulary used for the urban ruling elites (*nobiles, maiores, sapientes, prudentes*) is given a wider literal meaning. These terms may very often have been applied with a moral, rather than social or legal, sense (the noble men, the wise men and the older men) by a deferential populace naturally respectful of wealth and influence.[28] The language may then reflect prestige obtained through a certain talent (political, intellectual, financial, administrative or military) and not always membership of the 'nobility' or the enjoyment of any fixed legal privileges which went with that. Therefore, figures traditionally considered as non-noble – perhaps lower lay and ecclesiastical officials, medium-sized landowners, artisans, merchants – also formed, under different circumstances, the *nobiles et sapientes viri*. As a result, the civic elite had a noble and non-noble dimension, but both of these 'elements' and their activities were increasingly merging. This was certainly the case in northern Italy too. Here Rippe recently identified the composition of the urban aristocracy as extremely fluid, noting its integration with mercantile and artisan groups.[29] Any distinct split between an older established urban nobility – such as the eleventh-century *comites* of Salerno and Amalfi – and the newer non-noble elites was more perceived than real. There were various points of contact between both – intermarriage, the possession of public office and the ownership of land.[30] Some of the noble and non-noble elite enjoyed landed wealth and public service while also participating in trade. The noble solidarity of counts at Salerno may in many respects, according to Loré, have formed a true class. But equally the same scholar noted that it was never a closed group. The title, and the status attached to it, was not transmitted automatically from father to son, and there were cases of *gastald* and judicial families obtaining the rank.[31] Indeed, during the reign of Guaimar IV (1027–52), the number of attested counts increased to fifty-four, and this

---

[27] L. Genicot, 'The nobility of medieval Francia: continuity, break or evolution', in *Lordship and Community in Medieval Europe*, ed. F. Cheyette (New York, 1968), p. 129.

[28] This is especially likely when the descriptive noun is given in its comparative form, Reynolds, *Kingdoms and Communities*, p. 205; see the examples at Benevento: *nobiliores cives* (*Chron. S. Sophiae*, ii. 786–8 no. vi.37), *maiores ac nobiliores cives* (*Chron. S. Sophiae*, ii. 662–6 no. v.12).

[29] G. Rippe, *Padoue et son contado (Xe–XIIIe siècle)* (Rome, 2003), pp. 324–5.

[30] Jones, *Italian City-State*, pp. 103–7, 116–20, 143 emphasises the importance of landed wealth among the urban elites; Nicholas, *Growth of the Medieval City*, pp. 115–28.

[31] For example, in 1054 a Manso *comes*, son of Manso the *gastald*, *Pergamene di S. Nicola di Gallucanta*, pp. 190–1 no. 73.

was due largely to the emergence of people of non-comital origin.[32] Del Treppo has shown that even at Amalfi those considered to be part of the nobility (*nobiles* or *maiores natu*) were not entirely dissimilar from the *populares* – in this case a generic term for anybody else. People from both groups aspired to public office, disposed of economic resources that depended on a land base and took part (in varying forms) in mercantile activity.[33]

Alongside wealth, a common indicator of membership within the civic elite was the attainment of public office. This in itself brought an additional, powerful identity based on profession.[34] City judges and consuls were often addressed as a grouping alongside the *populus*.[35] The judges' status was always safeguarded within various charters of liberties. We have already noted their quotidian importance in civic affairs.[36] As a result, the urban community considered the office to be synonymous with the 'abstract' city and a symbolic guarantee of local custom. According to the Constitutions of Melfi prospective judges and notaries had to show 'letters from the men of the district in which they are to be appointed. These letters should contain testimony of the trustworthiness and the moral character of the judges or notaries to be appointed, as well as how well instructed they are in the customs of that district.'[37] From the late twelfth century there are also hints in the South that some individuals among the judiciary were acquiring a more professional legal training. This may have been on the back of a growing interest in Roman law, particularly at Bologna, and there are some charter references to individuals from the South studying there.[38] Some new and interesting titles also appear. At Troia we find a *magister legista* (lawyer) and a *magister Rao iudex iurisque professor* (judge and professor of law).[39] At Benevento in 1230 there was a *Saductus doctor iuris civilis iudex et scriba Beneventani palatii* (doctor of civil law, judge and scribe of the Beneventan palace).[40] A judge Saductus Canturbius *legum doctor* signed the recording of Benevento's statutes, also in 1230, as did the judge Roffred Epiphanio,

---

[32] Loré, 'L'aristocrazia salernitana', in *Salerno nel XII secolo*, pp. 66–7.

[33] Del Treppo and Leone, *Amalfi*, pp. 76–81.

[34] This can be seen among notaries who use additional images or marks to identify themselves in documents. See the Montevergine manuscript which forms the frontispiece of this book, where the Barese protonotary Lupo, a name which means 'wolf', uses the image of that animal as his notarial emblem.

[35] See Kehr, 'Una bolla inedita di Papa Celestino III', pp. 1–4; *PL* 214, cols. 513–4 no. 558.

[36] Although using the term 'judge', I follow Wickham's caution on the potential meaning of *iudex*, *Courts and Conflict*, p. 21 n. 11. For further discussion on the city judge see above pp. 103–5.

[37] *Liber Augustalis*, pp. 49–60 Bk I, title lxxix (62).   [38] See above p. 182 n. 95.

[39] *Le Cartulaire du chapitre du Saint Sépulchre de Jérusalem*, ed. G. Bresc-Bautier (Paris, 1984), no. 167; *Montevergine*, ix. no. 840; Clementi, 'Further documents', pp. 171–6 nos. 2–3.

[40] *S. Modesto*, pp. 94–7 no. 37; Borgia, *Memorie istoriche*, ii. 429–30

as *civilis scientie profexor* (professor of civil science).[41] Roffred was born at Benevento, studied at Bologna, taught at Arezzo and became an esteemed jurist. Honorius III promoted Roffred, in 1218, to judge *ordinarius* at Benevento, where he was often found.[42] He also acted in affairs at Pistoia and became a key figure at both the papal and imperial courts – he was present at Frederick's imperial coronation of 1220.[43] Little wonder that judges had such long careers that transcended political upheaval. Most, but by no means all, judges and notaries probably came from already relatively prominent families. Indeed, there are many instances of succeeding generations of a particular kin-group obtaining local offices. But the Constitutions of Melfi stated that 'any judge or public notary, who is of low rank, a *villani* or *angararius*, as well as the sons of the clergy and those who are spurious or in any way illegitimate, should not in the future be appointed or in any way promoted.'[44] This attempt to make the profession of judge and notary more socially restricted indirectly attests how open these offices actually became. Indeed, while there are many examples of judges or notaries who were themselves the sons of judges or notaries, there are equally as many references to those who were not, or whose origins simply cannot be traced. Likewise, it is almost impossible to determine what proportion of the undoubted wealth, especially of city judges, was accrued through their current position or via family inheritance. The confirmation of Trani's customs and privileges in 1215 provided for a customary payment to be made to the city judges, 'who putting their own private business aside give their attention to public business'.[45] This supports the idea of a 'special' connection between judge and city. But in reality it was not the case that the judge's 'private business' was entirely set aside. Judges can be seen participating in a variety of activities away from their public office, as will be seen later. For example, the will made by Peter the judge from Salerno in 1141 gave to Cava some pits outside Salerno with the fishing rights pertaining to them.[46] The judge Petracca Buffus of Bari was also the lay prior of the church of S. Nicola in 1183 and loaned money, in 1194, to the chapter to buy oil and wax. In addition, he acquired a prestigious share of the prebends and oblations originally conceded to the sailors who had brought St Nicholas to the city.[47]

[41] Borgia, *Memorie istoriche*, ii. 429–30: G. Ferretti, 'Roffredo Epifanio da Benevento', *Studi Medievali* 3 (1908–11), pp. 230–87.
[42] See *Regesta Honorii Papae III*, i. 215–6 nos. 1303–4 and appendix of Ferretti, 'Roffredo Epifanio'.
[43] *His. Dip. Friderici Secundi*, ii. 73, 121.   [44] *Liber Augustalis*, p. 141 Bk II, title lx (38).
[45] *His. Dip. Friderici Secundi*, i (ii). 375–7.   [46] Cava, *Arca* xxv.29.
[47] *CDBV*, nos. 148, 163, 164.

Those who obtained the office of consul were certainly already prominent individuals. There is little detailed information about the social status of individual consuls at Benevento – aside from their names, which can often be misleading. However, one consul, Jacob Sculdascio, was the grandson of the city's first papal rector.[48] The status of the consuls who appeared at Benevento in the early thirteenth century appeared to be generally high. We find individuals such as a *comes*, a *vicecomes*, a *compalatius*, a knight, a notary, a son of a notary, two sons of judges but also a goldsmith (*aurifex*) and perhaps a dyer (*tintunerus*).[49] At Gaeta several of the new families, identified by Skinner, who entered the civic elite in the eleventh century obtained the consulate in the early twelfth century.[50] In both cities the office was probably rotated on a yearly basis, and in Benevento a consul could not be re-elected within five years or succeeded by his father, brother or son.[51] This may not have markedly widened the pool of people eligible for the consulate. In northern and central Italy, the consulate rapidly developed into a self-perpetuating elite. However, at Naples the consular government of the early 1190s seems to have had a wider social composition and was not an institution dominated by a hereditary nobility. Aligernus Cotunus, the apparently leading figure in the consulate, appears to have been a 'new man' virtually untraceable before 1190.[52] Of the twenty consuls who signed the famous charter of privileges to the Amalfitans in 1190, Filangieri suggested that eleven were 'nobles', with the rest coming from the *mediani* or *popolani* (for what these imprecise labels are worth).[53]

In short, the civic elite was not a synonym for the noble class. It incorporated people of varying status who had achieved local influence. All that can be attempted in most cases is to recognise when a person exercised power and/or influence, and to suggest that this placed them among the city's leading figures. Classifying individuals or their kin-groups further only leaves a host of contradictions. It will be useful to give examples of influential families and to show in what ways they were

---

[48] See above p. 120.   [49] See above pp. 157–60.
[50] Skinner, *Family Power in Southern Italy*, pp. 197–9.   [51] Borgia, *Memorie istoriche*, ii. 424.
[52] The Cotunus family rose rapidly after 1190, gaining from both sides in the conflicts of the 1190s. As well as his position in Naples, Aligernus seems to have been given the title of 'prince of Sorrento' in 1194, presumably from Henry VI (*Codice diplomatico amalfitano*, i, ed. R. Filangieri di Candida (Naples, 1917), p. 450 no. 234). A brother of Aligernus was briefly awarded the county of Fondi in 1191 (*Rich S. Germano*, p. 13), while a son received the city of Lettere and the castle of Gragnano from the Empress Constance, and remained an influential figure in the region of Naples, *Constantiae Imperatricis et Reginae Siciliae Diplomata*, p. 301 no. 45; Jamison, *Admiral Eugenius*, pp. 90, 100–1, 112, 115, 124, 164, and cal. doc. no. 23 p. 349; Fuiano, 'Napoli normanna e sveva', p. 460.
[53] Filangieri, 'Note al *Privilegium Libertatis*', 107–16.

so. Some of their members may have belonged to the urban nobility, and others not. All that can be demonstrated for certain is that members of the kin-group wielded influence, and what its basis was. At Salerno the two main branches of the Guarna kin-group can be traced back to Romuald Grassus (died before 1109), who carried the title of *comes* and therefore appears to be of 'noble' standing. One branch produced a city *strategotus*, a city judge, an archdeacon, the Archbishop Romuald II (1153–81) and three local lords. The other offshoots included a city judge, a ducal chamberlain, two religious officials, the royal justiciar Lucas Guarna (1172–89 – who was related to a royal chamberlain) and the latter's son the *miles* Philip, who became count of Marsico.[54] A member of the Guarna family had attempted to negotiate Salerno's surrender to Henry VI in 1191 and another was briefly archbishop-elect in 1195–6.[55] The Guarna seem to have still been flourishing in the city in the thirteenth century – a certain judge Romuald Guarna, the son of the judge John Guarna, was attested acquiring a shop in Salerno from his relation, a *magister medicus*.[56] The family had vast rural and urban property, and members whose positions were based within the regional, civic or ecclesiastical administration, or on territorial lordship.[57]

Some even more high-profile cases show how, particularly from the twelfth century, seemingly non-noble individuals (along with their kin-groups) could rise to the very highest status, primarily through service. Matthew of Salerno became a notary at the royal court (first attested in 1156, when he drafted the famous Treaty of Benevento), then vice-chancellor of the kingdom (from 1169), a royal *familiaris* during King William II's reign and finally chancellor, until his death in 1193, under King Tancred.[58] But other members of Matthew's family attained high status. One of his brothers was the abbot of the monastery of SS. Trinità, Venosa (1157/9–67) and another was bishop of Catania (1168–9).[59] A cousin Philip was a royal chamberlain at Salerno (died in 1179), and he in turn was related to the city's *protoiudex*, while another notary at the royal court was also a relation.[60] It would seem that Matthew's rise was in part based on his own administrative skills – these obtained his

---

[54] Loud, *Age of Robert Guiscard*, genealogical table p. 305. *Documenti per la storia di Eboli*, p. 199 no. 431.
[55] See above p. 133.
[56] *CDS*, pp. 64–5 no. 14, pp. 88–9 no. 30, pp. 12–16 nos. 81–2, pp. 193–5 no. 96.
[57] See for example *CDS*, pp. 381–4 no. 238; *Catalogus Baronum commentario*, arts. 446, 517; Cava, *Arca* xxxxii.27; *Documenti per la storia di Eboli*, p. 111 no. 222, p. 126 no. 255, pp. 179–80 nos. 379–81.
[58] *Falcandus*, p. 81 n. 46.
[59] H. Houben, *Die Abtei Venosa und das Mönchtum im normannisch-staufischen Süditalien* (Tübingen, 1995), pp. 158–9.
[60] See above p. 95; *Falcandus*, p. 163.

release from a Palermitan prison in 1161, and Falcandus even refers to his intelligence and political competence.[61] Both could have been honed by a close association with Maio of Bari.[62] One wonders, however, whether Matthew hailed from an already powerful Salernitan kin-group or if his own advancement had opened up rewards for others in his family. Matthew and his extended kin-group were highly important within Salerno itself, as can be seen from some of the local offices they obtained. According to Falcandus this could be a double-edged sword for Salerno. The writer described Matthew as instrumental in persuading the king, in 1162, to spare the city following the uprising of a faction within it. Yet Falcandus equally reported an accusation that Matthew had also used the opportunity to take revenge upon an innocent man, who, because he had insulted his relatives, was falsely accused of leading the rebellion and subsequently executed. Another allegation asserted that Matthew 'used the authority and fear of the court' to compel a young man to marry his niece in the presence of the civic elite.[63] Later, back in Palermo, we are told that Salernus, 'a physician who was a close friend of Matthew', had been 'appointed a judge of the city of Salerno with his support'.[64] Whatever the veracity of such claims, it seems that Matthew's lofty status in the kingdom's governing hierarchy brought suspicion as much as respect from his fellow citizens. It may be that his civic interests were considered to have been compromised by his proximity to the centre of royal power. Matthew did maintain a connection with his native city – he made donations to the cathedral, where an inscription calls him *magnus civis*, invested in urban property and his name was recorded in the necrology of the *Liber Confratrum* of S. Matteo of Salerno.[65] Indeed of Matthew's sons, Nicholas was archbishop of Salerno (1182–1221) and a key figure within both city and kingdom, while Richard was made count of Ajello by Tancred. In 1193, Richard donated some property in Salerno to the cathedral fraternity, among which were stalls used for butchery and 'other business [*negotiatio*]'.[66]

Only a little more is known about the origins of Maio of Bari, who was recorded as a royal *scrinarius*, possibly a vice-chancellor, then chancellor, before becoming the supremely powerful 'great admiral of admirals' in 1154.[67] Maio's father, Leo de Rayza, had been a long-serving

[61] *Falcandus*, pp. 121, 149, 198.   [62] *Falcandus*, pp. 96–7, 121.

[63] *Falcandus*, pp. 131–3.   [64] *Falcandus*, p. 172.

[65] *Italia Sacra*, vii. 405; Cava, *Arca* xliii.78; G. A. Loud, 'The monastic economy in the principality of Salerno during the eleventh and twelfth centuries', *PBSR* 71 (2003), p. 168; *Necrologio del Liber Confratrum*, p. 100 line 1.

[66] *Italia Sacra*, vii. 412–13; *CDS*, pp. 99–101 no. 37, p. 128 no. 57.

[67] *Falcandus*, p. 60 n. 10; *Romuald*, pp. 234–5 (English translation in *Falcandus*, p. 220).

judge (1119–47) and leading figure in Bari.[68] If Falcandus' report that Maio was instead the son of an olive-oil seller has any veracity, it would be likely that his father took part in that lucrative trade as an entrepreneurial side venture to his judicial activity and was not solely a simple street-trader.[69] Maio was far from being of humble origins, but his emergence owed much, like Matthew of Salerno's, to his clear abilities, and even Falcandus recognised his 'intellect' and 'eloquence'.[70] In the 1150s his brother Stephen became master captain of Apulia along with his brother-in-law Simon, who was also recorded as a royal seneschal, while Maio's son Stephen was an admiral.[71] Maio's sister Eustochia was attested as the abbess of a nunnery at Bari in 1160, and another sister married a royal constable who founded a convent at Matera.[72] Especially in the case of Eustochia, it is not clear what role the local importance of the family or Maio's status played in her obtaining the position of abbess. After Maio's assassination, in 1160, his brother Stephen and son Stephen were arrested and they, along with Simon, disappear from the records.[73] However, Kamp has demonstrated that Eustochia remained as abbess until *c.* 1200 and that the family was still wealthy and prominent within Bari.[74] For example, at Bari in 1197, the master chamberlain Frederick of Hohenstadt assembled a court in the house of Roger de Amirato – perhaps the same as the Roger *Maioris magni Amirati filius* who signed a document later that same year.[75] In 1201 Roger *Madii Ammirati filius* was part of a delegation that established a commercial agreement between Bari and Ragusa. Moreover, Roger's son Maio de Amirato was a justiciar in the 1230s and had as son-in-law the 'nobleman' Richard of Montefusco.[76] The *de rayza* patronym, which was that of Maio's father Leo, was also still found in the city around 1200.[77]

Most elite families could not boast such big names among their ranks, but the circles in which they operated more than confirmed their local importance. This could be applied to the de Roccas at Troia. John de Rocca was present as a *strategotus* at a ducal court in 1123, while his son

[68] *Necrologio del Liber Confratrum*, p. 102 line 9.   [69] *Falcandus*, pp. 17, 69.

[70] *Falcandus*, p. 60. Maio had pious and literary interests, *Falcandus*, pp. 17–18, and authored a commentary on the Lord's Prayer, Matthew, 'Maio of Bari's commentary', 119–44. Romuald called Maio 'fluent of speech and prudent and careful', pp. 234–5 (English translation in *Falcandus*, p. 220).

[71] *Falcandus*, pp. 17, 77 nn. 39, 99.

[72] Martin, *Pouille*, p. 480, 671; N. Kamp, 'Su un nipote di Maione di Bari, che fu giustiziere di Federico II', in *Medioevo Mezzogiorno Mediterraneo*, p. 284 n. 4.

[73] *Falcandus*, p. 99.   [74] Kamp, 'Su un nipote di Maione di Bari', pp. 283–300.

[75] *CDBVI*, nos. 4, 5. A document of 1199 refers to certain *domos Rogerii de Amirato* in the Pusterola area of Bari, *Montevergine*, xi. no. 1062.

[76] See for example, *Acta Imperii Inedita*, i. 609 no. 769.

[77] *CDBV*, no. 162; *CBVI*, no. 70.

Rao was a royal baron and, in 1159, was attested as a royal justiciar.[78] One of Rao's sons, Lucas, was also a royal justiciar (and a *catepan*), while another, John, was by 1187 lord of Monterotaro (near Dragonara). In addition, a monastery near Monterotaro, called S. Maria de Rocca, was perhaps a family foundation and had an Abbot Rao who may have been a relative.[79] The de Roccas also acted as advocates for the bishop of Troia and the monastery of S. Angelo of Orsara in the city's *contado*.[80]

The Caputus and Collivaccinus families may be even more representative of the typical urban elite. At Salerno, members of the Caputus family repeatedly occupied the office of *strategotus* in the twelfth century. They also conceded and obtained an assortment of lands and properties in the region of Salerno.[81] Of a similar standing were the Collivaccinus kin-group at Benevento. In 1151, Ademarius Collivaccinus, son of Bernard Collivaccinus, stood as guarantor to a concession made by some men, one of whom was a relative by marriage, of water rights on the River Calore to S. Sofia of Benevento.[82] Ademarius was possibly the abbot recorded in the *Obituarium S. Spiritus*, and he and his brother Bernard appeared in 1159 as *mundoalds*.[83] In the same year, Vitalis, son of (perhaps another?) Ademarius Collivaccinus, received a guarantee from a certain Malfridus son of Rolegrimo that the latter would repay a loan of 20 *romanati*. In the meantime Vitalis would hold two shops in the *Iudicalia* area of the city in pledge and receive interest on the loan if the payment was delayed.[84] A judge called Drogo was attested in Benevento from 1162 to 1193, carrying the surname Collivaccinus for all but his first two appearances in 1162 and 1164, while alongside Drogo in 1193 we find a judge Bartholomew Collivaccinus.[85] Later, Bartholomew and Malfridus Collivaccinus, both city judges, signed the civic statutes of 1202 and were present at a high-profile court in 1216.[86] In a charter of 1212 a Bernard Collivaccinus held land outside the city at Iulianisi, near to the property of a church called *Sancte Marie qui dicitur*

---

[78] *Troia*, nos. 46, 67, 76; *Colonie cassinesi*, no. 30; Jamison, 'Norman administration', cal. doc. no. 31; *Catalogus Baronum*, art. 397.

[79] *Troia*, no. 87; *Cartulaire de S. Matteo*, i. 80–2 no. 45 (and also the appended note), 134–6 no. 75.

[80] *Troia*, nos. 65, 67, 76, 103.

[81] Cava, *Arca* xxiii.70, xxiii.119, xxiv.22, xxiv.54, xxiv.68, xxiv.69, xxiv.89, xxiv.95, xxv.119, xxvi.40, xxvi.82, xxvii.64, xxvii.66, xxviii.33, xxxii.46, xxxii.48; *Nuove pergamene*, pp. 26–8 no. 12

[82] Benevento, Museo del Sannio, Fondo S. Sofia, vol. 10 no. 5.

[83] *Obituarium S. Spiritus*, p. 48c. 23 b; *Montevergine*, iv. no. 383.

[84] *Cattedrale di Benevento*, no. 79.

[85] *Montevergine*, v. no. 414, vi. no. 524; Girgensohn, 'Documenti beneventani', pp. 302–4 no. 9; *S. Modesto*, nos. 13–6; *Cattedrale di Benevento*, no. 124.

[86] *Montevergine*, x. no. 915, xi. no. 1031; *Borgia, Memorie istoriche*, ii 178–83, 423, 427; *Abbazia di Montevergine*, p. 88 no. 1417, p. 89 no. 1421; Malfridus was still attested in the city in 1226, Benevento, Biblioteca Capitolare, 92 no. 15.

de Collivaccinis – perhaps a family foundation. The same document mentions Bernard's brother, Peter, as a subdeacon and notary of the pope and also *custos* of the church of *Sancte Marie qui dicitur de Aurificibus* (of the goldsmiths) which was also at Iulianisi.[87] This Peter was very likely the same Peter Collivaccinus from Benevento, a papal subdeacon, who compiled in 1209, on Innocent III's orders, the canon law collection known as the 'Compilatio Tertia', and who in 1217 became cardinal bishop of Sabina. He may also have been the author of the *Deeds of Pope Innocent III*.[88] The *Obituarium S. Spiritus* records the names of several Collivaccinus and thus their local importance.[89]

A final point can illustrate the assortment of individuals who could obtain prominence within the urban community. Rather unusually, at Troia streets were named after people, some of whom were known inhabitants of the city.[90] The first mention comes in 1085 of a house 'in platea puplica qui nominatur Iohanne iudice de Sabbo', a man who was active in Troia as a judge from 1039 to 1065.[91] In 1125 there is record of a *trasenda puplica* called 'Petri de Riso archidiaconi', who seems to have had a son named Urso who held land, in 1129, in the city's *contado*.[92] In 1127 we find a public passage 'que vocatur Amuri Caccisii' – a man who appears at Troia from 1091 to 1132 signing numerous private charters and twice acting as an epsicopal advocate.[93] In 1202 reference is made to a street named after a judge John Leporinus, who was attested in his office at Troia from 1156 to 1183.[94] Later still, in 1227, there is reference to a street called 'domini Guillelmi Menescalco'.[95] He signed an act of donation in 1159 to the bishop of Troia and owned a garden in the city.[96] As well as also possessing a fief in the county of Andria, William

---

[87] *S. Modesto*, no. 28.

[88] This Peter became cardinal deacon of S. Maria in Aquiro in 1212, was papal legate to southern France in 1214–15, and was raised in 1216 to cardinal priest of S. Lorenzo in Damaso before his promotion to cardinal bishop of Sabina: W. Maleczek, *Papst und Kardinalskolleg von 1191 bis 1216* (Vienna, 1984), pp. 172–4; J. M. Powell, 'Innocent III and Petrus Beneventanus: reconstructing a career at the papal curia', in *Pope Innocent III and his World*, ed. J. C. Moore (Aldershot, 1999), 51–62. A *magister Petrus Collivaccinus episcopus Sabinensis* can be found in the *Obituarium S. Spiritus*, p. 82 c. 37a.

[89] *Obituarium S. Spiritus*, p. 17 c. 8 a, p. 48 c. 23 b, p. 57 c. 28 a, p. 251 c. 109 b.

[90] There are a few other examples of similar street names in other cities but they are not nearly as concentrated. At Benevento there was a *trasenda publica* named after a judge Leo (1112, 1118, 1152, 1199), *Cattedrale di Benevento*, nos. 55–6, 72, 133, one called after a *gastald* called Zerone, *Cattedrale di Benevento*, no. 107, and another called after a *gastald* Gaido, *Abbazia di Montevergine*, p. 110 no. 1502.

[91] *Troia*, no. 19; see above p. 27.   [92] *Troia*, nos. 49, 54.

[93] *Troia*, no. 51; for the Caccise family see also *Troia*, nos. 25, 29, 40, 42, 46, 49, 59, 78: *Colonie Cassinesi*, no. 30.

[94] *Abbazia di Montevergine*, p. 26 no. 1144; *Colonie cassinesi*, no. 30; *Troia*, nos. 73, 76, 78, 80, 86, 94, 100; *Montevergine*, vi. nos. 551, 568, vii. no. 684.

[95] *Troia*, no. 143.   [96] *Troia*, no. 76; *Montevergine*, vi. no. 551.

had close connections with the monastery of S. Sofia of Benevento.[97] In 1164, he was present with high-ranking royal officials at Lesina, acting as a guarantor in a property dispute concerning S. Sofia, and in 1172 at Troia he acted as the monastery's advocate; on both occasions he was said to be from Troia.[98] However, in 1173, before various high royal officials at Capua, William was found in dispute with the monastery over property in the *castellum* of Toro.[99] Further street names carrying otherwise unattested names include – a 'platea diaconi Guydi' (1110), streets named after a Baldwin Truncamonis (1176) and a Walter Cambitor (1190, 1197) and another with the name of John de Pandulfo (1202).[100] It is possible that the latter was the John de Pandulfo who appeared at Troia in 1197 as a relation of a certain Seclina, herself part of a wealthy and prominent family.[101]

Those with streets named for them include two public officials, two ecclesiastics, a money-changer (*cambitor*) and various landowners. William Manescalsus enjoyed interests that took him beyond the city and ranged from high-profile court cases to the ownership of a humble city garden. As intriguing are those individuals, like Baldwin Truncamonis, who were clearly important figures and yet no other record of them appears to have survived. Some of the streets (perhaps those named after the two judges and also William) still carried the person's name after they had most probably died. Conversely, Amuris Caccise had a public passageway in his name while he was definitely alive, as he acted as an advocate in the very charter in which the street was mentioned. It can be assumed that these people, and their associated street names, were widely known in the city and that their memory was perpetuated after their death. In a relatively small and compact city, street names would have played a significant part in the daily vocabulary. All of these people must have attained an elevated position in the city through their career or wealth, which enabled their name to be attached to a public space. As a sample group they encapsulate the diversity of the civic elites and the difficulty in identifying and defining them.

IN THE 'MIDDLE' OF THE COMMUNITY

The civic elites were formed in varying circles of importance from an ever-changing number and miscellaneous range of people. The point at which an individual did not have the means or ability to be part of

[97] *Catalogus Baronum commentario*, art. 82.
[98] Pergamene Aldobrandini, II no. 5; *Troia*, no. 88.   [99] Pergamene Aldobrandini, II. no. 27.
[100] *Colonie cassinesi*, no. 18; *Montevergine*, vii. no. 606, ix. no. 840, xi. no. 1022, xii. no. 1161.
[101] *Montevergine*, xi. no. 1022.

that group is entirely unknown, as well as being subjective and specific to a given time and place. The charter material inevitably tends to record the activities of the wealthy and prominent and occasionally those, on the other hand, who suffered some form of poverty. The people who fell in between these categories, the greatest proportion of the urban population, are almost entirely hidden. It may be that we have glimpses of them in hundreds of charters – purchasing a plot of land or a house – and we may be led to believe that this formed part of a more extensive complex, whereas in reality it represented a modest whole. This extremely broad segment of the urban populace was in the middle, as it were, in terms of being financially comfortable and having reasonably stable occupations. Free individuals, who ranged from modest property-owners to tenants, from lower local officials to small entrepreneurs, semi-skilled and skilled workers. It is tempting to consider those at Aversa who called themselves *burgensis* as being within this range of people. Some may qualify under the above terms, yet we must be careful not to generalise here, given the inconsistent meaning, and then declining use, of the word.[102] There is little overall evidence for a defined *mediani* or 'middle class'. Where the term does appear in a non-narrative and distinct sense, at Naples, there is little chance of knowing who or what status it encompassed.[103] We have already seen that engagement in activities or professions traditionally connected with this 'middle group' could bring prominence and perhaps even membership of the elite. If it is often hard to specifically identify individuals from these 'middling ranks' who might have functioned in the highest circles, there is plenty of evidence to suggest that such people could enjoy real standing in their communities, enough to influence the elites, even if they themselves were not a part of them.

This problem of identification can be seen from evidence from the port city of Monopoli. Here, with growing regularity as the twelfth century progressed, men interested in varying forms of commerce and trade appear more prominently in the charter material, to such an extent that they might be considered to be among the city elite. We see people identified as *nauclerius* (skipper/sailor/merchant?), *negotiator* (businessman), *mercator* (merchant), *cambiator* and *magister bancarius* (banker/money-changer), purchasing real estate and acting as mediators.[104] Those with

---

[102] See above pp. 178–80.

[103] The word's use also seems to have been of short duration at Naples – it was not employed in the two important documents concerning Naples in 1190 (see above pp. 125–6), where the groupings referred to are *barones, cives, comestabuli, consules, milites, nobiles* and *universus populus.*

[104] *Conversano*, nos. 79, 160. In 1162 the advocate of the monastery of S. Benedetto of Conversano was Onorato *negotiator*, *Conversano* no. 107; in 1185 Catardus *mercator*, the son of Thomas

the title of *nauclerius* witnessed transactions seemingly in semi-public roles which did not always require the judge's presence. In 1168 the *nauclerius* Ciprianus and Hieronimus, the son of another *nauclerius*, oversaw a donation made by the abbot of the church of S. Nicola *de Portu Aspero* of Monopoli. The church's advocate was a Sbephizzio *cabiatorum* (money-changer?).[105] When, in 1189, a Ioannoccarus *nauclerius*, son of Athenasius *nauclerius*, bought two houses, the agreement was completed before a city judge and notary, but also another *nauclerius* and a Maio *cambiator*, son of Grimoald *cambiator*.[106] Again, in 1212 a house was sold before a knight and the *nauclerius* John Narro, with no judge present. In the following year, the receipt of a dowry was confirmed before the same *nauclerius* and the *nauclerius* Sebastian.[107] Elsewhere, *nauclerii* from Bari were wealthy enough to own slaves and to engage in a wide network of differing interests and relationships that clearly placed them within important circles, as evidenced through the records of the Barese *nauclerius* Otto, the son of John Melis de Regina.[108] Moreover, the expansion in numbers of local offices like the *baiulus*, and their farming out, was ideally suited to people from this type of background with liquid wealth. An investigation at Taranto in the 1230s showed that previously at least four men with the title/personal name of *nauclerius* had exercised that office in the city.[109]

On occasion skilled workers, or artisans, a group considered to be at the core of the so-called 'middle class', demonstrated standing within the community. With the development of production and enterprise in the eleventh and twelfth centuries, artisans gained in social prestige and were able to increasingly enter the land market, which brought its rewards.[110] They appear more regularly as witnesses in charters, alongside prominent local figures. Those who worked with metal (*ferrarii, caldararii*), and above all goldsmiths (*aurificii*), were often active members of the community.[111] In the records of Benevento's civic statutes we find one goldsmith as a consul (and also a dyer) and another as a *iuratus*,

---

negotiator, received, from the same monastery of S. Benedetto, a house in the suburb of Monopoli, *Conversano* no. 134 and see also nos. 115, 140, 142; a document of 1217 refers to an olive-press belonging to a Sconrus *nauclerius* and Pantaleone, sons of Leo *mercator*, a Kirizzius *nauclerius* who was a mediator, and a witness called Urso, son of John the merchant, *Conversano* no. 166.

[105] *Conversano*, no. 118. [106] *Conversano*, no. 140, [107] *Conversano*, nos. 162, 163.
[108] *CDBV*, nos. 36, 146; see Appendix, 'An example of a kin-group and its network of relationships', below.
[109] *Taranto*, pp. 62–6 no. 17.
[110] G. Galasso, 'Le città campane nell'Alto Medioevo', in *Mezzogiorno medievale e moderno* (Turin, 1965), pp. 95–8; R. Licinio, 'L'artigiano', in *Condizione umana*, pp. 168–9.
[111] Martin, *Pouille*, pp. 420–1, 424–5.

while in other cities they acted as mediators.[112] At Aversa from roughly
the 1130s onwards, high numbers of artisans operated in the city's most
prominent circles. Many charters from the city, some dealing with
important cases and involving leading officials and individuals, were
witnessed by several artisans.[113] Baldwin *corduanerius* (cordwainer) and
Jordan *parmentarius* (tailor) witnessed, usually together, a host of legal
and property transactions from the 1130s until 1150.[114] Perhaps their
activity in civic affairs was based on wealth. Jordan certainly had real
estate – in 1131 he donated land in the city to the cathedral and also had
a house nearby, while Baldwin had a house in the *platea pubblica de Sancta
Maria*.[115] Again in 1131, before Prince Robert II of Capua, another
parmentarius, Peter de Arnone, bought ten pieces of land and a *fundus*
from Rainfred, a knight of Aversa.[116] Interestingly, from 1141 to 1158
a Peter de Arnone is found as a witness in numerous charters, without
the epithet of tailor.[117] If this is the same Peter then the omission of
his occupation could have been the result of his land purchases, which
may have engendered a change in his activities or the way in which he
was identified by himself and others.

As with public officials, a person's profession clearly played a big part
in their identity, especially for those who incorporated it within their
name. One might surmise that solidarities focused on such identities
gave cohesion to the largely undetected middle (and lower) ranks of
urban society and transcended any common legal, financial or political
status. Urban topography certainly contributed to this. As markets often
emerged around city gates, many artisans lived, or owned property, in
close proximity within suburbs. Other trades had to be established on
the periphery of the urban environment for technical purposes. Tanners
were more likely to practise their craft outside the city walls because of
the noxious techniques involved. In 1222 Cava conceded to certain men
some land outside Salerno, 'near the ditch which was made for the
defence of the city', in order to establish a tannery.[118] Likewise, metal-
workers were often found on the urban fringe on account of their craft's

---

[112] Borgia, *Memorie istoriche*, ii. 427, 433; *Troia*, no. 59; *CDNA*, pp. 99–101 no. 57.
[113] For example *CDNA*, pp. 105–7 no. 61, pp. 113–14 no. 65, pp. 126–9 no. 73, pp. 150–2 no. 85,
pp. 157–60 no. 89, pp. 199–201 no. 108, pp. 333–5 no. 15, pp. 341–2 no. 19.
[114] *CDNA*, pp. 46–54 nos. 30–2, pp. 68–71 nos. 40–1, pp. 74–5 no. 43, pp. 83–8 nos. 48–50,
pp. no. 99–101 no. 57, pp. 313–5 no. 4.
[115] *CDNA*, pp. 43–4 no. 28, pp. 70–1 no. 41, p. 102 no. 59, pp. 162–4 no. 91.
[116] *CDNA*, pp. 46–50 no. 30.
[117] *CDNA*, pp. 74–5 no. 43, pp. 83–4 no. 48, pp. 113–14 no. 65, pp. 126–9 no. 73, pp. 333–5 no.
15, pp. 341–2 no. 19.
[118] *CDS*, pp. 139–41 no. 65 (and note 1). However, the *ruga* and *piscina tanatorum* at Aversa seem to
have been inside the city, or at least in a relatively built-up area, see below n. 122.

high fire risk, as also were fullers and dyers, who required large spaces and access to water.[119] Outside Troia a church called S. Nicola *de Ferrariis* could have been in a suburb of metalworkers, given that the son of a *ferrarius* sold a *casalinum* nearby in 1150.[120] Either way, the church's name suggests some common association among metalworkers, as does the church of S. Maria *de Aurificibus* (goldsmiths) outside Benevento.[121] Perhaps some informal associations did form in quarters where trades were concentrated, based on a mutual identity of interests and regulation of practice. There were areas such as the butchers' quarter (*bucheria*), the suburb of fishermen (*piscatorum*), the *ruga parmentariorum* (tailors' street), *ruga tanatorum* (dyers' street) and *ruga panecteriorum* (bakers' street) at Aversa and a *ruga* and *platea parmentariorum* at Salerno.[122] Other inter-dependent craftsmen, such as butchers, horners and skinners, were probably all located near to each other, and it was common for different artisans to live close together.[123] At Aversa, in 1151, when Richard *corviserius*, the son of Sicus *corviserius*, sold some property, it bordered the land of a *parmentarius* and the houses of a *corduanerius* and a *cultellerius*.[124] There is, however, no evidence of any legally formed guilds based on profession.[125] There was also no established specialist 'merchant class' with a fixed place in the social hierarchies of the South Italian cities. People from a variety of social backgrounds participated in commerce in a number of direct, indirect, permanent or occasional ways. This may explain the limited usage of the title 'merchant' in private documents, along with the lack of references to *mercatores* or *negotiatores* as an 'order'.[126]

There is certainly plenty more evidence to show how artisans or traders, or those who recognised an occupation as part of their heritage, as well as living in close quarters, also acted in close proximity. The earlier examples from Monopoli confirm this. Sometimes at least two artisans (usually more at Aversa), often with different occupations, appeared in some form in the same charter, suggesting that their interests often converged. In 1155 at Aversa the witnesses to a donation made by a *burgensis* included two tailors (three if one includes Peter de Arnone),

---

[119] K. D. Lilley, *Urban Life in the Middle Ages 1000–1450* (Basingstoke, 2002), pp. 234–5.

[120] *Troia*, no. 69.   [121] *S. Modesto*, pp. 73–8 no. 28.

[122] *CDNA*, pp. 115–17 no. 67, pp. 132–4 no. 76, pp. 185–7 no. 102, pp. 194–6 no. 106, pp. 333–5 no. 15; *CDS*, pp. 162–3 no. 81; *Tancredi et Willelmi III Regum Diplomata*, pp. 10–12 no. 4.

[123] Lilley, *Urban Life*, pp. 236–7.   [124] *CDNA*, pp. 102–3 no. 59.

[125] G. M. Monti, *Le corporazioni nell'Evo Antico e nell'Alto Medio Evo* (Bari, 1934) shows that a *societas* of St Nicholas, arising from the translation of 1087, did not exist in a legal sense, pp. 309–24.

[126] In contrast to general European literary references to these new groupings, which grew in frequency in the twelfth century, Fonseca, '"Ordines" istituzionali e ruoli sociali', pp. 14–17; Jones, *Italian City-State*, pp. 103–6; for more see pp. 253–5.

a tanner (*tanator*), a leather-worker (*corviserius*) and a man carrying the surname 'quarryman/sculptor' (*tallapetra*).[127] At Troia, in 1132, a goldsmith acted as a mediator in a property exchange involving a *caldararius* who received a garden near another *caldararius*.[128] A charter of 1144 was signed by the sons of a builder and of a metal-worker, while in an act of 1154, in which a *contiator* bought a garden, two fellow constructors are referred to, one of whom owned another garden nearby.[129] The two *mundoalds* in a document from Capua in 1176 were a *parmentarius* and *corviserius* respectively.[130] Succession of profession from father to son was widespread and perhaps became more so with the economic and commercial revival of the eleventh and twelfth centuries. A growing 'social and psychological investment in children' during this period may partly have been a response to the increased importance of learning a trade from a young age.[131] Familial links between different types of artisans and traders were also common.[132] At Aversa, in 1154, Beatrice the daughter of Lawrence the tailor, and wife of Goimerius *corviserius*, conceded an orchard in a suburb, and half of a house in the *ruga parmentariorum*, to the nunnery of S. Biagio.[133] At Monopoli, in 1199, we find that Asconia the wine-seller (*vini venditor*) was married to Bone, who was related to Iuzonose, who in turn was married to a *magister* John *faber* of Brindisi. Both Bone and Iuzonose were themselves related to a John the butcher (*buccerius*).[134] In 1209, Pantaleo of Monopoli, son of Citoleone the *negotiator*, married Citacarapresa the daughter of Stephen Crassus the *negotiator*. The brother of Citacarapresa's step-father was a *nauclerius*, as was her own brother Sanctorus, and their advocate was John *magister bambacarum* (master banker?), son of *magister* Thomas.[135]

The earlier example of Peter de Arnone encapsulates the problems of identifying people's social status by their occupation, and the dangers of stereotyping. We have already discussed, with particular reference to Amalfi, how individuals from seemingly diverse backgrounds took part in trade, as one of many activities, and as such chose not to identify themselves as merchants. The mere task of identifying a person's profession is not easy. The addition of an occupation to a forename could well be a family surname and not necessarily the person in question's

---

[127] *CDNA*, pp. 341–2 no. 19. However, the *tallapetra* 'surname', carried here by Clemens, may not represent a current occupation as he was also at one point a city *strategotus* (see above p. 99), but this is not to deny that he could not be involved in both professions. At the very least the name surely denotes that the occupation was practised by a family ancestor.

[128] *Troia*, no. 59.   [129] *Troia*, nos. 66, 71.   [130] *Pergamene normanne*, no. 15.

[131] D. Herlihy, 'Medieval children', in *Women, Family and Society in Medieval Europe. Historical Essays, 1978–1991* (Providence, 1995), p. 229.

[132] Martin, *Pouille*, pp. 420–1.   [133] *CDNA*, pp. 333–5 no. 15.

[134] *Conversano*, no. 147.   [135] *Conversano*, no. 160.

occupation. However, this should at least indicate that at some point an ancestor had followed that occupation. The examples used above were felt to be more likely to reflect current occupations. The use of the term *magister* can often help to identify someone as a current practitioner of the occupation associated with their name. On the other hand there will be many cases of individuals who chose not to record their occupation title in a given context. This must be borne in mind for those cities, like Benevento, Capua, Trani and even to some extent Bari, where fewer craftsmen or traders appear in the source material.

It is perhaps too easy to spot the artisan tag among a group of names and to pick out patterns and inter-relationships between them. This must be recognised in order not to overplay the sense of solidarity which did exist in the artisan world, and to avoid overlooking other relationship networks. The artisan 'class' was extremely heterogeneous and there could be huge financial and social disparity within it. Artisans and traders often had close associations with people who might be considered to belong to a different 'social group'. At Troia, in 1138, the son of a shoe-maker was related to a doctor's wife, while in 1183 the *mundoald* of the daughter of a metal-worker was the *cantor* of the city cathedral.[136] In the same city, in 1154, two construction workers (*contiator* and *murator*) were described as the *parentes* of both the wife and daughter-in-law of John de Boccio, a royal baron.[137] In Salerno, in 1206, John de Alto the goldsmith was married to Tande, who was the daughter of John the notary and advocate. Also related to Tande was a certain Alfanus, the son of the notary Matthew, who was the son of Alfanus the son of Lando *comes* – identifying therefore a 'noble' heritage.[138] In the thirteenth century a woman named Agnes had some very prominent family connections – she was the wife of judge Romuald Guarna, the sister of Palmerius, a cleric of the Salernitan archbishopric as well as chaplain and *medicus* of the pope, and daughter and niece of two doctors.[139] Interestingly Agnes's father was the son of a Solomon Parmentarius. If the surname does not represent a current occupation it would seem that an ancestor had been a tailor. Palmerius' will mentions land, with a shop, in the *platea parmentariorum*.[140] As this case and others, perhaps including that of Maio of Bari, suggest, the identities, activities and status of all types of kin-groups were constantly in flux. Indeed, while a variety of motives were responsible for sons often following

---

[136] *Troia*, nos. 61, 100; Martin, *Pouille*, p. 421 nn. 140 and 143.   [137] *Troia*, no. 71.
[138] *CDS*, pp. 65–7 no. 15.
[139] *CDS*, pp. 88–9 no. 30, pp. 162–6 nos. 81–2, pp. 193–5 no. 96.
[140] *CDS*, pp. 193–5 no. 96.

their father's profession, many did not. If from Aversa Roger the son of Pippin the tanner followed in his father's footsteps, it is not recorded in the material in which he appears. Roger's main interests revolved around land – by 1160 he held at least four separate units from the cathedral of Aversa in return for annual payments.[141] Acting as a witness in 1168, his name even appears as Roger Pipini without the *tanator* appended to his father's name.[142] There is nothing to indicate the profession of Amerusius the father of the *magister faber* Petracca of Conversano. Furthermore, in 1175 Petracca asked the monastery of S. Benedetto of Conversano to concede to him a dilapidated house which he wanted to rebuild. The abbot agreed on condition that he could call upon the skills of Petracca's, *and his heirs'*, trade to work for the monastery. A subsequent clause stipulated that should Petracca's heirs *not* follow their paternal trade then they would be obliged to pay a pound of wax annually instead.[143] Petracca's sons Amerusius and Maraldus appeared in 1207, when they divided some land at Marzano between them. Amerusius carried the generic title of *magister*, while Maraldus was a deacon.[144] Moreover, here again is an example, in Petracca, of an artisan who in the twelfth century had moved, if only on a limited scale, into the rural land market. In 1173 the monastery of S. Benedetto leased to him some small pieces of land, while in 1182 he sold land at Iniano.[145] Such individuals represent the more visible face of the emerging middling rank – the majority of which remain completely undetected.

ON THE EDGES OF THE COMMUNITY

Like the medieval commentators we are forced into arbitrary divisions of urban society. There was never a defined boundary between the elite and the middle ranks, and the same applies for any cut-off point between the latter category and those at the base of the urban community (the *minori* or sometimes simply the *populus*). Again we are dealing with mostly indeterminate groups which were neither isolated from the rest of society nor conformed to a given pattern. On the whole those of lower status rarely appear in the source material, or if they do are difficult to identify. Most were simply low income earners (labourers

---

[141] *CDNA*, pp. 124–6 no. 72, pp. 135–6 no. 77, pp. 139–40 no. 79.

[142] *CDNA*, pp. 157–60 no. 89; similarly a charter of 1207 mentions a 'domus Rogerii Pipini', *CDSA*, pp. 106–7 no. 51.

[143] *Conversano*, no. 129.

[144] *Conversano*, no. 156. The term *magister* when used on its own could represent a variety of meanings, most likely with the connotation of master or specialist of a particular profession.

[145] *Conversano*, nos. 128, 132.

and other non-skilled manual workers) who often had unstable occupations in that work was not permanently available. Consequently wealth, influence and privilege were limited at this social level. Moreover, the 'city air makes free' axiom did not apply to the entire urban community in southern Italy. Some inhabitants of the city were not legally free. Slaves/servants (*servus*, usually for males, and *ancilla* for females) were a relatively small but perceptible component of the city community within wealthy urban households in this period. Growing urbanisation and wealth revived the demand for urban slavery, particularly in the southern Mediterranean.[146] There is some evidence for slaves in Campania in the eleventh century and earlier, at places such as Amalfi, Gaeta and Salerno.[147] If it did continue in that region into the twelfth century and later, the sources provide only rare evidence. A charter of 1154, from the Cava archive, details the sale of an *ancilla* called Nubilia 'from the race of the Saracens' (*ex Saracenorum genere*), along with her child.[148] However, references to slaves, certainly from *c.* 1100, feature almost exclusively in the Apulian documentation, notably at Bari, but there are also scattered references from Foggia, Monopoli, Taranto, Trani and Troia.[149] Perhaps this results from the prohibition, which we learn from a Barese charter of 1127, against Christians being held as slaves except for those of Slavic origin (*qui ex sclavorum gente geniti sunt*).[150] Certainly the Apulian coastal cities had numerous contacts with the opposite shore of the Adriatic, which made it easier to acquire Slav people as slaves.[151] The documentation from Bari regularly identifies slaves as being Slavs (*sclavus* or *ex genere sclavorum*) or refers to some who seem to carry Slavic names.[152] Alternatively at Bari, in 1065, forming part of a dowry was 'una ancilla Setanna nomine cum filio suo Nicolula ex genere Sarracenorum'.[153] But there is no real evidence to suggest

---

[146] S. M. Stuard, 'Ancillary evidence for the decline of medieval slavery', *Past and Present* 129 (1995), pp. 8, 17.

[147] C. Verlinden, *L'Esclavage dans l'Europe médiévale* (Ghent, 1977), ii. 104–5, 110.

[148] Galasso, 'Le città campane', p. 87 (Cava, *Arca* xxviii.100).

[149] At Troia there is reference to slaves in a charter of 1202, *Montevergine*, xii. no. 1173, and also in clause 14 of the 1127 charter of privileges which deals with theft committed by *servi et ancillae*, *Troia*, no. 50. A similar theme is covered in the Barese customs, Petroni, *Storia di Bari*, ii. 492 Rubric XV. 1.

[150] *CDBV*, no. 74; O. R. Constable, 'Muslim Spain and Mediterranean slavery: the medieval slave trade as an aspect of Muslim–Christian relations', in *Christendom and Its Discontents. Exclusion, Persecution, and Rebellion, 1000–1500*, ed. S. L. Waugh and P. D. Diehl (Cambridge, 1996), pp. 264–84, emphasises the fact that master and slave were usually of different religions in the medieval period.

[151] Martin, *Pouille*, pp. 508–9; M. Spremić, 'La migrazione degli Slavi nell'Italia meridionale e in Sicilia alla fine del Medioevo', *Archivio storico italiano* 138 (1980), pp. 5–8, discusses the continued use of Slavs as slaves in Apulia in the thirteenth century.

[152] *CDBIV*, no. 36; *CDBV*, nos. 9, 66, 78, 79, 94, 119, 146, frag. no. 14.   [153] *CDBIV*, no. 42.

how widely this rule might have been enforced or that every documented slave was either Slav or non-Christian.

Slaves found themselves in a difficult position. They were usually considered as moveable property, while the aforesaid document from Bari in 1127 refers to those people who, 'pro peccatis' (for sins), are sold as 'servos et ancillae'.[154] Often references to slaves occur when they formed part of a dowry or passed into different ownership through a testament.[155] On other occasions the slave was being purchased, listed among a person's possessions or having their ownership disputed over.[156] In 1167, at Bari, among a man's *res*, in relation to a dowry, were 'clothes, *regimina domus*, male slaves, female slaves, horses, mares and all other livestock'.[157] In some transactions slaves are described as having healthy limbs (*cum sanis membris*) and being suitable for serving (*apti ad serviendum*), although the specific tasks required of them are rarely enumerated.[158] It appears that households usually had more than one slave, perhaps attached to individual family members, and at times they were mother and daughter or son.[159] It seems that medieval custom maintained that a slave woman's offspring would inherit their mother's status.[160] Again, the valuable document of 1127 from Bari reiterates this, for it records a dispute over whether a certain Lupo was of slave rank. Lupo argued that he was a freeman (*ingenuus*) because his mother was Bulgarian and that therefore he was not born from slaves.[161] Moreover, this highlights the probability that many slaves had been so from birth, and the sources speak of an *infantula*, a *filiolus*, *minores* and *iuvenes*.[162] Stuard's work highlights the persistence of female slavery, its difference from its male counterpart and the high demand for child slaves. It also emphasises the 'violent institution' that slavery represented, and that slaves suffered an 'almost complete deracination, for their culture was erased and replaced'.[163]

Some slaves were at least liberated by their owner. Liberation could occur at different stages – sometimes this occurred on the owner's death, but in some cases liberation could be delayed until the owner's surviving spouse died.[164] Alternatively, two dowry agreements, dealing with people from Monopoli, in 1128 and 1209, envisaged another way to free, in

---

[154] *CDBV*, no. 74.   [155] *CDBV*, nos. 9, 36, 78, 87; *Conversano*, nos. 79, 160.
[156] *CDBV*, nos. 66, 79, 94, 109, 119, 158.   [157] *CDBI*, no. 51
[158] *CDBIV*, no. 36; *CDBV*, nos. 78, 87; Conversano, nos. 79, 160.
[159] *CDBIV*, no. 42; *CDBV*, nos. 9, 66, 78, 87, 100, frag. no. 14.
[160] Stuard, 'Ancillary evidence', pp. 7–8.
[161] *CDBV*, no. 74; Martin, *Pouille*, p. 509 n. 131, suggests that Lupo's mother was from Butrint in southern Albania.
[162] See above n. 155.   [163] Stuard, 'Ancillary evidence', pp. 7–8.
[164] *CDBV*, no. 36, 100; *Trani*, nos. 86; *Troia*, no. 156.

these cases, female slaves.[165] In the 1209 case, the husband-to-be agreed to cast aside any mistress, and if that mistress should also be his *ancilla* he was to 'give her as a freewoman to a husband or [he] would give her into his hands for him to arrange the rod of manumission [*vindicta*]'. There was indeed a formal procedure to go through for the slave to be liberated. In 1103, at Bari, Nicholas the *nauclerius* decreed that on the day of his death, and before his body was buried, the *servus* Guarinulus was to be freed, for the sake of Nicholas's soul, by a religious official who should lead Guarinulus around a sacred altar and provide him with a *cartula liberationis*.[166] There are other examples of liberation in different contexts that show intermediate stages of freedom. In 1164, at Bari, a certain Melicaccia established that his *servus* Simeon would be freed. However, this involved an interim period of five years in which Simeon was to be an *aldius* (half-free) in the 'hands' of a priest. In that time Simeon was to still serve Melicaccia 'day and night on [his] every instruction just as a *servus* serves his master', and the latter would feed, clothe and shoe him. It seems that at the same time the priest would have some jurisdiction over Simeon, who could not flee or his *aldietas* would be cancelled. On the completion of that period, the priest should free Simeon 'from all tie and condition of servitude' before an altar and provide a charter of freedom.[167]

But as in so many areas, the fluidity of the vocabulary employed creates a constant obstacle to understanding the status attached to a given term.[168] In some cases it is far from clear if the language implies that a person was a slave or a servant.[169] As the state of *aldietas* suggests, there were varying grades of freedom. There are references to individuals who appear to be unfree or semi-free without carrying the title of slave/servant.[170] One such category was the *affidati*, who appear to have been semi-free. Public powers often granted the *ius affidandi*, the right to settle people as *affidati*, usually on rural settlements under the lordship

---

[165] *Conversano*, nos. 79, 160; see also *CDBIV*, no. 36.   [166] *CDBV*, no. 36.

[167] *CDBV*, no. 122; other similar examples, no. 146, frag. no. 14; for further references to liberation see *CDBVI*, nos. 26, 28, 38; *Trani*, no. 36.

[168] A point made clearly by Stuard, 'Ancillary evidence', pp. 8–9 and Verlinden, *L'Esclavage*, ii. 108–9; A. Rio, 'Freedom and unfreedom in early medieval Francia: the evidence of the legal formulae', *Past and Present* 193 (2006), pp. 7–40, has recently highlighted the similarly fluid and uncertain nature of unfree status in early medieval Francia.

[169] Servant or some type of dependant, rather than slave, seems more likely when terms like *serviens* are employed, *Pergamene sveve*, ii. no. 18.

[170] The prince of Capua granted some inhabitants of Capua to his chamberlain in 1121, and some more, with their children and heirs, to a monastery in 1129, *Pergamene di Capua*, i. 60–3 no. 24, 74–9 no. 31. Among the rural population there was a greater variety of terms which denoted some kind of dependant status such as *defensani*, *famuli*, *villani*, *censiles*; P. Corrao, 'Il servo', in *Condizione umana*, p. 67.

of ecclesiastical establishments.[171] The *affidatus* appears to have had Byzantine origins. The actual term, however, was used only within the Terra di Bari and Terra di Otranto and not before the Norman period, by which time it appears to have carried a specific legal status.[172] However, as already noted, some *affidati* do appear in an urban setting, at Bari. In 1094 a certain Regem was released *de affidatione puplica* by the city's *catepan* and was 'given', for forty *solidos michalatos bonos*, to the church of S. Nicola of Bari to be under its 'tutela et defensio atque affidatio'.[173] The act constituted Regem 'free, secure and immune' from the *pars publica*, in relation to duties and taxes, but now he was to pay the *census affidationis* to the church. We have already discussed the cases of the 'releasing' of *affidati* at Bari for a fee, in 1108 and 1113. These show that, following the transaction, the former *affidati* no longer had to pay various taxes linked to the *affidatura*, were considered 'free' among their fellow citizens and had access to civic custom. The case of 1108 also seemed to apply to Aldebertus' family.[174] In 1109 a certain Gemma asked Princess Constance for, and received, an *affidatus* of Prince Bohemond's called Simeon. The *affidatus*, along with all his heirs and family, was to be in Gemma's power and control and to pay all taxes to her.[175] Generally *affidati* appear more infrequently by the mid-twelfth century, at least in private charters.[176] Changes in terminology could be responsible, and it is likely that there were still people with a comparable status to the *affidatus* within South Italian cities. It is difficult to know where exactly the *affidatus* fitted within the urban community. Bari's charter of privileges of 1132 did not extend to the *affidati*, while the city's customs of *c.* 1200 stated that the *affidatus* was to provide galley service along with the *civis*, the *incola Barensis* and the *indigena*.[177]

Another group, the Jewish community, had some restrictions placed on its personal freedom and often fell under the authority of the public power. Many Jewish communities passed from the jurisdiction of the secular authorities to ecclesiastical ones. In 1086 Robert Guiscard's wife, Sichelgaita, donated Bari's Jewish quarter (*Iudeca*), and the Jewish community within it, to the archbishop of Bari.[178] Similar grants were

---

[171] See Roger Borsa's concession in 1092 to the monastery of S. Lorenzo of Aversa, *CDNA*, p. 12 no. 7; see also *Conversano*, no. 126; *Recueil des actes des ducs*, pp. 113–16 no. 36; Martin, *Pouille*, pp. 315–16; *CDBI*, no. 32.

[172] Tamassia, 'Ius Affidandi', pp. 221–3; Martin, *Pouille*, p. 313. In other areas, like the Capitanata, a similar right to settle *homines* appears without the use of the word *affidatus*, *Troia*, no. 36.

[173] *CDBV*, no. 18.   [174] See above pp. 174–5.   [175] *CDBV*, no. 54.

[176] *Affidati* are still mentioned more regularly in public charters such as *Constantiae Imperatricis et Reginae Siciliae Diplomata*, pp. 159–66 no. 44.

[177] *Rogerii II Regis Diplomata Latina*, pp. 54–6 no. 20; Petroni, *Storia di Bari*, ii. 440 Rubric II. 5.

[178] *CDBI*, no. 30.

made by Roger Borsa in the 1090s to the archbishop of Salerno and the bishop of Melfi respectively.[179] It was probably King William II who conceded the Jewish community of Trani to the city's archbishop, while the Church of Capua was granted the *iudaica* of the city, but not until 1198.[180] The grants usually included the variety of taxes and services to which the Jews were liable.[181] Despite the fact that all the region's Jewish communities remained in general under royal protection, Henry VI was required, in 1195, to specifically confirm it for the one in Trani. This suggests a deterioration of the position of the Jewish community in the city. Henry decreed against the molestation of, and extortion of money from, the Jewish population, and he also prohibited forced conversion.[182] As the Jews of Trani were under the jurisdiction of the city's Church they were to be judged in its court in all matters, except for those which related to imperial affairs, and had to pay an annual fee. It is possible also that the Jewish communities of southern Italy had to pay special taxes for royal protection and also in other special circumstances.[183] As Houben has demonstrated, there is no firm evidence to suggest that the Normans brought with them any concerted policy of intolerance towards the region's Jews. The legislation of King Roger generally maintained the usages, customs and laws of 'the variety of people' within the kingdom, while still displaying an underlying negativity towards Jews.[184] Overall, any 'tolerance' in the South was essentially a practical one distant from its modern, 'enlightened' sense. Indeed, with the revenues that were derived from the Jewish community there would have been little financial incentive, either for the king or bishops, to implement any strategies for conversion. Moreover, the Jewish community (and the Muslim one in Sicily) was seen as socially inferior.[185] Indeed, while in 1195 Henry VI urged that people 'should not be compelled to believe [in Christ] against their will', the protection and justice on offer was made 'without paying attention to the perversity [*pravitas*] of those people, which deserves to be condemned' – which is to be inferred, in this case, to be those of the Jewish faith. The Barese

---

[179] *Antiquitates Italicae Medii Aevi*, i. 899–900; *Italia Sacra*, i. 923.

[180] *Constantiae Imperatricis et Reginae Siciliae Diplomata*, pp. 217–19 no. 60. The Jewish community at Taranto had been under the jurisdiction of that city's archbishop since at least the reign of King William II, *Taranto*, pp. 75–85 no. 22, while that at Troia appears to have been conceded to the city's bishop by Duke Roger Borsa, *Troia*, no. 94.

[181] *Trani*, nos. 82, 83.   [182] *Trani*, no. 84; Houben, 'Gli ebrei', p. 208.

[183] A. Marongiu, 'Gli ebrei di Salerno nei documenti dei secoli X–XIII', *Archivio storico per le provincie napoletane* 62 (1937), pp. 23–4 [reprinted in A. Marongiu, *Byzantine, Norman, Swabian and Later Institutions in Southern Italy* (London, 1972)].

[184] Monti, *Stato normanno svevo*, p. 116 article I, p. 125 article XII.

[185] Houben, 'Gli ebrei', pp. 194–7, 200, 210.

customs of *c.* 1200 stipulated that the oaths of 'Jews or others, who profess idolatry and do not invoke the name of Christ' were not to be admitted in cases in which they claimed to have received injury from Christians, nor were they able to testify against the latter unless they could provide witnesses.[186]

In 1221 Frederick II promulgated a general ruling against dice-players, prostitutes, jugglers and Jews, who were to be 'distinguished from Christians in difference of dress and bearing'.[187] The regulation on Jewish dress followed closely that decreed at the Fourth Lateran Council of 1215, which aimed to prevent undue social integration and miscegenation between Christians and Jews.[188] Later, in attempting to protect the kingdom's religious minorities, Frederick II's Constitutions of Melfi, of 1231, imply that these communities had limited rights and were, at least by the thirteenth century, under real threat. One decree granted the right to impose defences for the Jewish community because 'we do not desire them to be harassed in their innocence because they are Jews'. Another legislated against Jews being 'defrauded of the power of our protection because a difference of religion renders them hateful and deprives them of all other help'. The fine for a secret murder or injury committed against a Christian was 100 *augustales*, while if the victim was Jewish it was only 50.[189] Frederick II's apparently tolerant attitude towards Judaism at times displayed typical Christian inconsistency. As Chazan observes, Jewish communities were protected, although in negative terms, while at the same time having limitations placed on their behaviour, which was historically perceived as a threat to Christianity.[190]

As the twelfth century moved into the thirteenth, Jewish communities, primarily in northern Europe but also in southern Italy, were subject to an ever-growing pressure that was both direct and indirect. It was the result of an increasingly aggressive Latin Christendom whose intolerant attitudes 'were rooted in broad societal malaise' and were guided by the papacy. Pope Innocent III's pontificate (1198–1216) was

---

[186] Petroni, *Storia di Bari*, ii. 502, 504 Rubric II.

[187] *Rich. S. Germano*, pp. 94–5; Abulafia, *Frederick* II, pp. 143–44. Jewish men had to wear beards.

[188] The Fourth Lateran Council of 1215 also forbade the building of new synagogues and prohibited Jews from holding office and owning slaves. It is not clear how far this was applied in southern Italy, and Frederick II did allow the building of new synagogues. Jews had been banned from owning Christian slaves in King Roger's legislation, Monti, *Stato normanno svevo*, p. 125 article XII.

[189] *Liber Augustalis*, pp. 21–2 Bk I, title xviii (21), pp. 29–30 titles xxvii–xxviii (31–2). All of these laws applied also to the Muslim community.

[190] R. Chazan, 'Pope Innocent III and the Jews', in *Pope Innocent III and His World*, ed. John C. Moore (Aldershot, 1999), pp. 187–204.

significant in diffusing, through innovative measures and highly negative stereotypes, 'the augmented twelfth-century sense of Jewish malevolence and harmfulness'.[191] The traditional balance between 'protection' and 'limitation' was increasingly tilting towards the latter. By the end of the thirteenth century growing anti-Semitic policies led to the (temporary) disappearance of most Jewish communities in Apulia. This had been achieved primarily through mass forced conversions and emigration resulting from the deteriorating conditions. Sources in the 1290s show that the Jewish communities of Naples, Trani and Salerno were compelled to convert and that the synagogue in the latter city was sold. At a similar period the surviving Muslim colony was also expelled from Lucera in Apulia.[192]

Despite this the Jewish communities of southern Italy, even in the thirteenth century, were more secure and integrated within the urban populace than was the case in northern Europe. The South Italian communities had been settled in their region far longer than their northern counterparts. While royal policy practised an ambiguous tolerance, and later hostility, towards the Jews, there is no clear evidence of any popular movements against them during our period. As can be seen from Benjamin of Tudela's survey, there was a notable, well-assimilated and largely prosperous Jewish population within many South Italian cities. Jewish communities had been established in many areas for centuries and were not, at least openly, forced to live together in Jewish quarters (*Iudaica*).[193] The Jewish communities may have been to some extent self-governing. There is some limited evidence that they applied their own law, although particularly in Salerno they usually lived according to Roman law.[194] There was freedom of worship and evidence

---

[191] Chazan, 'Pope Innocent III', pp. 201, 203.

[192] J. Cohen, *The Friars and the Jews. The Evolution of Medieval Anti-Judaism* (London, 1982), pp. 85–9; Marongiu, 'Gli ebrei', pp. 25–6 and appendix III, pp. 30–1; D. Abulafia, 'Monarchs and minorities in the Christian western Mediterranean around 1300: Lucera and its analogues', in *Christendom and Its Discontents*; J. Starr, 'The mass conversion of Jews in Southern Italy (1290–1293)', *Speculum* 21 (1946), pp. 203–11; key aspects of the developing relationships across medieval religious divides are analysed in R. Vose, *Dominicans, Muslims and Jews in Medieval Aragon, c. 1220–1320* (Cambridge, 2009).

[193] Houben, 'Gli ebrei', p. 210. There were also Jewish quarters in cities not already mentioned, such as at Benevento: Loud, 'A Lombard abbey', appendix I, pp. 303–4 no. 6; Girgensohn, 'Documenti beneventani', pp. 302–4 no. 9; *Cattedrale di Benevento*, no. 94; and at Aversa there is an interesting reference in 1189 to an area of the city where the *Iudaica* had formerly been, *CDNA*, pp. 259–61 no. 138.

[194] In 1272 at Salerno a Jewish man swore, in relation to upholding a contract, 'super librum legis quam Dominus dedit Moysii in Monte Synay', *CDS*, p. 404 no. 265; Marongiu, 'Gli ebrei', pp. 9–10; R. Chazan, 'The Jews in Europe and the Mediterranean basin', in *The New Cambridge Medieval History*, vol. IV, *c*. 1024–*c*. 1198, ed. D. Luscombe and J. Riley-Smith (Cambridge, 2004), pp. 640–4.

both of Jewish religious officials and synagogues within cities.[195] When the Jewish inhabitants of Bari's *Iudeca* were passed to the archbishop in 1086, the document mentioned a 'locum sinagoge'.[196] At Naples a synagogue was attested in the twelfth century and there was reference to a 'schola hebreorum', while a document of 1292 mentions a principal synagogue at Salerno.[197] Also at Salerno there are numerous documents in which land was let to Jews, usually in the *Giudayca*, for a period generally of nineteen or twenty-nine years.[198] The contract often allowed the recipient to build houses and live on the land, to remove any dwellings at the end of the term and provided the donor, often a church, with the right of pre-emption. This has been taken as proof of the incapacity of the Jewish community at Salerno to possess immobile goods. However, Marongiu has shown this not to be the case, suggesting that such temporary concessions were made also to Christians, and that Jewish people were entirely capable of possessing immobile goods.[199] Beyond this there was wider participation in the land market – for example in 1197, Seniorus, a Jew from Trani, purchased twenty-four olive trees from a man from Molfetta.[200]

As can be seen from a reference from Barletta in 1183 to a Samuel *ebreus Tranensis civis*, Jews could carry the citizen label alongside non-Jewish citizens, although the status this conferred is far from clear.[201] Moreover, Jews were able to stand as *fideiussores*.[202] In the early eleventh century, the prince of Capua had installed a Jewish man named Paltiel as governor and director of all civic affairs.[203] In Salerno, where one of the region's largest Jewish communities resided, a Jew called Sciamar acted in 1140 as Cava's *custodia decimationum* – supervising the collection of the monastery's revenues in the city's squares. It was a position that was given to Sciamar for life. In 1149 he received more property from Cava

---

[195] For example at Salerno, *Nuove pergamene*, nos. 14, 21, 32, 36; F. Cerone 'Sei documenti inediti sugli ebrei di Salerno dal 1125 al 1269', in *Studi di storia napoletana in onore di Michelangelo Schipa* (Naples, 1926), pp. 62–3 no. 3.

[196] *CDBI*, no. 30.

[197] *Monumenta ad Neapolitani Ducatus*, ii (i). 391 no. 629; N. Ferorelli, *Gli ebrei nell'Italia meridionale dall'età romana al secolo XVIII* (Turin, 1915) p. 40; Marongiu, 'Gli ebrei', pp. 25–6. In Troia there was a cemetery named S. Bartolomeo 'of the Jews', *Montevergine*, ix. no. 935, and outside Capua a Jewish cemetery, mentioned in 1112, *Regesto di S. Angelo in Formis*, pp.15–17 no. 7.

[198] *CDS*, pp. 126–7 no. 56, pp. 143–5 no. 69; *Nuove pergamene*, nos. 33, 35; Cava, *Arca* xxxii.56, xxxii.59, xxxvi.30.

[199] Marongiu, 'Gli ebrei', pp. 14–21; for example, *Pergamene di S. Nicola di Gallucanta*, no. 139; *Nuove pergamene*, no. 23; Cava, *Arca* xxi.110, xxiv.68.

[200] *Le carte di Molfetta (1076–1309)*, ed. F. Carabellese, *Codice diplomatico barese* VII (Bari, 1912), no. 76.

[201] *Pergamene di Barletta. Archivio Capitolare*, no. 141.

[202] Cerone, 'Sei documenti', pp. 62–3 no. 3; *CDS*, pp. 126–7 no. 56, pp. 143–5 no. 69; Cava, *Arca* xxxii.56, xxxvi.30.

[203] Milano, *Storia degli ebrei*, p. 62.

as a result of his 'good services' and 'on account of the love and prayers' of Philip the royal chamberlain.[204] Southern Italy's Jewish communities were culturally important, as is evident in the pun on Isaiah 2:3 made by the renowned twelfth-century Rabbi Jacob Tam: 'for out of Bari shall go forth the Torah and the word of the Lord from Otranto.'[205] Benjamin of Tudela spoke of 'great scholars and esteemed persons' in the Jewish community at Capua and 'men of learning' at Taranto.[206] On the other hand, only limited evidence exists for any commercial and money-lending activities among the Jewish communities in our period. Their primary activity in southern Italy appears to be as artisans, and they enjoyed monopolies in some cities over butchery, *auricellam* (jewellery-making?) and dyeing.[207] It should be briefly mentioned that there were no permanent Muslim communities on the mainland, before the transfer of the Sicilian Muslims to Lucera in the 1220s. The sources show only Muslim slaves and a couple of scattered but interesting references. In 1117, during the factional conflicts in Bari which often targeted private towers, one of these buildings was guarded by a 'Saracen' (*vigil Sarracenus*). Later in 1138 we find a certain Cafaro 'dwelling at Conversano and of Saracen origin', but who was clearly Christian as he donated himself and his goods to the monastery of S. Benedetto.[208]

In theory, the foreign resident, whether temporary or permanent, was also distinguished from the main core of the urban community. To be an *extraneus* usually carried a distinct status and limited access to the benefits of local customs and privileges within the city in which they were then present. In essence they could not hold public office, as evidenced by most of the civic charters of privileges, which reserved such positions for the native population. The Trani charter of liberties of 1139 distinguises the *extranei* from the *clerici* and *laici* of the city, but all have their goods safeguarded.[209] In the Troian charter of 1127 foreigners had to pay the *plateaticum*, while local inhabitants were exempt.[210] At Salerno Roger II agreed that he would not introduce other nobles to the *coetus nobilium* or *extranei* to the *numerum civium*. Within this sense of separate status it is often not clear to what extent foreigners were able to draw upon any of their own native customs or privileges that they might have. However, in line with the reality of assimilation, in a world of growing communication and social mobility, there is evidence for a willingness to incorporate the *extraneus* into the community. While

[204] Cerone, 'Sei documenti', pp. 59–61 no. 1; Cava, *Arca* xxvii.41.
[205] Cohen, *Friars and the Jews*, p. 85.   [206] *Itinerary Ben. Tudela*, pp. 7, 9.
[207] See below pp. 255–6.
[208] See above p. 206; *Anonymi Barensis Chronicon*, p. 155; *Conversano*, no. 85.
[209] *Trani*, no. 37.   [210] *Troia*, no. 50 clause 31.

a clause in the Barese customs of *c.* 1200 forbids foreigners to act as witnesses against citizens of Bari, the same article stated that 'those who have their residence in Bari are not regarded as *extraneus*'.[211] An earlier clause had already explained that anyone taking up residence in the city, and bringing with them the totality of their fortune, would immediately become a *Barensis* with the full enjoyment of civic custom.[212] Comparable clauses can be found in other documents, quoted earlier: Trani's charter of privileges of 1215, which allowed 'strangers' who came to live in the city to be henceforth assessed as citizens of Trani with all the privileges, customs and judicial protection that this entailed, and Pope Honorius III's order in 1216 on a similar subject concerning residence at Benevento.[213] Moreover, a plethora of charter evidence shows the extent to which people were moving between settlements – for marriage, work, residence, investment – and how familial connections stretched into different cities. This was growing more so as the twelfth century progressed.[214]

These networks of relationships primarily circulated within a radius of relatively close settlements, yet there were always distant contacts as well. There was great movement between inhabitants of the Apulian cities, particularly those on the coast. A document of 1199 from Monopoli shows an extended family which owned property in a suburb of that city, had one member married to a man from Brindisi and another who had made his will at Trani.[215] The will of Otto *nauclerius* of Bari, made in 1200 as he prepared to journey to Byzantium, showed that he owed money to a Jew from Trani and was owed money by a judge from Monopoli, a notary from Acquaviva and a man from Brindisi.[216] Also, in smaller inland cities movement was common. Some charters at Conversano contain a clause that foresaw the potential for people to leave (*exabitare*) the city of Conversano. It often provided for the land or property, which had been rented or conceded, to go back to the original owner/donor until the time when the tenant/proprietor returned to live in the city (*ad habitandum redire*).[217] At Troia there was a range of people who identified themselves or their parents as being from a different settlement. They came from relatively close communities like Bovino,

---

[211] Petroni, *Storia di Bari*, ii. 444 Rubric III. 4.

[212] Petroni, *Storia di Bari*, ii. 440 Rubric II. 8.   [213] See above pp. 174, 178.

[214] As with surnames relating to profession, the same caution must be used with those that are toponyms but which may still offer insight, at least on more distant family histories.

[215] *Conversano*, no. 147.

[216] Otto also appeared in Trani in 1205, see Appendix, 'An example of a kin-group and its network of relationships', document 6, below.

[217] *Conversano*, no. 151 and for variations nos. 123, 128, 129, 152.

Baselice and Ariano, as well as those more distant such as Melfi, Rapolla, Avellino, Alife, Salerno and Capua.[218] Some of these settlers obtained at least some influence within their new city. Baresanus, the son of a man from Baselice, was a notary at Troia from 1170 to 1198, while Peter de Rapolla witnessed, alongside important locals, a significant concord between the lord of Biccari and the bishop of Troia in 1177 and also owned a sizable amount of land in the city's *contado*.[219] Ecclesiastical careers may have brought some to the area: for example a deacon from Baselice in 1085 and a canon of the cathedral, mentioned in 1154, who carried the surname *Salernitanus*.[220] At the same time inhabitants from Troia were attested elsewhere. In 1156 a Richard of Troia appeared at Aversa, in 1170 a notary of the bishop of Agrigento in Sicily was called Roger of Troia and in 1195 the son of a Troian, born at Ascoli Satriano, was then living at Melfi.[221] Individuals often maintained simultaneous interests in different settlements. In 1125 a knight called Richard, resident in the Principate, sold a house in Troia, in 1129 a former inhabitant of Troia called Bella, then living in Rapolla, sold some land in the *contado* of Troia to her son-in-law, while in the 1190s a certain Seclina of Troia disposed of real estate at Dragonara, where her nephew was a constable.[222]

It was a similar picture in Campania with, for instance, people of Naples and Capua appearing at Aversa.[223] Further afield, the *strategotus* of Messina, from 1156–68, was a Richard of Aversa.[224] There was much interaction between the populaces of the Tyrrhenian coastal cities.[225] Perhaps the most distinct and sizeable community of 'outsiders' within the cities of southern Italy were Amalfitans and others from that surrounding region. As Amalfi's Mediterranean commercial network altered from the eleventh century, more colonies of Amalfitans and their neighbours, particularly from Ravello, appeared across southern Italy,

---

[218] Bovino: *Montevergine*, vi. no. 568; Baselice: *Troia*, nos. 19, 66 and below n. 219; Ariano: *Troia*, no. 39; Melfi: *Troia*, nos. 56, 93; *Montevergine*, x. no. 983; Rapolla: *Troia* nos. 73, 92, 94; Avellino: *Montevergine*, ix. no. 840; Alife: *Troia* nos. 52, 72; Salerno: *Troia* nos. 70, 109, 143; Capua: *Troia*, no. 21; in 1195 the niece of a notary called Roger *de Sicilia* appeared at Troia, *Montevergine*, x. no. 983.

[219] Baresanus: *Troia* nos. 86, 93, 108, 109, 118, 121; *Montevergine*, vii. no. 684, x. nos. 942, 974, 983; Peter: *Troia*, nos. 73, 94.

[220] *Troia*, nos. 19, 70. The city's bishop was often not a native of Troia, see below p. 229.

[221] *Montevergine*, iv. no. 348, x. no. 984; *Le più antiche carte dell'archivio capitolare di Agrigento (1092–1282)*, ed. P. Collura (Palermo, 1960), p. 53 no. 20.

[222] *Troia*, nos. 49, 54; *Cartulaire de S. Matteo*, i. 134–6 no. 75, 161–3 no. 90.

[223] CDNA, pp. 211–3 no 114 for a John who was 'unus de feodati militibus Averse' and a 'habitator' of Naples; p. 242 no. 130 for a Ligorio *civis Neapolitano et baro civitatis Averse*.

[224] *Falcandus*, pp. 117 and n. 96, 183–4.

[225] A general theme running through Skinner, *Family Power in Southern Italy*.

refocusing on regional overland trade. In many cities individuals carrying the toponym *Amalfitanus* or some form of the word Ravello can be found. At Aversa there was a *burgus* (suburb) and a *ruga* (street) *Amalphitanorum*, at Trani a *ruga Ravellensium* and at Benevento it was Amalfitans who lavishly decorated the city in anticipation of Pope Calixtus II's visit in 1120.[226] Also in Benevento, in 1184, the pope confirmed the ancient customs which the people of Scala, Ravello and others from the duchy of Amalfi, who dwelled in Benevento, had formerly enjoyed in the city. These 'Amalfitans' had judicial protection and could settle cases with Beneventans *extra curiam* and through Amalfitan judges.[227] At Bari the content of the city's charter of liberties of 1132 was not to apply to the Amalfitans. From the later redaction of that same city's customs the *Ravellenses* who lived in Bari were still identified as such, yet the customs elsewhere stated that anybody who had residence in the city would at once be a *Barensis*. The *Ravellenses* were not allowed to be heard in cases against Bari citizens 'unless they will have signed documents in the customary way'.[228] In a document of 1141, at Bari, a Mauro musceta *ravellensis* is called a *commorator* of the city, while a man named John *castaldus ravellensis* had been a *baiulus* in Bari sometime before 1223.[229] In 1190 the Neapolitans gave a grant to 'the most wise men of Scala and Ravello' and to other *negotiatores, campsores* and *apothecarii* from the duchy of Amalfi living and trading in Naples. The concession gave the 'Amalfitans' and their heirs complete freedom, just like the citizens of Naples, in 'the free and open practice of [their] businesses'. Furthermore, the 'Amalfitans' were permitted to appoint consuls in the city from among their number in Naples. These consuls could settle 'Amalfitan' disputes according to their old customs, without the interference of the Neapolitans. In certain ways the Amalfitans and their neighbours were very much an identifiable and separate group within many South Italian urban communities. But in many other ways they were an integrated and central component of the populace. Their role in the local trading network made them both indispensable and most likely affluent. With wealth came influence. Especially in the eleventh century at Salerno there were various important families carrying the toponym *Atranensis*, the name given in Salerno to descendants of Amalfitans who had settled in that city.[230] The *Atranenses* were found predominantly in the *vicus* Sancte Trofimene and Vietri regions, both

---

[226] *CDNA*, pp. 68–9 no. 40, pp. 341–2 no. 19; *Trani*, no. 103, *Falco*, pp. 54–6.
[227] Borgia, *Memorie istoriche*, iii. 163–6.   [228] Petroni, *Storia di Bari*, ii. 448 Rubric III. 11.
[229] *CDBV*, no. 94; *CDBVI*, no. 42.
[230] Among these many families were the Ioncatella, Sfagilla and Butrumiles; H. Taviani-Carozzi, *La Principauté lombarde de Salerne IXe–XIe siècle* (Paris, 1991), ii. 800–37 and appendix III, 1152–66.

areas suitable for the pursuit of commerce. They continued to live under Roman law, regularly married within their own group and invested together in property, often mills, as *consortes*. While remaining distinct, many *Atranenses* held a place in what Taviani-Carozzi calls the 'society of power' and the 'exercise of honours' at Salerno.[231] Intermarriage with Salernitan Lombards took place, and this form of integration may be one explanation for the declining usage of the *Atranensis* toponym in the twelfth century.[232]

The example of the Amalfitan communities may touch upon an important factor in the way outsiders were treated within their new environments. Their acceptance and subsequent experiences probably varied according to their skills and potential contributions. The sources mostly focus on the more affluent immigrants. Is it perhaps significant that the article in the Bari customs stating that residence in the city constituted someone as a *Barensis* is qualified with the requirement for the person to relocate all their wealth there as well? Indeed many *extranei* were found in a city because they were providing some relatively lucrative service or trade or enjoyed some useful family or patrimonial connections there. Yet we know little of those who did not have quite the same opportunities at their disposal – the rural immigrants who probably hailed from the city's immediate territories.[233] It has been observed that the populations of South Italian cities were larger than expected because of their propensity to incorporate rural inhabitants.[234] Galasso's study on the cities of Campania emphasises the great movement that occurred in this era from countryside to city, something of course particularly central to urban development in northern and central Italy.[235] Moreover, how were exiles or refugees of war absorbed? When Troia was destroyed by Roger II in 1133 its population was dispersed around the *contado*, and still further. Later in the decade the city developed into a place of refuge for opponents of the king, as also at varying points did Benevento and Naples.[236] In the years immediately following Bari's ruin in 1156 some 'former' *Barenses* are found in places like Giovinazzo and Trani.[237] There are two key questions here. Firstly, at what point, if ever, was the foreigner no longer a foreigner within his or

---

[231] Taviani-Carozzi, *Principauté lombarde de Salerne*, ii. 828.

[232] P. Skinner, 'Daughters of Sichelgaita: the women of Salerno in the twelfth century', in *Salerno nel XII secolo*, p. 125 discusses other possible explanations.

[233] G. Barni, '*Cives* e *rustici* a Milano alla fine del XII secolo e all'inizio del XIII secondo il *Liber Consuetudinum Mediolani*', *Rivista storica italiana* 69 (1957), pp. 5–60 offers a detailed discussion of the relationship between the urban and rural inhabitant at Milan, and its imbalance in favour of the former.

[234] Pounds, *Economic History*, p. 260 [235] Galasso, 'Le città campane', pp. 61–135.

[236] See above pp. 167–8. [237] *CDBV*, nos. 114, 123.

her new civic community? Secondly, what change in status did such a transition encompass? Which brings us back to the earlier discussion on citizenship, where fixing upon any concrete findings is highly problematic.

Finally, poverty, particularly for the lower and less privileged ranks, was a constant threat. Precipitating factors, such as lack of work, disease, natural disasters and warfare, undoubtedly hit the lower classes the hardest. A frequent military tactic was not only to target the city but also to burn the surrounding crops and vines. This could induce famine and sickness and raise the price of basic foodstuffs, as happened during the siege of Salerno in 1076/7.[238] The effects of extreme environmental changes could be the same. The famine of 1102 resulted in a bushel of grain being sold for 100 *denarii*, according to the *Annales Beneventani*.[239] In all cases the lowest earners, and least privileged, were likely to have suffered the most.

It must be remembered, however, that these factors affected the entire populace and that poverty was a threat to people of all social ranks.[240] When a donation or sale was made to relieve a person's poverty this does not signal that the individual was of the lowest status or indeed had become so as a result of their current condition. Poverty affected noble, artisan and labourer, although in clearly different ways and to different degrees, without immediately denuding any of them of their social identity. It could indicate an absolute status, lacking the basics of life, or a relative one, in the sense of a person who was no longer able to enjoy their pre-existing socio-economic position.[241] Poverty was neither gender- nor age-specific, even though many declarations of poverty concerned women, usually widows, and their children.[242] But some of these cases may be misleading, as they dealt with women living under a rigid Lombard law which made it difficult to utilise their property. The mother could circumvent this legal obstacle through her child

---

[238] According to *Amatus*, the combination of Guiscard's siege and Gisulf II's actions led to 'great hunger in Salerno. Those who had no provisions could find none to buy, nor were alms given at the doors of the houses, for the poverty was great.' Amatus goes on to describe the further horrors which the besieged inhabitants suffered; their resort to eating the 'flesh of horses, dogs and cats', the rising price of foodstuffs and bodies that were left unburied. In response to this, Guiscard, when in possession of the city (but not the citadel), 'saw the poverty of the people of Salerno' and set up a market where cheap food could be bought, pp. 194–200.

[239] Bertolini, 'Gli '*Annales Beneventani*', p. 152; famine struck Naples during its blockade by royal forces in the mid-1130s, Falco, p. 176; *Alex. Tel.*, Bk III.23 pp. 71–2.

[240] M. Mollat, *The Poor in the Middle Ages – An Essay in Social History*, trans. A. Goldhammer (Yale, 1986), pp. 65, 70, 105.

[241] S. Fodale, 'Il povero', in *Condizione umana*, pp. 46–7.

[242] P. Skinner, 'Gender and poverty in the medieval community', in *Medieval Women in their Communities*, ed. D. Watt (Cardiff, 1997), 204–21.

alienating, if need could be demonstrated, its own property. Women and children were certainly among the most vulnerable in the community, but there were as many women who were neither dependent nor unable to be financially successful. In its own relative way, poverty could affect those seemingly of the highest status. In 1149 Lauretta, the granddaughter of Stephen Sculdascio, the former rector of Benevento, donated vines and land to her young cousin Jacob. Lauretta acted 'because he [Jacob] suffers great need' (*multa indigentia*).[243] By 1193 Jacob was in a position to donate a house with shops within Benevento to Montevergine, having already presented the monastery with some land and vines.[244] Jacob even attained the consulship in the city.[245] Numerous transactions contain clauses dealing with the possibility of falling into poverty and show it to be an ever-present concern to a variety of people. At Aversa, in 1159, Stephen Russingolo, an inhabitant of the suburb of the fishermen, received four lands from the canons of the cathedral. A clause gave the canons the right of pre-emption on the lands if Stephen's heirs should suffer 'great poverty' (*inopia*).[246] Debt, in particular, could be accrued by anybody of any rank and at times could affect the next generation. At Bari, in 1140, the children of the deceased Meliacca feared that the interest on their father's unpaid debts, which was growing daily, would lead to the loss of their inherited possessions.[247] At Troia, in 1132, the *infantula* Iurneda, along with her mother Duchilia and a relative, had to sell some lands. Iurneda had been prompted to act by the death of her father and his 'large debt [which has] placed me [Iurneda] under pressure from his creditors, and I am now suffering severe shortage [. . . from which . . .] I am by no means able at this very bad time to extricate myself.'[248]

Debt was common and did not always lead to such hardship, but accumulating it may have served to keep poverty in the forefront of people's minds. At Bari and Benevento, for example, there are a number of twelfth-century charters dealing with loan contracts, repayments of debts and pledges made against them.[249] In 1132, the will of Gilbert

---

[243] *Montevergine*, iii. no. 291.

[244] *Montevergine*, ix. no. 897 and also iv. no. 375. The shop had previously belonged to Stephen Sculdascio.

[245] See above p. 120.   [246] *CDNA*, no. 76, p. 133.   [247] Cava, *Arca* xxv.2.

[248] *Troia*, no. 58. It is worth noting that this document was redacted at a time of great disruption for the city. It may be that the 'very bad time' is both a reference to Iurneda's and Troia's condition; in 1126 at Bari, the minor Leo sold some land to relieve himself of the debt left by his deceased father, *CDBV*, no. 72. In 1191, the will of John, son of Gafuri Bernardi, disposed to pay both his and his father's debts which burdened them, *CDBV*, no. 158.

[249] *CDBV*, nos. 105, 110, 123, 132, 138, 140, 141, frag. nos. 13, 15, 17–18; *Cattedrale di Benevento*, nos. 68, 79, 133, which speaks of a 'law and custom of pledge (*pignus*) of this city'.

Amalfitanus, who lived at Aversa and perished in the Battle of Nocera, bequeathed half of his house and property to the cathedral and the other half to be sold to pay off his debts.[250] At Benevento, in 1193, city judges ordered a certain Sebastian to take possession of a house belonging to Andrea. The latter had pledged the house against a loan received from Sebastian and the date of repayment had passed.[251] Many individuals provided alms and other assistance for the poor, often in their testaments. The will of John, son of Disigius of Trani, in 1138, left 200 *miliarenses* 'for paupers, widows, orphans and poor clerics'.[252] At Salerno, in 1164, Cava donated some baths to a man who had to provide a warm fountain each month for the *pauperes* to wash in.[253] Part of the bequest of Andreas *medicus* of Capua, in 1181, was 'for the poor and the works/repair of bridges'.[254] In the testament of Otto *nauclerius* from Bari in 1200 a plantation of olives and some vines were to be left, if the family succession failed, to the church of S. Lazaro, 'where the lepers stay outside Bari'.[255] Indeed, attitudes influenced by theological ideas emerged in the twelfth century to confer a 'new social standing' on the poor.[256] That people of all ranks were vulnerable, and that the commercial and economic revival could rapidly gain or lose fortunes, would not have contradicted that belief. Hospitals devoted to supporting the poor were established within cities. Outside Salerno could be found a 'xenodochium pro substantione pauperum' and, by 1183, a hospital of St John of Jerusalem.[257] A variety of hospitals were also documented at Capua, mostly in the suburbs.[258] By the end of the twelfth century, prayer unions and associations emerged in some cities, with lay participation and certain similarities to confraternities, which placed emphasis on charity and care for the poor.[259] The foundation charter of S. Spirito of Benevento established that 'from the *census* of the possessions of the

---

[250] *CDNA*, p. 53 no. 32.　　[251] *Cattedrale di Benevento*, no. 124.　　[252] *Trani*, p. 92 no. 37.
[253] C. A. Garufi, 'Di uno stabilmento balneare in Salerno nel secolo XII', *Studi Medievali* 1 (1904–5), pp. 276–80.
[254] *Pergamene normanne*, no. 23. Capua's location on the bend of the Volturno made bridges a particularly important component of urban life.
[255] *CDBVI*, no. 10.　　[256] Mollat, *Poor in the Middle Ages*, p. 106.
[257] Jamison, 'Norman administration', cal. doc. no. 57; *Italia Sacra*, vii. 406; G. Vitolo, 'Città e chiesa nel Mezzogiorno medievale: la processione del santo patrono a Salerno (sec. XII)', in *Salerno nel XII secolo*, p. 143.
[258] The *xenodochium S. protomartiris Stephani et Agathes* in a suburb near the *pontem Casolini*, the *hospitalis S. Iohannis Hierosolimitani* near the city's *castellum novum*, the *hospitalis S. Iacobi de Alto Passu* to the west of the city, the *domus infirmorum ecclesie S. Lazari* not far from the castle, and the *hospitalis ad opus et hutilitatem pauperum* near the cemetery of the church of S. Maria outside Capua; *Pergamene normanne*, nos. 12, 30; *Pergamene sveve*, ii. no. 8; *Pergamene di Capua*, i. 110–2 no. 52; G. Bova, *La vita quotidiana a Capua al tempo delle crociate* (Naples, 2001), pp. 81–2.
[259] See below pp. 234–5.

fraternitas . . . half be given to *pauperes, viduas et orfanos*', while the *con-fratres* of S. Bartolomeo of Naples gathered every Tuesday and Saturday to distribute alms to the poor.[260] While the theoretical sanctity of poverty may have been growing, Fodale is correct to recognise that most people aimed to avoid such a condition, and also to ask how many individuals appearing in documents were not identified as 'poor' for personal reasons.[261] Poverty was at the core of the community's consciousness, and although it was a socially eclectic phenomenon it carried the most impact for the lower ranks.

Thus there was an entire gamut of individuals who could find themselves on the margins of the urban community. In Bresc's survey Jews, Muslims, the ill, the deformed, sinners, exiles, travellers, foreigners, the poor, practitioners of certain trades, criminals, illegitimates, the elderly, children and women could all qualify as 'le marginal'.[262] But, as seen above, the notion of social inclusion or exclusion can be viewed in a more nuanced way. Within these 'marginal' groups were individuals who were often actually far better integrated within the urban community than has usually been imagined. At the same time these conditions for 'marginality' could also include the wealthy and seemingly privileged.

SOLIDARITIES AND SOCIAL CONFLICT

The main thread of this chapter has emphasised the complex and ever-changing 'communities' that formed the urban populace in southern Italy. Our discussion of the three arbitrary groupings of the higher, middle and lower ranks shows how often they overlapped. This is far from surprising, given the array of 'solidarities' that any individual could be part of at any one time. As Reynolds noted, medieval people were 'remarkably vague about the particular collective group in which they were acting and its membership'.[263] An individual could be a member of a number of solidarities formed out of origin, culture, occupation, urban topography, religion, personal friendship and above all family. Many of these were horizontal relationships which intersected the vertical hierarchic ones. Of course the most fundamental one was the family – 'the

---

[260] Houben, 'Confraternite e religiosità', appendix, pp. 374–5; G. Vitolo, 'Esperienze religiose nella Napoli dei secoli XII–XIV', in *Medioevo Mezzogiorno Mediterraneo*, appendix I, pp. 26–31.

[261] Fodale, 'Il povero', pp. 56, 59.

[262] H. Bresc, 'Le marginal', in *Condizione umana*, pp. 20–1.

[263] S. Reynolds, 'English towns of the eleventh century in a European context', in *Die Stadt im 11. Jahrundert*, ed. P. Johanek (Münster, 1995), p. 6 [reprinted in her *Ideas and Solidarities of the Medieval Laity* (Aldershot, 1995)]; and also Reynolds, *Kingdoms and Communities*, pp. 167, 184–8.

building block of larger social structures'.[264] It too was a flexible entity, and indeed there was no medieval Latin word for 'family'. Many kin-groups in the South Italian documentation can be traced only over two or three generations. The survival rate of the documentation is partly responsible for this as are the problems of tracing families who have not yet adopted fixed surnames. Following lead-names, forenames that are commonly used within a family, can be a useful way of overcoming this but only in limited cases. Moreover, the continued process of inter-marriage between families adds to the problems. At Amalfi, many prominent families which appeared for the first time in the twelfth and thirteenth centuries were not 'new' but branches of ancient kin-groups which had adopted an intermediate surname from their extensive genealogy.[265] Likewise, at Gaeta we can see some of those new 'sur-named' families, which emerged from the mid-eleventh century to form the civic elite, intermarrying with other kin-groups and thus disap-pearing themselves.[266] As a result, a family name may have disappeared, but the family itself continued in an organic sense within the new unit. Kin-groups in their widest sense clearly had more longevity than our sources suggest. In reality every individual represented a unique point within one branch of various converging family trees, out of which only one kin-group name could be adopted. The South Italian medieval family could be both 'extended' and 'nuclear', with considerable diver-gence in those who were considered members at a particular moment.[267] In most cases the origins or disappearances of families are inevitably concealed from us by the nature of naming patterns and the ways in which kin-groups were constantly evolving and redefining themselves.[268] Therefore, when a kin-group name seemingly disappears, war, regime change, natural disasters and infertility are not the only explanations.

The fluidity of kin-groups, perhaps the smallest communities within the civic populace, and the inter-relationships between them mirror the nature of those larger urban groupings that were discussed earlier. These solidarities were not shaped by any rigid legal ordering. It is especially vital to dispel the idea that within a city's component groups (the *nobiles*, *mediani* and *minori* – such as they are) the mentalities, activities and interests were somehow entirely homogenous, and that this homogeneity

---

[264] D. Herlihy, 'The making of the medieval family: symmetry, structure and sentiment', in *Women, Family and Society in Medieval Europe. Historical essays, 1978–1991* (Providence, 1995), p. 136.
[265] Del Treppo and Leone, *Amalfi*, pp. 112–15.
[266] Skinner, *Family Power in Southern Italy*, p. 237.
[267] J. Drell, 'The aristocratic family', in *The Society of Norman Italy*, pp. 104–5.
[268] Herlihy, 'The making of the medieval family', p. 145.

was itself inevitably at odds with that prevailing in other groups within the same city.[269] The medieval mind was more than capable of identifying a sense of self and an awareness of being separate. Above all we have to caution against erroneous generalisations when discussing broad social movements and class conflict. The internal clashes that emerged within South Italian cities never pitted one discrete class against another. The multiplicity of identities that an individual could choose from precluded this. The conflicts at Benevento in the early twelfth century are often portrayed as an aristocratic faction against a popular one, implying that there was an inevitable tension and separation between them.[270] Likewise at Bari, after the events of 1087, a 'middle-class' party supposedly supported the church of S. Nicola against the aristocrat-backed cathedral.[271] But were these really coherent, long-established entities with definable, long-term interests, or, more likely, were they temporary and *ad hoc* solidarities formed from a variety of ranks for a relatively immediate purpose? Factions may have been identified with their leading (or most vociferous) protagonists, but we should not see their entire social make-up reflected in them. William of Apulia commented that at the siege of Bari (1068–71) 'the *maiores* [were] able to lead the spirit of the *minores* to whatever end they wished.'[272] This does not mean that both groups were previously opposed in their interests, but rather that the lower ranks felt a natural deference towards the leading men of their city, and that the two 'groups' could coalesce.[273] To further complicate matters, Argirizzus, the apparent leader of the pro-Norman faction at Bari during the siege, signed a document, in March 1071, in Greek and listed his range of Byzantine titles.[274] Care should be taken not to assume that a given identity or status made certain actions and behaviour inevitable. The civil strife in Benevento, described so vividly by Falco, produced factions whose often-changing social composition made it hard to differentiate between them. It must have been a similar story for those factions which arose in many cities at times of war and

---

[269] S. Reynolds, 'Social mentalities and the case of medieval scepticism', *Transactions of the Royal Historical Society*, series 5, 41 (1991), pp. 21–41.

[270] G. Intorcia, *La comunità beneventana nei secoli XII–XVIII. Aspetti istituzionali. Controversie giurisdizionali* (Naples, 1996), speaks of a 'partito popolare' struggling against a 'partito aristocratico', pp. 24–5; W. Holtzmann, 'Un nuovo documento riguardante il rettore Ansone di Benevento', *Samnium* 31 (1958), pp. 125–32, sees the disorders after 1101 as factional fighting between the *patriziato* and the *classi inferiori*, and argues that Landulf Burellus led a popular party against Anso's aristocratic one, p. 128; Vergineo, *Storia di Benevento*, pp. 194–222, includes a discussion of these different factions and social movements.

[271] Nitti di Vito, *La ripresa gregoriana*, pp. 7, 261, 482.

[272] *Will. Apulia*, Bk III lines 144–8, p. 172.   [273] See above pp. 188–9.

[274] *CDBIV*, no. 45; von Falkenhausen, *La dominazione Bizantina*, p. 174.

unrest. The so-called revolt of the *mediani* against the *nobili* at Naples in 1156, the apparently pro- and anti-Byzantine factions at Monopoli and Bari in 1155–6 and the strife at Salerno in 1162, where a group called the *capiturinos* emerged, all show the persistence of civic discord.[275] But little, beyond the broadest conclusions, can be deduced from the coalitions and their apparent aims, which formed during such tumults. Evidence from northern and central Italian cities tends to confirm the problems of identifying innate 'class' conflict. Here overt violence and discord appear as a more persistent feature of the urban landscape, but one whose contours are no easier to decipher.[276] The participation in the early thirteenth century, for example, of 'nobles' within the *popolo* movement is emblematic of the hazy social boundaries.[277] Personal rivalry between families, and the means employed by particular individuals within the community to accumulate wealth and power, may often have lain behind many wider factional conflicts. At Bari, in the early twelfth century, some of the city elite owned private towers which were targeted by opponents; a smaller-scale development, perhaps, of the *consorterie* so widespread in central and northern Italy, where towers could act as statements of kin-group prestige and the focal point for local solidarities and friction between them.[278] Privately owned towers were also attested in other cities such as Benevento, Salerno, Troia and Trani.[279] It becomes then all the more remarkable that, despite the variety of 'solidarities' and conflicts that emerged, the urban community, as we have seen, could still act together, with some sort of consensus, particularly in its role in government. Above all, a sense of transcendent civic consciousness may go far in explaining this.

---

[275] Fuiano, 'Napoli normanna e sveva', pp. 424–32.

[276] For a general discussion see, L. Martines (ed.), *Violence and Civic Disorder in Italian Cities 1200–1500* (Berkeley, 1972).

[277] Tabacco, *Struggle for Power*, pp. 226–7; E. Coleman, 'Cities and communes', in *Italy in the Central Middle Ages 1000–1300*, ed. D. Abulafia (Oxford, 2004), pp. 53–4.

[278] *Anonymi Barensis Chronicon*, pp. 155–6; Vitolo, *Città e coscienza cittadina*, pp. 21–3.

[279] Benevento, Museo del Sannio, Fondo S. Sofia, vol. 21 no. 1; Salerno: *CDS*, pp. 103–4 no. 39; Troia: *Troia*, nos. 20, 72; *Colonie cassinesi*, no. 18; *Montevergine*, vi. no. 568; Trani: *Trani*, nos. 33, 63.

Chapter 8

THE CHURCH, BISHOP AND CIVIC IDENTITY

In John of Salisbury's well-known analogy of the 'republic' as a human entity, it was 'those who direct the practice of religion' who should be considered as representing the body's 'soul'.[1] In the medieval urban world this was certainly apt, as the Church was at the core of the city's make-up: it dictated the community's accepted belief system, it sculpted the streets and squares with its buildings and dominated the skyline with its cathedral, its wealth percolated through the urban economy, its officials provided guidance, both spiritual and political, and through its ceremonies it offered a framework in which the urban community could socially commune. The city and the Church in medieval southern Italy very much merged into, and were reliant on, each other, no doubt much to the chagrin of some of the more radical Church reformers of the day.

It is apparent that, despite initial complaints of depredations against the Church, Norman rule augmented episcopal and monastic power in the South, both politically and materially. This made the Church a participant in local administration and bound it, in a position of dependency, to the ruling lay powers. Additionally, in conjunction with papal reformers, the Norman rulers encouraged the establishment of firmer ecclesiastical hierarchies and also assisted leading monastic houses in the construction of territorial lordships, with similar results. Ramseyer has demonstrated this in the Salerno region for the city's archbishopric and the monastery of Cava, and evidence elsewhere suggests comparable developments.[2] SS. Trinità, Venosa, received, from Robert Guiscard, rule of half the city of Venosa in 1074, and other houses such as S. Lorenzo of Aversa, S. Benedetto of Conversano, S. Sofia of Bevenento

---

[1] John of Salisbury, *Policraticus*, ed. and trans. C. J. Nederman (Cambridge, 1990), Ch. 2, Bk V, pp. 66–7.
[2] Ramseyer, *Transformation of a Religious Landscape*, pp. 151, 157, 161, 172, 177.

and S. Nicola of Bari obtained similar secular patronage. This further bolstered these establishments' influence on urban life.[3]

Within this framework, bishops and abbots stood at the centre of many of the currents of interaction which flowed between Church and community. The bishop enjoyed little formal legal jurisdiction over the lay urban community, aside from cases (such as incest and blasphemy) that fell under the authority of the ecclesiastical court. However, those individuals who resided within the bishopric's (often increasing) landed patrimony, and also, in many cases, the Jewish community, fell under ecclesiastical jurisdiction. In this way at least some small part of the urban community was directly subject to a religious institution. A royal privilege of 1156 allowed the bishop of Troia the powers of a justiciar over all his men (including the Jewish population) and to hold courts to judge adulterers, sorcerers and doctors (probably unqualified ones) throughout the diocese.[4] In 1220 Frederick II granted the archbishop of Salerno the power to act as a justiciar over Church lands and people within his archdiocese.[5] The addition of a variety of other lucrative incomes, tithes from public revenues, trade monopolies and exemptions from customs taxes, made some ecclesiastical institutions vital components of the urban economy and administration. However, it was only a minority of the larger, favoured sees (and leading religious houses) that received the full range of these special privileges, and only a few bishoprics ever developed substantial territorial lordships.[6] Yet even in the many small South Italian sees which did not receive as much patronage, the bishop's diminished political and financial clout was offset by an even more intimate relationship with the citizenry. This meant that maintaining the loyalty of churchmen was still vitally important for secular rulers. As a result of their increasing activity in the land and property markets, bishops, abbots and other ecclesiastics were in constant contact with the lay community, buying, selling, donating, exchanging and receiving goods. These transactions often took place in secular courts before local officials and other leading men. Some of these laymen acted as advocates for religious institutions during such legal procedures; however, churchmen also acted as advocates for laypeople. Interaction between churchmen and laymen in secular matters was a daily affair. In 1214 the abbot of S. Benedetto of Conversano leased some land to the local judge, William, who was described as being 'in

---

[3] *Recueil des actes des ducs*, pp. 85–7 no. 22; Loud, 'A Lombard abbey', pp. 273–306; Houben, 'I Benedettini in città: il caso di Bari (sec. X–XIII)', in *Mezzogiorno normanno-svevo*, p. 292.

[4] *Troia*, no. 75; the abbot of Cava was given the right to be a justiciar over its men and lands in 1209, *Hist. Dip. Friderici Secundi*, i. 151–2.

[5] *CDS*, pp. 124–5 no. 53.   [6] Loud, *Latin Church*, pp. 318–23, 391.

every way a loyal helper and advisor in all the requirements and business of us and our church'.[7] But the relationship was not always so tranquil, and dealings between church and laymen could easily lead to dispute and legal process. Churches and monasteries contributed to civic, and royal, defence, which further entwined them with the lay community.[8] A document of 1189 shows that the cathedral congregation of Aversa made financial contributions towards the fortification of the city walls.[9] Conversely, in 1197 the officials and people of Bari were ordered not to force the men of S. Nicola of Bari to provide galley service, an exemption that had stood from the 'time of the kings'.[10] The implication is that such institutions could otherwise be liable to military obligations, perhaps especially after 1139, but in truth the exact extent and nature of this service remains uncertain. In any case, all of this required a larger body of administrative officials – guardians, procurators and bailiffs. A more complex hierarchy of ecclesiastical functionaries was also needed to minister to the needs of the ever-growing urban population.

Many of these church officials were drawn from the local community, providing a further bond between the two. The arrival of the Normans did not greatly alter the social and ethnic composition of the episcopate and even less so that of the cathedral chapters.[11] Moreover, most monasteries remained filled by native monks. At Salerno John Mansella, cousin of the royal chamberlain Atenolf, and the archdeacon Robert, from the Guarna family, were canons of the cathedral.[12] In the thirteenth century, the brother-in-law of judge Romuald Guarna was a Salerno cleric and also a papal chaplain and doctor. Among many other examples, the son of Petracca, a *magister faber* of Conversano, was a deacon, while one of the three sons of the judge Petracca Buffus of Bari was a priest.[13] The Collivaccinus family of Benevento supplied a local abbot and canon, not to mention a high-ranking cardinal bishop at Rome.[14] Like the de Roccas at Troia, it is quite likely that they also founded their own religious establishment near Benevento.

---

[7] *Conversano*, no. 164; the advocates of S. Benedetto, in the late twelfth and early thirteenth centuries, included a son of a notary (*Conversano*, no. 123), a former judge (no. 134), a knight (no. 137) and a judge (nos. 151–2, 154, 157, 164, 169).

[8] See G. A. Loud, 'The Church, warfare and military obligation in Norman Italy', *Studies in Church History* 20 (1983), pp. 31–45; for an extended discussion see Loud, *Latin Church*, pp. 340–62.

[9] *CDNA*, pp. 253–5 no. 135.   [10] *CDBVI*, no. 3.

[11] This, and the ensuing, section on the episcopate, draw on the following invaluable works: Loud, *Latin Church*; Kamp, *Kirche und Monarchie*, vols. I and II; Kamp, 'The bishops of southern Italy', pp. 185–209.

[12] G. Sangermano, 'La cattedrale e la città', in *Salerno nel XII secolo*, pp. 153–4; Another Guarna, John, had also previously been an archdeacon, Loud, *Age of Robert Guiscard*, p. 305.

[13] See above p. 205; *CDBI*, no. 82.   [14] See above pp. 196–7; *PL* 215, col. 721 no. 141.

The community itself played an implicit role in the election of the bishop. Archbishop Elias of Bari revealed that his election in 1089 was made through the common vow and agreement of all the populace of the city (who were later identified as making an earnest entreaty on this matter to the pope when he visited the city), its clergy and Duke Roger.[15] Bishop Gerard of Troia (1090–7) was also chosen with the consent of the duke, the clergy and the people of the city.[16] In the 1130s the Capuans and Beneventans gave their assent to the election of new archbishops.[17] In the case of the larger and wealthier sees, some of which like Capua also had a strategically valuable location, the appointment of the bishop was of prime importance to the papacy and lay rulers in the region; both took greater interest in filling these types of sees. Not only civic but regional and even international factors had to be taken into account. Before the mid- to late eleventh century some cities like Capua and Benevento had recruited their archbishops primarily from the princely family and local nobility.[18] By the late eleventh century there was a growing tendency in some cities for the episcopate to be filled by (possible) Normanno-French or other foreign bishops; however, in many cases we can only rely on unsatisfactory onomastic evidence. At Troia, in the last twenty years of the eleventh century, the see was occupied by three Frenchmen and a north Italian. At Capua, Archbishops Hervey (1078–82), Robert (1088) and Sennes (1097–1116) were all Normanno-French, as were the early bishops of Aversa and probably Archbishop Drogo of Taranto (1071).[19] It would seem that non-native bishops were most likely to be found in areas of greater Norman settlement and that this was the prime reason for their election. But there was certainly no Norman drive to displace the indigenous episcopate, and in many other cases the Norman rulers opted for or retained native bishops. In any case, by the mid-twelfth century the question of 'Norman' influence on the episcopate would become irrelevant in the face of widespread assimilation with the indigenous population. Moreover, the Normans undoubtedly recognised the utility of the local connections of men such as the hugely popular Archbishops Alfanus I of Salerno (1058–85) and Elias of Bari (1089–1105).[20]

After 1130 the monarchs monitored episcopal elections, although the monarchy's grip over the Church was not the tyrannical one portrayed

---

[15] *CDBI*, no. 34.   [16] *Troia*, nos. 134–5.   [17] *Alex. Tel.*, Bk III.32 p. 77; *Falco*, p. 190.

[18] For example, Archbishop Roffred I of Benevento (1076–1107) was a relative of the prince of Benevento, *Chron. S. Sophiae*, ii. 747–50 no. vi.25.

[19] Fonseca, 'La chiesa di Taranto', pp. 83–114.

[20] Loud, *Latin Church*, pp. 115–27 offers a comprehensive analysis of the possible origins of some of the episcopate in the decades either side of 1100.

by some contemporaries.[21] The twelfth-century episcopate in southern Italy maintained its mixed composition of international and native prelates, although there was a greater trend towards the latter after *c.* 1150.[22] Bishops William III and IV of Troia were from Normandy and Poitou respectively, and Archbishop Geoffrey of Capua was formerly bishop of Dol.[23] Archbishop William of Salerno was from Ravenna and Archbishop Lombardus of Benevento was a famous canonist from Piacenza. The majority, however, were South Italians like Lambert of Aversa (1192), who had risen through that city's ecclesiastical ranks from at least 1158.[24] The Salernitan archbishops of the twelfth century were, except for one, all drawn from the local elite.[25] Native prelates were just as likely to be appointed to sees of great strategic and financial importance, and they often came from influential families in the higher social strata with a tradition of administrative service. Romuald II of Salerno (1153–81) was from the Guarna family, which boasted a royal justiciar in its ranks. Nicholas of Salerno (1182–1222) was the son of the vice-chancellor Matthew and brother of Count Richard of Aiello. Roger of Benevento (1179–1225), from San Severino, was the son of a count and royal justiciar, and also the cousin of the powerful master justiciar Count Robert of Caserta. Similarly, Rainald of Capua (1199–1212) was the son of Count Peter of Celano, a highly influential master justiciar. Samarus of Trani (1192–1201) was a native of the city and probably rose through the ecclesiastical ranks of Trani from the 1160s. He was the son of a royal chamberlain and was related to another, as well as to two justiciars.[26] Archbishop Alfanus of Capua (1153–80) was the uncle of the royal justiciar Florius of Camerota.[27]

Some prelates obtained the powerful position of royal *familiaris* at Palermo, including Romuald II of Salerno, Matthew of Capua (1183–99) and Nicholas of Salerno. Walter Pagliaria of Troia (1189–1201/8), from the noble Manopello family of the Abruzzi, was also a *familiaris* and rose to be royal chancellor and a powerful force in the kingdom. Other incumbents of the see of Troia also undertook royal business: William III of Troia helped negotiate the Treaty of Benevento in 1156 between King William I and the pope, while Elias of Troia was sent to England in the 1170s to arrange King William II's marriage.[28] The latter mission

---

[21] Loud, *Latin Church*, pp. 255–339.   [22] Loud, *Church and Society*, p. 213.
[23] *Italia Sacra*, vi. 326.   [24] Loud, *Church and Society*, p. 213; Loud, *Latin Church*, pp. 370–2.
[25] *Italia Sacra*, vii. 380–416.
[26] Kamp, *Kirche und Monarchie* (Rainald), vol. I, pp. 112–16, (Roger) 203–8, (Nicholas) 425–32, (Samarus) II, pp. 548–50.
[27] *PL* 200, cols. 332–3 no. 303.
[28] William III: 'The Treaty of Benevento' is translated in additional texts of *Falcandus*, pp. 248–52. Helias: *Romuald*, p. 268; *Troia*, no. 94.

took place after an earlier attempt in 1167 at a marriage alliance with Constantinople had failed. On that occasion it had been Bertrand of Trani who had been dispatched to the Byzantine capital.[29] William, archbishop of Salerno acted as a royal justiciar, and Romuald II of Salerno numbered the leadership of the king's diplomatic mission to the Peace of Venice (1177) among his many royal services.

At the same time, the papacy had its own requirements of the episcopate, and Loud has extensively highlighted the growing contact between the papacy and South Italian churchmen in the twelfth century. South Italian prelates were strongly represented at Church councils (aided by their proximity to Rome). While papal jurisdiction over the South Italian Church expanded, assisted by close relations with the monarchy after 1156 and later Innocent III's role as *baiulus* of the kingdom, it was still the South Italian prelates themselves who mostly dispensed these political and administrative duties in the name of Rome. Bishops and abbots were dispatched on numerous extra-diocesan investigative missions to resolve disputes within or between religious houses.[30] On occasion the assignment had a much higher profile. For example, Archbishop Sennes of Capua was an apostolic legate from 1113 onwards, as were the archbishops of Naples and Taranto under Innocent III. In 1124, Roffred II of Benevento was preparing to journey as papal legate 'to the illustrious emperor of Constantinople', and in the 1160s Henry of Benevento went on a similar mission.[31] In 1127/8 Archbishop Walter of Taranto was given special governing duties at Benevento, and in the early thirteenth century Bishop Philip of Troia held the position of rector in the papal city.[32] Bishops thus had varied demands placed upon them which often entailed absences from their dioceses.

Important external responsibilities, the patronage of secular rulers and the papacy, and economic strength made the Church a powerful force. Yet, owing to the diocesan structure, bishops in southern Italy always

---

[29] *Romuald*, p. 254; J. Parker, 'The attempted Byzantine alliance with the Sicilian kingdom, 1166–1167', *PBSR* 24 (1956), 86–93; Kamp, *Kirche und Monarchie*, ii. 545–6.

[30] Loud, *Latin Church*, pp. 181–254 notes other ways in which a close relationship with the papacy was cultivated: papal consecrations of bishops, dedication of religious houses, both of which were made easier by geographic closeness, and a reasonably consistent presence of South Italians in the college of cardinals. There were also, vice versa, cardinals who appeared as papal legates in the South, particularly under Innocent III.

[31] *Cattedrale di Benevento*, no. 60; *Italia Pontificia*, ix. 68–9 nos. 65–6; Girgensohn, 'Documenti beneventani', pp. 302–4 no. 9; Henry acted as an intermediary in negotiations between the Byzantine emperor Manuel I and the Capetian Louis VII in the 1160s, Tolstoy-Miloslavsky, 'Manuel I Komnenos and Italy', appendix.

[32] See above pp. 77, 156–7.

maintained their local position more firmly than their northern European counterparts. The resultant close, spiritual connection with the populace, combined with their evident connection to external secular authorities, allowed bishops (and some abbots) to act as a real bridge between local and central government. Consequently the bishop acquired a leading role in local governance, particularly at times when central authority was weak. In Benevento, Archbishop Landulf II (1108–19) headed a faction that favoured political accommodation with the Normans and played a key role in the city's government.[33] Later, in the 1130s, we see Archbishop Landulf III participating in alliance negotiations with Roger II's enemies, while Falco claimed that Archbishop Rossemanus was 'in command' of the city in 1137.[34] At Bari, Archbishop Elias was a hugely influential figure to whom it seems the whole population had taken a general oath.[35] His successor Archbishop Riso (1112–17) was actually nominated by the populace to be their 'leader'. He was to organise the city's defence and in 1113 was found collecting revenues in Bari in order to finance a civic militia. Riso's involvement within the city's factional strife ultimately led to his murder by a rival. At Troia, Bishop William II (1106–41) took a similar position and in the 1120s and 1130s acted as the city's spokesman. Indeed, when the city was left without a ruler in 1127, and subsequently received its charter of privileges from the pope, it would seem that William became ever more central to urban government. A private charter from Troia of 1127 was dated by the bishop's ruling years and called him 'the saviour of the city of Troia' (*Troiane civitatis servator*).[36] An inscription on the doors of Troia cathedral also called William 'Liberator Patriae'.[37] In 1133 the bishop apparently 'persuaded all the people [of Troia] not to abandon their fealty to the king' and later headed a procession of the clergy and people of Troia out of the city in a doomed attempt to placate the monarch. The bishop was prone to the odd volte-face. In 1139 he was 'in floods of tears' when burying Rainulf of Caiazzo, Roger II's main opponent, in his cathedral. Yet shortly afterwards he was found pleading with the king to count him and the city 'among his *fideles* and friends'.[38] Like many of the local administrative functionaries, William II maintained his office after 1139, highlighting the strength of his position at Troia. Within the greater order of the kingdom the episcopate's role in local and papal administration continued. Bishops

---

[33] See above pp. 51–3.   [34] See above p. 80.
[35] *Anonymi Barensis Chronicon*, p. 154.   [36] *Troia*, no. 51.
[37] Carabellese, *L'Apulia ed il suo comune*, p. 413 n. 2. Similarly, on his tomb, Bishop Nicholas of Monopoli (1118–44) was described as 'Defensor Patriae', *Italia Sacra*, i. 963.
[38] *Falco*, pp. 150, 154, 216, 224.

remained important advisers and unofficial leaders of the community. This becomes more apparent after 1189 and the weakening of royal power. As before 1139, bishops seem to have enhanced their roles in local government during periods of political collapse. In 1190 Bishop Walter of Pagliaria was among the leaders of an attack by the people of Troia on Foggia. Archbishop Nicholas of Salerno directed the defence of his city in 1191, and in taking up the sword was accused by Peter of Eboli of having 'forgotten religious scruples [and of spoiling] his hands'.[39] In 1199, Archbishop Roger of Benevento was charged with stirring up trouble among the Beneventans, resulting in violence, fatalities and the accusation that he was 'a participant in, and master of, civil war'.[40] In 1201, Paganus, bishop of Monopoli, along with some local officials and the populace, agreed a trading treaty with Ragusa.[41] During Otto IV's intervention in southern Italy, both the bishop of Melfi and the archbishop of Sorrento were reprimanded for their role in encouraging the local community to side with the Welf.[42]

Northern and central Italy provides useful comparison. Here the relationship between bishop and community was complicated by a number of factors not present in the same way in the South. In the tenth and eleventh centuries many bishops had accumulated vast temporal powers (fiscal, military, judicial) within the city walls; they acted as imperial representatives and some carried the title of count. The bishop's power base was consolidated through the construction of a clientele network consisting of the powerful landed class residing in the surrounding territories. The imperial–papal clash of the late eleventh century, the ideals of the reform and the increasing organisation of urban communities altered the position of many bishops. It would be wrong, however, to see communal formation in opposition to episcopal power. Certainly there were episodes of intense friction, caused by both parties' claim to significant power and privileges. At times the papacy, as at Milan, also supported the community's efforts to increase its power at the expense of the bishop. But often there was real co-operation, arising from the fact that bishops had real temporal power that could not be negotiated away overnight. Also, the communes structured their organisation on the foundation of earlier episcopal civic organs of government and made territorial claims founded on the extent of the diocese.[43] Thus, to create a legitimising tradition of continuity, communes

---

[39] *Peter of Eboli*, p. 34, Bk I.XV lines 388–9.   [40] *Register Innocenz*, pp. 434–6 no. 227.
[41] *Acta et Diplomata Ragusina*, no. 12.
[42] *PL* 214 no. 115 cols. 625–7; *PL* 216 no. 139 cols. 928–30.
[43] Thompson, *Cities of God*, pp. 44–6.

were keen to associate with important symbols such as the bishop, cathedral and civic saints.[44] The commune gradually superseded many of the bishop's temporal powers, leaving the prelate with more informal, but still significant, influence. Bordone, for example, has shown in the Piemonte region how communal and episcopal government could be integrated within the same city; a process 'which although safeguarding the eminent position of the bishop, left by its nature a wide range for manoeuvre to the commune'.[45]

In the South, bishop and community did not lay claim to quite the same potential levels of power, thus negotiating a working relationship was much easier. During periods of political vacuum, it does not seem that South Italian bishops aimed for outright rule over their communities, with the possible exception of Benevento in the 1130s. As we shall see shortly, episodes of conflict between both parties were rarely, at least overtly, about the power relationship between bishop and community and their respective share in government. Often disagreement was sparked by involvement within local factions, or by external pressure. South Italian bishops did acquire notable duties and responsibilities. Yet perhaps more emphasis should in fact be placed on the bishop's spiritual functions, which created the strongest connection with the community. While we cannot understand the real nature of individual private faith, many people demonstrated a public one. While motivations other than solely spiritual ones may have been involved, numerous charters contain bequests to a variety of religious establishments, and some people adopted the monastic habit in later life. Often such acts were said to have been made in the hope of saving the soul of the donor or loved ones or for the annual celebration of the anniversary of deceased relatives and friends.[46] Vitolo has recently, and quite rightly, questioned the conviction 'that southern Italy remained extraneous to the new and more advanced religious experiences, which the laity was engaging with elsewhere in the peninsula'.[47] Indeed, from the later twelfth century a number of prayer unions and associations appeared in the South which incorporated, to differing extents, lay members and displayed similarities to confraternities (S. Matteo at Salerno, S. Bartolomeo

---

[44] E. Coleman, 'Sense of community and civic identity in the Italian communes', *The Community, the Family and the Saint: Patterns of Power in Early Medieval Europe: Selected Proceedings of the International Medieval Congress, University of Leeds, 4–7 July 1994, 10–13 July 1995*, ed. J. Hill and M. Swan (Turnhout, 1998), pp. 53–6; Hyde, *Society and Politics*, pp. 58–9.

[45] Bordone, ' "Civitas Nobilis et Antiqua" ', p. 56 and pp. 49–61.

[46] Loud, *Latin Church*, pp. 430–93 discusses the important role of patronage, by both the Norman and indigenous aristocracy as well as urban elites, in the rapid expansion of monasticism in southern Italy.

[47] Vitolo, 'Esperienze religiose nella Napoli', p. 3.

at Naples, S. Spirito, S. Bartolomeo and S. Euphemia at Benevento).[48] These associations were concerned with charitable and pious endeavours. Like guilds they seem to have incorporated an element of mutual support and offered a relationship which cut across other traditional vertical ties.[49] S. Bartolomeo at Naples was certainly by 1179, and probably earlier, a mixed association of priests and lay people. The lay members participated fully in all activities of the association and had their own priest.[50] S. Spirito, founded in 1177, was open to all clergy and lay people of Benevento and represented a city-wide 'spiritual union'. Of the names recorded in the necrology of the confraternity of S. Spirito, which was started in 1198, 35 per cent were those of lay-people. Another confraternity at Benevento, S. Bartolomeo, appears in 1179 and seems to already have incorporated lay members, while a third, S. Euphemia, may well have had a lay component by the second decade of the thirteenth century.[51] There is much debate on whether S. Matteo of Salerno was a confraternity. Either way its *Liber Confratrum* contains the names of a vast range of lay people who claimed some spiritual association with the renowned cult centre, and this is in itself important.[52]

However, we must not assume that faith was at the root of all things for all people. Individuals were capable of doubt, scepticism, 'unbelief' and non-conformity towards views, including religious ones, which were supposedly conventional and accepted.[53] At Trani, before his death and subsequent canonisation as the city's saint, Nicholas the Pilgrim was considered to be insane and was derided. This may be a literary model of the suffering of holy men but still suggests that such reactions could be commonplace. Later references to Nicholas's miracles after his

---

[48] Houben, 'Confraternite e religiosità', pp. 355–77; G. Vitolo, *Istituzioni ecclesiastiche e vita religiosa dei laici nel Mezzogiorno medievale. Il codice della confraternita di S. Maria di Montefusco (Sec. XII)* (Rome, 1982), pp. 12–19; T. Frank, *Studien zu Italienischen Memorialzeugnissen des XI. und XII. Jahrhunderts* (Berlin, 1991), pp. 73–94, 156–79.

[49] A. Black, *Guilds and Civil Society in European Political Thought from the Twelfth Century to the Present* (London, 1984), pp. 4–5, 26–9.

[50] Vitolo, 'Esperienze religiose nella Napoli', pp. 3–34; C. D. Fonseca, ' "Congregationes clericorum et sacerdotum" a Napoli nei secoli XI e XII', in *La vita del clero nei secoli XI e XII. Atti della I settimana di studio* [La Mendola, 1959], 2 vols. (Milan, 1962), ii. 265–83. Both authors also briefly discuss the mysterious 'associations' in Naples known as *staurite*, which were often formed by leading families and included the people of a particular city quarter.

[51] Loud, 'Politics, piety and ecclesiastical patronage', pp. 309–10; *Cattedrale di Benevento*, no. 106; Girgensohn, 'Documenti beneventani', pp. 310–13 no. 13.

[52] Vitolo, 'Città e chiesa nel Mezzogiorno medievale', p. 141 and n. 26; Frank, *Studien zu Italienischen Memorialzeugnissen*, pp. 91–4.

[53] Reynolds, 'Social mentalities', pp. 21–41.

death suggest that some people doubted his role in them.[54] Also, after the initial flurry of the First Crusade, South Italians generally took little direct part in the crusading movement, although we do know of a few pilgrims to the Holy Land and other sites.[55] The populace did not always blindly follow its prelate and there could often be disharmony between bishop and community. A party in Bari successfully resisted Archbishop Urso's attempts to place the relics of St Nicholas in the cathedral. The archbishops at Benevento led factions in the early twelfth century that were opposed by rival groups. Political tensions resulted in the murder of both Archbishop Riso of Bari (1117) and Peter of Benevento (1155) by citizens. In 1208 the Capuans submitted to the count of Fondi as a result of their loathing for the count of Celano, the father of Rainald their archbishop. The latter assisted his father the next year to recover the citadel of Capua. At Troia, in the 1210s, the community sided with Emperor Otto IV against the wishes of their Bishop Philip; and this type of tension between city and bishop seems to have been repeated else-where (Naples and perhaps Trani and Bari) during the invasion.[56]

Nevertheless, through the confluence of his spiritual and secular responsibilities, the bishop usually came to be considered as the emblematic representative and protector of the community, as well as of the city in an abstract sense. This 'marriage', one that according to Church tradition should be for life, explains the limited cases of translations of bishops between sees.[57] This was given more resonance in the way the Church shaped not only the mental but also the physical landscape. Churches and monasteries, some of which were family foundations and still privately owned by lay people, permeated the urban environment. An organised urban parish network was slow to develop. At Capua, aside from a solitary reference in 1178, parishes are not mentioned until the mid-thirteenth century.[58] But in some cities their presence can be detected more conspicuously in the twelfth century.[59] The second

---

[54] *Vita Nicolai Peregrini et Relatio Adelferii*, in *Acta Sanctorum*, June i (Paris, 1867), cols. 238–9, 240, 244; see also P. Oldfield, 'St Nicholas the Pilgrim and the city of Trani between Greeks and Normans, *c*. 1090–*c*. 1140', *Anglo-Norman Studies 30. Proceedings of the Battle Conference 2007*, ed. C. P. Lewis (Woodbridge, 2008), pp. 168–81.

[55] G. A. Loud, 'Norman Italy and the Holy Land', in *The Horns of Hattin*, ed. B. Z. Kedar (Jerusalem, 1992), pp. 49–62; see also *Vita Nicolai Peregrini*, col. 244; P. Oldfield, 'The Iberian imprint on medieval Southern Italy', *History* 93 (2008), pp. 324–6 discusses South Italian pilgrims to the shrine of St James at Compostella.

[56] Oldfield, 'Otto IV and southern Italy'.   [57] Loud, *Latin Church*, pp. 237–9.

[58] Loud, *Church and Society*, pp. 221–2; *Pergamene normanne*, no. 19. See also C. E. Boyd, *Tithes and Parishes in Medieval Italy. The Historical Roots of a Modern Problem* (Cornell, 1952).

[59] At Troia, for example, archpriests, officials responsible for local parish churches, are attested as early as 1087 and 1105; *Colonie cassinesi*, no. 14; *Troia* no. 37; Martin, *Pouille*, pp. 641–7.

half of the *Obituarium* of the confraternity of S. Spirito of Benevento, compiled *c.* 1200, catalogued the inserted names by city parishes.[60] At Aversa a 'parrochia ecclesie Sancti Crucis' was attested in 1124 and one called 'Sancti Antonini' in 1126.[61] The city had other parishes named S. Andrea, S. Giovanni, S. Maria *de Platea*, S. Nicola and S. Audoeno.[62] It is notable that when these parish names appear in documents they often were used as a means for individuals to identify themselves more specifically, and they seem akin to urban quarters.[63] This is just one way in which the Church was physically present in the urban community's everyday life beyond provision of a space and calendar for worship.

The centrality of the cathedral, both topographically and psychologically, was of great importance.[64] The later eleventh century was a period in which the cathedral developed and articulated old messages in new ways.[65] It was a phase that witnessed the construction or reconstruction of many city cathedrals throughout Apulia and Campania. The cathedrals at Taranto (after 1060), Salerno (1080), under the aegis of Robert Guiscard, and Capua (*c.* 1080 to the 1120s) were all rebuilt. New buildings at Trani and Troia were also begun in the 1090s.[66] These projects required the co-operation of the urban inhabitants; supplying labour, craftsmanship and, in many cases, their nearby properties to enable completion of the 'new' cathedral complex. An inscription at the cathedral at Trani states that it was constructed by the 'gens pia Tranensis'.[67] At the same time, a series of translations or inventions of civic patron saints took place; most of whom were housed in these new buildings, bringing prestige and revenue. All of this would have encouraged the community's identification of the cathedral as both a public space and sanctuary for them; indeed it is more than likely that civic assemblies took place within the cathedral or at least before its doors. While saints' cults had been strong in southern Italy in the early

---

[60] *Obituarium S. Spiritus*, xxii.   [61] *CDNA*, pp. 368–70 no. 35, pp. 373–5 no. 37.

[62] S. Andrea: *CDNA*, pp. 43–4 no. 28; S. Maria: *CDNA*, pp. 113–4 no. 65; S. Giovanni: *CDNA*, pp. 68–70 no. 40; S. Nicola: *CDNA*, pp. 174–6 no. 98; S. Audoeno, *CDSA*, pp. 22–4 no. 11; Gallo, *Aversa normanna*, pp. 71–4.

[63] For example, *CDNA*, pp. 266–7 no. 141, 'ego Lisiardus filius quondam Iudicis palmenterii, habitator civitatis Averse, scilicet in parrochia Sancte Marie'.

[64] Delogu, 'I Normanni in città', pp. 173–205.

[65] M. C. Miller, *The Bishop's Palace. Architecture and Authority in Medieval Italy* (Cornell, 2000), pp. 86–8.

[66] R. Colapietra, 'Profilo storico-urbanistico di Trani dalle origini alla fine dell'ottocento', *Archivio storico pugliese* 33 (1980), p. 9; E. Bertaux, *L'Art dans l'Italie méridonale*, 3 vols. (Paris, 1903), i. 353–8; Martin, *Pouille*, p. 619, lists the dates of other newly constructed cathedrals such as Brindisi, Conversano and Melfi.

[67] Bertaux, *L'Art dans l'Italie méridonale*, i. 372.

medieval period, the later eleventh century witnessed a resurgence.[68] In 1080 St Matthew's relics were rediscovered and placed in the refounded cathedral of Salerno, while in 1087 St Nicholas was brought from Myra to Bari and was eventually placed in a new basilica. In the 1090s Archbishop Bisantius of Trani appealed to the pope to recognise the recently deceased Nicholas the Pilgrim as a saint and patron of the cathedral, while the invention of St Cataldus also took place at Taranto after 1060.[69] In 1104 the relics of saints Eleutherius, Pontianus and Anastasius the Confessor found their way to the cathedral at Troia.[70]

It is easy to see how attached the urban community was to their saints. Falco of Benevento's work offers vivid descriptions of the widespread euphoria that holy relics could induce. On such occasions endemic faction in the city was put aside. In 1119 the archbishop of Benevento placed a number of saintly relics on public display. Falco, in ecstatic tones, described the city-wide effect of the event, the spectacle of the religious processions that took place and noted 'something unheard of for many years, the city of Benevento moved only by honour and love for the saints'.[71] In 1125 the invention of St Barbatus took place in the city's cathedral before a crowd of citizens, and for the following eight days the clergy and laity of each quarter of the city undertook celebratory candlelit processions. Falco was so fully immersed in these events that he was even able to kiss St Barbatus' bones, just as he had done those relics which were displayed in 1119. When in the following year Benevento was struck by a nocturnal earthquake some of its terrified inhabitants fled to the cathedral, others to the monastery of S. Sofia, and they 'stayed in the places of the saints groaning and weeping'.[72] Equally, the arrival of St Nicholas at Bari created such a highly-charged atmosphere that warfare erupted over where the relics should be placed, a faction successfully resisting Archbishop Urso's attempts to house the relics in his cathedral. It is important to note also that the expedition to Myra was very much a civic enterprise with a largely lay contingent of sailors and merchants. While some priests and clerics participated, the mission was achieved without the knowledge of the archbishop.[73] The

---

[68] T. Head, 'Discontinuity and discovery in the cult of saints: Apulia from late Antiquity to the high Middle Ages', *Hagiographica* 6 (1999), pp. 171–211; Vitolo, *Città e coscienza*, pp. 5–16.

[69] *Trani*, no. 25; Martin, *Pouille*, p. 620; A. Galdi, 'I santi e la città. Agiografie e dedicazioni', in *Salerno nel XII secolo*, p. 180; Head, 'Discontinuity and discovery', pp. 193–7.

[70] A. Poncelet, 'La Translation des SS. Éleuthère, Pontien et Anastase', *Analecta Bollandiana* 29 (1910), pp. 409–26; *Romuald*, p. 204.

[71] *Falco*, pp. 48–50.   [72] *Falco*, pp. 78, 82.

[73] See the account of Nicephorus, cleric of Bari, Jones, *Saint Nicholas of Myra*, pp. 176–93; See generally Nitti di Vito, *La ripresa gregoriana di Bari*; Cioffari, *Storia della basilica di S. Nicola di Bari*, p. 50; P. J. Geary, *Furta Sacra: Thefts of Relics in the Central Middle Ages* (Princeton, 1978), pp. 115–27.

miracle stories attached to St Nicholas often note an attempted robbery of some part of his relics.[74] The distress of the citizens of Bari on learning of the theft and their ineffable joy on the relics' return is a common feature.

Elsewhere, at Troia the arrival of holy relics in 1104, which was recorded in a work written in the twelfth century, was apparently greeted outside the city by 10,000 inhabitants.[75] At Trani, the death of St Nicholas the Pilgrim saw the 'whole city gathered in one'. Later the author of a wider account of the saint's life and miracles, Amandus the deacon, described the saint's saving of a ship from wreck. As proof against detractors Amandus said that a waxen model of the ship with Nicholas at its helm could now be seen hanging in the saint's church, donated by the grateful captain of the vessel.[76] In 1162, according to the chronicle attributed to Romuald, the city of Salerno was saved from King William I's wrath by a timely storm brewed up by St Matthew, 'who has been given by God to the city of Salerno as patron and defender'.[77] The poetry of Archbishop Alfanus I of Salerno had already exalted Matthew's protection and affinity with the *cives*.[78] As we can see, many of the details of this new emphasis on the patron saint come from the range of concomitant hagiographical works, which reinforced their power. Some of the earlier works were fashioned by writers linked to Montecassino in its golden age (*c.* 1050–*c.* 1100). Archbishop Alfanus of Salerno had briefly been a monk at the abbey, as was Guaiferius, who wrote (*c.* 1059–*c.* 1080) an expanded *vita* of Secundinus, another saint of Troia.[79] Of course, myth and exaggeration are central to all these saints' stories. But regardless of this, the bond between the holy patron and the community is a recurrent message that should not be overlooked.

Indeed, other evidence emphasises the connection between community and saint. The very first clause in Bari's privileges of 1132 detailed Roger II's promise not to remove the relics of St Nicholas from the city, while its Customs of *c.* 1200 named Nicholas as 'our guard and saint'.[80]

---

[74] Poncelet, 'Miracula Sancti Nicolai', pp. 405–32, especially pp. 424–7.

[75] Poncelet, 'Translation', p. 422. [76] *Vita Nicolai Peregrini*, cols. 240, 244.

[77] *Romuald*, p. 251; A. Galdi, 'La diffusione del culto del santo patrono: l'esempio di S. Matteo di Salerno', in *Pellegrinaggi e itinerari dei santi nel Mezzogiorno medievale*, ed. G. Vitolo (Naples, 1999), pp. 181–91; Vitolo, 'Città e chiesa nel Mezzogiorno medievale', pp. 134–48.

[78] *I carmi di Alfano*, particularly pp. 84–5 no. 7, pp. 225–6 no. 58.

[79] A. Mirra, 'I versi di Guaiferio monaco di Montecassino nel secolo XI', *BISME* 46 (1931), pp. 104–6; A. Mirra, 'Guaiferio monaco poeta a Montecassino nel secolo XI', *BISME* (1932), pp. 199–208; Vitolo, *Città e coscienza*, pp. 16–17; H. E. J. Cowdrey, *The Age of Abbot Desiderius. Montecassino, the Papacy, and the Normans in the Eleventh and Early Twelfth Centuries* (Oxford, 1983), pp. 19–27; Head, 'Discontinuity and discovery', pp. 186–92.

[80] *Rogerii II Regis Diplomata Latina*, pp. 54–6 no. 20; Petroni, *Storia di Bari*, ii. 434 Rubric I.3.

In the later twelfth century the sculptor Barisanus of Trani crafted the bronze doors of his local cathedral. On one panel he portrayed himself kneeling before St Nicholas the Pilgrim, thus making clear his own attachment to the saint.[81] At some point either side of 1100, the Salernitan Landulf Butrumiles, bearing the Byzantine title of *protosebastos*, donated to the city's cathedral a bronze door produced in Byzantium. The door, which was dedicated to St Matthew, depicted Landulf and his wife in the same panel as the saint and beseeched Matthew to intercede with Christ on their behalf.[82] St Matthew's effigy appeared on Salernitan coinage, as did other saints elsewhere, and some churches insisted that the payment of rents should occur on their saints' feast days.[83] Thus the saint was intrinsically meshed into the mundane everyday. Ecclesiastics clearly perceived the importance of civic cults for establishing their authority and claims to ancient traditions.[84] So too did lay rulers understand the power of the saint. Prince Grimoald of Bari attributed his title to Nicholas and in doing so emphasised the saint's protection of the city.[85] In 1216 Frederick II's wife made a donation to the archbishop of Salerno 'on account of reverence for blessed Matthew'.[86] On the other hand Falco told how in 1133 a procession that went out of Troia carrying the bodies of saints failed to deter Roger II's ferocious punishment of the city.[87]

The social and geographic range of those affected by the pull of the saint is interesting. Again such information needs to be used with caution, but is still useful. The saint in the medieval world was 'socially amphibious' and could often be identified with all social classes.[88] Those who were cured by Barbatus at Benevento included a shoemaker, a peasant from Montefusco and a woman. On each occasion the urban populace hurried joyously to see the healed, and Falco himself was able to touch the shoemaker's cured arm. The holy relics deposited at Troia drew people from Ariano, Montecorvino, Telese, Ascoli and Manopello in the Abruzzi. Also mentioned were a 'youth' from Rome who was

---

[81] D. A. Walsh, 'The iconography of the bronze doors of Barisanus of Trani', *Gesta* 21 (1982), pp. 91–106.

[82] M. English Frazer, 'Church doors and the gates of paradise: Byzantine bronze doors in Italy', *Dumbarton Oaks Papers* 27 (1973) p. 160; D. F. Glass, *Romanesque Sculpture in Campania. Patrons, Programs and Style* (Pennsylvania, 1991), pp. 66–7, covers Landulf's donation to the cathedral along with those of other leading Salernitans, including the vice-chancellor Matthew of Salerno.

[83] L. Travaini, *La monetazione nell'Italia normanna* (Rome, 1995), pp. 44, 86, 262, 274; see below pp. 260–1.

[84] Head, 'Discontinuity and discovery', pp. 186, 209–11.

[85] *CDBV*, nos. 69, 71; Dacomarius seems to have cultivated a similar connection with Nicholas at Benevento, see above 42.

[86] *CDS*, pp. 107–9 no. 43.   [87] Falco, p. 154.   [88] Murray, *Reason and Society*, pp. 383–404.

living in the *Terra Fundana*, a Spaniard and two *infantuli Troiani* (one of whom was described as a pauper's daughter).[89] Those attracted to the shrine of St Nicholas the Pilgrim at Trani included locals, among them an *indigena* and a youth 'born from noble stock', as well as an *incola* from Calabria and a man from Flanders.[90] The expedition to obtain St Nicholas's relics did not just include Baresi but seemingly also men from Monopoli and Taranto.[91] At Bari, St Nicholas healed, among the many, a 'very noble' person from Bari, an Armenian, a Pisan and someone from Taranto.[92] Would-be-thieves of Nicholas's relics were to include a goldsmith and Frenchmen, and to some the city even became known as the port of St Nicholas.[93] Thus, while the saints protected the urban community, their powers stretched further afield.[94] This accentuated the importance of saints and, while it underlines a common devotion regardless of a person's origin or status, it could also create friction and rivalry. As seen at Bari, this friction could be within the urban community, but it could also be between cities. It could be that rivalry, or imitation, influenced the composition in Benevento, in the 1090s, of a work which staged Nicholas's miraculous works principally within that city. So too could Trani's acquisition of its own saint, Nicholas (the Pilgrim), in the 1090s, be viewed.[95] Around 1200, in the continuing dispute between Troia and Foggia, the archpriest of Foggia accused the Troians of stealing his settlement's relics – which, if true, was no trifling matter.[96] It was also surely irksome to the Foggians that their clerics were obliged to send to the Church of Troia a cart laden with produce and livestock 'for the honour of the saints who are in Troia'.[97]

South Italian urban communities used virtually the same symbols to express their collective identity as did those in northern and central Italy, and for similar reasons.[98] The patron saint, cathedral and those religious

---

[89] Poncelet, 'Translation', pp. 424–6.   [90] *Vita Nicolai Peregrini*, col. 241.

[91] *CDBV*, no. 164, provides a list with sixty-two names of those who took part; Cioffari, *Storia*, p. 50.

[92] Jones, *Saint Nicholas of Myra*, p. 192, Cioffari, *Storia*, pp. 78–80, lists other visitors, including people from Amalfi, Ancona and Aquitaine.

[93] See above n. 74; *The Ecclesiastical History of Orderic Vitalis*, 6 vols., trans. M. Chibnall (Oxford, 1968–80), iv. 70, 72 Bk VII.13, relates stories of attempted thefts by men from Angers and Noyon.

[94] St Nicholas was very much a 'universal saint' and was particularly popular with merchants and sailors in the Mediterranean. Bari had faced competition from Venice and Genoa in acquiring Nicholas's relics, G. Petralia, 'Santi e mercanti nel Mediterraneo latino medievale: note diacroniche', *Medioevo Mezzogiorno Mediterraneo*, pp. 89–110.

[95] Jones, *Saint Nicholas of Myra*, pp. 207–8; Oldfield, 'St Nicholas the Pilgrim', pp. 179–80.

[96] *Documenti tratti dai registri vaticani*, pp. 49–55 no. 53.   [97] *Troia*, p. 386 no. 139.

[98] D. Webb, *Patrons and Defenders: The Saints in the Italian City States* (London, 1996), especially pp. 60–92; Thompson, *Cities of God*; Coleman, 'Sense of community', pp. 45–60.

officials associated with them were hugely important channels through which civic identity could be articulated. In fact, the twelfth century saw a growing popularity and diffusion of the names Nicholas and Matthew, not just in Bari and Salerno but throughout the peninsula.[99] But civic consciousness in twelfth-century southern Italy was not purely a product of religious passion. It may be that the growing size of urban communities demanded a wider civic awareness. Demographic growth and urbanisation was apparent in southern Italy from at least the eleventh century. More suburbs appeared outside cities, and the charter documentation evidences a high density of urban dwellings in places like Bari and Salerno. With this growth, the 'limits of face to face communities' were surpassed and there was a greater need for an 'imagined community'.[100] There were other reasons too for an emergent civic pride. The unstable political environment of southern Italy in the mid-eleventh century dictated the region's urban communities becoming more involved in civic self-government.[101] External 'threats' fortified the internal sense of communal togetherness. These two developments intensified as urban governments became increasingly autonomous, for notable periods of the twelfth century, amidst political fragmentation, rebellion and civil war.[102]

As a result, the relationship between the urban inhabitant and the 'abstract' city grew more intimate. The repeated desire for the recognition of 'ancient' civic customs nurtured the feeling of a shared past and common identity, as did their continued use. Also, as already discussed, the twelfth century saw a marked growth in awareness of the idea of citizenship in southern Italy and of people identifying themselves as *cives*. The reasons for this are manifold, but whether a cause or consequence, the use of the language of citizenship fortified civic awareness by carrying a claim for inclusion within a community. While not consistently as intense, or on the same level, as the communal cities of the North, in some cases rivalries developed between neighbouring South Italian settlements, often ostensibly revolving around religious jurisdictions.

---

[99] M. Villani, 'Il contributo dell onomastica e della toponomastica alla storia delle devozioni', in *Pellegrinaggi e itinerari dei santi nel Mezzogiorno medievale*, ed. G. Vitolo (Naples, 1999), p. 256. Perhaps the judge Secundinus (see above p. 70) of Troia (1125–69) was named after the seventh-century bishop of *Aecae* (the classical settlement from which Troia claimed descent), who was later to be a civic saint at Troia, Mirra, 'I versi di Guaiferio monaco', pp. 104–6.

[100] Lynch, *Individuals, Families, and Communities*, pp. 15–16.

[101] For a general discussion see Vitolo, *Città e coscienza*.

[102] When, amidst political upheaval in 1201, a group of *Baresi* entered a local monastery (the precise circumstances of the episode remaining vague) they apparently did so 'out of enthusiasm for loyalty to the king and for the honour and comfort of the city of Bari and all its territory', *CDBI*, no. 70.

For many, particularly churchmen, these may have been real issues in themselves, but for others the ecclesiastical subordination of nearby settlements, alongside the possession of a prestigious patron saint, was the most tangible way to express the desire for local ascendancy and, by proxy, urban pride. Aversa's attempts to avoid the ignominy of being a suffragan of the archbishops of Capua or Naples fall into this category. Similar are the hints at popular participation in the conflicts that erupted between the Churches of Troia and Foggia from around 1190 onwards. In reality, this desire for local ascendancy meant more than prestige and turned on the question of wealth and economic superiority. This was certainly at the root of the conflict between Troia and Foggia, while a document of 1125 refers to 'war' and 'enmity' between Salernitans and Gaetans, which probably relates to commercial competition.[103] As a consequence of all these currents, rival settlements would go so far as to side with opposing contenders in periods of war. The issue of local rivalry, which suggests some sort of collective response by the community, is a compelling one. This is all the more so when we consider the diverse composition of these urban communities, the evidence for internal conflict and violence within them and the regular movement of people between settlements through trade and familial and social relationships.[104]

Certainly before the foundation of the kingdom there were some urban-orientated, local narrative works which suggest evidence of urban identity. The work of Lupus Protospatharius (ends 1102), the Bari Annals (1043) and the so-called anonymous Bari Chronicle (1118) were all variants of a set of annals focusing on Bari.[105] At Benevento there were the *Annales Beneventani* (1129), again in three different versions, and Falco of Benevento's extraordinary chronicle (1140). Certainly these types of works seem to disappear after 1139 to be replaced by broad-based efforts, which one might even say have a royal orientation. Although the monarchy was willing to allow urban freedoms to continue in return for the political submission of cities, it is possible that royal government considered the continued production of city-focused works to have been one dangerous step too far in this 'bargain'. Given the peninsula's disparate history and component parts, sanctioning such works may have been seen as a potential stimulus to separatist tendencies.[106] But we may

---

[103] *Cod. Dip. Caietanus*, ii. no. 307.   [104] See above pp. 222–5 for more on internal conflict.
[105] *Annales Barenses*, ed. G. H. Pertz, *MGH SS* V (Hanover, 1844); *Lupus Protospatharius, Annales*; *Anonymi Barensis Chronicon*. These and other Barese sources, with their varied translations, are collected in one useful volume, *Antiche cronache di Terra di Bari*, ed. G. Gioffari and R. Lupoli Tateo (Centro Studi Nicolaiani – Memorie e Documenti 5) (Bari, 1991).
[106] Brown, 'The political use of the past', pp. 197–8.

be reading too much into the apparent paucity of this type of material. Even before 1139 there was only a handful of such works, which are primarily brief annals. We also have to ask: why was Falco's legacy not continued at Benevento, which was outside the kingdom?[107] Indeed, if city-focused works should supposedly appear in periods of greater political autonomy one would have expected them to have been produced under Prince Grimoald at Bari, or at Gaeta when consular officials first appeared, or perhaps at Naples in the 1130s when that city resolutely resisted Roger II. Vitolo perceptively pointed out the lack of any extant civic chronicle at Bologna before the mid-thirteenth century in a highly cultured city with a communal government.[108] More likely at the root of this is a much wider issue. The civic chronicle in medieval Italy, at least in a secular form and going beyond earlier annalistic accounts, was only just emerging in the twelfth century. The two earliest examples were the remarkable works of Caffaro at Genoa, who seems to have started his work at some point in the first half of the twelfth-century, and Falco's chronicle itself, the composition of which appears to have started in the early 1120s.[109]

A side question also emerges on the survival of such material.[110] Falco's discussion, for example, of the establishment of the commune at Benevento implies that other historical works existed on the subject. The chronicle attributed to Romuald of Salerno may have utilised some now lost annals from Troia in its early twelfth-century section, and Lupo Protospatharius' work seems to employ some similarly lost annals from Matera.[111] With this in mind, it is not implausible that similar works were produced after 1139, while the monarchy would have struggled to monitor all literary output in distant mainland cities. Considering that works may have been copied in only very small numbers and have reached a relatively small audience, we may well be overestimating their contribution to civic identity, as opposed to their content, which is highly important in recording the fact that such feelings already existed. In this context, the importance of Falco's work lies not in how far it further fanned the flames of urban identity. It is rather in that it was written by a member of the community, who understood and recorded

---

[107] Falco's work, which ended abruptly in 1140, seems to have a now lost section up to 1144 preserved in the Chronicle of S. Maria di Ferrara, see above p. 12 n. 32.

[108] Vitolo, *Città e coscienza*, pp. 37–9.

[109] Loud, 'Genesis and context', pp. 189–92; R. Face, 'Secular history in twelfth-century Italy: Caffaro of Genoa', *JMH* 6 (1980), pp. 169–84; see also A. Placanica, 'L'opera storiografica di Caffaro', *Studi Medievali*, ser. 3, 36 (1995), pp. 1–62.

[110] This historiographical void is covered by Vitolo, *Città e coscienza*, pp. 29–34.

[111] D. Matthew, 'The chronicle of Romuald of Salerno', *The Writing of History in the Middle Ages. Essays Presented to Richard William Southern*, ed. R. H. C. Davis (Oxford, 1981), pp. 250–6.

events first and foremost in relation to how they impacted upon *his* city and *his* community. As a valuable byproduct of this he provided reams of evidence that suggested his fellow citizens thought in similar ways and were provoked to express this in a number of formats. When Falco, or the anonymous author of the Bari Chronicle for that matter, put down their pens for the last time, their local communities did not at that same point lose their civic consciousness. The development of patron saint cults, the growth of ideas of citizenship, the consequences of demographic expansion, the community's new role in self-government and the dynamics of local rivalry all suggest that a civic identity existed and had strong outlets which depended on many things beyond literary output and the extent of a city's political autonomy.

Chapter 9

THE URBAN ECONOMY

Medieval southern Italy was seen by contemporaries as a fertile and affluent region. Evidence of a mature, profit-based economy, guided by wealthy elites in growing cities, is apparent in southern Italy well before the Norman arrival.[1] Amatus' land of milk and honey of the eleventh century survived the disruptions resulting from the Norman infiltration and later periods of strife.[2] By creating a more organised framework which tended to dissolve regional barriers, the monarchy did not suppress the region's economy and prosperity.[3] In the twelfth century, the kingdom offered at least a more stable and unified internal market.

As no location was more than 50 miles from the coast, the sea always played an important role both in communication and the economy. Most port cities enjoyed a relatively vibrant coastal trade with each other. But given southern Italy's position in the Mediterranean it is not surprising that some had more extensive commercial links. Southern Italy was largely an exporter of oil (particularly Apulia), grain and other unfinished products of the land, while imports consisted mostly of manufactured and luxury goods from the Eastern market; a document from Bari of 1223, for example, refers to the import of linen from Syria and Alexandria.[4] Amalfi and Gaeta both famously enjoyed prosperous trading networks, especially within the eastern Mediterranean.[5] Certainly the Geniza documents from Cairo demonstrate the close links between North Africa and the ports of Sicily and southern Italy into the eleventh century, and these links continued.[6] While a city like Naples

---

[1] A. Guillou, 'Production and profits in the Byzantine province of Italy (tenth to eleventh centuries): an expanding society', *Dumbarton Oaks Papers* 28 (1974), pp. 97–105.

[2] *Amatus*, Bk I.19, p. 50.   [3] Matthew, *Norman Kingdom*, pp. 71–85.   [4] *CDBVI*, no. 42.

[5] Among the many works see, for example, A. O. Citarella, 'Patterns in medieval trade: the commerce of Amalfi before the Crusades', *Journal of Economic History* 28 (1968), pp. 531–55.

[6] S. D. Goitein, *Letters of Medieval Jewish Traders* (Princeton, 1973), pp. 40–4; *Will. Apulia*, Bk III, p. 190 lines 480–5 noted *Arabes, Libi, Siculi* and *Afri* at Amalfi.

might not have been a centre for long-distance trade until after our period, Salerno certainly seems to have been. However, a tariff list of 1128 does demonstrate the presence of Neapolitans, alongside Gaetans, Amalfitans, and Salernitans, in Genoa.[7] King William I's pact with the Genoese in 1156 shows again that Salernitans traded in that city.[8] Elsewhere, a charter of 1105 speaks of Salernitans 'in navigatione in terras Sarracenorum', while one of 1125 shows a Salernitan in 'Tunisia' transporting hides and wax to Gaeta through the agency of a man from the latter city.[9] King Roger's charter of concessions of 1137 not only remitted to the Salernitans the tax on 'sandalium et linearum', which came from Calabria, Lucania and Sicily, but also reduced 'the tithes and other merchant rights, which the *Salernitani* had hitherto been accustomed to pay in Alexandria', to the customary level enjoyed there by Sicilians.[10] The coastal cities of Apulia also showed signs of long-distance commercial activity. It is from Trani that, if dated correctly at 1063, the oldest surviving maritime law code of the Latin West hails and perhaps hints at a sailors' corporation.[11] The translation of the relics of St Nicholas from Myra to Bari not only opened up that city to pilgrims from all over Europe but showed that the Baresi were active in the eastern Mediterranean, particularly at Antioch. It has been argued that the translation was Bari's response to its declining commercial position, as a result of the break with Byzantium and the rise of Venice.[12] Nevertheless, the development of the crusading movement established the Apulian coastal ports as major centres in the twelfth century for traffic and commerce bound for the Holy Land.[13] Many of the First Crusade armies passed through Bari and Brindisi. The English pilgrim Saewulf sailed to the Holy Land from Monopoli in 1102 on a ship bound for Corinth which stopped to trade at various settlements on the way. Saewulf mentioned ships also at Bari, Barletta, Siponto, Trani and Otranto.[14]

---

[7] *Codice diplomatico della repubblica di Genova*, 3 vols., ed. C. Imperiale di Sant'Angelo, *FSI* LXXVII, LXXIX, LXXXIX (Rome, 1936–42), i. no. 51; D. Abulafia, *Two Italies: Economic Relations between the Norman Kingdom of Sicily and the Northern Communes* (Cambridge, 1977), p. 74.

[8] *Cod. Dip. Genova*, i. no. 279; also in *Guillelmi I Regis Diplomata*, pp. 47–8 no. 17.

[9] Cava, *Arca* xviii.31; *Cod. Dip. Caietanus*, ii. no. 308.

[10] *Rogerii II Regis Diplomata Latina*, pp. 129–31 no. 46.

[11] *Ordinamenta et Consuetudo Maris*, appendix, part iv, pp. 521–43; G. Coniglio, 'La societa di Trani e gli "ordinamenta"', *Archivio storico pugliese* 24 (1981), pp. 75–88.

[12] See above pp. 33, 238–9, 241; although in 1130 a Genoese went to Constantinople on a Barese ship, Abulafia, *Two Italies*, p. 75.

[13] Loud, 'Norman Italy and the Holy Land', pp. 53–4.

[14] *Peregrinationes Tres: Saewulf, John of Würzburg, Theodericus, Corpus Christianorum. Continuatio Mediaevalis* 139, ed. R. B. C. Huygens, with a study of the voyages of Saewulf by J. H. Pryor (Sydney, 1994), pp. 35–7, 59 lines 6–12; Fulcher of Chartres notes Hugh of Vermandois passing

Following the establishment of the kingdom, South Italian cities lost a certain freedom of action in their maritime trade, the inevitable consequence of commercial policy having to fall in line with the monarchy's foreign political relations. At the same time the burgeoning north Italian maritime cities, not restricted in the same way, attained greater prominence in South Italian ports. King William I's pact with Genoa, in 1156, confirmed Genoese privileges within South Italian cities since King Roger's time and established rates of duty. The main coastal cities of southern Italy always enjoyed long-distance trading contacts and were relatively bustling entrepôts. However, they were not able to attain the same level of long-distance commerce as their North Italian counterparts, and they largely tended to become more passive transit stages within a wider Mediterranean trading nexus supervised by the Genoese, Pisans and Venetians. Salerno became the key mainland port of the kingdom in the mid- to late twelfth century, largely because it was on the North Italians' route to Alexandria. Abulafia has pointed to the importance of a variety of Genoese commercial contracts which concerned Salerno, and it would seem that the latter city succeeded, to some extent, to Amalfi's previously prime position.[15] However, it has been shown that commercial relations between both these South Italian cities were so intertwined, and that Amalfitans were so conspicuous in and around Salerno, that this may not be as clear-cut as it seems.[16] In the Adriatic, Venice had close contacts with Apulian cities and contracted pacts with Bari in 1122 and Brindisi in 1199.[17] Venetian commercial contracts were drawn up in Bari, Trani and Brindisi or concerned voyages to and from these cities.[18] Other Venetian documents speak more generally of commercial ventures in Apulia, while one of 1179 envisages a round of voyages which might include Acre, Alexandria and Apulia.[19] A royal directive to customs officials in Trani and Barletta, in 1231,

---

through Bari on the First Crusade and also says that he himself went there and prayed in the church of S. Nicola, *The First Crusade: The Chronicle of Fulcher of Chartres and Other Source Materials*, ed. E. Peters (Philadephia, 1971), Bk I.6, p. 35, Bk I.7, p. 38; Guibert of Nogent, speaking of the crusaders, said that 'many went to Brindisi, pathless Otranto received others, while the fishy waters of Bari welcomed others', *The Deeds of God through the Franks: A Translation of Guibert de Nogent's Gesta Dei per Francos, trans.* R. Levine (Woodbridge, 1997), Bk II, p. 55.

[15] Abulafia, *Two Italies*, pp. 102, 106, 111, 113, 119–21, 158, 162 and also pp. 228–30, where the place of Sicily, and by extension the mainland, in the north Italian trading network is covered.

[16] V. von Falkenhausen, 'Il commercio di Amalfi con Constantinopoli e il Levante nel secolo XII', in *Amalfi, Genova, Pisa e Venezia. I commercio con Constantinopoli e il vicino Oriente nel secolo XII*, ed. O. Banti (Pisa, 1998), pp. 34–5.

[17] *CDBV*, no. 68; *Acta Imperii Inedita*, i. 470–1 no. 583.

[18] *Documenti del commercio Veneziano nei secoli XI–XIII*, 2 vols., ed. R. Morozzo della Rocca and A. Lombardo (Rome, 1940), i. nos. 41, 63, 325, ii. nos. 544, 626.

[19] *Documenti del commercio Veneziano*, i. nos. 136, 306, 391, 397, 409–10, 437, ii. no. 569.

envisaged Venetians trading there.[20] It has also recently been suggested that silk and silk cloth might have been produced in Apulia at this time and was one reason for Venetian commercial activity in the region.[21] However, this northern Italian 'infiltration' was not necessarily the result of a coherent royal policy that was inherently suspicious of allowing too much commercial freedom to its own cities. Rather, it was more part of a wider northwards shift of the Western economy. North Italian cities were better placed than their southern counterparts to take advantage of this and were able to link the Norman kingdom into a more dynamic trading network. In this context their presence in the South Italian external market did not drastically stifle the region's prosperity at this point and may have even stimulated the local economy.[22] It is also worth noting that Genoa, Pisa and Venice had been noticeably strengthening trading contacts with the South from at least the early to mid-eleventh century. Their more conspicuous presence within the kingdom was far from a novel development. The South's long-distance trade did increasingly come to be dominated by northern Italians.[23] But it was probably not until well into the thirteenth century that South Italian 'merchants' felt the full ramifications of this and started to focus increasingly on landed interests.[24]

Moreover, scattered references to South Italian ventures in longer-distance commerce continue after the mid-twelfth century. Amalfitans still appeared in Muslim territories, at Constantinople and in the Holy Land; at Acre, for example, in 1190 they were allowed commercial liberty, fiscal exemptions and their own court supervised by Amalfitan consuls.[25] There is evidence for Salernitans trading at Genoa in 1191, while in 1196 the inhabitants of Trani were given commercial freedom

---

[20] *Acta Imperii Inedita*, i. 619 no. 792 and no. 793 for a similar letter, also in 1231, referring to *mercatores Romani* at Naples.

[21] By T. Goskar in her paper, 'Material culture and local exchange – Apulia and Venice', which was read at the International Medieval Congress (10–13 July 2006) at Leeds.

[22] Houben, *Roger II*, pp. 163–5.

[23] See for example the grant made to Genoa in the name of Frederick II in 1200 of *fondachi* and houses in Messina, Trapani, Syracuse and Naples, exemption from import and export duties (specifying grain) and the re-establishment of consuls throughout the kingdom, *Cod. Dip. Genova*, iii. no. 72; D. Abulafia, 'Southern Italy, Sicily and Sardinia in the medieval Mediterranean economy', in *Commerce and Conquest in the Mediterranean, 1100–1500* (Aldershot, 1993), pp. 1–32.

[24] Matthew, *Norman Kingdom*, p. 74; R. Pavoni, 'Il mercante', in *Condizione umana*, pp. 238–44, 248–50.

[25] M. Camera, *Memorie storico-diplomatiche dell'antica città e ducato di Amalfi*, 2 vols. (Salerno, 1876–81), i. 201, see also i. 200, 202–4; *Regesta Regni Hierosolymitani (1097–1291)*, ed. R. Röhricht (Innsbruck, 1893), i. nos. 35, 253, 372, 380; Pavoni, 'Il mercante', pp. 228–31; a *ruga Amalfitani* was first attested at Antioch in 1098 and still mentioned in 1164, *Cod. Dip. Genova*, i. no. 12; von Falkenhausen, 'Il commercio di Amalfi', pp. 36–8.

in the kingdom of Cyprus.[26] Other hints are provided by references to individuals described as being absent or who were preparing to go abroad (like Otto *nauclerius* of Bari preparing a journey to Byzantium in 1200).[27] Apulia's coastal cities maintained long-distance contacts through the continued crusading and pilgrimage movements. Benjamin of Tudela said that at Trani 'all the pilgrims gather to go to Jerusalem', while in 1189 three German pilgrims were at Bari preparing for the same journey.[28]

While there was a gradual overall shift in the nature of the region's long-distance commercial activity, the cities of southern Italy were still active in the flourishing regional and internal trade. Amalfitan activity, rather than declining as such, was refocused. It concentrated even more on an already prominent role as supplier to an internal market which was linked into the wider international trading network of the North Italian cities.[29] Amalfitan communities developed within many South Italian cities.[30] In the 1160s Benjamin of Tudela still spoke of the inhabitants of Amalfi as 'merchants engaged in trade [who] buy everything for money'.[31] Gaetans continued to trade at Rome and along the Tyrrhenian coast.[32] In Tancred's privilege of 1191, the city's inhabitants were exempt from paying certain commercial taxes, the *falangagium* on the coast from Gaeta to Palermo and the *dirictum* which they had been held to pay on return from Sicily, Sardinia and 'Barbaria'. Another clause refers to Gaetans bringing corn from Sicily.[33] Bari's position in long-distance commerce declined in the later twelfth century, not helped by its destruction in 1156. But coastal trade between the Apulian ports remained important. In 1215 Frederick II ordered that the people of Trani should not pay *scalaticum* or *ancoraticum* (probably docking taxes) at Brindisi and throughout 'maritime Apulia'.[34] Exchanges with the opposite shore of the Adriatic were also regular. From a document of 1186, referring to a curia of King William in the Dalmatian city of Ragusa, it seems that the Norman monarchy enjoyed some sort of protectorate there. An administrative connection may have strengthened an already existing economic one.[35] Ragusa had treaties with Molfetta

---

[26] Abulafia, *Two Italies*, p. 186; *Regesta Regni Hierosolymitani*, i. no. 729.

[27] See Appendix, 'An example of a kin-group and its network of relationships', document 5, below.

[28] *Itinerary Ben. Tudela*, p. 9; *CDBV*, no. 154.   [29] Del Treppo and Leone, *Amalfi*, pp. 169–70.

[30] There is no need here to join the long debate on Amalfi's changing trade patterns, and the main consensus upon the city will be followed; see above pp. 216–8, 246 n. 5, and above n. 29 for general works on Amalfi.

[31] *Itinerary Ben. Tudela*, p. 9.   [32] Abulafia, 'Southern Italy, Sicily and Sardinia', p. 18.

[33] *Tancredi et Willelmi III Regum Diplomata*, pp. 42–6 no. 18.

[34] *Hist. Dip. Friderici Secundi*, i (ii). 375–7.

[35] *Acta et Diplomata Ragusina*, no. 5; Abulafia, 'Dalmatian Ragusa', pp. 412–28.

(1148 and renewed in 1208), Monopoli (1201), Bari (1201), Termoli (1203) and Bisceglie (1211).[36] These provided the Ragusans with a combination of customs exemptions and security within the Apulian ports and suggest that ties had been forged well before the written pacts. In 1195 the inhabitants of Dalmatian Cattaro, a suffragan of the archbishopric of Bari, were exempted from the *ancoraticum* and *plateaticum* levied on their ships and goods in the port of Bari.[37] Moreover, slaves from central and eastern Europe were traded through the Adriatic ports en route to Bari and beyond.[38]

The real strength of South Italian urban economies lay not in the international commercial connections of the peninsula's key ports but in the produce and crafts that were found within their local markets.[39] Many of the major cities had highly productive hinterlands and were usually located along key communication and trading routes. From classical times Campania had a reputation for fertility, especially in the Capuan plain, which later took the suggestive name of Terra di Lavoro. Alexander of Telese's description of Capua supports this, although Benjamin of Tudela mentions that the city had 'bad water' and that the countryside was 'fever-stricken'.[40] The city was ideally sited on a bend on the navigable Volturno, which was replete with mills.[41] Peter of Eboli emphasised Capua's fecundity; to him it was an 'ancient city, most rich in its fields, mother of resources . . . a land that flourishes with fruitfulness'.[42] According to Benjamin of Tudela, even Amalfi, in its precipitous location, enjoyed an abundance of fruit, vineyards and olives.[43] Vines and fruit-trees, particularly chestnuts, were common in the region. It was similar inland at Benevento, situated within a fertile basin. In addition, the city stood on an important route, lying between the Sabato and Calore valleys, on the most easily traversable east–west communication path between the Tyrrhenian and Adriatic coasts.[44] Across the Apennines within the Capitanata, Troia had been founded in 1021 on the edge of the large, but sparsely populated Tavoliere plain. In the course of the twelfth century the whole area began to be systematically cultivated, and numerous settlements developed within Troia's *contado*. Most notable was Foggia, which by *c.* 1200 had emerged as

---

[36] *Acta et Diplomata Ragusina*, nos. 12–16.   [37] *CDBI*, no. 65.
[38] See above pp. 206–8.   [39] Matthew, *Norman Kingdom*, p. 77.
[40] For Alexander of Telese's description of Capua see below p. 261 n. 118; *Itinerary Ben. Tudela*, p. 7.
[41] Di Resta, *Capua*, pp. 4, 16, 30–2.   [42] *Peter of Eboli*, p. 60 XXVI lines 773–8.
[43] *Itinerary Ben. Tudela*, p. 9.
[44] *Italy*, 4 vols., ed. K. Mason, Geographical Handbook Series, Naval Intelligence Division (London, 1944–5), vol. I, pp. 333–4.

a real urban centre, complete with thriving market and located at the heart of the rich grain-fields of the Tavoliere.[45] In central Apulia a highly fertile strip roughly 12 miles wide ascended from the coast to the Murge tableland. A dense network of cities ran along this belt, primarily on the coast, like Bari, but there was also a second chain of settlements, like Conversano, found within 4–8 miles from the coast. On this coastal plain olives and vines were grown in abundance, while further inland cereals were the primary crop.[46]

The local market was a forum for the foodstuffs and raw materials produced in the city's immediate territory as well as for city-based artisan products; it was another point at which urban and rural boundaries blurred. Some of the goods named in 1223, on which the church of S. Nicola of Bari claimed a share of the city's customs taxes, demonstrate the connections with both the neighbouring rural and long-distance markets. They were bread (only if imported), wine (both exported and imported), honey, ricotta, fresh cheese, all fruits, figs, garlic, onions, fine herbs, eggs, fish both salted and fresh and only if marketed by *extranei*, linen (imported and exported), with the exception of imports from Alexandria or Syria, worked wood from the mountains, worked glass, cushions, mattresses and a variety of ceramics.[47] Markets, of which there could be more than one in (or outside) a city, were key places of communal interaction. Despite this there are only limited references to the markets themselves. A 'Saturday market' formed as a district in Aversa, while the main market in Capua was near the cathedral.[48] Often markets were referred to according to the product sold there: Falco's chronicle mentions a meat market of S. Lorenzo in Benevento, a charter from Salerno of 1197 refers to the *platea maior* 'where herbs are sold' and one from Bari of 1212 mentions a 'field in which grain is sold'.[49] More revealing is a donation in 1136 by Pope Anacletus II to the archbishop of Benevento which included a *paradisus* (enclosed park) near the church of S. Maria. The document refers to the damage frequently occasioned to the church 'on account of the large numbers and noise of those selling and buying [there]'. It goes on to grant also the 'revenues of those who sit and sell vegetables and fruit in that *paradisus*'.[50]

---

[45] Oldfield, 'Rural settlement', pp. 327–45.   [46] *Italy*, vol. I, pp. 374–80.

[47] *CDBVI*, no. 42; R. Iorio, R. Licinio and G. Musca, 'Sotto la monarchia normanno-sveva', in *Storia di Bari – dalla conquista normanna al ducato sforzesco*, ed. F. Tateo (Bari, 1990), p. 76.

[48] Di Resta, *Capua*, p. 19.

[49] *Falco*, p. 102; *CDS*, pp. 179–82 no. 89 (also in *Pergamene del monastero benedettino di S. Giorgio (1038–1698)*, ed. L. Cassese (Salerno, 1950), no. 16); *CDBI*, pp. 158–9; Cava, *Arca* xxii.33 mentions a market in a *platea* at Salerno.

[50] *Cattedrale di Benevento*, no. 62.

Trading activity clearly took place in a variety of formal and informal locations throughout a city. Trade shaped the urban landscape. As we have seen, fellow craftsmen often congregated within the same street or suburb, which often took their name. Others had to practise their craft in certain quarters owing to the very nature of it. Transactions may well have taken place in these places. Documents are littered with references to *apothecae*, which could be anything from a small shop to a warehouse, and particularly at Aversa to *sedilia*, which appear to be stalls.[51] The 1136 document from Benevento also conceded the *plateaticum* of four *apothecae* which were within the house of John de Civitate. In short, contemporary descriptions of the vitality of South Italian markets are more than mere encomia. In the Muslim geographer al-Idrisi's description of the kingdom's resources, Naples had 'markets with merchandise traffic, and an overabundance of goods and material of all types', Otranto had '[well-] frequented markets and lively commerce', likewise Trani and Taranto, where there were many 'merchants and travellers', and Salerno had 'flourishing markets'.[52] Indeed, medieval Salerno acquired the sobriquet *opulenta*.[53]

Identifying from the sources any individuals or groups who were the commercial suppliers, buyers and sellers in these markets is difficult. Public documents, especially the Constitutions of Melfi, do mention the generic 'merchant'. Another decree of Frederick II in 1231 refers to those 'who come to Trani to buy *panni* (fabrics) from the merchants' shops'.[54] However, in private documents, people who identified themselves specifically as merchants were rare, yet not unknown. As previously indicated, the presence of Amalfitans and their neighbours in cities, especially in the twelfth century, may well indicate trading activity.[55] The agreement concluded between the Amalfitan community and Naples in 1190 certainly suggests this to be the case. The document refers to *negotiatores*, *campsores* and *apothecarii*, although we should not assume that all *Amalfitani* dwelling in other cities were engaged in commerce.[56] South Italian Jews seemed to play only a minor role in commerce by the twelfth century, which perhaps reflected wider Mediterranean changes in Jewish trading patterns.[57] The region's Jews were almost certainly still

---

[51] *Italia Sacra*, vii. 412–3; *CDS*, pp. 99–101 no. 37, p. 128 no. 57, refers to stalls at Salerno used for butchery 'and other business (*negotiatio*)'.

[52] *L'Italia descritta nel 'Libro del re Ruggero'*, pp. 74–6, 95, 103–4.

[53] See above p. 25 n. 44.   [54] *Acta Imperii Inedita*, i. 620 no. 795.

[55] See above pp. 216–8.   [56] Filangieri, 'Note al *Privilegium Libertatis*', pp. 107–16.

[57] E. Ashtor, 'Gli ebrei nel commercio mediterraneo nell'Alto Medioevo (sec. X–XI)', in *Gli ebrei nell'Alto Medioevo. 30 marzo–5 aprile 1978, Settimane del Centro italiano di studi sull'Alto Medioevo* xxvi (Spoleto, 1980), vol. I, pp. 401–87 and especially the discussion, pp. 465–87.

active commercially, but there are only occasional indirect inferences to suggest this.[58] However, in 1231, when Frederick II established a monopoly on the purchase of silk in the kingdom, this was placed in the hands of some Jewish associates from Trani.[59] While in places like Trani, Troia and Salerno the *mercator* title does not seem to appear, at inland Benevento it is found. In 1169, Pope Alexander III enacted a command to protect 'mercatores et viatores et peregrini' coming to the city, although of course this uses the broad language so often found in public documents.[60] Perhaps also the use of the word in Benevento owes more to the northern Italian pope who employs it here. In the same city, in 1182, we see a John de Montecalvo *mercator* preparing for a pilgrimage to the shrine of St James at Compostella and establishing a Riso *mercator* as one of the tutors of his children.[61] Given the quantity of documentation, one would expect to find more 'merchants', especially in places like Amalfi. Why more are not attested is entirely open to conjecture. The idea that individuals could take part in a variety of activities, of which commerce was only one, may be a useful point from which to approach the problem. Perhaps this diversity of interests, and the growing dominance of northern Italians within the commercial market, explains the limited identification with the merchant tag. In the South no legally defined 'specialist' merchant class, or associations, seem to have developed in the way they did further north. By 1150 there were, for example, 'consuls of the merchants' at places like Pisa and Milan, who also played a role in communal government. That said, the idea of merchant solidarity should not be over-played.[62]

The suspicion must be that 'merchants' are there but not in the guise we would expect. *Nauclerii* appear often in cities like Bari, Trani, Monopoli and Taranto. In most cases these 'sailors' appear to be reasonably affluent, inter-connected and prominent members of the civic community.[63] It may be that *nauclerius* carried the more generic sense of merchant.[64] Whatever the meaning, their activities were lucrative and centred around the sea. The will of Nicholas *nauclerius* of Bari, in 1103, mentioned his shares (*sortiones*) in a ship jointly owned with a nephew and 'other men of the city'. The document referred to potential profits

---

[58] Such as in Goitein, *Letters of Medieval Jewish Traders*, pp. 327–8.
[59] *Acta Imperii inedita*, i. 614 no. 785. The document also mentions 'other Jews from Trani' who were 'throughout other provinces of the kingdom'.
[60] *Cattedrale di Benevento*, no. 89.   [61] *Cattedrale di Benevento*, no. 112.
[62] Pavone, 'Il mercante', p. 217; Nicholas, *Growth of the Medieval City*, p. 162; A. Castagneti, 'Feudalità e società comunale', in *Medioevo Mezzogiorno Mediterraneo*, p. 218.
[63] See above pp. 199–200.
[64] *Nauclerius* derives from the Greek *naukleros*, which in classical Greek could mean 'shipowner', 'merchant', 'skipper'.

gained as a result of the ship's voyage (*taxidium*).[65] Likewise, the testament of Otto *nauclerius* of Bari showed that he was engaged in maritime ventures, was both creditor and debtor to a number of people from various Apulian settlements and was, it seems, part of a commercial group of associates (*socii*).[66] Monopoli stands out for the frequency of individuals carrying titles connected to commerce and who also, at times, appear in the same document as *nauclerii*. In 1189 the *nauclerius* Iohannocarrus bought a house near one belonging to Catardus *mercator* and did so in the presence of Maio *cambiator*.[67] Later, Sconrus *nauclerius*, son of Leo *mercator*, acted in the presence of Urso, son of John *mercator*.[68] Besides *mercatores* and *cambiatores* there were also *negotiatores* and *magistri bancarium* in the city.[69] At Trani, in 1165, a *cambiator* collected a loan from a *negotiator*.[70] Inland in the emerging settlement of Foggia, in the early thirteenth century, there appear a *mercator*, *olearius* (oil-trader) and *speciarius* (spice-trader).[71] In some cities we find wine-sellers (*vini venditores*), and their activities found their way into the city's statutes of 1202 at Benevento.[72] But we do not know whether any of these types of traders were 'merchants' engaged in large-scale commerce or were simply operating within local markets.

Money-changers/lenders (*campsores*, *cambiatores*) and bankers (*bancarii*, *banbacarii*) suggest commercial activity and investment. Indeed credit agreements appear more developed in southern Italy from the late eleventh century.[73] In Troia there was a street named after a Walter *cambitor* and at Salerno a *ruga* (lane) *banbacariorum*. Other bankers and money-changers are found, mostly from the late twelfth century onwards, at Bari, Foggia, Trani and Monopoli.[74] It is worth mentioning that there is little evidence of the Jewish community's involvement in such activity. Although references, in 1183, 1200 and 1205, show non-Jews owing money to Jews, documents concerning Jewish activity in money-lending

---

[65] *CDBV*, no. 36.
[66] See Appendix, 'An example of a kin-group and its network of relationships', document 5, below.
[67] *Conversano*, no. 140.
[68] *Conversano*, no. 166. Urso appeared earlier in 1199 exchanging lands with olive-trees, no. 149.
[69] *Conversano*, nos. 107, 115, 134, 137, 142, 149, 160.
[70] *CDBV*, no. 123; see similar references at Bari, *CDBI*, no. 61.
[71] Martin, *Foggia*, p. 52; *Regesto di S. Leonardo di Siponto*, ed. F. Camobreco (Rome, 1913), no. 173; *Troia*, no. 152.
[72] *Conversano*, no. 147; Cava, *Arca* xliii.109; *CDBV*, no. 84; Borgia, *Memorie istoriche*, ii. 426.
[73] On credit see Martin, *Pouille*, pp. 477–85.
[74] *CDBI*, nos. 61, 77, 78, 84; *CDBVI*, nos. 7, 38, 50; *Cartulaire de S.Matteo*, ii. 502–5 no. 285; *Pergamene del monastero benedettino di S. Giorgio*, no. 15; people with a 'bambacarius' surname appear at Benevento: *Montevergine*, viii. no. 786, ix. no. 835.

in southern Italy are rare.[75] Moreover, if some credit agreements charged interest, particularly at Bari, it is clear that these transactions could be made between people of any faith, at least before the Constitutions of Melfi allowed Jews alone to practise usury.[76] Indeed, in 1193 at Salerno, Manuel *hebreus* owed 15 ounces of gold to a *civis Romanus* called Barono.[77] Many individuals lent (and handled) money without employing a professional title. The aforesaid Otto *nauclerius* also had various debts to call in, while the testator of a will written in 1183 had deposited 499 *perpari*, under seal, with John the tailor of Salerno.[78] The records of a man like Stephen Sclavus, son of Melus, from Bari show the ubiquity of money-lending. He first appeared in 1085 owning a *curtis* (court?), in 1089 he paid back a loan (at a lower figure than had originally been agreed) and in *c.* 1099 took out another against his house and some vines in Bari.[79] Perhaps these loans allowed Stephen to invest further. In 1104 he is found loaning money to a man from Rome and another from Toulouse, described as *commoratores* in Bari, who were surely some sort of merchants. Another undated document shows that Stephen had loaned out more money, this time to a relative.[80] Growing wealth may have brought social promotion, and Stephen's activities in local affairs certainly begin to appear more conspicuous. In 1107 Stephen was one of two witnesses called in a case involving a relation, the other being a man who was called a *comes* and was the son of a *turmarch*.[81] In 1108 Stephen witnessed three documents relating to the church of S. Nicola of Bari, and in 1109 his wife received a donation from the *catepan* of Bari, on account of her husband's loyalty towards Prince Bohemond.[82] A picture emerges of the informality of banking, local trade and exchange and the opportunities it offered.

By far the greatest suppliers to the urban market were local rural producers and city-based artisans. The market was above all a space for locally produced goods. Although craftsmen are relatively rare in the source material, there is still regular enough mention of them to discern a variety of manufacture, retail and service trades. The documentation from Aversa, in particular, reveals an unusually high number of artisans for an average-sized inland city. There is reason to suppose then that

---

[75] *Pergamene di Barletta. Archivio Capitolare*, no. 141; *CDBVI*, nos. 10, 18 (see also Appendix, 'An example of a kin-group and its network of relationships', document 6, below). The latter charter, which does foresee a potential interest charge, also interestingly allows the contract to be altered only on production of a document written in Hebrew.

[76] *Liber Augustalis*, pp. 11–3 Bk I title vi (8–9); Houben, 'Gli ebrei', pp. 206–7.

[77] Cerone 'Sei documenti inediti', pp. 62–3 no. 3.   [78] Cava, *Arca* xxxviii.112.

[79] *CDBV*, nos. 5, 10, 29.   [80] *CDBV*, no. 38, frag. no. 11.   [81] *CDBV*, no. 46.

[82] *CDBV*, nos. 48, 53, 54, frag. no. 10. Also at Bari see the activities of Felix, son of Maio de Tasselgardo, over the period 1153–89, *CDBV*, nos. 106, 132, 141, 149, 152.

larger cities, like Bari and Salerno, were home to far more crafts than the sources disclose.[83] The ecclesiastical nature of much of the material and the problems with the way individuals identified themselves certainly contribute to their apparent scarcity.[84] Also, the informality of much of the production process must be taken into account. Many homes doubled as workshops, while craftsmen relied on the assistance of their family.[85] Women and children were vital components of this largely domestic enterprise, and 'many households were multi-occupational units.'[86] Female workers occasionally appear in the sources. In 1202 at Salerno, for example, Rodolenda *fornaria* (baker), the wife of Matthew Barbatu, rented from Peter Calvarusus some property with an oven. Rodelenda was able to 'make bread in the oven day and night' and had to pay an oven-tax (*fornaticum*).[87] Generally there is no real sign that any one urban centre specialised in a particular craft. The presence of metal-workers (*ferrarius, faber, cultellerius, caldararius*) is almost universal, and there are also quite regular references to the more high-status goldsmiths (*aurifex*). Otherwise, among the most common trades were builders (*fabricator, murator*), carpenters (*carpentarius*), saddlers (*sellarius*), tailors (*parmentarius*), cloth-workers (*bardarius*), leather-workers (*corviserius, cor-duanerius*), skinners (*pelliparius*), tanners (*tannator*) and butchers (*buccer-ius*). However, some urban economies must have focused trade around a particular commodity. The olive-oil trade seems especially lively at Bari; the claim that Maio of Bari's father was an olive-oil seller was meant as a pejorative swipe, but suggests that the city and the oil-trade were so inter-connected as to encourage outsiders to create stereotypes. Bari also had a standardised olive oil measure (*ad stare puplicum barense*), and payments could be made in the commodity. In the case of Salerno, with its famous medical school, a host of medical and pharmaceutical trades and suppliers must have emerged. Developed manufacturing or industry in the cities was essentially small scale. There were various salt-works, particularly along the Adriatic coasts, and their revenues were mentioned

---

[83] Galasso, 'Le città campane', pp. 88–107, 116–21.

[84] The difficulty of identifying artisans is typified in two charters from Salerno. In one from 1228, Cava rented land and a house in the city to John Cassanella, who if he wished may live and 'practise his craft' (*ars*)' there. *CDS*, pp. 148–9 no. 73. A charter of 1120 gave John, son of Cristofoli, the right to draw water 'for the purpose of tanning skins', Cava, *Arca* xxi.33. It is only these chance qualifying statements which suggest that both men might be artisans. For further discussion see above pp. 203–4.

[85] A charter of 1220 from Aversa refers to a house 'in which the *tincta* of Aversa is practised', *CDSA*, pp. 195–7 no. 96.

[86] H. Swanson, *Medieval Artisans. An Urban Class in Late Medieval England* (Oxford, 1989), pp. 6–7, 128.

[87] *CDS*, pp. 49–50 no. 5.

in documents at Taranto and Naples.[88] Elsewhere, al-Idrisi refers to ship-building at Bari and Gaeta.[89] Dye-works were attested at Aversa, Salerno, Taranto and Troia. At Salerno, the Jews had a monopoly on making and selling *auricella* (jewellery?) and slaughtering four-legged animals, and at Taranto and Troia they were active in the *tinctoria* (dyeworks).[90] Jewish dyers were also referred to at Brindisi, and in 1231 Frederick II appointed two Jews at Capua to establish conventions on the dyeing industry.[91]

We have discussed elsewhere the possibility that there may have existed informal associations based on trade. But there is no evidence for any legally defined bodies.[92] In his Constitutions of Melfi, Frederick II, who seemed opposed to any such corporate organisations, legislated for the strict supervision of artisan trading standards. A number of these constitutions suggest the monarchy's belief in corruption among artisans and merchants and offer no hint of organised corporations.[93] Here we find a notable difference with central and northern Italy, where, particularly from the mid-twelfth century, legally defined 'merchant' and 'artisan' guilds crystallised. By the early thirteenth century, some guilds had created their own consular officials and acquired overt political functions. Some played significant roles in the rise of the *popolo* and developed a military dimension too.[94] This, combined with other evidence such as the development of an *ordo mercatorum* and the use of the *commenda*, confirms the greater commercial sophistication of the North. But their absence in South Italian cities does not mean they themselves were commercially undeveloped. The evidence, for example on Otto *nauclerius* of Bari, suggests that complex commercial activities and organisation could exist without the need to create defined corporations and practices or indeed to commit these norms to writing.[95] As we noted earlier, the status and use of literacy in the twelfth century did not yet require implicitly understood actions and traditions to be recorded on paper.[96]

Public power maintained a large degree of control over the region's markets and drew taxes from them, ever more so under the monarchy.

[88] *Taranto*, pp. 49–54 no. 13; *Pergamene di San Gregorio Armeno*, no. 44; Matthew, *Norman Kingdom*, p. 339.

[89] *Italia descritta nel 'Libro del re Ruggero' compilato da Edrisi*, pp. 94, 103,

[90] *Pergamene salernitane (1008–1784)*, ed. L. E. Pennacchini (Naples, 1941), no. 12; *Taranto*, pp. 58–9 no. 15, pp. 75–85 no. 22; *Troia*, no. 75.

[91] *Itinerary Ben. Tudela*, p. 9; *Acta Imperii Inedita*, i. 621 no. 796.   [92] See p. 224 n. 123.

[93] *Liber Augustalis*, pp. 132–6 Bk III, title xlix (26) (1), (27), (28), title l (29), title li (30), title lii (31).

[94] Hyde, *Society and Politics*, pp. 73–4, 108; Coleman, 'Cities and communes', pp. 52–3.

[95] See Appendix, 'An example of a kin-group and its network of relationships', below.

[96] See above pp. 76–7.

The indirect tax system was maintained at least until near the end of the twelfth century. The *plateaticum*, a charge on transactions within the *plateae* (squares), was taken over by the Norman rulers from their Lombard predecessors. Exemptions from paying the *plateaticum*, or grants of a share of it, were highly sought after and suggest lucrative profits. The monastery of S. Benedetto of Conversano was freed by Count Geoffrey from payments on transactions in that city and in 1107 was exempted by an official of Bohemond from the 'price . . . of the *plazze* and *pesatura*' when buying and selling in Bari.[97] At Salerno the monastery of Cava seems to have obtained the tithe of market revenues from an initial grant by Roger Borsa in 1100, which was extended by later rulers.[98] The church of S. Nicola of Bari claimed a third of the *plateaticum* on certain goods in the *duana* from the time of King William I.[99] At Taranto it seems the archbishop had enjoyed, since the reign of King William II, the tithe from all *introitus* and *proventus* of the *baiulatio*.[100] Examples of non-ecclesiastical recipients of such grants were rare. The charter of privileges from Troia exempted all inhabitants, but not *extranei*, from the *plateaticum*.[101] In 1195 Queen Constance granted to the archbishop of Bari the tithe of all revenues from Bari, which had previously been offered by William II to Tasselgardus, a royal chamberlain.[102] The public authorities charged additional trade-related taxes: the *portaticum* charged on entering the city gates and a slaughter-tax known as the *ius macelli*, while in port cities taxes such as the *anchoraticum* and *scalaticum* were levied by *baiuli* and sometimes by officials known as *portulani*.[103] Towards the end of the period other types of customs taxes, which are difficult to distinguish between, were also employed. The *ius dohane* and *ius fundici* appear alongside officials known as *dohanerii* and *fundicarii*.[104] Permission to practise certain trades, or to receive the revenues drawn from them, could also pertain to the public authority. In 1109 the prince of Capua granted out the dyeing rights over a wide area to two *burgenses* of Aversa.[105] It may well be that the Norman kings attempted to form monopolies on some trades. The archbishop of Taranto received from royal grant a portion of the revenues from the city's butchery and dyeing trades.[106] In 1190 the archbishop of Salerno requested from the king the entire revenues of the city's dyeworks. In return the archbishop offered

[97] *Conversano*, nos. 45, 59, 62.   [98] See above p. 30; *CDS*, pp. 227–30 no. 125.
[99] *CDBVI*, no. 42.   [100] *Taranto*, pp. 62–6 no. 17.
[101] *Troia*, no. 50; Martin, *Pouille*, pp. 428–33.
[102] *Constantiae Imperatricis et Reginae Siciliae Diplomata*, pp. 19–23 no 5.
[103] For example, Cava, *Arm. Mag.*, F.2; *Trani*, no. 88; *Acta Imperii Inedita*, i. 619 no. 792.
[104] *Acta Imperii Inedita*, i. 619–20 no. 793.   [105] *Pergamene di Capua*, i. 25–6 no. 10.
[106] *Taranto*, pp. 75–85 no. 22, pp. 90–1 no. 24, pp. 94–101 no. 26.

the Church's tithe in Salerno and nearby Tusciano, as well as other possessions including a *fundicus*, shops and buildings.[107] In 1191 Tancred confirmed to the 'commune' of Gaeta the right of *tintura*.[108] We have already seen that certain Jewish communities were given a monopoly on this activity, as well as on others such as the slaughtering of four-legged animals. Frederick II certainly aimed at establishing state monopolies on the dyeing and salt industries, as well as for the purchase of silk, and public power had 'general responsibility for controlling the use of natural resources'.[109] Timber, water, fishing and pasturage rights were among these.

The public powers also controlled the coinage in circulation.[110] The monetary system of the South was quite different from the rest of western Europe, where silver dominated until the thirteenth century. Southern Italian coinage by contrast essentially consisted of gold and copper, with silver only notably entering from the time of the Staufen. Moreover, the monetary system of the South was far from unitary. In the eleventh century there were ostensibly separate systems operating in Byzantine Apulia, with the gold *solidi*, silver *miliaresia* and copper *follari*, and in Campania, where imitation gold *tarìs* of Arabic origin and local forms of copper *follari* began to be minted. Within the northern sector of Campania, Gaeta, and to a lesser extent Capua and Naples, were also connected to the North Italian monetary system, with the use of imperial silver from Pavia and Lucca. Importantly, coinage from each of these South Italian regions seems to have circulated among the others. The Normans in essence maintained the local forms of currency, but there was some increased use of silver *denarii* from Rouen.[111] King Roger's monetary reform of 1140 attempted to introduce an indigenous silver coin (the *ducalis*) and aimed to bring some unity and order. However, there may have been little practical difference: the *ducalis* was eventually overrun by the infiltration of silver *provesini* from Champagne, and more importantly there still remained notable regional variations in currency.[112] Local forms of coinage were still minted at important centres

---

[107] *Tancredi et Willelmi III Regum Diplomata*, pp. 10–5 nos. 4–5, pp. 20–3 nos. 7–8 (Jamison, *Admiral Eugenius*, appendix I no. 4).

[108] *Tancredi et Willelmi III Regum Diplomata*, pp. 42–6 no. 18.

[109] *Acta Imperii Inedita*, i. 621 no. 796 and *Taranto*, pp. 58–9 no. 15, pp. 75–85 no. 22; Matthew, *Norman Kingdom*, pp. 81, 339–40.

[110] The following discussion on coinage utilises the excellent P. Grierson and L. Travaini, *Medieval European Coinage*, vol. XIV, *Italy (III) (South Italy, Sicily, Sardinia)* (Cambridge, 1998), pp. 1–177, appendix 1 pp. 401–4, appendix 3 pp. 436–41; see also Martin, *Pouille*, pp. 443–77.

[111] Loud, 'Coinage, wealth and plunder', pp. 819, 821, 831–3.

[112] Houben, *Roger II*, pp. 159–61.

like Amalfi and Salerno, and it would seem also briefly at Bari.[113] Gaeta and Naples enjoyed their own copper *follari*, continuing in the former city even after 1194, when they were abolished in the rest of the kingdom. The presence of a local mint and coinage type carried more than mere economic significance. To Falco of Benevento, Roger's reform was a 'terrible edict' which led to death and poverty. The chronicler's almost hysterical response shows how significant the status of coinage could be, and not just fiscally. Falco reports the pope's ardent attempts to assure the 'frightened' Beneventans that Roger's new coinage was merely a 'transitory' phenomenon.[114] Coinage communicated a statement of power by bearing a ruler's title. Alternatively, in some cases the coinage could emphasise protection and civic identity by carrying effigies of local saints: St Matthew at Salerno, St Nicholas at Bari, St Gennarus at Naples and St Erasmus at Gaeta. The agreement of Duke Richard in 1123 not to alter Gaeta's copper *follari* was at the tearful request of the populace. It perhaps reflected a combined awareness of the fiscal and symbolic importance of coinage.[115] Later, Gaeta received the freedom to strike its own *follari* and to keep the mint in the city for its 'general advantage' as before.[116] It is in its multi-layered relationship with the community, incorporating power, wealth and identity, that the significance of the South's coinage lay. Equally, as Loud observed, 'the monetarisation of south Italian society is striking', demonstrating that the South was prosperous, and wealth was not solely dependent on landholding, inheritance or violence.[117] A perusal of the charter material more than bears this out.

Commentators from the eleventh and twelfth centuries tend to confirm this. They offer us a variety of glowing images of the mainland's cities. We are told by one chronicler that the city of Capua was 'a real metropolis ... with an extensive suburb ... overflowing with grain, wine and meat, as well as with all sorts of other merchandise'.[118] Another source describes Bari as 'the most powerful city of Apulia, celebrated by fame and immensely rich, proud in its noble citizens and remarkable in the architecture of its buildings'.[119] Elsewhere, Trani is portrayed as 'a city of illustrious name, full of riches, arms and many people', while it was claimed that Salerno, in the 1160s, was a 'highly regarded city,

---

[113] L. Travaini, 'Le zecca e le monete di Salerno nel XII secolo', in *Salerno nel XII secolo*, pp. 346–9; the mint at Salerno was disbanded in 1194 and that of Amalfi in 1222, for which *Rich. S. Germano*, p. 103.

[114] *Falco*, p. 234.   [115] *Cod. Dip. Caietanus*, ii. 215–17 no. 301.

[116] *Tancredi et Willelmi III Regum Diplomata*, pp. 42–6 no. 18.

[117] Loud, 'Coinage, wealth and plunder', pp. 841–2.   [118] *Alex. Tel.*, Bk II.66, p. 55.

[119] *Falcandus*, p. 74.

which brought considerable prestige to the entire realm'.[120] Although these descriptions contain a concoction of literary formula, embellishment and underlying agendas, the admiration for South Italian civic life, its vitality and significance to contemporaries are inescapable. The image of southern Italy as a prosperous, if dangerous, region certainly gained currency among outsiders.[121] The Englishman Robert of Howden described how in 1194 Henry VI's army was 'made rich from the spoils of the Salernitans', following the discovery of 'a great treasure worth 200,000 ounces of gold' in the city's main tower.[122] The German chronicler Otto of St Blasien also noted Henry VI's unearthing of the public treasury in Palermo, where there was stored 'the riches of Apulia, Calabria and Sicily, which are lands with an abundance of metals, bearing a glorious store of precious stones and all types of gems'.[123] Of course this wealth was in no way shared across the social spectrum. A large majority of the populace lived at subsistence level and a sizeable group even below that, their fortunes subject to climate and war. Yet for others there were at least prospects of sharing in some of the huge wealth that southern Italy could potentially generate.

---

[120] *Will. Apulia*, Bk III, p. 184 lines 371–2; *Falcandus*, p. 131
[121] For a stimulating discussion of medieval English attitudes towards the 'exotic' and 'alien' South Italians see G. A. Loud, 'The kingdom of Sicily and the kingdom of England, 1066–1266', *History* 88 (2003), pp. 540–67.
[122] Roger of Howden, *Chronica*, iii. 269.
[123] *Die Chronik Ottos von St. Blasien und Die Marbacher Annalen*, Ch. 40, p. 118.

CONCLUSION

To understand fully the nature of urban society in twelfth-century southern Italy we must question, as Susan Reynolds has more generally, the assumption that 'liberty, equality and community go together'.[1] In other words, we need to acknowledge that although the Norman rulers established a closer supervision of the cities, this need not have been undesirable to the urban community or precluded its freedom of action, and to recognise that social and economic inequality was an accepted principle among the civic population which did not prevent it acting as a 'communal' group. Moreover, in understanding South Italian urban life one has to quickly come to terms with the limited and imprecise vocabulary which has been left by the sources, while at certain points to analyse what has not been said can be as useful as analysing what has. The collective role of the community was so widely acknowledged, and one might even say so unremarkable, that medieval commentators saw no need to elucidate it further. It accounts, for example, for the limited information they offer us on how cities functioned during the frequent periods of political unrest. Conversely, a more precise terminology does not suddenly bring something into existence. This applies for instance to the 'commune' at Benevento, which suddenly, and only, appears in Falco's chronicle from 1128 to 1130, and to the *societas* first recorded in a charter at Naples in 1129/30. The likelihood is that in both cases these 'associations' existed in some format before and after these dates, even though they were not specifically attested in other source material. At all points it is crucial to keep in mind the generally conservative wording and formulas used by medieval notaries in their documents. When 'innovations', be they novel official titles or social vocabulary, appear in the written record it is likely that they had been in place in the 'real world' for quite some time before. Indeed, it would seem that novelties

[1] Reynolds, *Kingdoms and Communities*, xi.

may have been dressed in the guise of traditional terminology to make them easier to accept by potentially suspicious authorities.[2] Parallels can be drawn with the increasing awareness of the informality of the early communal institutions of northern Italy, where urban government was supposed to be precociously structured. There the cities acquired autonomy 'in much more fragmentary, inconsistent, indeed contradictory ways' and 'to pin down a single moment of origin for this autonomy . . . can be a meaningless imposition of external order.'[3]

From this approach a different and more complex picture of South Italian urban life emerges. One key development, which has to some extent previously been recognised, is the evolution in the cities of Campania and Apulia (and one coterminous with those in central and northern Italy) of innovative methods of self-government during the disorder of the eleventh century and the period of early Norman domination. But this evolution did not stop, let alone reverse, after the 1130s, and this has received much less consideration. These developments continued throughout the twelfth century in a different yet no less intriguing way. The cities were active participants in, not the supine victims of, wider, volatile events. Their role in the civil war in the 1130s and during the period from 1189 to 1220, as well as the rebellions of the 1150s and 60s, and the manner in which all these cities were incorporated into a new kingdom after 1139 bear witness to this. South Italian urban communities were constantly in a position to make choices, and choices brought a voice and power. The whole period is characterised by continuity at all levels, yet within the cities significant internal developments still took place. We need only note the creation of an independent principate at Bari, the constitution of a 'commune' at Benevento in the 1120s and the emergence of consuls at Benevento, Gaeta and Naples. At the same time there is greater evidence of the fluidity of the social ordering of urban communities, while the notion of citizenship and civic identity acquired greater articulation. Southern Italy was also notable for its wealth, and the urban economy continued to flourish, although in a different format, under the monarchy. Modern conceptions of a poverty-stricken South should not be projected back onto the medieval period.[4] The formation of the kingdom was neither as disruptive for the urban population and its traditions of government, nor was it thereafter as intrusive or bureaucratic, as has been imagined. A rather different monarchy emerges from the one which, according to

---

[2] As noted in a different context by S. A. Epstein, *Wage Labor and Guilds in Medieval Europe* (North Carolina, 1991), p. 50.

[3] Wickham, 'The sense of the past', pp. 176, 185–7.   [4] Filangieri, *Territorio e popolazione*, pp. 177–9.

Marongiu, had 'no institutional limitations, and [offered] no concessions to its subjects'.[5] The creation of the monarchy, although a highly significant moment, did not represent such a massive turning-point for urban society. Wickham cautioned against the meaningless imposition of external order to determine when autonomy was acquired, and the same can be said of identifying a given moment in which it could be lost.

If it is right to see the idea of 'liberty' in the medieval period as 'not the right to vote or express political opinions', but instead as the 'power to act in the affairs of the community and to exert influence on one's fellows, free from the interference of the sovereign government', then South Italian city-dwellers may well have felt far more free than we have previously allowed them to be.[6] It is important to recognise also that urban communities in the South were more than capable of expressing political opinions, and that this often coincided with extended periods when central government collapsed and cities were forced to fill the void. Yet even during phases of order (such as 1139–89, though even then there were also rebellions) the practicality of governing the mainland from Sicily left much of day-to-day government untouched under the surface and in the hands of local people. While this work has explored South Italian cities collectively it remains evident that there existed notable cultural and social divergences among them. This is particularly the case for the major centres (Bari, Benevento, Naples and Salerno) with their own varied historical traditions; a diversity that was perhaps not evident in quite the same way among the North Italian cities, especially those along the Po Valley.

In many ways the history of southern Italy's cities in the twelfth century is a history driven by the people who lived within them; by those who walked through their city's alleyways and squares; by those who sat in local courts acting with the peculiarities of their civic customs embedded in their mind; by those who knew the fragrances and noises of the market-place; by those who knew the soil and the seasons; by those who drank with their companions in the tavern or who prayed before their local saint. It was they who brought the city to life – enjoyed it and suffered in it, welcomed newcomers or turned them away. For them, kings and rulers came and went, issued their orders, exacted their demands and at times unsheathed their swords. But none of this could ultimately break or distort the bond between the community and its city; a bond that reshaped and renewed itself with every passing day, but which was continuous and which wrote its own history.

---

[5] Marongiu, 'A model state', p. 308.
[6] A. Harding, 'Political liberty in the Middle Ages', *Speculum* 55 (1980), p. 423.

Appendix

AN EXAMPLE OF A KIN-GROUP AND ITS NETWORK OF RELATIONSHIPS: THE FAMILY OF OTTO *NAUCLERIUS* OF BARI

(1) December 1136 – Bari – Marriage agreement between John, son of Melis de Regina, of Bari and Dumnana, son of Melis Randi, of Bari. John gives a pledge to Ascone and Maio, brothers and sons, of Melis Randi. John's mediators are his father Melis, his *barbanus* Maraldus, son of Luponis, and his cousin Torcinia, son of the aforesaid Maraldus. John gives as *meffium* (marriage gift) to Dumnana 100 gold *solidi* and two young slaves.[1]

(2) February 1191 – Bari – Otto, son of John Melis de Regina, purchases land from Stephen, son of Kurisergius de Malocore, for 4 ounces of gold tari. The document mentions vines already belonging to Otto.[2]

(3) 1191 – Bari – Otto purchases half a house in Bari from his brother Senior, whose wife is Alfarana, daughter of Maralditius *nauclerius*.[3]

(4) 24 August 1197 – Bari – Otto, called a *nauclerius*, purchases from Nicholas de Suppo 3.5 vines 'in pertinentiis Caucini' with 11 olive trees there, as well as 69 more olive-trees and a *curticellam* of olives nearby, for 42 ounces of gold tari.[4]

(5) December 1200 – Bari – Otto *nauclerius* makes his will as he prepares to journey 'in partibus Romanie'. Otto appoints his son-in-law, Nicholas Struzzius, as one of the executors of his will. The will provides a dowry 'iuxta morem barensem' for his daughter, who was the wife of Jacob, son of Peter de Leone, one for his daughter Boliarina, the wife of the aforesaid Nicholas Struzzius, and one for his *neptis*, who was the wife of Grimoalditius. It pays money to Sabbatus the Jew of Trani, Paunesse the widow of Henry, Domnulus de Asconia, Iaspido Emmanuel and to the aforesaid Nicholas Struzzius. It orders the reclamation of money from John Emmanuel, the judge Lucas of Monopoli, John the notary of Acquaviva, and the heirs of Nicholas Striccius. The latter also (?) had been for a long time under an obligation, contracted by their father, to pay back money to Otto and Peter Crassus, Virgilio, Iohannocarrus Kirici, Epifanius, Maralditius, Pandus and John de Gualandra. Otto claimed repayment of a seventh part of money owed to him and his *socii* by Spironus of Brindisi.

[1] *CDBV*, no. 87. [2] *CDBV*, no. 157.
[3] *CDBV*, no. 159; *CDBV*, frag. no. 24, is a document of land division from 1194 which refers to *Oto f. domini Iohannis . . .* This could be our Otto, and the fragmentary charter mentions an 'ecclesia Sancte Agnetis', while Otto's will mentions olives 'in pertinentis Sancte Agnetis'.
[4] *CDBVI*, no. 7.

Further monetary repayments were claimed by Otto from John de Russano de Campulo, John de Ioa (a part of which was owed also to Angelus of Modugno), John *putator*, Petronus Dardanus, the heirs of Kiri Asconie, Nicholas Asconie de Melis Rando, Nicodemus Stefani *medie brachie*. Payments to be made in *starea* of oil were claimed from Bartholomew de Simbulo, the *sacerdos* John de Carrone, Disigius Petrinee, John Sanctus Agnetis, Romacca Celiarum, Sanduzza the widow of Oggerius (who receives also a payment of 13 gold tari). More money claimed from the heirs of judge Eustratius, Matthew de Skisico. [The details in the mid-section of the document are particularly unclear – it seems to deal with possible insurance payments concerning maritime ventures ('ex calamitate maris et gentis') and it is not always apparent whether the person mentioned was a creditor or debtor.] Individuals who appear in this section are Pintus, Peter Crassus (again), Nicholas Iohannacius, Geromanus *nauclerius* and Leo Peter de Laya. The latter seems to be obliged to pay on his safe return to Bari ('in Barum salvus reddiderit') money to the aforesaid Sabbatus the Jew, Nicholas Iohannacius, Petracce de macino and Nicholas Struzzius (again). The will orders further payments to Leo *grecus* and Bisantius the priest of Monopoli. Otto makes payments for *quarantinis* to be sung on his behalf and an ounce of gold is to be given to the church of Bari for *officiando* (celebrating his anniversary?). The same amount is given to the church of S. Nicola and to each monastery in Bari as well as to the church of S. Lazaro. Provision is made for Otto's wife to remain secure, and all the rest to go to his son Nicholas. If Nicholas and then Otto's daughters die without heirs, Otto's plantation of olive-trees 'in pertinentiis Sancte Agnetis' and the vines 'in pertinentiis Sancte Martini' shall go to the 'church of S. Lazaro where outside Bari the lepers dwell'. All Otto's old olive trees 'in pertinentiis Sancte Agnetis' shall go to the clerics of the archbishopric of Bari, for annually celebrating his anniversary. All Otto's olive trees in Caucini shall go to his nephew John, the son of his already deceased brother Senior. If John dies without heirs the olives also will go to the clerics of the archbishopric of Bari. The house of Otto at Bari 'in vicinia sancti Theodori' shall go to the children of the brothers Domnulus and Nicholas de asconia Melis Randi. The document was signed by the aforesaid Leo Peter de Laya, Peter of Bari, John Gadeleto, Nicholas Sergii cavallerio, Nicholas Andritii, Nicholas Gradelonii.[5]

(6) 22 August – 1205 – Trani – Otto *nauclerius* agrees to repay money to Sabbatus *hebreus*, son of Musce, of Trani, with the potential for interest.[6]

(7) 19 February 1208 – Bari – Iacoba daughter of the late Leo Petri Romani and widow of Otto *nauclerius barensis*, along with her son Nicholas and the *epitropi* Peter Crassus and Nicholas Struzzius, pledge to pay money to Bisantius, son of Petracca Struzzius (apparently the brother of Nicholas Struzzius), within a year. As security they pledge olive-trees 'in loco Sancte Agnetis' (formerly belonging to Otto) which were near those of Nicholas de Iohannicius.[7]

(8) 1224 – Bari – Testament of Nicholas, son of Otto *nauclerius*, before Agralistus de Cernello. Nicholas's *epitropi* are John Petri Crassi, who seems to have been married to a daughter of Otto's, and Rosemannus de Tafuro. Nicholas makes

---

[5] *CDBVI*, no. 10   [6] *CDBVI*, no. 18.   [7] *CDBVI*, no. 22.

bequests to the clerics and the fabric of the Church of Bari, to Lupo his 'spiritual father', to a female named Iennensis and to the clerics of S. Nicola *Maior*. His sister Maralda should make an annual payment to the clerics of the Church of Bari to sound the bells annually on his behalf. Nicholas' mother Iacoba and sister Boliarina are to supervise, with the *epitropi*, all his immoveable property.[8]

(9) 27 February 1233 – Bari – Alferada, son of Mirus de Agralisto, and her son Grisoiohannes promise not to disturb thereafter Boliarina, daughter of [Otto] *Nauclerius barensis* and widow of *sire* Nicholas Struzzius.[9]

★ ★ ★

If we take Otto *nauclerius* as the central character here, we can see the varied interests of an individual and his family and the operation of a number of different relationships. Otto's first appearances in the 1190s are ventures into the land market, although it is clear (document 2) that he already had landed property. In fact, Otto's father in the 1130s had been wealthy enough to offer slaves and a large quantity of *solidi* as a marriage-gift to his wife, and other charters from the decade show him possessing land, mostly outside Bari at Noia.[10] Moreover, a charter of 1151 shows that King Roger had given, 'pro regalibus', to certain inhabitants of Bitonto some vines which Melis de Regina of Bari had in 'loco Sancti Martini'. It is not clear why these lands were transferred, if Melis was still alive and indeed was Otto's grandfather, but it is notable that in his will Otto disposed of vines at a place with the same name (document 5).[11] Otto first took the title *nauclerius* in the 1190s, and lacking other evidence we cannot say whether this was a family 'profession'. Indeed, of his relatives, only his son-in-law Nicholas Struzzius certainly took part in similar activities. The will of 1200 suggests his involvement in some associated investments with Otto, while two charters of 1203 specifically call Nicholas a *nauclerius* (interestingly these are the only occasions when he is so named).[12] It might be noted, however, that Otto's sister-in-law Alfarana was the daughter of a Maralditius *nauclerius* (docment 3). Otto's evident commercial activity supports the likelihood that *nauclerius* carried the wider sense of merchant rather than simply sailor. Otto's extraordinary will demonstrates an extensive network of commercial activity; he himself was preparing to travel to Byzantium, he had acted with a group of associates (*socii*) and seems to have operated some form of maritime insurance. The vast list of people who owed money to him, or whom Otto provided payments for, included a Jew from Trani (with whom we later find Otto at Trani in document 6), a judge from Monopoli and a notary from Acquaviva. While the will reveals that a large amount of Otto's extensive wealth was moveable (in money and oil), it also documents, alongside earlier evidence (documents 2–4), some notable vine and olive holdings. Otto's bequests to local religious houses, one of which was associated with lepers, reveal the man's spiritual concerns, as do his son's testament (document 8).

Otto was keen to provide for his wife and children in his will. Provision was also made for John, the son of Otto's deceased brother Senior. Later, Otto's own son

---

[8] *CDBVI*, no. 43.   [9] *CDBVI*, frag. no. 3.   [10] *CDBV*, nos. 86, 88, 90.   [11] *CDBV*, no. 104.
[12] *CDBVI*, nos. 14, 15, in which Nicholas purchased olive trees at Modugno, some of which had at one time been owned by his own father, Petracca.

An example of a kin-group and its network of relationships

Nicholas gave important duties to his mother and sisters in his will of 1224. Marriages linked in other families and formed close relationships. The provision in the 1200 will for the children of the brothers Domnulus and Nicholas de asconia Melis Randi is interesting, as this seems to be the family from which Otto's mother came (document 1). The will also shows that Otto had loaned money to (the aforesaid) Nicholas de asconie de Melis Rando. Otto's son-in-law Nicholas Struzzius, himself a landowner and *nauclerius*, was established as an *epitropos* in Otto's will; Nicholas took on the same role for Otto's widow in 1208.[13] Other names that appear are also rather interesting. They hint at long-standing extra-familial relationships and suggest that Otto rubbed shoulders with some of the Barese elite. Iohannoccarus Kirici was a witness in document 3 in 1191 and was one of Otto's *socii* in 1200. Peter Crassus, another business associate identified in Otto's will, may well have been the notary of the same name attested in Bari and part of an important kin-group.[14] Certainly Peter remained close to the family: he acted as an *epitropos* for Otto's widow in 1208, as did his son John, who, it seems, married a daughter of Otto's (documents 7 and 8). Otto's purchase of land in 1191 was from Stephen de Malecore, the same man who witnessed document 7, was later a *catepan* of Bari and again part of a wealthy family. Indeed, the share of the house that Otto obtained from his brother in 1191 (document 3) was located next to the 'domus filiorum Sergii de malocore' – Sergius being Stephen's father. Another one-time *catepan* of Bari, Bartholomew de Simbulo, owed oil to Otto in the 1200 will.[15] The numerous other names that appear once in the documentation concerning Otto or his family may well convey countless other relationships. It may or may not be coincidence, for example, that Nicholas Iohannacii, who seems to have a business association with Otto in his will, also owned olives in 'loco Sancte Agnetis', near Otto and his family's holdings (document 7). Similarly a John Emmanuel witnessed document 2 in 1191, and a man with the same name owed Otto money according to the 1200 testament.

---

[13] For Nicholas and his family see the above n. 12, document no. 7 and also *CDBI*, no. 84.

[14] Peter Crassus the notary: *CDBV*, nos. 138, 141; other references to people with the name 'Crassus': *CDBI*, nos. 53, 70, 77, 78, 99, 106, *CDBVI*, nos. 24, 32, 55, 60, 83, 93, 95, frag. no. 4.

[15] For Stephen and Bartholomew see above pp. 137–8, 151.

BIBLIOGRAPHY

MANUSCRIPT SOURCES

Benevento, Biblioteca capitolare.
Benevento, Museo del Sannio, Fondo S. Sofia.
Cava dei Tirreni, Archivio della badia di SS. Trinità.
Pergamene Aldobrandini (formerly of the Biblioteca Apostolica Vaticano).

PRINTED PRIMARY SOURCES

Abbazia di Montevergine. Regesto delle pergamene, vol. II, 1200–49, ed. G. Mongelli (Rome, 1957).

Acta et Diplomata Ragusina, ed. J. Radonić (Belgrade, 1934).

Acta Imperii Inedita Saeculi XIII et XIV, 2 vols., ed. E. Winkelmann (Innsbruck, 1880–5).

Alexandri Telesini Abbatis Ystoria Rogerii Regis Sicilie Calabrie atque Apulie, ed. L. De Nava, *FSI* CXII (Rome, 1991).

Annales Barenses, ed. G. H. Pertz, *MGH SS* V (Hanover, 1844).

Annales Casinenses, ed. G. H. Pertz, *MGH SS* XIX (Hanover, 1846).

Annales Cavenses, ed. G. H. Pertz, *MGH SS* III (Hanover, 1839).

Annales Ceccanenses, ed. G. H. Pertz, *MGH SS* XIX (Hanover, 1866).

Annali genovesi di Caffaro e de' suoi continuatori, 5 vols., ed. L. T. Belgrano, *FSI* XI, XII, XIII, XIV, XIV (ii) (Genoa, 1890–1901, Rome 1923–9).

Annalista Saxo, ed. L. C. Bethman, *MGH SS* VI (Hanover, 1844).

Anonymi Barensis Chronicon (855–1149), ed. C. Pellegrino, *RIS* V (Milan, 1724).

Antiche cronache di Terra di Bari, ed. G. Gioffari and R. Lupoli Tateo, Centro Studi Nicolaiani – *Memorie e Documenti* V (Bari, 1991).

Antiquitates Italicae Medii Aevi, 6 vols., ed. L. A. Muratori (1738–42).

L'archivio diocesano di Salerno. Cenni sull'archivio del capitolo metropolitana, ed. A. Balducci (Salerno, 1959–60).

O. Bertolini, 'Gli *Annales Beneventani*', *BISME* 42 (1923), pp. 9–163.

G. Cangiano, 'L'*Adventus Sancti Nycolai in Beneventum*', *Atti della societa storica del Sannio* 2 (1924), pp. 131–62.

I carmi di Alfano I, arcivescovo di Salerno, ed. A. Lentini and F. Avagliano, *Miscellanea Cassinese* XXXVIII (Montecassino, 1974).

Bibliography

Le carte che si conservano nello archivio dello capitolo metropolitano della città di Trani (dal IX secolo fino all'anno 1266), ed. A. Prologo (Barletta, 1877).

Le carte di Molfetta (1076–1309), ed. F. Carabellese, *Codice diplomatico barese* VII (Bari, 1912).

Le Cartulaire de S. Matteo di Sculgola en Capitanate (registri d'istrumenti di S.Maria del Gualdo) (1177–1239), 2 vols., ed. J-M. Martin, *Codice diplomatico pugliese* XXX (Bari, 1987).

Le Cartulaire du chapitre du Saint Sépulchre de Jérusalem, ed. G. Bresc-Bautier (Paris, 1984).

Catalogus Baronum, ed. E. M. Jamison, *FSI* CI (Rome, 1972).

Catalogus Baronum commentario, ed. E. Cuozzo, *FSI* CI (ii) (Rome, 1984).

F. Cerone, 'Sei documenti inediti sugli Ebrei di Salerno dal 1125 al 1269', in *Studi di storia napoletana in onore di Michelangelo Schipa* (Naples, 1926), pp. 59–73.

Les Chartes de Troia. Edition et étude critique des plus anciens documents conservés à l'archivio capitolare, I (1024–1266), ed. J-M. Martin, *Codice diplomatico pugliese* XXI (Bari, 1976).

Chronicon Ignoti Monachi Cisterciensis Sanctae Mariae de Ferraria, ed. A. Gaudenzi (Naples, 1888).

Chronicon Monasterii Casinensis, ed. H. Hoffman, *MGH SS* XXXIV (Hanover, 1980).

Chronicon Sanctae Sophiae, 2 vols., ed. J-M. Martin, *Fonti per la storia dell'Italia medievale* (Rome, 2000).

Die Chronik Ottos von St. Blasien und die Marbacher Annalen, ed. and trans. F-J. Schmale (Darmstadt, 1998).

D. R. Clementi, 'Calendar of the diplomas of the Hohenstaufen Emperor Henry VI concerning the kingdom of Sicily', *QF* 35 (1955), pp. 86–225.

D. R. Clementi, 'An administrative document of 1190 from Apulia', *PBSR* 24 (1956), pp. 101–6.

D. R. Clementi, 'Further documents concerning the administration of the province of *Apulia et Terra Laboris* during the reign of the Emperor Henry VI', *PBSR* 27 (1959), pp. 170–82.

Codex Diplomaticus Caietanus, 2 vols. (Montecassino, 1887–92).

Codex Diplomaticus Cavensis, vol. IX, 1065–72, and vol. X, 1073–80, ed. S. Leone and G. Vitolo (Cava, 1984, 1990).

Codice diplomatico amalfitano, 2 vols., ed. R. Filangieri di Candida (Naples, 1917, Trani, 1951).

Codice diplomatico brindisino, vol. I, 492–1299, ed. G-M. Monti (Bari, 1977).

Codice diplomatico della repubblica di Genova, 3 vols., ed. C. Imperiale di Sant'Angelo, *FSI* LXXVII, LXXIX, LXXXIX (Rome, 1936–42).

Codice diplomatico normanno di Aversa, ed. A. Gallo (Naples, 1926).

Codice diplomatico salernitano del secolo XIII, vol. I, 1201–81, ed. C. Carucci (Subiaco, 1931).

Codice diplomatico svevo di Aversa [parte prima], ed. C. Salvati (Naples, 1980).

Codice diplomatico verginiano, 13 vols., ed. P. M. Tropeano (Montevergine, 1977–2000).

Il Codice Perris. Cartulario amalfitano. Sec. X–XV, 3 vols., ed. J. Mazzoleni and R. Orefice (Amalfi, 1985).

Bibliography

Le colonie cassinesi in Capitanata. IV. Troia, ed. T. Leccisotti, *Miscellanea Cassinese* XXIX (Montecassino, 1957).

Constantiae Imperatricis et Reginae Siciliae Diplomata (1195–1198), ed. T. Kölzer (Codex diplomaticus regni Siciliae, Ser. II.i (2)) (Cologne, 1983).

De Rebus Gestis Rogerii Calabriae et Siciliae Comitis, Auctore Gaufredo Malaterra, ed. E. Pontieri, *RIS* V (Bologna, 1927–8).

The Deeds of Frederick Barbarossa, by Otto of Freising and His Continuator Rahewin, trans. C. C. Mierow (New York, 1966).

The Deeds of God through the Franks: A Translation of Guibert de Nogent's Gesta Dei per Francos, trans. R. Levine (Woodbridge, 1997).

Deeds of John and Manuel Comnenus by John Cinnamus, trans. C. M. Brand (New York, 1976).

I diplomi greci ed arabi di Sicilia, ed. S. Cusa (Palermo, 1868–82).

Diplomi inediti dei principi normanni di Capua, conti di Aversa, ed. M. Inguanez, *Miscellanea Cassinese* III (Montecassino, 1926).

Documenti del commercio veneziano nei secoli XI–XIII, 2 vols., ed. R. Morozzo della Rocca and A. Lombardo (Rome, 1940).

Documenti per la storia di Eboli. I. (799–1264), ed. C. Carlone (Salerno, 1998).

I documenti storici di Corato (1046–1327), ed. G. Beltrani, *Codice diplomatico barese* IX (Bari, 1923).

Documenti tratti dai registri vaticani (da Innocenzo III a Nicola IV), ed. D. Vendola (Trani, 1940).

The Ecclesiastical History of Orderic Vitalis, 6 vols., trans. M. Chibnall (Oxford, 1968–80).

Falcone di Benevento, Chronicon Beneventanum, ed. E. D'Angelo (Florence, 1998).

The First Crusade: The Chronicle of Fulcher of Chartres and Other Source Materials, ed. E. Peters (Philadephia, 1971).

D. Girgensohn, 'Documenti beneventani inediti del secolo XII', *Samnium* 40 (1967), pp. 262–317.

Guillaume de Pouille, La Geste de Robert Guiscard, ed. and trans. M. Mathieu (Palermo, 1961).

Guillelmi I Regis Diplomata, ed. H. Enzensberger (Codex Diplomaticus Regni Siciliae, Ser. I.iii) (Cologne, 1996).

Historia Diplomatica Friderici Secundi, 6 vols., ed. J. L. A. Huillard-Bréholles (Paris, 1852–61).

La Historia o Liber de regno Sicilie e la Epistola ad Petrum Panormitane Ecclesie Thesaurium di Ugo Falcando, ed. G. B. Siragusa, *FSI* XXII (Rome, 1897).

The Historia Pontificalis of John Salisbury, ed. and trans. M. Chibnall (Oxford, 1986).

The History of the Normans by Amatus of Montecassino, trans. P. Dunbar and G. A. Loud (Woodbridge, 2004).

The History of the Tyrants of Sicily by 'Hugo Falcandus', 1154–1169, trans. G. A. Loud and T. Wiedemann (Manchester, 1998).

W. Holtzmann, 'Un nuovo documento riguardante il rettore Ansone di Benevento', *Samnium* 31 (1958), pp. 125–32.

H. Houben, 'Urkunden zur italienischen Rechtsgeschichte. Abschriften aus dem Staats-archiv Neapel im Nachlass Julius Ficker', *QF* 79 (1999), pp. 28–98.

Bibliography

L'Italia descritta nel 'Libro del re Ruggero' compilato da Edrisi, ed. and trans. M. Amari and C. Schiaparelli (Rome, 1883).

Italia Pontificia, 10 vols., ed. P. F. Kehr (Berlin, 1905–74) [vol. IX: Apulia-Samnium, ed. W. Holtzmann (1963)].

Italia Sacra, ed. F. Ughelli (2nd edn by N. Colletti, 10 vols., Venice, 1717–21).

The Itinerary of Benjamin of Tudela, ed. and trans. M. N. Adler (London, 1907).

John of Salisbury, *Policraticus*, ed. and trans. C. J. Nederman (Cambridge, 1990).

P. F. Kehr, 'Una bolla inedita di Papa Celestino III per la città di Benevento', *Samnium* 13 (1940), pp. 1–4.

Liber ad honorem Augusti di Pietro da Eboli, ed. G. B. Siragusa, *FSI* XXXIX (Rome, 1906).

Liber ad honorem Augusti sive de rebus Siculis: Codex 120 II der Bürgerbibliothek Bern, ed. T. Kölzer and M. Stähli (Sigmaringen, 1994).

The Liber Augustalis or Constitutions of Melfi promulgated by the Emperor Frederick II for the Kingdom of Sicily in 1231, trans. J. M. Powell (New York, 1971).

G. A. Loud, 'A calendar of the diplomas of the Norman Princes of Capua', *PBSR* 44 (Rome, 1981), pp. 99–143.

Lupus Protospatharius, Annales, ed. G. H. Pertz, *MGH SS* V (Hanover, 1845).

Miscellanea Giovanni Mercati: le pergamene di Melfi all'archivio secreto vaticano, ed. A. Mercato (Vatican City, 1946).

Monumenta ad Neapolitani Ducatus Historiam Pertinentia, 2 vols., ed. B. Capasso (Naples, 1885).

Necrologio del Liber Confratrum di S. Matteo di Salerno, ed. C. A. Garufi, *FSI* LVI (Rome, 1922).

Nuove pergamene del monastero femminile di S. Giorgio di Salerno. I. [993–1256], ed. M. Galante (Salerno, 1984).

L'Obituarium S. Spiritus della biblioteca capitolare di Benevento (sec. XII–XIV), ed. A. Zazo (Naples, 1963).

Ordinamenta et Consuetudo Maris edita per Consules Civitatis Trani, ed. and trans. Sir T. Twiss in *The Black Book of the Admiralty, Monumenta juridica* 55 (London, 1876), appendix, part iv, pp. 521–43.

Patrologia Latina, 221 vols., ed. J. P. Migne (Paris, 1844–64).

Peregrinationes Tres: Saewulf, John of Würzburg, Theodericus, Corpus Christianorum. Continuatio Mediaevalis 139, ed. R. B. C. Huygens with a study of the voyages of Saewulf by J. H. Pryor (Sydney, 1994).

Le pergamene del duomo di Bari (952–1264), ed. G. B. Nitto de Rossi and F. Nitti di Vito, *Codice diplomatico barese* I (Bari, 1867).

Le pergamene dell'archivio arcivescovile di Taranto, i (ii) (1083–1258), ed. F. Magistrale (Lecce, 1989).

Le pergamene delle cattedrale di Terlizzi (971–1300), ed. F. Carabellese, *Codice diplomatico barese* III (Bari, 1899).

Pergamene del monastero benedettino di S. Giorgio (1038–1698), ed. L. Cassese (Salerno, 1950).

Le pergamene di Barletta. Archivio capitolare (897–1285), ed. F. Nitti de Vito, *Codice diplomatico barese* VIII (Bari, 1914).

Pergamene di Barletta del Reale Archivio di Napoli (1075–1309), ed. R. Filangieri di Candida, *Codice diplomatico barese* X (Bari, 1927).

Bibliography

Le pergamene di Capua, 3 vols., ed. J. Mazzoleni (Naples, 1957–8).

Le pergamene di Conversano, I (901–1265), ed. G. Coniglio, *Codice diplomatico pugliese* XX (Bari, 1975).

Le pergamene di Gaeta. Archivio storico comunale 1187–1440, ed. P. Corbo (Gaeta, 1997).

Le pergamene di San Gregorio Armeno (1141–1198), ed. R. Pilone (Salerno, 1996).

Le pergamene di S. Nicola di Bari. Periodo greco (939–1071), ed. F. Nitti di Vito, *Codice diplomatico barese* IV (Bari, 1900).

Le pergamene di S. Nicola di Bari. Periodo normanno (1075–1194), ed. F. Nitti di Vito, *Codice diplomatico barese* V (Bari, 1902).

Le pergamene di S. Nicola di Bari. Periodo svevo (1195–1266), ed. F. Nitti di Vito, *Codice diplomatico barese* VI (Bari, 1906).

Le pergamene di S. Nicola di Gallucanta (secc. IX–XII), ed. P. Cherubini (Salerno, 1990).

Le pergamene normanne della Mater Ecclesia capuana (1091–1197), ed. G. Bova (Naples, 1996).

Pergamene salernitane (1008–1784), ed. L. E. Pennacchini (Naples, 1941).

Le pergamene sveve della Mater Ecclesia capuana, 2 vols., ed. G. Bova (Naples, 1998–9) [vol. I (1201–28), vol. II (1229–39)].

R. Piattoli, 'Miscellanea Diplomata (III)', *BISME* 57 (1941), pp. 151–204.

Le più antiche carte dell'abbazia di San Modesto in Benevento (secoli VIII–XIII), ed. F. Bartolini (Rome, 1950).

Le più antiche carte dell'archivio capitolare di Agrigento (1092–1282), ed. P. Collura (Palermo, 1960).

Le più antiche carte del capitolo della cattedrale di Benevento (668–1200), ed. A. Ciarelli, V. de Donato and V. Matera (Rome, 2002).

A. Poncelet, 'Miracula Sancti Nicolai a Monacho Beccensi', *Catalogus Codicum Hagiographicorum Latinorum Bibliotheca Nationali Parisiensi* (1890), vol. II, pp. 405–32.

'La Translation des SS. Éleuthère, Pontien et Anastase', *Analecta Bollandiana* 29 (1910), pp. 409–26.

Recueil des actes des ducs normands d'Italie [1046–1127]: I., Les Premiers ducs (1046–1087), ed. L-R. Ménager (Bari, 1980).

Regesta Honorii Papae III, 3 vols., ed. P. Presutti (Rome, 1888–95).

Regesta Regni Hierosolymitani (1097–1291), 2 vols., ed. R. Röhricht (Innsbruck, 1893).

Regesto di S. Angelo in Formis, ed. M. Inguanez (Montecassino, 1925).

Regesto di S. Leonardo di Siponto, ed. F. Camobreco (Rome, 1913).

Die Register Innocenz III – 2. Pontifikatsjahr, 1199/1200, ed. O. Hageneder, W. Maleckzek and A. A. Strnad (Vienna, 1979).

The Register of Pope Gregory VII – 1073–1085, trans. H. E. J. Cowdrey (Oxford, 2002).

Roberti de Monte Cronica, ed. L. C. Bethmann, *MGH SS* VI (Hanover, 1844).

Roger of Howden, *Chronica*, ed. W. Stubbs (4 vols., Rolls Series, 1868–71).

Rogerii II Regis Diplomata Latina, ed. C-R. Bruhl (Codex Diplomaticus Regni Siciliae, Ser. I.ii (1)) (Cologne, 1987).

Romualdi Salernitani Chronicon, ed. C. A. Garufi, *RIS* VII part i (Città di Castello, 1935).

Rycardi de Sancto Germano Notarii Chronica, ed. C. A. Garufi, *RIS* VIII part ii (Bologna, 1937).

Bibliography

F. Schneider, 'Neue Dokumente vornehmlich aus Süditalien', *QF* 16 (1914), pp. 1–54.
Storia documentata della scuola medica di Salerno, ed. S. De Renzi (Naples, 1857).
Syllabus Graecarum Membranarum, ed. F. Trinchera (Naples, 1865).
Tancredi et Willelmi III Regum Diplomata, ed. H. Zielinski (Codex Diplomaticus Regni Sicilae, Ser. I.v) (Cologne, 1982).
Vita Nicolai Peregrini et Relatio Adelferii, in *Acta Sanctorum, June* i (Paris, 1867).
Vita S. Iohannis a Mathera, in *Acta Sanctorum, June* v (Paris, 1867).
Walter of Thérouanne, *Vita Karoli Comitis Flandriae*, ed. R. Köpke, *MGH SS* XII (Hanover, 1856).
William of Tyre, *A History of Deeds Done Beyond the Sea, 2 vols.*, ed. E. A. Babcock and A. C. Krey (New York, 1976).

SECONDARY SOURCES (★ INDICATES THAT THE ITEM CONTAINS EDITED DOCUMENTS)

★G. Abignente, 'Le consuetudine inedite di Salerno', in *Studi e documenti di storia e diritto*, 9 fasc. 4 (Rome, 1888), pp. 305–87.
D. Abulafia, 'Dalmatian Ragusa and the Norman kingdom of Sicily', *The Slavonic and East European Review* 54 (1976), pp. 412–28.
Two Italies: Economic Relations between the Norman Kingdom of Sicily and the Northern Communes (Cambridge, 1977).
'The Crown and the economy under Roger II and his successors', *Dumbarton Oaks Papers* 37 (1983), pp. 1–14.
'Southern Italy, Sicily and Sardinia in the medieval Mediterranean economy', in *Commerce and Conquest in the Mediterranean, 1100–1500* (Aldershot, 1993), pp. 1–32.
'Monarchs and minorities in the Christian western Mediterranean around 1300: Lucera and its analogues', in *Christendom and Its Discontents. Exclusion, Persecution, and Rebellion, 1000–1500*, ed. S. L. Waugh and P. D. Diehl (Cambridge, 1996), pp. 234–63.
Frederick II. A Medieval Emperor, 2nd edn (London, 2002).
E. Ashtor, 'Gli ebrei nel commercio mediterraneo nell'Alto Medioevo (sec. X–XI)', in *Gli ebrei nell'Alto Medioevo. 30 marzo–5 aprile 1978, Settimane del Centro italiano di studi sull'Alto Medioevo* xxvi (Spoleto, 1980), vol. I, pp. 401–87.
F. Baethgen, *Die Regentschaft Papst Innocenz III. im Königreich Sizilien* (Heidelberg, 1914).
G. Barni, '*Cives* e *rustici* a Milano alla fine del XII secolo e all'inizio del XIII secondo il *Liber Consuetudinum Mediolani*', *Rivista storica italiana* 69 (1957), pp. 5–60.
R. Bartlett, *Trial by Fire and Water: The Medieval Judicial Order* (Oxford, 1986).
E. Bertaux, *L'Art dans l'Italie méridonale*, 3 vols. (Paris, 1903).
E. Besta, 'Il diritto consuetudinario di Bari e la sua genesi', *Rivista italiana per le scienze giuridiche* 36 (1903), pp. 3–113.
A. Black, *Guilds and Civil Society in European Political Thought from the Twelfth Century to the Present* (London, 1984).
R. Bordone, '"Civitas Nobilis et Antiqua". Per una storia delle origini del movimento comunale in Piemonte', in *Piemonte medievale. Forme del potere e della società. Studi per Giovanni Tabacco* (Turin, 1985), pp. 29–61.

Bibliography

'L'amministrazione del regno d'Italia', *BISME* 96 (1990), pp. 133–56.

★S. Borgia, *Memorie istoriche della pontificia città di Benevento dal secolo VIII al secolo XVIII*, 3 vols. (Rome, 1763–9).

G. Bova, *La vita quotidiana a Capua al tempo delle crociate* (Naples, 2001).

W. M. Bowsky, 'Medieval citizenship: the individual and the state in the commune of Siena, 1287–1355', *Studies in Medieval and Renaissance History* 4 (1967), pp. 193–243.

C. E. Boyd, *Tithes and Parishes in Medieval Italy. The Historical Roots of a Modern Problem* (Cornell, 1952).

H. Bresc, 'Le marginal', in *Condizione umana e ruoli sociali nel Mezzogiorno normanno-sveve. Atti delle none giornate normanno-sveve. Bari, 1989*, ed. G. Musca (Bari, 1991), pp. 19–41.

T. S. Brown, 'The political use of the past in Norman Sicily', in *The Perception of the Past in Twelfth-Century Europe*, ed. P. Magdalino (London, 1992), pp. 191–210.

F. Calasso, *La legislazione statutaria dell'Italia meridionale: le basi storiche; le libertà cittadine dalla fondazione del regno all'epoca degli statuti* (Rome, 1929).

'La città nell'Italia meridionale durante l'età normanna', *Archivio storico Pugliese* 12 (1959), pp. 18–34.

★M. Camera, *Memorie storico-diplomatiche dell'antica città e ducato di Amalfi*, 2 vols. (Salerno, 1876–81).

F. Carabellese, *L'Apulia ed il suo comune nell'Alto Medio Evo* (Bari, 1905).

Il comune pugliese durante la monarchia normanno-sveva (Bari, 1924).

M. Caravale, *Il regno normanno di Sicilia* (Rome, 1966).

★G. Cassandro, 'La *Promissio* del duca Sergio e la *Societas* napoletana', *Archivio storico italiano* 100 (1942), pp. 133–45.

'La fine del ducato', in *Storia di Napoli* (Naples, 1969), vol. II (i), pp. 3–408.

A. Castagneti, 'Feudalità e società comunale', in *Medioevo Mezzogiorno Mediterraneo – studi in onore di Mario Del Treppo*, ed. G. Rossetti and G. Vitolo (Naples, 2000), pp. 205–39.

F. Chalandon, *Histoire de la domination normande en Italie et en Sicilie*, 2 vols. (Paris, 1907).

R. Chazan, 'Pope Innocent III and the Jews', in *Pope Innocent III and his World*, ed. J. C. Moore (Aldershot, 1999), pp. 187–204.

'The Jews in Europe and the Mediterranean basin', in *The New Cambridge Medieval History, vol. IV, c. 1024–c. 1198*, ed. D. Luscombe and J. Riley-Smith (Cambridge, 2004), pp. 623–87.

J-C. Cheynet, *Pouvoir et contestations à Byzance (963–1210)* (Paris, 1990).

G. Cioffari, *Storia della basilica di S. Nicola di Bari. I. L'epoca normanno sveva* (Bari, 1984).

A. O. Citarella, 'Patterns in medieval trade: the commerce of Amalfi before the Crusades', *Journal of Economic History* 28 (1968), pp. 531–55.

M. T. Clanchy, 'Remembering the past and the good old law', *History* 55 (1970), pp. 165–76.

From Memory to Written Record. England 1066–1307, 2nd edn (Oxford, 1993).

D. R. Clementi, 'Some unnoticed aspects of the Emperor Henry VI's conquest of the Norman kingdom of Sicily', *Bulletin of the John Rylands Library* 36 (1953–4), pp. 328–59.

Bibliography

'The circumstances of Count Tancred's accession to the kingdom of Sicily, duchy of Apulia and the principality of Capua', in *Mélanges Antonio Marongiu – Studies Presented to the International Commission for the History of Representative and Parliamentary Institutions* 34 (Brussels, 1968), pp. 57–80.

J. Cohen, *The Friars and the Jews. The Evolution of Medieval Anti-Judaism* (London, 1982).

R. Colapietra, 'Profilo storico-urbanistico di Trani dalle origini alla fine dell'ottocento', *Archivio storico pugliese* 33 (1980), pp. 3–107.

E. Coleman, 'Sense of community and civic identity in the Italian communes', in *The Community, the Family and the Saint: Patterns of Power in Early Medieval Europe: Selected Proceedings of the International Medieval Congress, University of Leeds, 4–7 July 1994, 10–13 July 1995*, ed. J. Hill and M. Swan (Turnhout, 1998), pp. 45–60.

'The Italian communes. Recent work and current trends', *JMH* 25 (1999), pp. 373–97.

'Representative assemblies in communal Italy', in *Political Assemblies in the Earlier Middle Ages*, ed. P. Barnwell and M. Mostert (Turnhout, 2003), pp. 193–210.

'Cities and communes', in *Italy in the Central Middle Ages 1000–1300*, ed. D. Abulafia (Oxford, 2004), pp. 27–57.

G. Coniglio, 'La societa di Trani e gli "ordinamenta"', *Archivio storico pugliese* 24 (1981), pp. 75–88.

O. R. Constable, 'Muslim Spain and Mediterranean slavery: the medieval slave trade as an aspect of Muslim–Christian relations', in *Christendom and Its Discontents. Exclusion, Persecution, and Rebellion, 1000–1500*, ed. S. L. Waugh and P. D. Diehl (Cambridge, 1996), pp. 264–84.

P. Corrao, 'Il servo', in *Condizione umana e ruoli sociali nel Mezzogiorno normanno-sveve. Atti delle none giornate normanno-sveve. Bari, 1989*, ed. G. Musca (Bari, 1991), pp. 61–78.

H. E. J. Cowdrey, *The Age of Abbot Desiderius. Montecassino, the Papacy, and the Normans in the Eleventh and Early Twelfth Centuries* (Oxford, 1983).

B. Croce, *History of the Kingdom of Naples*, trans. H. Stuart Hughes (Chicago, 1970).

P. Delogu, *Mito di una città meridionale (Salerno, secoli VIII–XI)* (Naples, 1977).

'I normanni in città: schemi politici ed urbanistici', in *Società, potere e popolo nell'eta di Ruggero II. Atti delle terze giornate normmano-sveve, Bari, 1977* (Bari, 1980), pp. 173–205.

P. Delogu and P. Peduto (eds.), *Salerno nel XII secolo. Istituzioni, società, cultura. Atti del convegno internazionale [June 1999]* (Salerno, 2004).

J. Drell, 'Cultural syncretism and ethnic identity. The Norman conquest of southern Italy and Sicily', *JMH* 25 (1999), pp. 187–202.

'The aristocratic family in Norman southern Italy', in *The Society of Norman Italy*, ed. G. A. Loud and A. J. Metcalfe (Leiden, 2002), pp. 97–113.

Kinship and Conquest: Family Strategies in the Principality of Salerno during the Norman Period, 1077–1194 (Ithaca, 2002).

'Family structure in Salernitan society', in *Salerno nell XII secolo. Istituzioni, società, cultura. Atto del convegno internazionale* [June 1999], ed. P. Delogu and P. Peduto (Salerno, 2004), pp. 103–18.

Bibliography

M. English Frazer, 'Church doors and the gates of paradise: Byzantine bronze doors in Italy', *Dumbarton Oaks Papers* 27 (1973), pp. 145–62.

H. Enzensberger, 'Chanceries, charters and administration in Norman Italy', in *The Society of Norman Italy*, ed. G. A. Loud and A. J. Metcalfe (Leiden, 2002).

S. A. Epstein, *Wage Labor and Guilds in Medieval Europe* (North Carolina, 1991).
Genoa and the Genoese 958–1528 (North Carolina, 1996).

R. Face, 'Secular history in twelfth-century Italy: Caffaro of Genoa', *JMH* 6 (1980), pp. 169–84.

G. Fasoli, *Scritti di storia medievale* (Bologna, 1974).
'Città e ceti urbani nell'età dei due Guglielmi', in *Potere, società e popolo nell'età dei due Guglielmi. Atti delle quarte giornate normanno-sveve. Bari, 1979* (Bari, 1981), pp. 147–72.

L. Feller, 'The northern frontier of Norman Italy, 1060–1140', in *The Society of Norman Italy*, ed. G. A. Loud and A. J. Metcalfe (Leiden, 2002), pp. 47–74.

N. Ferorelli, *Gli ebrei nell'Italia meridionale dall'età romana al secolo XVIII* (Turin, 1915).

G. Ferretti, 'Roffredo Epifanio da Benevento', *Studi Medievali* 3 (1908–11), pp. 230–87.

A. Filangieri, *Territorio e popolazione nell'Italia meridionale* (Naples, 1980).
'La struttura degli insediamenti in Campania e in Puglia nei secoli XII–XIV', *Archivio storico per le provincie napoletane* 103 (1985), pp. 61–86.

R. Filangieri, 'Note al *Privilegium Libertatis* concesso dai Napoletani agli Amalfitani in 1190', *PBSR* 24 (1956), pp. 107–16.

S. Fodale, 'Il povero', in *Condizione umana e ruoli sociali nel Mezzogiorno normanno-sveve. Atti delle none giornate normanno-sveve. Bari, 1989*, ed. G. Musca (Bari, 1991), pp. 43–59.

C. D. Fonseca, '"*Congregationes clericorum et sacerdotum*" a Napoli nei secoli XI e XII', in *La vita del clero nei secoli XI e XII. Atti della I settimana di studio* [La Mendola, 1959], 2 vols. (Milan, 1962), pp. 265–83.
'La chiesa di Taranto tra il primo e il secondo millennio', *BISME* 81 (1969), pp. 83–114.
'"*Ordines*" istituzionali e ruoli sociali', in *Condizione umana e ruoli sociali nel Mezzogiorno normanno-sveve. Atti delle none giornate normanno-sveve. Bari, 1989*, ed. G. Musca (Bari, 1991), pp. 9–18.

D. Foote, 'How the past becomes a rumor: the notarialization of historical consciousness in medieval Orvieto', *Speculum* 75 (2000), pp. 794–815.

P. E. Fornaciari, 'Beniamino da Tudela in Italia', *Archivio storico italiano* 147 (1989), pp. 415–34.

J. France, 'The occasion of the coming of the Normans to Italy', *JMH* 17 (1991), pp. 185–205.

T. Frank, *Studien zu Italienischen Memorialzeugnissen des XI. und XII. Jahrhunderts* (Berlin, 1991).

M. Fuiano, 'Napoli normanna e sveva', in *Storia di Napoli* (Naples, 1969), vol. II (i), pp. 411–518.

M. Galante, 'Il giudice a Salerno in età normanna', in *Salerno nel XII secolo. Istituzioni, società, cultura. Atti del convegno internazionale* [June 1999], ed. P. Delogu and P. Peduto (Salerno, 2004), pp. 46–60.

Bibliography

G. Galasso, *Mezzogiorno medievale e moderno* (Turin, 1965).

A. Galdi, 'La diffusione del culto del santo patrono: l'esempio di S. Matteo di Salerno', in *Pellegrinaggi e itinerari dei santi nel Mezzogiorno medievale*, ed. G. Vitolo (Naples, 1999), pp. 181–91.

'I santi e la città. Agiografie e dedicazioni', in *Salerno nel XII secolo. Istituzioni, società, cultura. Atti del convegno internazionale* [June 1999], ed. P. Delogu and P. Peduto (Salerno, 2004), pp. 170–87.

A. Gallo, *Aversa normanna* (Naples, 1938).

J. F. Gardner, *Being a Roman Citizen* (London, 1993).

★C. A. Garufi, 'Di uno stabilmento balneare in Salerno nel secolo XII', *Studi Medievali* 1 (1904–5), pp. 276–80.

'Sullo strumento notarile nel Salernitano nello scorcio del secolo XI', *Archivio storico italiano* 46 (1910), pp. 53–80, 291–343.

J. Gay, *L'Italie méridionale et l'empire Byzantin*, 2 vols. (Paris, 1904).

P. J. Geary, *Furta Sacra: Thefts of Relics in the Central Middle Ages* (Princeton, 1978).

S. Gelichi, 'The cities', in *Italy in the Early Middle Ages*, ed. C. La Rocca (Oxford, 2002), pp. 168–88.

L. Genicot, 'The nobility of medieval Francia: continuity, break or evolution', in *Lordship and Community in Medieval Europe*, ed. F. Cheyette (New York, 1968), pp. 128–36.

L. Genicot, 'Recent research on the medieval nobility', in *The Medieval Nobility*, ed. T. Reuter (Oxford, 1978).

D. F. Glass, *Romanesque Sculpture in Campania. Patrons, Programs and Style* (Pennsylvania, 1991).

S. D. Goitein, *Letters of Medieval Jewish Traders* (Princeton, 1973).

P. Grierson and L. Travaini, *Medieval European Coinage, vol. XIV, Italy (III) (South Italy, Sicily, Sardinia)* (Cambridge, 1998).

★P. Guillaume, *Essai historique sur l'abbaye de Cava* (Cava dei Tirreni, 1877).

A. Guillou, 'Production and profits in the Byzantine province of Italy (tenth to eleventh centuries): an expanding society', *Dumbarton Oaks Papers* 28 (1974), pp. 91–109.

A. Guillou *et al.* (eds.), *Storia d'Italia*, vol. III, *Il Mezzogiorno dai Bizantini a Federico II* (Turin, 1983).

A. Harding, 'Political liberty in the Middle Ages', *Speculum* 55 (1980), pp. 423–43.

C. H. Haskins, 'England and Sicily in the twelfth century', *English Historical Review* 26 (1911), pp. 433–47, 641–65.

T. Head, 'Discontinuity and discovery in the cult of saints: Apulia from late Antiquity to the high Middle Ages', *Hagiographica* 6 (1999), pp. 171–211.

H. Hearder, *Italy in the Age of the Risorgimento 1790–1870* (Harlow, 1983).

D. Herlihy, 'The making of the medieval family: symmetry, structure and sentiment', in *Women, Family and Society in Medieval Europe. Historical Essays, 1978–1991* (Providence, 1995), pp. 135–53.

'Medieval children', in *Women, Family and Society in Medieval Europe. Historical Essays, 1978–1991* (Providence, 1995), pp. 215–43.

C. Holmes, *Basil II and the Governance of Empire (976–1025)* (Oxford, 2005).

★H. Houben, *Die Abtei Venosa und das Mönchtum im normannisch-staufischen Süditalien* (Tübingen, 1995).

Bibliography

Mezzogiorno normanno-svevo: monasteri e castelli, ebrei e musulmani (Naples, 1996).

Roger II of Sicily. A Ruler between East and West (Cambridge, 2002).

B-U. Hucker, *Kaiser Otto IV* (Hanover, 1990).

J. K. Hyde, *Society and Politics in Medieval Italy – The Evolution of Civil Life, 1000–1350* (London, 1973).

★G. Intorcia, *Civitas beneventana. Genesi ed evoluzione delle istituzioni cittadine nei sec. XIII–XVI* (Benevento, 1981).

G. Intorcia, *La comunità beneventana nei secoli XII–XVIII. Aspetti istituzionali. Controversie giurisdizionali* (Naples, 1996).

R. Iorio, R. Licinio and G. Musca, 'Sotto la monarchia Normanno-Sveva', *in Storia di Bari – dalla conquista normanna al ducato sforzesco*, ed. F. Tateo (Bari, 1990), pp. 57–94.

★E. Jamison, 'The Norman administration of Apulia and Capua more especially under Roger II and William I, 1127–1166', *PBSR* 6 (1913) pp. 211–481 [reprinted as a separate volume, Aalen, 1987].

'The Abbess Bethlem of S. Maria di Porta Somma and the barons of the Terra Beneventana', *Oxford Essays in Medieval History Presented to Herbert Edward Salter* (Oxford, 1934), pp. 33–67.

Admiral Eugenius. His Life and Work and the Authorship of the Epistola ad Petrum and the Historia Hugonis Falcandi Siculi (London, 1957).

★C. W. Jones, *Saint Nicholas of Myra, Bari and Manhattan. Biography of a Legend* (Chicago, 1978).

P. Jones, *The Italian City-State: From Commune to Signoria* (Oxford, 1997).

E. Joranson, 'The inception of the career of the Normans in Italy – legend and history', *Speculum* 23 (1948), pp. 353–96.

N. Kamp, *Kirche und Monarchie im staufischen Königreich Sizilien. 1. Prosoprographische Grundlegung. Bistümer unde Bischöfe des Königsreich 1194–1266*, 4 vols. (Munich, 1973–82) [vol.I, *Abruzzen und Kampanien*; vol. II, *Apulia und Kalabrien*].

'Su un nipote di Maione di Bari, che fu giustiziere di Federico II', in *Medioevo Mezzogiorno Mediterraneo – studi in onore di Mario Del Treppo*, ed. G. Rossetti and G. Vitolo (Naples, 2000), pp. 283–300.

'The bishops of southern Italy in the Norman and Staufen periods', in *The Society of Norman Italy*, ed. G. A. Loud and A. J. Metcalfe (Leiden, 2002), pp. 185–200.

★K. A. Kehr, *Die Urkunden der Normannisch-Sizilischen Könige – eine diplomatische Untersuchung* (Innsbruck, 1902).

E. Kennan, 'Innocent III and the first political crusade', *Traditio* 27 (1971), pp. 231–49.

F. Kern, *Kingship and Law in the Middle Ages* (Oxford, 1968).

J. Kirshner, 'Civitas sibi faciat civem; Bartolous of Sassoferato's doctrine on the making of a citizen', *Speculum* 48 (1973), pp. 694–713.

B. Kreutz, *Before the Normans – Southern Italy in the Ninth and Tenth Centuries* (Philadelphia, 1991).

A. Leone, 'Particolarismo e storia cittadina nella Campania medievale', *Quaderni Medievali* 9 (1980), pp. 236–56.

R. Licinio, 'L'artigiano', in *Condizione umana e ruoli sociali nel Mezzogiorno normanno-sveve. Atti delle none giornate normanno-sveve. Bari, 1989*, ed. G. Musca (Bari, 1991), pp. 153–85.

K. D. Lilley, *Urban Life in the Middle Ages 1000–1450* (Basingstoke, 2002).

Bibliography

G. A. Loud, 'How "Norman" was the Norman conquest of southern Italy', *Nottingham Medieval Studies* 25 (1981), pp. 13–34.

'Nunneries, nobles and women in the Norman principality of Capua', in *Annali canossani 1* (Reggio Emilia, 1981), pp. 45–62 [reprinted in G. A. Loud, *Conquerors and churchmen in Norman Italy* (Aldershot, 1999)].

'Royal control of the Church in the twelfth-century kingdom of Sicily', *Studies in Church History* 18 (1982), pp. 147–59.

'The Church, warfare and military obligation in Norman Italy', *Studies in Church History* 20 (1983), pp. 31–45.

Church and Society in the Norman Principality of Capua, 1058–1197 (Oxford, 1985).

'The medieval records of the monastery of St Sophia, Benevento', *Archives* 19 (1991), pp. 363–73 [reprinted in G. A. Loud, *Montecassino and Benevento in the Middle Ages* (Aldershot, 2000)].

'Monarchy and monastery in the Mezzogiorno: the abbey of St. Sophia, Benevento and the Staufen', *PBSR* 59 (1991), pp. 283–318.

'Norman Italy and the Holy Land', in *The Horns of Hattin*, ed. B. Z. Kedar (Jerusalem, 1992), pp. 49–62.

'The genesis and context of the Chronicle of Falco of Benevento', in *Anglo-Norman Studies 15. Proceedings of the Battle Conference 1992*, ed. M. Chibnall (Woodbridge, 1993), pp. 177–98.

'Continuity and change in Norman Italy: the Campania during the eleventh and twelfth centuries', *JMH* 22 (1996), pp. 313–43.

'William the Bad or William the Unlucky? Kingship in Sicily – 1155–1166', *The Haskins Society Journal* 8 (1996), pp. 99–113.

'A Lombard abbey in a Norman world; St. Sophia, Benevento, 1050–1200', in *Anglo-Norman Studies 19. Proceedings of the Battle Conference 1996*, ed. C. Harper-Bill (Woodbridge, 1997), pp. 273–306.

'Politics, piety and ecclesiastical patronage in twelfth-century Benevento', in *Cavalieri alla conquista del Sud. Studi sull'Italia normanna in memoria di Léon-Robert Menager*, ed. E. Cuozzo and J-M. Martin (Bari, 1998), pp. 283–312 [reprinted in G. A. Loud, *Montecassino and Benevento in the Middle Ages* (Aldershot, 2000)].

'Coinage, wealth and plunder in the age of Robert Guiscard', *English Historical Review* 114 (1999), pp. 815–43.

'A provisional list of the papal rectors of Benevento, 1101–1227', in *Montecassino and Benevento in the Middle Ages* (Aldershot, 2000), pp. 1–11.

The Age of Robert Guiscard. Southern Italy and the Norman Conquest (Harlow, 2000).

'The monastic economy in the principality of Salerno during the eleventh and twelfth centuries', *PBSR* 71 (2003), pp. 141–79.

'The kingdom of Sicily and the kingdom of England, 1066–1266', *History* 88 (2003), pp. 540–67.

The Latin Church in Norman Italy (Cambridge, 2007).

G. A. Loud and A. J. Metcalfe (eds.), *The Society of Norman Italy* (Leiden, 2002).

K. A. Lynch, *Individuals, Families, and Communities in Europe, 1200–1800. The Urban Foundations of Western Society* (Cambridge, 2003).

P. Magdalino, *The Empire of Manuel I Komnenos, 1143–1180* (Cambridge, 1993).

W. Maleczek, *Papst und Kardinalskolleg von 1191 bis 1216* (Vienna, 1984).

Bibliography

A. Marongiu, 'Gli ebrei di Salerno nei documenti dei secoli X–XIII', *Archivio storico per le province napoletane* 62 (1937), pp. 3–31 [reprinted in A. Marongiu, *Byzantine, Norman, Swabian and Later Institutions in Southern Italy* (London, 1972)].

'A model state in the Middle Ages: The Norman and Swabian kingdom of Sicily', *Comparative Studies in Society and History* 6 (1963–4), pp. 307–20.

J-M. Martin, 'Les Communautés d'habitants de la Pouille et leur rapports avec Roger II', in *Società, potere e popolo nell'età di Ruggero II. Atti della terza giornate normanno-sveve. Bari 23–25 maggio 1977* (Bari, 1980), pp. 73–98.

'Les Communes en Italie méridionale aux XII et XIII siècles', in *Villes, bonnes villes, cités et capitales: mélanges offerts à Bernard Chevalier* (Tours, 1989), pp. 201–10.

'Troia et son territoire au XI siècle', *Vetera Christianorum* 27 (1990), pp. 175–201.

'Foggia, Lucera', in *Itinerari e centri urbani nel Mezzogiorno normanno-svevo. Atti delle decime giornate normanno-sveve. Bari 1991*, ed. G. Musca (Bari, 1993), pp. 333–63.

La Pouille du VI au XII siècle (Rome, 1993).

'Le città demaniali', in *Federico II e le città italiane*, ed. P. Toubert and A. Paravicini Bagliani (Palermo, 1994), pp. 179–95.

'L'Administration du royaume entre Normands et Souabes', in *Die Staufer im Süden. Sizilien und das Reich*, ed. T. Kölzer (Sigmaringen, 1996), pp. 113–40.

Foggia nel Medioevo (Rome, 1998).

'Historiographie récente de l'Italie méridionale pendant le haut moyen age', *Cahiers de civilisation medievale X-XII siècles*, 41 (1998), pp. 331–51.

'L'Occident Chrétien dans le *Livre des Cérémonies*, II, 48', *Travaux et mémoires* 13 (2000), pp. 617–46.

'L'Empreinte de Byzance dans l'Italie normande. Occupation du sol et institutions', *Annales. Histoire, Sciences Sociales* 4 (July–August 2005), pp. 733–65.

J-M. Martin and G. Noyé, *La Capitanata nella storia del Mezzogiorno medioevale* (Bari, 1991).

L. Martines (ed.), *Violence and Civic Disorder in Italian Cities 1200–1500* (Berkeley, 1972).

K. Mason (ed.), *Italy*, 4 vols., Geographical Handbook Series, Naval Intelligence Division (London, 1944–5).

D. Matthew, 'The Chronicle of Romuald of Salerno', in *The Writing of History in the Middle Ages. Essays Presented to Richard William Southern*, ed. R. H. C. Davis (Oxford, 1981), pp. 239–74.

'Maio of Bari's commentary on the Lord's prayer', in *Intellectual Life in the Middle Ages. Essays Presented to Margaret Gibson*, ed. C. Smith and B. Ward (London, 1992), pp. 119–44.

The Norman Kingdom of Sicily (Cambridge, 1992).

'Semper fideles. The citizens of Salerno in the Norman kingdom', in *Salerno nel XII secolo. Istituzioni, società, cultura. Atti del convegno internazionale* [June 1999], ed. P. Delogu and P. Peduto (Salerno, 2004), pp. 27–45.

★L-R. Ménager, 'Les Fondations monastiques de Robert Guiscard, duc de Pouille et de Calabre', *QF* 39 (1958), pp. 1–116.

Amiratus – Ἀμηρᾶς – L'Emirat et les origines de l'amirauté (XIe–XIIIe siècles) (Paris, 1960).

'La Legislation sud-italienne sous la domination normande', in *Settimane di studio del Centro italiano di studi sull'Alto Medioevo xvi, Spoleto 1968* (Spoleto, 1969) [reprinted in L-R. Menager, *Hommes et institutions de l'Italie normande* (London, 1981)], pp. 439–96.

Bibliography

'Pesanteur et étiologie de la colonisation normande de l'Italie', in *Roberto il Guiscardo e il suo tempo (Relazioni e communicazioni nelle prime-giornate normanno-sveve, Bari 1973)* (Bari, 1975), pp. 189–215 [reprinted in L-R. Menager, *Hommes et institutions de l'Italie Normande* (London, 1981)].

'Inventaire des familles normandes et franques émigrés en Italie méridionale et en Sicile (XI–XII siècles)', in *Roberto il Guiscardo e il suo tempo (Relazioni e communicazioni nelle prime-giornate normanno-sveve, Bari 1973)* (Bari, 1975), pp. 259–390 [reprinted with additions in L-R. Menager, *Hommes et institutions de l'Italie normande* (London, 1981)].

A. Milano, *Storia degli ebrei in Italia* (Turin, 1963).

M. C. Miller, *The Bishop's Palace. Architecture and Authority in Medieval Italy* (Cornell, 2000).

A. Mirra, 'I versi di Guaiferio monaco di Montecassino nel secolo XI', *BISME* 46 (1931), pp. 93–107.

'Guaiferio monaco poeta a Montecassino nel secolo XI', *BISME* 47 (1932), pp. 199–208.

N. Moe, '"This is Africa": ruling and representing southern Italy, 1860–61', in *Making and Remaking Italy – The Cultivation of National Identity around the Risorgimento*, ed. A. R. Ascoli and K. von Henneberg (Oxford, 2001), pp. 119–53.

M. Mollat, *The Poor in the Middle Ages – An Essay in Social History*, Trans. A. Goldhammer (Yale, 1986).

G. M. Monti, *Le corporazioni nell'Evo Antico e nell'Alto Medio Evo* (Bari, 1934).

★G. M. Monti, *Lo stato normanno svevo. Lineamenti e Ricerche* (Trani, 1945).

J. Morris, 'Challenging *Meridionalismo*: constructing a new history for southern Italy', in *The New History of the Italian South – The Mezzogiorno Revisited*, ed. R. Lumley and J. Morris (Exeter, 1997), pp. 1–19.

R. Morris, 'Dispute settlement in the Byzantine provinces in the tenth century', in *The Settlement of Disputes in Early Medieval Europe*, ed. W. Davies and P. Fouracre (Cambridge, 1986), pp. 125–47.

J. H. Mundy, 'In praise of Italy: the Italian republics', *Speculum* 64 (1989), pp. 815–34.

A. Murray, *Reason and Society in the Middle Ages* (Oxford, 1978).

G. Musca (ed.), *Condizione umana e ruoli sociali nel Mezzogiorno normanno-sveve. Atti delle none giornate normanno-sveve. Bari, 1989* (Bari, 1991).

G. Musca and P. Corsi, 'Da Melo al regno normanno', in *Storia di Bari dalla conquista normanna al ducato sforzesco*, ed. F. Tateo (Bari, 1990), pp. 5–55.

D. Nicholas, *The Growth of the Medieval City: From Late Antiquity to the Early Fourteenth Century* (New York, 1997).

J. F. Niermeyer, *Mediae Latinitatis Lexicon Minus* (Leiden, 1976).

F. Nitti di Vito, *La ripresa gregoriana di Bari (1087–1105); e i suoi riflessi nel mondo contemperaneo politico e religioso* (Trani, 1942).

P. Oldfield, 'Rural settlement and economic development in southern Italy: Troia and its *contado*, c.1020–c.1230', *JMH* 31 (2005), pp. 327–45.

'St Nicholas the Pilgrim and the city of Trani between Greeks and Normans, c. 1090–c. 1140', in *Anglo-Norman Studies 30. Proceedings of the Battle Conference 2007*, ed. C. P. Lewis (Woodbridge, 2008), pp. 168–81.

'The Iberian imprint on medieval southern Italy', *History* 93 (2008), pp. 312–27

'Otto IV and southern Italy', *Archivio normanno-svevo* 1 (forthcoming).

Bibliography

J. Parker, 'The attempted Byzantine alliance with the Sicilian kingdom, 1166–1167', *PBSR* 24 (1956), pp. 86–93.

R. Pavoni, 'Il mercante', in *Condizione umana e ruoli sociali nel Mezzogiorno normanno-sveve. Atti delle none giornate normanno-sveve. Bari, 1989*, ed. G. Musca (Bari, 1991), pp. 215–50.

G. Petralia, 'Santi e mercanti nel Mediterraneo latino medievale: note diacroniche', in *Medioevo Mezzogiorno Mediterraneo – studi in onore di Mario Del Treppo*, ed. G. Rossetti and G. Vitolo (Naples, 2000), pp. 89–110.

★G. Petroni, *Della storia di Bari dagli antichi tempi sino all'anno 1856*, 2 vols. (Naples, 1857–8).

A. Placanica, 'L'opera stroriografica di Caffaro', *Studi Medievali* 36 (1995), pp. 1–62.

F. Porsia, 'Vita economica e sociale', in *Storia di Bari – dalla conquista normanna al ducato sforzesco*, ed. F. Tateo (Bari, 1990), pp. 189–227.

J. M. Powell, 'Medieval monarchy and trade. The economic policy of Frederick II in the kingdom of Sicily', *Studi Medievali* 3 (1962), pp. 420–524.

'Innocent III and Petrus Beneventanus: reconstructing a career at the papal curia', in *Pope Innocent III and His World*, ed. J. C. Moore (Aldershot, 1999), pp. 51–62.

N. J. G. Pounds, *An Economic History of Medieval Europe* (London, 1994).

V. Ramseyer, *The Transformation of a Religious Landscape. Medieval Southern Italy 850–1150* (Ithaca, 2006).

I. Di Resta, *Capua (Le città nella storia d'Italia)* (Rome and Bari, 1985).

T. Reuter (ed.), *The Medieval Nobility* (Oxford, 1978).

S. Reynolds, 'Social mentalities and the case of medieval skepticism', *Transactions of the Royal Historical Society*, series 5, 41 (1991), pp. 21–41.

'English towns of the eleventh century in a European context', in *Die Stadt im 11. Jahrhundert*, ed. P. Johanek (Münster, 1995), pp. 1–12 [reprinted in *Ideas and Solidarities of the Medieval Laity* (Aldershot, 1995)].

Kingdoms and Communities in Western Europe 900–1300 (Oxford, 1997).

A. Rio, 'Freedom and unfreedom in early medieval Francia: the evidence of the legal formulae', *Past and Present* 193 (2006), pp. 7–40.

G. Rippe, *Padoue et son contado (Xe–XIIIe siècle)* (Rome, 2003).

G. Rossetti and G. Vitolo (eds.), *Medioevo Mezzogiorno Mediterraneo – studi in onore di Mario Del Treppo* (Naples, 2000).

B. Ruggiero, 'Per una storia della pieve rurale nel Mezzogiorno medievale', *Studi Medievali* 16 (1975), pp. 583–626.

G. Sangermano, 'La cattedrale e la città', in *Salerno nel XII secolo. Istituzioni, società, cultura. Atti del convegno internazionale* [June 1999], ed. P. Delogu and P. Peduto (Salerno, 2004), pp. 14–69.

P. Scheffer-Boichorst, 'Urkunden und Forschungen zu den Regesten der staufischen Periode', *Neues Archiv der Gesellschaft für ältere deutsche Geschichtskunde* 27 (1902), pp. 71–124.

M. Schipa, 'Nobili e popolani in Napoli nel Medioevo in rapporto all'amministrazione municipale', *Archivio storico italiano* 83 (1925), pp. 3–44.

A. N. Sherwin-White, *The Roman Citizenship* (Oxford, 1973).

P. Skinner, *Family Power in Southern Italy: The Duchy of Gaeta and Its Neighbours 850–1139* (Cambridge, 1995).

'Gender and poverty in the medieval community', in *Medieval Women in their Communities*, ed. D. Watt (Cardiff, 1997), pp. 204–21.

Bibliography

'Room for tension: Urban life in Apulia in the eleventh and twelfth centuries', *PBSR* 66 (1998), pp. 159–76.

'When was southern Italy "feudal"?', in *Il feudalismo nell'Alto Medioevo, 8th–12th April 1999. Settimane di studio del Centro italiano di studi sull'Alto Medioevo* 47 (Spoleto, 2000), vol. I, pp. 309–40.

'Daughters of Sichelgaita: the women of Salerno in the twelfth century', in *Salerno nell XII secolo. Istituzioni, società, cultura. Atto del convegno internazionale* [June 1999], ed. P. Delogu and P. Peduto (Salerno, 2004), pp. 119–33.

M. Spremić, 'La migrazione degli Slavi nell'Italia meridionale e in Sicilia alla fine del medioevo', *Archivio storico italiano* 138 (1980), pp. 3–15.

Joshua Starr, 'The mass conversion of Jews in southern Italy (1290–1293)', *Speculum* 21 (1946), pp. 203–11.

B. Stock, *The Implications of Literacy: Written Language and Models of Interpretation in the Eleventh and Twelfth centuries* (Princeton, 1983).

S. M. Stuard, 'Ancillary evidence for the decline of medieval slavery', *Past and Present* 129 (1995), pp. 3–28.

W. Stürner, *Friedrich II. Teil 1. Die Königsherrschaft in Sizilien und Deutschland 1194–1220* (Darmstadt, 1992).

H. Swanson, *Medieval Artisans. An Urban Class in Late Medieval England* (Oxford, 1989).

G. Tabacco, *The Struggle for Power in Medieval Italy – Structures of Political Rule* (Cambridge, 1989).

H. Takayama, *The Administration of the Norman Kingdom of Sicily* (New York, 1993).

N. Tamassia, '*Ius Affidandi*. Origine e svolgimento nell'Italia meridionale', *Atti del reale istituto veneto di scienze, lettere ed arti* 72 [part 2] (1912–13), pp. 343–90.

H. Taviani-Carozzi, *La Principauté lombarde de Salerne, IXe–XIe siècle*, 2 vols. (Paris, 1991).

H. Taviani-Carozzi, B. Vetere and A. Leone, *Salerno nel Medioevo* (Rome, 2000).

★G. Tescione, *Caserta medievale e i suoi conti e signori* (Caserta, 1990).

A. Thompson, *Cities of God. The Religion of the Italian Communes 1125–1325* (Pennsylvania, 2005).

D. N. Tolstoy-Miloslavsky, '*Manuel I Komnenos and Italy: Byzantine Foreign Policy, 1135–1180*' (Unpublished PhD thesis, Royal Holloway, University of London, 2008).

L. Travaini, *La monetazione nell'Italia normanna* (Rome, 1995).

'Le zecca e le monete di Salerno nel XII secolo', in *Salerno nel XII secolo. Istituzioni, società, cultura. Atti del convegno internazionale* [June 1999], ed. P. Delogu and P. Peduto (Salerno, 2004), pp. 337–54.

M. Del Treppo and A. Leone, *Amalfi medioevale* (Naples, 1977).

T. C. van Cleve, *Markward of Anweiler and the Sicilian Regency* (Princeton, 1937).

O. Vehse, 'Benevent als Territorium des Kirchenstaates bis zum Beginn der avignonesischen Epoche' [2 parts], *QF* 22–3 (1930–2), pp. 87–160, 80–119.

G. Vergineo, *Storia di Benevento e dintorni, vol. I, Dalle origini mitiche agli statuti del 1230* (Rome, 1985).

C. Verlinden, *L'Esclavage dans l'Europe medievale*, 2 vols. (Ghent, 1977).

★C. Vetere, *Le consuetudini di Napoli – Il testo e la tradizione* (Salerno, 1999).

M. Villani, 'Il contributo dell onomastica e della toponomastica alla storia delle devozioni', in *Pellegrinaggi e itinerari dei santi nel Mezzogiorno medievale*, ed. G. Vitolo (Naples, 1999), pp. 249–66.

Bibliography

★G. Vitolo, *Istituzioni ecclesiastiche e vita religiosa dei laici nel mezzogiorno medievale. Il codice della confraternita di S. Maria di Montefusco (sec. XII)* (Rome, 1982).

G. Vitolo, *Città e coscienza cittadina nel Mezzogiorno medievale (sec. IX–XIII)* (Salerno, 1990).

'Esperienze religiose nella Napoli dei secoli XII–XIV', in *Medioevo Mezzogiorno Mediterraneo – studi in onore di Mario Del Treppo*, ed. G. Rossetti and G. Vitolo (Naples, 2000), pp. 3–34.

'Città e chiesa nel Mezzogiorno medievale: la processione del santo patrono a Salerno (sec. XII)', in *Salerno nel XII secolo. Istituzioni, società, cultura. Atti del convegno internazionale* [June 1999], ed. P. Delogu and P. Peduto (Salerno, 2004), pp. 134–48.

V. von Falkenhausen, 'Taranto in epoca bizantina', *Studi Medievali* 9 (1968), pp. 133–66.

'I ceti dirigenti prenormanni al tempo della costituzione degli stati normanni nell'Italia meridionale e in Sicilia', in *Forme di potere e struttura sociale in Italia nel medioevo*, ed. G. Rossetti (Bologna, 1977), pp. 321–71.

La dominazione bizantina nell'Italia meridionale dal IX all'XI secolo (Bari, 1978).

'A provincial aristocracy: the Byzantine provinces in southern Italy (9th–11th century)', in *The Byzantine Aristocracy IX to XIII Centuries*, ed. M Angold, BAR international series 221 (Oxford, 1984), pp. 211–35.

'Die Städte im byzantinischen Italien', *Mélanges de l'école française de Rome* 101 (1989), pp. 401–64.

'Un inedito documento greco del monastero di S. Vito del Pizzo (Taranto)', *Cenacolo*, n. s. 7 (19) (1995), pp. 7–20

'Il commercio di Amalfi con Constantinopoli e il Levante nel secolo XII', in *Amalfi, Genova, Pisa e Venezia. I commercio con Constantinopoli e il vicino Oriente nel secolo XII*, ed. O. Banti (Pisa, 1998), pp. 19–38.

R. Vose, *Dominicans, Muslims and Jews in Medieval Aragon, c. 1220–1320* (Cambridge, 2009).

D. Waley, *The Italian City-Republics* (London, 1969).

Siena and the Sienese in the Thirteenth Century (Cambridge, 1991).

D. A. Walsh, 'The iconography of the bronze doors of Barisanus of Trani', *Gesta* 21 (1982), pp. 91–106.

D. Webb, *Patrons and Defenders: The Saints in the Italian City States* (London, 1996).

C. Wickham, 'The sense of the past in Italian communal narratives', in *The Perception of the Past in Twelfth-Century Europe*, ed. P. Magdalino (London, 1992), pp. 173–89.

Courts and Conflict in Twelfth-Century Tuscany (Oxford, 2003).

'City society in twelfth-century Italy and the example of Salerno', in *Salerno nel XII secolo. Istituzioni, società, cultura. Atti del convegno internazionale* [June 1999], ed. P. Delogu and P. Peduto (Salerno, 2004), pp. 12–26.

H. Wieruszowski, 'Roger II of Sicily, *Rex Tyrannus*, in twelfth-century political thought', *Speculum* 38 (1963), pp. 46–78.

R. B. Yewdale, *Bohemond I, Prince of Antioch* (Princeton, 1917).

A. Zazo, 'Professioni, arti e mestieri in Benevento nei secoli XII–XIV', *Samnium* 32 (1959), pp. 121–77.

★L. Zdekauer, 'Le franchigie concesse da Onorio II alla citta di Troia (1127)', *Rivista italiana per le scienze giuridiche* 25 (1898), pp. 242–57.

INDEX

Abruzzi, 1, 20, 56, 84, 93, 129, 169, 230, 240

Acquaviva, 215, 266, 268

Acre, 248, 249

Adrian IV, pope (1154–9), 117, 121

affidati, 35, 174–5, 176, 208–9

Agrigento, 216

Aimo of Argentia, 68, 72, 89, 94

Alexander III, pope (1159–81), 93, 117, 118, 120, 121, 254

Alexander, count of Conversano, 37, 38, 64

Alexander of Telese, chronicler, 12, 56, 58, 74, 82, 251, 261

Alexandria (Egypt), 75, 246, 247, 248, 252

Alfanus, archbishop of Capua (1153–80), 95, 230

Alfanus I, archbishop of Salerno (1058–85), 25, 173, 229, 239

Alife, 115, 216

Aligernus Cotunus of Naples, 126, 132, 147, 192

Amalfi, 1, 9, 11, 17, 20, 23, 39, 54, 73, 84, 86, 98, 106, 108, 168, 169, 170, 186, 187, 189, 190, 203, 206, 223, 246, 248, 250, 251, 254, 261

    Amalfitan diaspora, 116, 118, 121, 126, 154, 175, 177, 178, 187, 192, 216–18, 221, 247, 249, 250, 253

Amatus of Montecassino, chronicler, 12, 22, 23, 171, 219, 246

Anacletus II, [anti]pope (1130–8), 56, 59, 60, 65, 66, 68, 77, 78, 79, 80, 177, 252

Anagni, 43

Anfusus, prince of Capua and duke of Naples (d. 1144), 66, 73, 87

Anso of Benevento, 42, 51, 54, 224

Antioch, 247, 249

Apulia, 1, 5, 7, 9, 10, 11, 13, 18, 19, 20, 21, 22, 26, 27, 33, 38, 39, 54, 61, 62, 64, 67, 73, 75, 84, 85, 86, 88, 94, 96, 100, 103, 108,

110, 111, 112, 113, 132, 134, 135, 141, 144, 148, 153, 166, 169, 170, 188, 206, 212, 215, 237, 246, 247, 248, 249, 250, 252, 255, 260, 261, 262, 264

Argirizzus of Bari, 22, 23, 26, 224

Ariano, 216, 240

artisans/traders, 199–205, 252–8

Ascoli Satriano, 92, 94, 116, 130, 168, 175, 216, 240

Auletta, 93

Avellino, 216

Aversa, 8, 9, 10, 19, 24, 40, 44–5, 54, 64, 66, 72, 73, 81, 84, 87, 90, 92, 93, 94, 95, 97, 99, 102, 103, 104, 107, 108, 114, 124, 125, 126, 129, 131, 134, 138, 139, 143, 144, 145–6, 146, 166, 167, 170, 176, 178–80, 185, 186, 187, 188, 201, 202, 203, 205, 212, 216, 217, 220, 221, 228, 229, 237, 243, 252, 253, 256, 257, 258, 259, see also de Rebursa kin-group

    bishops of, see Lambert

    customs/privileges of, 105, 133, 179

    S. Biagio, nunnery of, 43, 54, 203

    S. Lorenzo, monastery of, 39, 130, 136, 209, 226

baiuli/bailiffs, 76, 100, 101–2, 115, 119, 129, 133, 137, 138, 139, 146, 149, 150–1, 155, 161, 174, 217, 231

Bari, 9, 10, 13, 18, 20, 21, 22–3, 26, 27, 29, 30, 33–6, 38, 43, 46–9, 54, 58, 59, 62, 63, 66, 71, 73, 81, 83, 84, 86, 87, 88, 92, 93, 95, 96, 97, 100, 101, 103, 104, 105, 109, 110, 111, 129, 131, 132, 134, 135, 136, 137–8, 138, 140, 149, 150–3, 154, 155, 167, 168, 171, 174–6, 180, 184, 186, 188, 190, 191, 195, 200, 204, 206, 208, 209, 213, 214, 217, 218, 220, 221, 224, 225, 228, 229, 232, 236, 241, 242, 243, 246, 247, 248,

Index

Index

Index

Index

Index

9590627R00173

Printed in Great Britain
by Amazon.co.uk, Ltd.,
Marston Gate.